BUSINESS EDUCATION AND EMERGING MARKET ECONOMIES

BUSINESS EDUCATION AND EMERGING MARKET ECONOMIES

PERSPECTIVES AND BEST PRACTICES

Edited by

Ilan Alon
Crummer Graduate School of Management, Rollins College, Winter Park, Florida

John R. McIntyre
DuPree College of Management, Georgia Institute of Technology, Atlanta, Georgia

Kluwer Academic Publishers
Boston/New York/Dordrecht

Distributors for North, Central and South America:
Kluwer Academic Publishers
101 Philip Drive
Assinippi Park
Norwell, Massachusetts 02061 USA
Telephone (781) 871-6600
Fax (781) 681-9045
E-Mail <kluwer@wkap.com>
Distributors for all other countries:
Kluwer Academic Publishers Group
Post Office Box 17
3300 AH Dordrecht, THE NETHERLANDS
Tel: +31 (0) 78 657 60 00
Fax: +31 (0) 78 657 64 74

E-Mail <services@wkap.nl>

Electronic Services <http://www.wkap.nl>

Business Education and Emerging Market Economies:
Perspectives and Best Practices
By Ilan Alon and John R. McIntyre
p.cm.
Includes bibliographical references and index.
ISBN 978-1-4419-5467-1 ISBN 978-1-4020-8072-2 (eBook)
DOI 10.1007/978-1-4020-8072-2

Dedication

From Ilan Alon:
To my loved Zipi

From John McIntyre:
To Genevieve Anna-France Mayent, dear friend and close relative

Contents

II. CURRICULAR AND COURSE CONTENT INNOVATIONS

III. STRATEGIC INTERNATIONAL EDUCATIONAL ALLIANCES

List of Figures

List of Tables

Foreword
Business Education in Emerging Economies

Dan LeClair
Director of Knowledge Services, A.A.C.S.B. International

Business education is crucial in emerging economies because competitive industries demand leadership from skilled, knowledgeable managers. So it is not surprising that the last decade has brought explosive growth in graduate business education around the world: the burgeoning economies of China and India; transitioning economies of the former Soviet republics; and developing economies of Latin America and sub-Saharan Africa. But we have much to learn about business education in these economies. How can business schools and other providers meet their needs? What curricula and pedagogical approaches will work best? Is there a role for business schools to create entrepreneurial cultures or drive economic reform? To what extent should school develop corporate partnerships and collaborate across borders to deliver education? Can technology applications expand the reach of management education?

By addressing these and other questions, the contributors to this volume substantially enhance our understanding of business education in emerging economies. As a whole, the articles demonstrate an appreciation for the complexity and breadth of business education and cover a broad range of business education topics and regions. The editors, Ilan Alon and John McIntyre, have organized an excellent compilation of articles that will be of keen interest to practitioners and students of management education alike.

My position in directing research on business schools worldwide may offer some insight to understanding specific challenges in emerging economies. I offer five observations to keep in mind when considering the contributions in this book.

1. Business curricula should be relevant locally.

Too often, curricula from U.S. programs are copied without regard for the differences that apply in foreign settings. Although logical given the maturity of management education in the U.S. and scarcity of resources in developing countries, this approach often doesn't work simply because the curriculum doesn't fit. Business education is inseparable from the historical, political, demographic, technological, and social realities in any country or region. Parts of any curriculum might be global, but seeking generic content that is "applicable across cultures" or "culturally sensitive" might conflict with the goal of relevance. Rather than importing generic business curricula, business educators in emerging economies must involve local business leaders to develop relevant learning goals and objectives, curricula to achieve these objectives, and educational resources to support the educational process.

2. Educational achievement depends on process as much as content.

Traditional lectures and rote learning methods still characterize instruction in many emerging economies. For students to master management skills, educators must apply interactive, experiential learning models and integrate learning with business practice. The dearth of local business alumni, scarce faculty resources, and academic traditions make applying these models particularly challenging in emerging markets.

3. Student and faculty qualifications must be appropriately matched to business programs.

Business programs must be consistent with the educational backgrounds and experience of targeted students. However, among schools in emerging markets, it is not uncommon to find, for example, inexperienced students recruited to programs best suited to executives. Furthermore, the recruitment and retention of qualified faculty is extremely challenging in emerging markets due to the lack of domestic business doctoral programs, attractive private sector employment opportunities, and low academic salaries. To advance business education under these conditions, business school leaders must create innovative solutions to develop and maintain qualified faculties.

4. Adequate educational resources and physical infrastructure are necessary to provide high-quality business education.

Many schools in emerging markets suffer insufficient educational resources (e.g., textbooks, cases, networked computers, databases, etc.) and poorly-designed facilities that were originally designed for other purposes and can't support interactive or technology-based instruction. Some approaches to business education may be impossible to apply in such settings.

5. Business education goes beyond producing qualified graduates.

To fully contribute to emerging economies, business educators must apply the resources of higher education to meet the needs of local business organizations and other domestic institutions. They must share relevant management knowledge with businesses and governmental agencies in their regions, and they must assist in building entrepreneurial environments that will help their economies grow. Through education and outreach, business schools have a responsibility to contribute to the local, national, and international communities of which they are part.

This book is of enormous interest to A.A.C.S.B. International -- the Association to Advance Collegiate Schools of Business -- a network of close to 900 business schools dedicated to advancing business and management education worldwide. Although best known for delivering the premier global accreditation for business schools, A.A.C.S.B. International also develops management education leaders through conferences and seminars. It assists member schools to improve by providing benchmarking services and publishing research about business education trends, practices, and issues. Like A.A.C.S.B. International, this book has the goal of strengthening business education worldwide. Readers are encouraged to apply the articles to reflect on current approaches to business education, explore new ideas for developing managerial talent, and debate the challenges and opportunities faced by business education in emerging economies.

Dan LeClair
Director of Knowledge Services
A.A.C.S.B. International

Acknowledgements

This book is a culmination of work that extends beyond the efforts of the primary editors. We wish to acknowledge the participation, review, and support of the following people: Dr. Raj Agrawal, Professor of Economics and International Business, Institute for Integrated Learning in Management, New Delhi, India; Mr. Mark Ballam, Associate Director, Georgia Tech C.I.B.E.R.; Mr. H. E. Jose Octavio Bordon, Ambassador of Argentina to the United States of America and Former Executive Director, Social and Economic Development Program – a joint initiative of the Government of Argentina and the Inter-American Development Bank; Dr. Michael R. Bowers, Professor of Marketing, Crummer Graduate School of Business, Rollins College; Dr. David Bruce, Professor of International Business, Institute of International Business, Georgia State University; Dr. Lee Caldwell, Professor of Strategy and Associate Dean, DuPree College of Management; Dr. Mauricio Cardenas, Professor of International Management, Tec de Monterrey, Mexico; Dr. Rajesh Chakrabarti, Assistant Professor of International Finance, DuPree College of Management; Dr. Alka Citrin, Assistant Professor of Marketing, DuPree College of Management; Dr. David M. Currie, Professor of Economics and Finance, Crummer Graduate School of Business, Rollins College; Dr. Abraham M. George, Founder and President, The George Foundation and Chairman, eMedexOnline L.L.C.; Dr. Robert G. Hawkins, past president of the Academy of International Business, Professor Emeritus of Economics and Management, past Dean of the Ivan Allen College, Georgia Tech; Dr. James Johnson, Associate Professor of International Business, Crummer Graduate School of Business, Rollins College; Dr. Saul Klein, Lansdowne Professor of International Business, University of Victoria; Dr. Rich Lee, Assistant Professor of English, S.U.N.Y. Oneonta; Dr. Shaomin Li, Professor of Management, Old Dominion University; Dr. Craig M. McAllaster, Dean and Professor of Management, Crummer Graduate School of Business, Rollins College; Dr. Cecilia McInnis-Bowers, Professor of Marketing and International Business, Rollins College; Dr. David L. McKee, Professor of Economics, Kent State University, President of the International Academy of Business Disciplines; Dr. Sergio Postigo, Cátedra Karel Steuer de Entrepreneurship, Universidad de San Andrés; Dr. Penelope Prime, Director, China Research Center, Professor of Economics and Finance, Coles College of Business, Kennesaw State University; Dr. R. Reeves-Ellington, Professor Emeritus, Binghamton University; Dr. Barry R. Render, Professor of Management Science and Operations Management, Crummer Graduate School of Business, Rollins College; Dr. Francis Ulgado, Associate Professor of International Marketing and Faculty Director, G.T. C.I.B.E.R.; Dr. Thomaz Wood Jr., Associate

Professor, Escola de Administração de Empresas de São Paulo; Ms. Tracy Wooten, Visiting Instructor of Composition, University of Central Florida.

In addition to the people above, the following institutions were instrumental in providing the resources for making this book a reality: A.G.L. Resources Inc.; the Brazilian-American Chamber of Commerce; the Consulate General of Argentina in Atlanta and the Embassy of Argentina in Washington, D.C.; the Crummer Graduate School of Business, Rollins College; the DuPree College of Management's Dean's Office, Georgia Tech, Atlanta, Georgia; the Georgia Tech Center for International Business Education and Research at the DuPree College of Management; the National Association of Chinese Americans; the U.S. Department of Education C.I.B.E.R. Programs; World Times, Inc.

I. Developing a Knowledge-Based Economy

Chapter 1
Introduction

Ilan Alon
Crummer Graduate School of Business, Rollins College

John R. McIntyre
DuPree College of Management, Georgia Institute of Technology

INTRODUCTION

This book is a by-product of a research conference on the trends and prospects of business education and emerging market economies co-organized by the Georgia Tech Center for International Business Education and Research (G.T. C.I.B.E.R.), the DuPree College of Management, Georgia Institute of Technology, and the Crummer Graduate School of Business, Rollins College.

Containing refereed chapters relating to the intersection of two streams of research -- business education and emerging markets -- the book contributes to the respective literatures by exploring the role of business education in emerging market economies, the impact of political transitioning and economic development on the educational environment of selected emerging markets, the challenges and opportunities facing educators and educational institutions in emerging markets, and pedagogical and curricular innovations relating to emerging market environments. The book discusses the business education conditions in various regions of the developing world including Asia, Latin America, Eastern Europe, the Middle East, and Africa. Furthermore, the large emerging markets of Argentina, Brazil, India, China, Vietnam, Russia, and South Africa are explored in more detail in individualized chapters.

Emerging markets consist of about 80% of the world's population and 60% of its natural resources and are thought to be important foreign markets for international trade and investment (Welsh and Alon, 2003). While no one accepted definition of emerging market has been agreed upon, certain dimensions of emerging markets have been established along with their impact on the economic, political, and social environments. Welsh and Alon identified three characteristics associated with emerging market economies:

level of economic development, economic growth, and market governance. Per capita G.D.P. in emerging markets are significantly lower than those of the developed markets. Emerging markets' G.D.P. per capita lie between those of the less developed world (L.D.C.s) and the developed markets, but their income per head varies widely. For example, three of the big emerging markets (B.E.M.s) -- India, China, and Vietnam -- fall in the lowest per capita income class as classified by the World Bank (World Bank, 2001). Yet others, such as South Korea, have G.D.P. per capita income well over $10,000.

Despite the lower per capita G.D.P., emerging markets have received an increasing share of investment and trade in recent years due in part to their growing economies. As these economies grew, so did their demand for Western lifestyles, infrastructure development, and educational reform. Aspirations to technological leadership and political influence in the world have stimulated emerging market governments to invest in their transportation systems, communications industry, health sector, finance industry, and educational systems, and to further liberalize their economies to induce economic growth.

The third factor associated with emerging markets is market governance changes led in part by economic liberalization and political transitioning as emerging market governments have started to relinquish control of state-owned enterprises and have allowed market mechanisms and economic freedom to flourish. To adapt to the emergent market and governance structure of the global capitalist market, emerging markets have focused on developing their educational institutions to be able to compete on a worldwide basis. Higher education in general and business education in specific have played an important role in modernizing the countries' human resources and implementing global economic integration.

The World Economic Forum's annual Global Competitiveness Reports shed abundant light on the relationships between societal institutions and global economic growth (2004). The global growth competitiveness rankings and annual reports -- the most authoritative and comprehensive assessment of the comparative strengths and weaknesses of national economies around the world kept since 1979 -- have focused on three central pillars and sub-indices: the macroeconmic environment index, the quality of public institutions index, and the technological innovation index. The annual rankings indicate the gradual march forward of emerging market economies on two, if not three, of the sub-indices and the foundational relationship that exists between investment in basic and professional education and improvements in global growth indices over recent years.

In their book *The Emerging Markets and Higher Education: Development and Sustainability*, McMullen and his colleagues have underlined the impact of higher education on emerging markets (2000). The thrust of their analysis suggests that higher education in emerging markets has enabled these countries to achieve sustainable economic growth, develop and train their future private and public sector leaders, construct a rule of law and a legal infrastructure, and pursue cultural openness and the development of a middle class. Furthermore, higher education has allowed for the creation of a knowledge-based economy that reduces illiteracy, advances technical skills and innovations, promotes democratic citizenship, and upgrades the skills of the population. Evidence of this is reflected in foreign direct investment flows. In sum, emerging market economies, following the well-known stages of the economic development model, will be able to move up the value-added chain by investing in their educational systems and physical infrastructure and by strengthening their political and economic market institutions.

Business education remains a nascent phenomenon in many of the emerging markets where economic elites have been heretofore trained overseas. We may be seeing a makeshift "import substitution" approach in the development of the requisite business education infrastructure in emerging market economies. The fast changing demographics and endogenous market dynamics more than justify a scholarly review and analysis of a policy area now clearly identified as critical by scholars, public policy makers, and business executives. Recent increases in business activity in emerging markets has raised the need of emerging markets for home grown cadres of managers and business professionals. Moreover, the industrialized markets are increasingly required to understand the unique conditions in these dynamic, developing, and transitioning economies. This book addresses both needs. It is divided into four parts relating to business education and emerging markets:

I. Developing a Knowledge-based Economy
II. Curricular and Course Content Innovation
III. Experiential and Virtual Educational Models
IV. Strategic International Educational Alliances

PART I: DEVELOPING A KNOWLEDGE-BASED ECONOMY

The first section of the book focuses on knowledge transfer to emerging markets. This knowledge transfer, particularly in the fields of business and management education, has been critical to emerging market industrialization and integration into the global innovation-driven economy.

Chapter 2, written by McKee, McKee, and Garner, examines the impact of business knowledge passed on from multinational consultants and, more specifically, large accounting firms to emerging market economies. Multinational consultants and major accounting firms provide facilitative services and specialized education, both formal and practical in industrializing countries. The authors begin with an overview of business service roles, followed by a discussion of the internationalization of the services in question. Subsequent to that, the educational impacts of such services are considered. Their discussion concludes with a final appraisal of such impacts, and the potential for their being provided by a wider menu of service firms.

In chapter 3, Reeves-Ellington discusses the content of business education in the context of emerging markets. He argues that there is a missing link in the traditional methods of teaching business in the context of these complex and dynamic markets. The author argues that business in many emerging markets is becoming a key player in society and its involvement with other communities. However, traditional business education fails to prepare graduates for operating fully in such complex environments. To do so requires the learning of new cultural and analytical skills as well as the ability to apply them in ways that empower a broader managerial audience to undertake change. The chapter calls for a successful emerging market-focused business curricula which provide traditional business skills along with instruction in the underlying business and societal value assumptions, theories, and models suitable for a culturally diverse and global environment.

In chapter 4, Fey and Zimmerman review educational reform in the largest and most populous emerging market, China. In China, the business curriculum includes the core disciplines of economics, mathematics, and behavioral science. Beyond that language, management sciences, psychology, and law are essential. Educational reform as it applies to business and management still faces serious challenges. Chinese education emphasizes conformity as much as specialized skills. It may, in fact, undermine the ability of students to apply their knowledge creatively. This suggests that in addition to content, certain skill issues should be addressed to meet the needs of a market economy. Despite a highly successful transition economy and an education system that receives high marks among developing countries, the Chinese educational system nonetheless has one of the lowest rates of return to education in both the developed and the developing worlds. The authors advocate a model originally developed for the "internationalization" of the business curriculum in the U.S., report on their survey interviews with managers at successful market oriented businesses in and around Shanghai, and examine the curriculum of the College of International Business at Shanghai University as an illustrative case.

In contrast to the emerging market economies of Asia and China, Bruce, Sombra, and Carrillo report on the educational performance of Latin America and Brazil in chapter 5. According the authors, the region has fallen behind much of Asia in the most basic measures of educational performance. This may be a major contributor to lessened success in economic development as well. The authors delineate a number of trade-offs in educational reform and development that exist between:

- primary/secondary education versus tertiary education,

- general higher education and technical training,
- teaching vs. scholarship,
- liberal vs. professional education,
- graduate professional vs. academic programs,
- degree programs vs. non-degree offerings, and
- public vs. private institutions.

A case study focuses on Brazil, adding a country-specific example of the issues and problems confronting educational reform in Latin America. Executive education is further discussed in detail.

Chapter 6 by Wood and Paula dovetails with Chapter 5 by augmenting the discussion of Brazil, the largest economy in Latin America, and focusing on the master's level education in business. In Brazil, as in other emerging markets, the development of business administration as a teaching and research field can be identified fairly closely with the industrialization process. In the 1990s, management education underwent considerable expansion and diversification. In the year 2000, there were, according to the Ministry of Education, 969 undergraduate programs, 28 master's programs, and ten doctorate programs in Brazil. In August 2002, the number of undergraduate programs had grown to an astonishing 2,687! The authors describe an important form of graduate business education in Brazil that is differentiated from the M.B.A. program of North America -- the M.P.A. programs (Professional Master in Business Administration). The M.P.A.s were officially authorized by the Brazilian Ministry of Education in 1998 and accredited in 2001. The authors' field work involves document analysis and in-depth interviews with ten coordinators and key-persons involved in six Brazilian M.P.A. programs, developed by five different institutions in four different states.

PART II: CURRICULAR AND COURSE CONTENT INNOVATIONS

The internationalization of business followed by the post 1980s wave of globalization have, in a very real sense, stimulated a parallel internationalization of business education as emerging markets have sought to learn and master the ways of the advanced industrialized nations. With increased internationalization of business education, the need for a global curriculum responsive to the local environment has become increasingly important. Business schools across the world are challenged with the dual task of developing universal skills for the global economy and well-honed curricula which address the local realities of their particular regions and countries. Part II discusses replication of business education models across countries, unique features of business education in emerging markets, application of Western educational models for teaching business in emerging markets, specific models for teaching students from emerging markets, and training heritage students for doing business in their chosen emerging market environment.

In chapter 7, Yonkers discusses research which divides educational systems across the world based on socio-cultural types and the applicability of an American model across culturally diverse countries. Her research reveals that there are various factors affecting the replication of American business education programs in emerging countries. These include language of instruction, educational funding sources, government educational policy, and local versus global education. Five cultural systems of education are discussed based on their educational values: Humanism, Rationalism, Naturalism, Universal and Comprehensive Naturalism, and Confucianism. It is argued that a country's educational philosophy will affect teacher/student relationships, choice of curricula, instructional designs, and school/business relationships. Keeping these factors in mind is important for successfully replicating programs in emerging countries.

Lyudmila and Lee, in chapter 8, discuss the development and unique features of the Ukrainian business educational environment, showing how innovations in emerging markets facilitate the county's increased integration in the global economy. The chapter examines the challenges of teaching and learning business and English at the same time in Ukrainian universities, techniques for incorporating cross-cultural education into the business-English curriculum, and acquisition of cultural intelligence through language and literature. The paper advocates a desirable link between linguistic competence, cultural understanding, and business education in the development of a globally equipped managerial cadre. Business education curricula in advanced industrialized economies can learn from emerging markets such as Ukraine methods to instill cultural intelligence in their students using language and literature. Lyudmila and Lee's arguments echo the call for the more liberal education advocated in chapter 3 by Reeves-Ellington.

Gillespie and Riddle, in chapter 9, discuss the implementation of a teaching methodology largely developed in and for the United States in the context of the Arab Middle East and North Africa (M.E.N.A.). This area of the world has suffered from lower economic growth and traditionally insular cultural elements, differentiated sharply in values from Western orthodoxy. In M.E.N.A. countries, trade liberalization has not generated substantial increases in employment opportunities, and many of the countries still depend on trade in commodities. Cultural factors such as Islamic values and collectivism as well as educational factors such as the number of students per class and traditional pedagogical approaches denote a sharp cultural divide which makes a Western style pedagogical approach perhaps challenging. The authors analyze the suitability of the case method in M.E.N.A. countries and its applicability in this distinctly differing cultural framework. Middle East business leaders often complain that the M.E.N.A. workforce is ill-prepared for today's business environment. The Middle East would not achieve its full economic potential unless the region revolutionizes its educational system and adopts a total change in approaches. The authors argue that the case method can provide students with an opportunity to exercise problem-solving and decision-making skills, which are crucial to coping with the changing business environment that M.E.N.A. managers face.

McInnis-Bowers, Chew, and Bowers, in Chapter 10, evolve a model for educating students from emerging markets in the United States, using experiences from graduate management education in a small, private, liberal-arts college. A specially designed curriculum for students with undergraduate degrees from foreign universities was developed to meet the challenges of attracting international students, developing meaningful and practical experiences, teaching leadership skills, and developing cultural competence. The program features a business internship experience and cultural immersion. From this curricular platform, the college was able to partner with a university overseas to create a study-exchange program, which enabled the working professionals studying in the part-time graduate management program to attend classes and live from one week to up to one month in an international community. The program design lends itself to partnering opportunities with institutions of higher learning in emerging markets. Elements contributing to the success of the program are identified so that the program's heuristic values may be replicated at other domestic and foreign universities.

In line with chapter 10, Laufer discusses in chapter 11 a response to emerging market business education in the United States, but the target market for this type of training is differentiated by focusing on heritage students, who often form an important link to emerging market trade and investment. These so called heritage students are diaspora members living in industrialized countries and who are considering returning to their former homelands where they may pursue careers as managers or entrepreneurs. The demand for such an educational approach proposed by Laufer stems from international migration, market liberalization in emerging markets, the growth of diaspora communities in industrialized countries, and opportunities derived from globalization. The paper describes Professor Laufer's experience teaching a course focused on the business environment in Israel over a five-year period at the University of Texas at Austin, providing guidance to educators about creating this type of course for other emerging markets. The success of the Israel course at the University of Texas at Austin is a clear indication that courses targeting heritage groups can be successful and serve as a valuable source of training for managers and entrepreneurs who could, in the future, be living in emerging markets.

In chapter 12, Wood describes the application of an experiential Internet-based pedagogical tool to teach business in developing nations and to improve existing student skills in forming businesses and entrepreneurships. The United Nations has repeatedly emphasized the need for developing countries to leverage information and communication technology (I.C.T.) as a potential means of improving quality of life as measured by G.D.P. per capita, gender equity, and protection of local culture. There is a corresponding need for educational tools in developing countries that demonstrate how profitable micro business models using Internet technology can be put into practice. Using common e-commerce based platforms for teaching business in emerging markets, Wood demonstrates to students how to develop competitive intelligence and market locally sourced products. The online auction pedagogical approach in emerging markets proves to combine the best in state-of-the-art management education: technology, globalization, and experiential based entrepreneurship.

In chapter 13, Jones and McCann continue Wood's line of exploration into internet-based technologies in emerging market education. The authors tellingly acknowledge the need for developing countries to provide opportunities for larger numbers of employees to undertake education in a broad range of business issues, if these countries are to develop competitive industries in a globally networked business world, and recommend virtual situated learning environments to fulfill, at least in part, this need. The chapter exemplifies a Virtual Situated Learning Environment (V.S.L.E.) developed for emerging markets by the University of the Royal Melbourne Institute of Technology (Australia) to underpin a Leadership and Management course. In 2003, the School of Management was asked to prepare a business course on Leadership and Management Skills for on-line delivery as part of an M.B.A. program to be delivered in various developing countries, commencing with Vietnam and China. The Leadership and Management course is the introductory course in the M.B.A. that is delivered generally and in industry specific formats in both Australia and overseas, in a F2F experiential learning environment. The course is designed to maximize experiential group learning opportunities through small and large group international interactions designed to encourage students to reflect upon the real-world working environment in which they seek to become leaders and managers of the future.

Chapters 14, 15, and 16 form a cohesive framework for internationalizing the curriculum with respect to developing skills in Western-based students relevant to business practices in emerging markets. In chapter 14, Doh and Vachani suggest that because most students in North America have had less exposure to emerging markets and are therefore less familiar with their particular features, experiential exercises are a particularly valuable tool in helping underscore the unique characteristics of these economies and the sometimes unusual situations facing managers operating in these emerging market environments. The authors provide brief descriptions of eight cases and exercises they developed to underscore the concepts and themes of emerging markets and elaborate on two of them in further detail. From their framework, instructors can choose among a range of materials depending on the emerging market issues they wish to uncover and the level of analysis they would like to target. The countries used in their simulation case studies include Mexico, South Africa, China, South Korea, Chile, India, and Russia.

Unlike the experiential exercises and simulations described in the previous chapters, chapter 15, written by Johnson, and chapter 16, authored by Currie, Krbec, and Matulich, address learning by doing, involving travel to emerging markets and face-to-face interactions with individuals of differing cultures and from less developed economies.

In chapter 15, Johnson focuses on how experiential learning in emerging markets through travel, experience, lectures, and company visits can augment American M.B.A. student knowledge of the global economy. Johnson critically evaluates the role of the foreign experience in international business education in emerging markets by applying experiential learning theory to seven types of foreign experiences: (1) in-class foreign experience; (2) study tour; (3) integrated study tour; (4) overseas practicum/project; (5) foreign language training; (6) foreign exchange program; and (7) overseas internship. The author advocates that integrated study tours and global practica, on the one hand, offer a compromise between minimizing the cost of overseas training and providing students with a realistic learning experience while, on the other hand, offering students exposure to the foreign environment in a short period of time, allowing minimal foreign interactions, iteration, and application.

Focusing more narrowly on the global practicum experience, Currie and his colleagues explain the benefits and the application of this unique, hands-on learning model utilizing global work-directed teams. According to these authors, higher levels of education for international business require that students experience what it is like to work in another country, and the global practicum provides exactly that experience. The chapter reports the results of a collaborative practicum between universities in the United States and Croatia. The practicum achieves several goals on the part of students, faculty, the universities, and the government of Croatia – a win-win collaboration that can be replicated across different universities.

In chapter 17, Potigo and Tamborini detail how academic institutions in emerging markets are proceeding in building up a local cadre of entrepreneurs as well as the skills and abilities appropriate to a dynamic and changing world. It is argued that the educational system of Argentina does not generate vocations or capacities to undertake new ventures; the citizenry is not educated with an entrepreneurial mindset; and current education and social aspirations are more oriented to work in large corporations. However, in the last decade, this situation has begun to change since economic opportunities in large corporations seemed less guaranteed. The chapter overviews the field of entrepreneurship education among the universities in Argentina and evokes the experience of the first Argentinean chair in entrepreneurship supported by a donor. Furthermore, it reviews the teaching methods and underlying pedagogical models used and the results they yield. This educational system rivals the best in world in sophistication and integration of the state-of-the-art in entrepreneurship education.

PART III: STRATEGIC INTERNATIONAL EDUCATIONAL ALLIANCES

To upgrade their skills and to deploy the latest and most impactful business education technologies, pedagogy, and curricula, emerging market universities have partnered with universities in advanced industrialized nations. The chapters in this section examine such cooperation in India, Russia, Vietnam, and South Africa, and each advance various prescriptive lessons leading to an evolving paradigm.

In chapter 18, Potter and Farah consider the educational alliance linking Eastern Michigan University's College of Business in developing and implementing a program of cooperation with Osmania University in Hyderabad, Andhra Pradesh, India. According to the authors, such strategic partnerships among the business programs of American and Indian universities began in 1959 and continue to flourish in the age of globalization. The first American partners were "mainline" research universities whose business schools still rank in the top 50 within the United States. Such is the case in most emerging markets. There are now over 1,200 business programs in the United States, and every one is challenged to demonstrate relevance in a global economy where emerging markets are the next wave of globalization. Today, there are nearly 800 business programs in India. Among these programs, there is great diversity. The process of selecting a partner and building a partnership has become very complex. At the same time, the potential value of collaboration for partners has grown tremendously. The strategic considerations that shaped the approach and commitments of the respective institutions in the United State and India are discussed, and the outlines of the resulting program are examined.

In chapter 19, Erickson, Insinga, and Kureshov map out a successful partnership between a small U.S. teaching institution, S.U.N.Y. College at Oneonta, and the Higher Business School of the Siberian Aerospace University in Krasnoyarsk, Russia. The program has internationalized both curricula through exchange of faculty and students. The specific characteristics of Russia and its people, Krasnoyarsk, and the Higher Business School are analyzed in this case study. Lessons can be drawn from the factors that brought the program to this point. Similarly, the chapter provides a useful study of how a curriculum can be adapted to the special needs and wants of a partner in emerging markets.

In chapter 20, Napier and Mai examine the educational strategic alliance between the National Economics University of Vietnam and Boise State University. The two universities have been partners since 1994 when Boise State was invited to offer its M.B.A. program in Vietnam and develop university teachers able to lead Vietnam into a market-oriented economy. The nine-year relationship included joint teaching, training, research, and cooperation in establishing and building the N.E.U. Business School. The development and capacity building stemmed from the financial support of the Swedish International Development Cooperation Agency (Sida) and the U.S. Agency for International Development (U.S.A.I.D.). In this context, the chapter examines three critical aspects of the relationship: (1) how a state university in Idaho became involved in a $2 million Swedish funded project to deliver a "train-the-trainer" M.B.A. to 30 lecturers at the N.E.U., which ultimately became a $8.5 million project to create a business school at the National Economics University; (2) how to manage such a joint educational venture and insure that it benefits both institutions; and (3) how the universities built a solid cooperative relationship through exchanges and internships, joint teaching and research, training programs offered in the U.S. and Vietnam, university and college administrative support and guidance, as well as professional staff mentoring and support. Finally, the paper comments on "lessons learned" from organizational and individual perspectives.

In contrast to the emerging markets of India, Russia, and Vietnam, South Africa is more economically advanced. In South Africa, economic liberalization was accompanied by political liberalization and pressures to transform the economic and institutional base of the country to make it more demographically representative. This mix was combined with pressure to respond to the needs of retaining and attracting global business firms. Klein and Ward, in chapter 21, analyze the changing context of business education in South Africa and the specific conditions affecting the Wits Business School of the University of the Witwatersrand in Johannesburg, South Africa's leading business school. Formally the Graduate School of Business Administration at the University of the Witwatersrand, Johannesburg, Wits Business School (hereafter W.B.S.) was established under the guidance of faculty from Harvard and Stanford Business Schools. W.B.S. began offering executive programs in 1968, followed in 1970 by M.B.A. degrees. The institution is an example of an emerging market institution that has succeeded in the new South African context. This success, as reflected in rankings of business schools, has developed based on a strong commitment to internationalization. Klein and Ward review the challenges faced by the institution in faculty recruiting, curriculum changes, international study tours, diverse program offerings, local case development, and international partnerships. The South African experience offers both lessons and cautionary notes for similar business schools in other emerging markets, balancing the imperatives of globalization and localization.

CONCLUSION

There is a sense of dynamism and excitement relating to prospects for increased cooperation in trade, investment, and cultural exchange between emerging market nations and the developed countries of the world economy. There is also a sense of uncertainty and instability inherent in the transitioning into more responsive economic systems and the shifting power bases which have come to characterize economic globalization. This has created a dual need, shared by developed countries and emerging markets alike, to understand dynamic international business environments and to learn from each other.

Emerging markets are propelled by the need to catch up with the developed countries in the areas so well delineated by the World Economic Forum's Global Competitiveness Reports -- technological innovation, predictable public institutions, labor standards, capital utilization, and efficiency. Business education provides one of the key and necessary ingredient in this third wave of globalization, as it has come to be termed. Professors from overseas are often invited as foreign experts to teach, develop curricula, and train the trainers. Simultaneously, developed countries want to tap the potential of emerging markets as evidenced in differing wages, cost advantages, and resource acquisition. Multinational companies and mini-multinationals, whether through efficiency or resource or market-seeking, are keen on sourcing products and services overseas and selling their products and services to the same destinations. This virtuous cycle fuels the economic growth so evident in emerging market dynamism and provides the impetus for new models of educational cooperation.

REFERENCES

McMullen, Matthew S., Mauch, James E., and Donnorummo, Bob, eds. (2000). *The Emerging Markets and Higher Education: Development and Sustainability*, New York: RoutledgeFalmer.

Welsh, Dianne and Alon, Ilan, eds. (2001). *International Franchising in Emerging Markets: Central and Eastern Europe and Latin America*, Chicago IL: C.C.H. Inc. Publishing.

World Bank. (2001). *World Report Development Report 2000/2001: Attacking Poverty*, Oxford, U.K.: Oxford University Press.

World Economic Forum. (2004). *Global Competitiveness Report 2003-2004*, http://www.weforum.org/.

Chapter 2
Multinational Consultants as Contributors to Business Education and Economic Sophistication in Emerging Markets

David L. McKee
Kent State University

Yosra A. McKee
Kent State University

Don E. Garner
California State University, Stanislus

INTRODUCTION: THE ROLE OF FACILITATIVE BUSINESS SERVICES

The concept of various service cadres as facilitators of business operations in advanced economies is hardly novel among students of service ascendancy in such economies. Indeed services designed to meet the needs of business clients have been prominent among the service sub-sectors leading the overall expansion of services in those economies. If this is true of advanced economies, a progression to the global economy seems logical: "Once Services emerged as facilitators in both the operation and expansion of modern economies, the extension of that role beyond national boundaries was all but inevitable" (McKee and Garner, 1992, 65). Since services have assumed a major facilitative role in the global economy, they themselves have often become internationalized. In the light of such advances it seems reasonable to ask what role business services may be shouldering in emerging nations.

The current authors have held ongoing interests in the role of international consulting firms, notably the major accounting firms, in facilitating business operations in various regional cadres of emerging nations. It seems evident that large international accounting firms have become major facilitators of business in the nations previously grouped as the Third World.

Clearly, the traditional accounting and auditing services offered by the firms in question provide some homogeneity in business practices to individuals and firms, not to mention nations operating in the global economy. By doing so they facilitate business operations in that economy and its constituent jurisdictions. The major accounting firms have been found to be doing just that in a wide range of locations (McKee, Garner, and McKee, 1998, 1999, 2000, and 2002).

Beyond the traditional accounting offerings, the firms in question have developed extensive menus of consulting service offerings aimed at assisting individuals, firms, and governments in their business related activities. Those offerings are aimed at facilitating the operations of the clients using them. Thus it seems reasonable to regard such offerings as facilitative business services. Indeed it seems quite clear that all business services by their very existence are performing facilitative roles. Were they doing less, their ongoing existence would have already been threatened.

Facilitative business services, as they are marketed internationally, are not solely the preserve of major accounting firms. Major banks, insurance firms, legal firms, and various consulting agencies may also be involved in numerous jurisdictions. Accounting examples are highlighted in the present discussion since they represent the segment of the facilitative business service sector most familiar to the current authors.

The scope of the menu that such firms can offer can be made more obvious by an example. For that purpose the authors have chosen K.P.M.G. Indonesia. Clearly K.P.M.G. ranks among the largest accounting firms operating in the post Pacific crisis, post Enron/Andersen debacle, and Indonesia is one of the larger nations in the former Third World grouping.

K.P.M.G. Indonesia consists of Siddharta, Siddharta and Harsono, and Siddharto Consulting Services (KPMG Indonesia, 2000). Combined, the two domestic firms claim to be one of the largest practices in Indonesia and offer their services to multinational corporations, joint ventures, and domestic companies (K.P.M.G. Indonesia, 2000). They market themselves as a source of international expertise in Indonesia, offering access to the global network of K.P.M.G. (K.P.M.G. Indonesia, 2000). To identify them as a purveyor of facilitative business services seems appropriate.

The firms offer a range of assurance services composed mainly of auditing, accounting, and risk management. To "ensure that management goals and objectives are achieved efficiently, effectively and economically" (K.P.M.G. Indonesia, 2000, 2), the firms pursue a system based approach driven by risk assessment models (McKee, Garner, and McKee, 2002). The firms note that accounting services are developed to assist with the preparation and management of underlying records and that they (the firm) specialize in outsourcing financial records (K.P.M.G. Indonesia, 2000).

Information and management services consist in the main of business support and compliance services, concerned with information systems

(K.P.M.G. Indonesia, 2000). The aim is to ensure adequate internal controls for systems and, beyond that, that systems applications are effective (K.P.M.G. Indonesia, 2000). "Recommendations for improving accounting systems, controls and other operational aspects of the business are made in a management letter at the conclusion of each audit" (McKee, Garner, and McKee, 2002, 128).

The firms can also assist with tax matters. In Indonesia non-compliance vis a vis taxation can elicit significant penalties. Thus the comprehensive range of tax services offered by the firms are popular with both businesses and individuals (McKee, Garner, and McKee, 2002). Beyond taxation, financial advisory services are also available, consisting mainly of corporate finance and corporate recovery/restructuring (McKee, Garner, and McKee, 2002). In the field of corporate finance the firm deals with acquisitions, takeovers, or mergers and also disposals and the identification of businesses to be bought or sold.

Beyond such matters the firms can assist with business appraisals, valuations, and advice on initial public offerings as well as share issues and flotations and project structured finance (McKee, Garner, and McKee, 2002). All such services are provided by a team of executives, well versed in the capital market, the securities industry, and investment banking (McKee, Garner, and McKee, 2002). "Such expertise combined with an understanding of local business, legal and cultural issues gives the firms the ability to facilitate the business operations of clients in Indonesia" (McKee, Garner, and McKee, 2002, 129).

Consulting services offered by the firm range from human resources to business strategies and from information systems to financial management (K.P.M.G. Indonesia, 2000). The goal in mind is to help clients to improve the effectiveness and profitability of their enterprises (K.P.M.G. Indonesia, 2000). Assistance is available in corporate management including such things as strategic planning, organizational restructuring, and economic assessment and forecasting, not to mention investment appraisal and feasibility (K.P.M.G. Indonesia, 2000). Attention can also be given to supply chain management and improving overall effectiveness, efficiency, and financial performance (K.P.M.G. Indonesia, 2000).

Marketing assistance can include research and planning the forecasting of sales and market trends, pricing, sales administration, and customer service (K.P.M.G. Indonesia, 2000). Operations management can cover such matters as facilities planning and production methods, and also production and materials requirements (K.P.M.G. Indonesia, 2000). The firm can also assist with quality control, inventory management, distribution management, and clerical productivity (K.P.M.G. Indonesia, 2000).

The firm also offers services in the area of human resource management, including personnel planning, executive selection, staff recruitment, performance appraisal, and personnel management systems.

Help is also available with respect to job evaluation, salary administration, and management training and development (K.P.M.G. Indonesia, 2000).

Financial management is also on the menu of service offerings. In this regard, matters pertaining to financial planning and budgeting, performance evaluation, and control and responsibility accounting can be dealt with as can product and service costing, capital expenditure and control, financial analysis, and financial management reporting (K.P.M.G. Indonesia, 2000).

The service menu of the firm also contains offerings relating to system integration, including information service strategy, operation strategy, system architecture, system selection, and evaluation. Related offerings include enterprise infrastructure technology review, enterprise resource planning, supply chain management, and change management. Still more assistance involves custom application development, data warehousing, secure electronic commerce, enterprise system integration, and program or project assurance (K.P.M.G. Indonesia, 2000).

Certainly K.P.M.G. and its Indonesian partner firms are offering a wide array of services designed to facilitate business. Such services have been seen to assist clients with four major issues (McKee, Garner, and McKee, 2002). They can help with the making of better informed decisions on strategy and policy issues related to change. They can assist in setting up effective management structures supported by sound personnel policies. They can help in ensuring that management information systems cover the needs of the organization. They can also help organizations to become more competitive by improving marketing, reducing manufacturing and distribution costs, and enhancing the supply of useful information (K.P.M.G. Indonesia, 2000).

Clearly this firm provides a good example of the scope of involvement such an enterprise can generate. K.P.M.G. or similar firms may well offer different service menus in different locations. What seems to be clear is that K.P.M.G. Indonesia irrespective of the level of its expertise on site has access to the vast resources of K.P.M.G. globally. Of course this illustrates one of the major strengths that large international accounting firms can bring to bear in specific settings. They do have access to the resources of their international networks, which of course strengthens their facilitative capabilities.

THE INTERNATIONALIZATION OF THE SERVICES IN QUESTION

Michael Porter has referred to the internationalization of competition in service pursuits (1990). He suggested that firms supplying such services could easily adjust their offerings to local needs, thus retaining a competitive edge over potential local competitors (Porter, 1990). Indeed the competitive needs of such service firms have prompted them to expand the number of jurisdictions from which they operate. Whether or not such an expansion may embrace settings in emerging nations will undoubtedly reflect client needs. According to Porter "a more fluid movement of information ... fast transportation and increasing ease and familiarity with international travel ... make buyers more likely to seek out the world's best service firms" (Porter, 1990, 251). In turn the market potential of domestic service firms in some locations may be impeded because "buyers with a more international outlook are increasingly willing to hire leading foreign firms" (Porter, 1990, 251).

If Porter's logic is correct, an expanding global economy has fostered a climate for the emergence of major multinational service firms facilitating the operations of client corporations through their offerings. Such offerings bring to bear predictably skilled international operators that may leave little room for the emergence of local practitioners in similar pursuits. Clearly such international service networks homogenize and make predictable the quality of their offerings, an attractive set of circumstances for potential corporate clients, but perhaps a mixed blessing for host jurisdictions.

As early as 1988 Thiery J. Noyelle and Anna B. Dutka suggested that with respect to the movement of U.S. based service firms into foreign jurisdictions, such firms often found local firms to have very little expertise and thus "U.S. firms played a key role in many countries in creating a domestic market" (29). In the light of such observations it has been suggested that "such firms ... have had a good deal to do with the structure and perhaps the growth or development of the economies in question" (McKee and Garner, 1992, 68).

According to a United Nations report, the general impact of international services may be difficult to measure because a whole range of services penetrates international boundaries within transnational corporate systems (1987). Included on occasion are such things as advertising, accounting, management, research, data processing, and legal services. In light of corporate secrecy practices, host nations may be hard pressed to assess local impacts. Beyond that "the internationalized services of international business units may preclude the development of domestic service groups" (McKee and Garner, 1992, 68).

Such impacts may be most noticeable in smaller emerging nations and increasingly significant where the services are aimed at international rather than strictly domestic concerns. However "even services aimed directly at the world economy may have significant impacts on small, local economies" (McKee and Tisdell, 1990). Indeed many smaller jurisdictions have included such service strategies in their development plans, witness widespread efforts at developing offshore financial centers.

It has been recognized that exposure to various business related services has been enhanced as such services are put in place to meet the production needs of multinational firms (McKee and Garner, 1992). Where such production units are positioned to deal with local markets, the impact of the service groups that they generate may be substantial (McKee and Garner, 1992). If the service groups themselves are international, then service-operating modes may bear a foreign imprint "which, depending upon the size and influence of the implanted service establishments, may have considerable impact upon the shaping of the local business service sector and the local economy in general" (McKee and Garner, 1992, 69).

Few would dispute the need for various services if a particular nation wishes to maintain or augment its operations in the global economy. In pursuing such a goal, the nation concerned may make irrevocable adjustments in its domestic economy. In jurisdictions where sophisticated cadres of business services are limited, developmental processes may be impacted adversely (United Nations, 1987). Clearly, various business services are needed by nations wishing to strengthen their linkages to the global economy. While contributing to such international linkages the services in question may come with a price to be exacted upon the domestic economy. That price may include the emergence of a foreign business service establishment, which may impair the development of a domestic counterpart. Whether such an occurrence is good or bad is, of course, jurisdiction specific and much dependent upon the emergence of a local business culture reflecting sound economic practices. Both formal and practical educational elements in this equation can hardly be ignored.

The significance of business services to the global economy is hardly in dispute. "Within and between national economies, services facilitate the passage of materials, personnel and funds within and between business units" (McKee, Amara, and Garner, 1995, 255). Accounting, financial and legal practitioners, not to mention a host of other specialized service groups, have generated combined impacts that have made global business more efficient and better integrated.

Although a positive role for facilitative business services in the global economy appears to be self-evident at this juncture, such a role in locations within emerging nations may require further consideration. Clearly the purveyors of the service needs of multinational firms in the global economy are facilitating the operations of those firms and thus strengthening the economy. Those purveyors have frequently become multinational firms in their own right and as such have been able to provide the expertise of their global networks to corporate and other clients in specific jurisdictions. In doing so they can guarantee a homogeneity to the nature and quality of their offerings. Clearly this would seem to benefit clients and host economies alike. The hiring of foreign consultants may be cost effective and at the same time may tap the efficiency of international service networks. However it will undoubtedly retard certain domestic career paths and employment opportunities. Such issues can be alleviated to some extent by jurisdictions that require the hiring of domestic onsite consulting partners.

International consultants may augment their domestic impacts in emerging nations in cases where they opt to open domestic offices. Such decisions are influenced by the size of the domestic economy in question, its relationship to other nations and jurisdictions, and, of course, the nature of the type of consulting activity contemplated.

Generally speaking, one might expect firms offering facilitative services in the global economy to consider branch offices in larger emerging nations as compared to offices in smaller jurisdictions. To begin with the larger nations in question would be more likely to house production units associated with multinational manufacturing firms. Facilitative consultants are known to favor locations giving access to potential clients. Consulting branch offices located to service multinational corporate clients would also be in a position to offer their services to domestic businesses as well as government agencies and others who might benefit from their expertise.

International service purveyors may also be prompted to open branch offices in jurisdictions that are the seat of concentrations of activity aimed at the global economy irrespective of the size of the jurisdictions concerned. Examples of such activities abound among actual or would be offshore financial centers (McKee, Garner, and McKee, 2000). Many such centers are emerging nations that have chosen the hosting of international business services as a path to economic development. Such centers, when successful, house banks and other business service groups, whose major responsibilities lie well beyond the boundaries of the jurisdictions in question. Branches of multinational service firms contribute significant employment opportunities to the domestic economy. Those employment opportunities are filled by both foreign and domestic workers. Certainly successful offshore financial centers boast economies that are larger and more sophisticated than might have been the case had they opted for an alternative route for development.

The nature of the consulting activity also has some bearing upon whether the firms offering it opt to open branch offices and where those branch offices may locate. Sophisticated scientific and engineering firms appear least likely among consultants to opt for wide arrays of branch offices embracing settings in emerging nations. Such consulting groups are more likely to operate out of locations in major international service centers from which teams of specialized professionals can be dispatched on project specific bases. This may be reflected in a lack of domestic firms capable of replicating their services and also in a lack of pressure for training domestic professionals.

EDUCATIONAL IMPACTS IN EMERGING NATIONS

Clearly various international accounting firms and other consultants offering facilitative services to business clients have major impacts in the global economy. Such impacts are both international and jurisdiction specific. Some such impacts are self evident, stemming from the successful completion of consulting roles of various descriptions. Others are much more difficult to assess. Examples of this last category often relate to education. Certainly international business consultants through their operations impinge in various ways upon educational concerns.

As Michael Porter has suggested, such consultants by their very existence may discourage the development of local consultants in the domestic economies of emerging nations. If successful international consultants were readily available, what need would there be for domestic counterparts? The expertise offered may serve clients and their economies well while simultaneously retarding the need for the development of domestic expertise.

The accounting firms may enjoy an advantage over other consultants since they have opened branches in multiple jurisdictions in order to service the traditional auditing and accounting needs of clients. Of course such branches afford local platforms from which to launch various consulting offerings.

In cases where multinational consultants open branch offices in emerging nations, the picture changes to some extent. To begin with such consultants tend to operate with a mix of foreign and domestic personnel. Typically there are positions for both professional and paraprofessional employees. Both types of employees benefit from the on-the-job training opportunities available from participation in specific projects.

Such firms are also incubators in the sense that domestic employees leave them to accept positions in the economy at large. In doing that, they take with them experience gleaned in the branch operations. Procedures learned generate demonstration effects, which in matters of business expertise contribute to stronger operating practices in domestic firms. In some cases the existence of the consulting firms generates spin off domestic firms. The whole process has a tendency to strengthen the service sectors of domestic economies.

The needs of the expanding economy generate a demand for academic programs as well. Post secondary business and professional education is encouraged. It is much easier to argue for expanded academic offerings when positions exist for graduates. Indeed, a distinct symbiosis can emerge between post secondary and technical education and the business community.

The potential for such developments can perhaps be demonstrated through a closer evaluation of the activities of specific business consultants.

In that regard, the current authors have been intrigued by the operations of major international accounting firms. While continuing to perform their traditional accounting and auditing functions, those firms have expanded their operations to include an ever-widening array of services to business.

"The importance of what international accounting firms are about in the global economy can be seen in a recent internet release by Independent Accounting International (1998)" (McKee, Garner, and McKee, 2002, 25). That group saw themselves "as an organization conceived and structured specifically for cross border operations" (Independent Accountants International, 1998). With respect to their consulting activity they suggested "we offer the same authority and reliability that business leaders already recognize in IA's extensive international accounting and auditing network, drawing on our well established offices in over 70 countries in all continents" (Independent Accountants International, 1998). This description could, of course, be replicated to illustrate the operations of a number of major international accounting firms and/or networks. Such organizations have developed wide menus of services provided on a consulting basis that far surpass their traditional accounting and auditing functions. An example of this was detailed earlier with respect to K.P.M.G. and its operations in Indonesia.

Independent Accountants International envisage a special advantage to both themselves and their clients from their supply of reliable data and advice on the country of interest, not to mention their ability to assign in-house I.A. business managers with direct experience with local business cultures as well as other nations (Independent Accountants International, 1998). In describing their personnel they stated that "each of I.A.'s Business Services affiliates is equipped to provide complete, swift response to your local business needs, identify potential pitfalls and opportunities during all phases of your venture" (Independent Accountants International, 1998).

The aims enumerated were to be accomplished through providing market research, strategic planning, and merger and acquisitions assistance and through coordinating legal and tax advising services (McKee, Garner, and McKee, 2002). Offerings also included administrative services covering accounting services as well as comprehensive management of subsidiaries. Independent Accountants International also stood ready to conduct executive searches and to provide professional staffs for subsidiaries with guarantees related to unbiased reporting, external hands on management, professional levels otherwise unattainable, and flexibility in scope and cost (1998).

As suggested "If such a network can successfully deliver on this menu of assistance, it speaks to the power they can wield in the global economy" (McKee, Garner, and McKee, 2002, 25). Beyond that, of course, is the power that they can wield in individual host jurisdictions, particularly those in emerging nations. Clearly they provide very practical facilitative business inputs to clients in such jurisdictions. Their presence provides local business training and experience to domestic employers. The services they render to clients strengthen such businesses. When their domestic employees move on to other endeavors in the local economy, they take with them their experience and expertise. The network in question provides a wide range of para-professional and professional employment opportunities in the local labor market.

Since the network in question can hardly be assumed to be the sole competitor in emerging nations hosting them, they, together with their rivals, magnify the potential for positive impacts. The availability of employment opportunities in turn encourages post secondary educational institutions to expand their business offerings. Major accounting organizations are hardly alone in generating such impacts. Various service groups aimed at facilitating business share in such positive overspills.

Independent Accountants International saw cross border operations as becoming unavoidable realities for medium sized firms (1998). "The breaking down of trade barriers, marketing integration and ever shortening distances within the global economy, are combining to bring this multinational challenge to the doorstep of companies that once could rely on a single national market" (Independent Accountants International, 1998). Beyond that they suggest that large firms are struggling with costly obstacles in foreign markets, irrespective of the depths of their experience and knowledge vis a vis home markets. Clearly the implication is that their network is capable of rendering assistance. In emerging nations that have elected a development strategy based upon manufacturing for export, the potential for assistance from such a firm seems obvious. Of course what is also obvious is the potential for expanding post secondary educational programs aimed at facilitating such concerns.

The network suggested that such international considerations see the firms concerned involved with a costly learning curve and a loss of time, effort, and money (Independent Accountants International, 1998). The most obvious issues, such as fiscal and auditing arrangements, are infrequently the sole cause of managerial problems. Included as a key element is "the supply of prompt, accurate and relevant financial and economic data on an ongoing and permanent basis" (Independent Accountants International, 1998). In addition is a needed understanding of the human, cultural and economic context of the new operating environment (Independent Accountants International, 1998). Another set of issues relates to developing the appropriate scale and costs of the management of subsidiaries, which is an issue that may benefit little from home country experience (Independent Accountants International, 1998).

Independent Accountants International is a global consulting corporation that offers business advice "on issues that involve transnational inquiries or management advisory services in many areas" (1998). Specialized services offered by member firms include market surveys, investigations and analyses, and productivity analysis and improvement (Independent Accountants International, 1998). Legal, administrative, and secretarial services are offered, as are human resources services and advice on mergers and acquisitions (Independent Accountants International, 1998). Assistance is also available concerning personal computer and software consulting services, health care consulting, and translation services (Independent Accountants International, 1998). The network can also provide information on individual or corporate investments as well as assistance on asset management involving representing troubled companies, acting as trustees and handling asset disposal (Independent Accountants International, 1998).

The network also helps with tax matters and government contracts and offers business valuation services and litigation support services (Independent Accountants International, 1998). Certainly it is involved globally in facilitating the operation of international business interests. Clearly it has much to offer to the economies of emerging nations. Its branch offices not only provide services to local markets, they are in fact a practical training ground for local personnel. They provide job opportunities for such personnel and also provide a rationale for expanding the programs offered by domestic academic institutions. They represent a good illustration of the symbiosis referred to earlier between consulting firms and local educational programs, a symbiosis that can only strengthen the economies of emerging nations concerned.

CONCLUSION: A FINAL OVERVIEW

In summary, it seems clear that services designed to facilitate business activities in the global economy have the lowest positive educational impacts in jurisdictions where they are employed as consultants on a project specific basis. In such cases, the services are provided by recruiting foreign personnel who complete their responsibilities and return to their home base. Unless the jurisdiction concerned mandates the hiring of local residents in tandem with the foreign consultants, little immediate positive impact can be expected in local labor markets. Indeed, to the extent that the operations of foreign consultants are successful, the emergence of local consulting groups may be retarded. The same can be said for the need for certain types of academic and/or technical training. Such circumstances are most likely to emerge in developing nations with respect to highly technical skills that can be acquired from international markets.

In cases where multinational consulting firms actually open branch offices in emerging nations, as do the accounting firms, the picture changes. Such offices in providing their services also offer opportunities for employment and indeed on-the-job training to local professional and para-professional personnel. Such employees, in cases where they move on to other positions in the local labor force, take with them skills sharpened by experience, which may generate demonstration effects that are potentially transmitted throughout the local economy. Such circumstances where they emerge can be expected to strengthen local economies. In some cases local employees matriculating from branches of foreign consulting firms are actually able to open viable local consulting firms.

With respect to impacts on local post secondary education, it seems clear that the types of activities referred to in the above paragraph should encourage program development. Certainly the need for expanding programs in accounting and other business disciplines to provide personnel for an increasingly specialized job market appears to be self-evident. Pressures for such programs should arise at both the university and the para-professional levels. It would appear that facilitative business services beyond their obvious situation specific impacts in emerging economies are also providing very positive pressures upon educational processes and programs both job related and academic.

REFERENCES

Independent Accountants International. (1998). *IA Accounting: A Global Approach.* (On-line). Available: http://www.iai.org/consulting/BODY.cfm

K.P.M.G. Indonesia. (2000). *KPMG Indonesia.* (On-line), Available: http://www.aspac. Kpmg.com/country/Indonesia.htm.

McKee, D. L. & Garner, D. E. (1992). *Accounting Services, the International Economy, and Third World Development.* Westport, CT: Praeger.

McKee, D. L. & Tisdell, C. (1990). *Developmental Issues in Small* Island *Economies.* New York: Praeger.

McKee, D. L., Amara, Y. A., & Garner, D. E. (1995). International services as facilitators. *Foreign Trade Review, 29* (4), 254-264.

McKee, D. L., Garner, D. E., & McKee, Y. A. (1998). *Accounting Services and Growth in Small Economies: Evidence from the Caribbean Basin.* Westport CT: Quorum.

McKee, D. L., Garner, D. E., & McKee, Y. A. (1999). *Accounting Services, the Islamic Middle East, and the Global Economy.* Westport CT: Quorum.

McKee, D. L., Garner, D. E., & McKee, Y. A. (2000). Offshore Financial Centers, Accounting Services and the Global Economy. Westport CT: Quorum.

McKee, D. L., Garner, D. E., & McKee, Y. A. (2002). *Crisis, Recovery, and the Role of Accounting Firms in the Pacific Basin.* Westport CT: Quorum.

Noyelle, T. J. & Dutka, A. B. (1988). *International Trade in Business Services.* Cambridge: Ballinger Publishing Company.

Porter, M. E. (1990). *The Competitive Advantage of Nations.* New York: The Free Press.

United Nations Center on Transnational Corporations. (1987). *Foreign Direct Investment, the Service Sector and International Banking.* New York: United Nations Center on Transnational Corporations.

Chapter 3

What Is Missing from Business Education? Meeting the Needs of Emerging Market Business Education

Richard Reeves-Ellington
State University of New York at Binghamton

INTRODUCTION

This paper argues that, regardless of the supplier, successful emerging market business curricula must provide traditional business skill set instruction, mental skill instruction, and the teaching of underlying business and societal value assumptions, theories, and models in ways that permit students to learn to be effective in culturally diverse social and organizational settings and that such a program is better served through a liberal education that provides a business major rather than a B.S. degree in business.

EMERGING MARKET NEEDS

Business, in many emerging markets, is becoming a key player in society and its involvement with other communities (Redding, 1996; Segal, 2000). However, traditional business undergraduate education fails to prepare graduates for operating socially in such complex environments (Doeriat, 1990; Henning, 1980; Pedersen, V., 1996). To do so requires the learning of new cultural analytical skills and the ability to apply them in ways that enhance a broader audience to undertake change. There is a vast and burgeoning culture-specific literature that tries to brief managers on how to act and what to expect in specific national settings (Mole, 1991). However, university intercultural materials tend to be theoretical and not action oriented (Ashkanasy, Wilderrom, and Peterson, 2000; Boyd and Richerson, 1985; Reeves-Ellington and Andersen, 1997) and general cultural consulting books list either what to do or not to do in random ways (Brislin, Craig, and Young, 1986; Dahlen, 1997). Other materials, in the form of case studies (Gordon, et. al., 1996; Horswell, 1996) provide post facto analysis that leads to understanding of the past but little guidance as to how to use the material for future actions. Hofstede provides excellent cultural information that informs but does not provide a simple method whereby practitioners can expand on his value analysis (1980). Also, some of his categories of analysis have been discredited as being culturally biased (Reeves-Ellington, 1998, 1999).

For emerging markets, undergraduate business education serves three distinct markets: local and non-local companies operating within the confines of traditional markets; local and non-local companies operating in the global market; and local companies operating in other emerging market environments. Each of these business segments requires business education that provides understanding and working skills that permit graduates to operate efficiently in any one or combination of the three markets. These skill sets must also allow business graduates to be able to influence their employers to make substantial changes in the organizations in which they work and in the markets and social environments in which their organizations participate. The skill sets required for successful negotiation in these complex environments include business function skills, mental and social skills, and organizational and societal and cultural skills. The latter skill sets are particularly important for emerging market business education, as they often have radically different operating environments that are inappropriate for the complex bureaucratic global economy.

Emerging market educational needs attest to the great and continuing requirement to understand how to do business in transcultural organizations and markets when the cultural contexts are in constant flux, and foreign organizations and local partner industries keep shifting and reinterpreting their practices. Understanding and working in such environments requires substantial student understanding and an ability to apply that understanding. Such understanding and applications requires a pedagogy of culture and society that requires learners to develop analytical cultural skills applicable to the business and social environments in which they find themselves (Keizer, 1999; Segal, 2000).

Within emerging markets, then, the need for quantitative functional business skills is indisputable, but while it is necessary, it is not sufficient (Jensen, 2000; Onyefulu, 2001; Pupo, 1985). However, more formal education in mental (Greenwalt, 1999) and interpersonal skill teaching (Isbell, 1999) and learning methods (Munday, 2002) is necessary, as is societal and cultural skill recognition and use (Khishtan, 1990). All three skill sets must provide students with usable, meaningful workplace skills (Ojeda, 1999; Rosenbloom, 1995). The substantially different business and educational requirements of emerging markets requires substantive changes in business education for these markets (Ashley, 1999; Matveev and Serpilin, 1999; Segal, 2000). Emerging markets require business education to graduate students who can work in domestic, global, and other emerging markets.

LIBERAL AND BUSINESS EDUCATION

I agree with Searle (1996) that liberal education's primary outcome is to liberate graduates from the contingencies of their background, which I argued is the foundation for successful business education in emerging markets. Defining successful business education as a part of liberal education flows naturally. While the content of liberal education may vary, one must understand its roots in Renaissance concepts and thoughts (Hale, 1993; Kristeller, 1980), a tradition that provides critical thinking, knowledge to use critical thinking, and professional skills to use the knowledge (Grendler, 1989; Kristeller, 1980), a tradition that uses texts to teach the branches of study most concerned with the secular human condition (including business activities) (Hale, 1993). Emerging markets education must not be based on more than pure business but rather must include societal commerce (Reeves-Ellington and Anderson, 1997). The transition into the world economy is based on more than economics but also requires broader societal support and integration in the form of a liberal economy (Zakaria, 2003).

Reeves-Ellington (1996) argues that often graduates must change one or all of these environments in ways that are socially acceptable to institutions in all three markets. Further, he states that within these markets, business curricula should be based on two fundamental assumptions: business is a social science – not a quantitative science; successful businesses, in the early 21st century, function in interdependent realities (realities that integrate the cultural norms, ethics, and values of the local, regional, and global cultures in which business organizations operate). Such a curriculum must provide an education that permits students to have the knowledge and skill to lead others in making necessary structural and process changes and place these changes in a wider social context. The curriculum must provide the thinking skills that permit graduates to develop new mental models (Senge, 1990) and cultural logic, analytical models that permit their users to understand deep-rooted normative and prescriptive values. These new thinking skills permit graduates to (1) identify key constituencies (customers) with whom they work, (2) benchmark their value systems, (3) use communications methodologies required by key constituencies, and (4) thereby either extend Western business practices and training or amend it to work within more traditional markets. Liberal education is the foundation for graduates gaining the thinking skills requisite for both the quantitative and qualitative segments of business education.

Purposes and Sources of Current Business Education

Current business education and literature acknowledge the importance of three traditional outcomes: an understanding of a body of knowledge based on business functions; providing business with graduates who are professionally trained, with a focus on a specific function; and the ability to produce work jointly with others as a business organization (team work). B.S. business degrees are grounded on quantitative methodologies and economic logic and limit critical thinking, logic, and reasoning to business problems that have been quantified for solution. The qualitative aspects of these metal skills as expressed in socio-cultural applications are largely ignored. Professors trained to work independently and in limited dyadic relationships with their advisors are ill-equipped to teach undergraduates about team work and team building. Arguably, business education and its curriculum are informed by perceived needs of complex, bureaucratically designed, Western business structures. There are other skills that students are expected to acquire, usually without formal instruction, in undergraduate business programs (Hudson, 1998). Analytical thinking, team work among students, in-class discussions, cooperation, shared learning, and open knowledge access are universally acclaimed, but usually are assumed to be learned by osmosis (Carnevale, 2000; Oblinger and Vervelle, 1998; Rao and Sylvester, 2000).

The American business education model, and its variants, provides the basis of many emerging market business programs, either through importation of such programs from Western universities or by adapting local educational programs to fit the model. The United States leads the way in developing tertiary undergraduate business education programs that are being exported to other countries (Austin, 2000). Austin also points out that most of these programs are either accredited by the most widely recognized accrediting body in the United States, The Association to Advance Colligate Schools of Business, commonly known today as A.A.C.S.B. International, or they are seeking such accreditation. In the sample of colleges and universities used in this paper, all are A.A.C.S.B. accredited. The combination of A.A.C.S.B. sanctioned U.S. undergraduate education expanding into emerging markets and the expansion of A.A.C.S.B. into accreditation of Universities outside the U.S. fundamentally influences the global world of undergraduate business education.

What is the A.A.C.S.B.?

A.A.C.S.B. International was founded in 1916 and began its accreditation function with the adoption of the first standards in 1919. A.A.C.S.B. International (2003) members approved the current mission-linked accreditation standards and peer review process in 1991 based on a common body of knowledge, an assumption that this body of knowledge is rooted in business functions, and learning the body requires two years of upper division tertiary education. Even with recent changes in A.A.C.S.B. accreditation statements, the old body of knowledge paradigm (Austin, 2000; Boothman, 2000) still prevails, thus limiting the ability to introduce curricula change. Second, the concept of international business (and its newly emergent name, globalization) has an underlying premise of international being "other." The internationalization of business education takes three tacks: globalizing economic assumptions (Nehrt, 1993), incorporating "international" issues into existing functional courses, and integrating business systems outside the Western market economy structure into it (Wharton, 2003; A.A.C.S.B., 2003). All programs have a primary purpose of providing employees to large bureaucratic organizations (Hugstad, 1983).

Business School Education Assumptions

The U.S. B.S. model focuses on understanding corporate functions and tools of analysis to appreciate their performance, fails to ground business activities in a wider social context, and provides little to no practical skills, training, and experience. Within this model, business faculty expect students to learn needed mental and social skills earlier in a liberal education provided independently of the business education. I offer three reasons for narrow concepts of business that exist in both curricula and statements of purpose in business schools: American business education needs to drive both (Cameron, 1980; Cavusgil, 1993; Boothman, 2000; Locke, 1999); U.S. accreditation requirements almost universally drives both; and U.S. business education has a dearth of cultural data that precludes meaningful instruction in cultural mores (Gordon, Haddad, Chow, Hwang, and We, 1996).

An alternate model of business education exists, one that closely integrates liberal and business education, but in which business is a major within liberal education rather than an independent entity (Reeves-Ellington, 1996). This program also provided classroom skill training and experience in soft mental skills, cultural skills, and social responsibility skills. The next section of this paper reviews existing business school programs and a program that offers a business major as a part of liberal education.

BUSINESS PRGRAM REVIEW

I reviewed 40 undergraduate business school programs (Yahoo, 2003) and one business major program that is offered as a case study of how to integrate business and liberal education.. The business school review included land grant and other state university programs, public and private college programs, religious affiliated and non-affiliated programs, and programs located in Australia, Germany, India, Ireland, Pakistan, New Zealand, the United Kingdom, and the United States. All programs selected worked with emerging market undergraduate students, either at their home institution, in country in conjunction with a local University, or independently in an emerging market. The business major program reviewed was selected based on my two year teaching and administrative experience at the American University in Bulgaria (A.U.B.G.).

Using the key variable headings of traditional business skills, mental skills, and socio-cultural skills, I examined web sites and printed material contents of curricula structure, curricula content, and desired outcomes as expressed through missions and statements of purpose. The skills and methods chosen reflect the needs of emerging market business education. Table 3.1 lays out the headings -- traditionally taught business skills, mental skills, socio-cultural skills, and methods of addressing issues -- and compares three programs that typify U.S. business school education, European business school education, and liberal business education. The descriptors of program strengths are subjective and range from excellent, strong, acceptable, weak, poor, through unknown.

Traditional Business Skills: Curricula Structure and Content Schools of Business

Universally, U.S. business school programs' emphasize finance, marketing, operations, accounting, and organization development and the body of knowledge that they represent (Baruch, 2003; Boothman, 2000; Brigham Young University, 2002; Cal State, 2003; Christ Church, 2003; Notre Dame, 2003; Ohio State University, 2003). Even schools, such as the Weatherhead School of Management (2003), that focus on organizational behavior and business fields of endeavor, reflect the same bias toward functional skill development to the exclusion of cultural and value understanding and use in organizations. All these schools have a two year component of liberal education, but it is separated from the two year business degree. Baylor University's (2003) curriculum for undergraduate business study exemplifies the functional bias (see Table 3.2).

We see that functional sets of a body of business knowledge absorb the entire curriculum, with no curriculum attention to soft mental skills that address non-business issues or to cross cultural interactions, understanding that would inform the emerging market world.

Other schools, of which Wharton (2003) is a good example, maintain the basic business school education at their core, but they do modify it by including some course work on the environment of business. Business remains the focus of the non-functional courses, however. They have

Table 3.1: Selected Business Education Comparisons for Emerging Market Needs

Skill Component of Business Education	Curriculum Component	Baylor Assessment	Edinburgh Assessment	A.U.B.G. Assessment
Traditional Business Focus	Addressed Through			
Functional body of knowledge	Curriculum construction	Excellent	Excellent	Strong
Professional education	Classroom activities based on case body of knowledge	Excellent	Excellent	Strong
Team work	Corporate structured functional education	Poor	Excellent	Excellent
Mental Skills	Addressed Through			
Social analysis	Liberal/business education	Poor	Poor	Excellent
Cultural knowledge	Field work/internships	Poor	Weak	Strong
Social reasoning	Liberal/business education/case studies	Weak	Acceptable	Excellent
Social judgment	Integrated education, internships	Weak	Acceptable	Excellent
Socio-Cultural Skills	Addressed Through			
Team Building	Formal/social interaction training and liberal/business education	Poor Weak	Poor Poor	Strong Strong
Social responsibility (ethics)	Case studies, volunteer work and internships	Weak	Weak	Strong
Societal understanding	Liberal education, societal interactions.	Poor	Weak	Acceptable
Open learning	Third party teaching	Weak	Acceptable	Excellent

followed the A.A.C.S.B. direction on claiming inclusion of ethic questions in other courses without stating which ones and what the content might be. In fact, they offer the following disclaimer:

> "The Ethics Project does not guarantee that all Wharton graduates will behave ethically. Rather the goal is to teach an approach for handling ethical questions and to dispel a common attitude among business students that the bottom line is the only relevant consideration. The intellectual understanding of ethical

obligations may not be sufficient to insure ethical behavior, but can be an important contributor to that goal. With the potential for exposure to ethics in nearly all their Business Fundamentals courses, many of their upper level courses, and in the courses they must take to fulfill the Social Environment bracket, Wharton students receive repeated and varied experience, grappling with ethical questions in realistic contexts."

Outside the United States, business school programs use functional designs to drive the curricula, but they do include some liberal education in conjunction with the business course offerings. The University of Edinburgh (2003) exemplifies a program that modifies the single mindedness of the U.S. application of business education. As

Table 3.2: Baylor University Curriculum (2003) -- Final Two Years

AND	QBA 2023	Intro to Quantitative Methods
	QBA 2025	Business Data Analysis
	ECO 2306	Principles of Microeconomics
	ECO 2307	Principles of Macroeconomics
OR	Bus 3303	Managerial Communications
	MKT 3310	Professional Selling & Comm.
	CSS 1302	Speech for Busi. & Profn'l Students
	Lower Level Business Core	
AND	ACC 2303	Financial Accounting
	ACC 2304	Managerial Accounting
	BUS 1301	Busi. Economy, & World Affairs
OR	ISY 1305	Intro Information Tech. & Processing
	ISY 3325	Busi. Applications on Microcomputer
	Upper Level Business Core	
AND	BL 3305	Legal Environment of Business
	BUS 3315	Integrated Business Writing
	BUS 4385	Strategic Mgmt & Business Policy
	FIN 3310	Intro. To Financial Management
	ISY 3305	Management Information Systems
	MGT 3305	Fundamental Concepts of Mgmt.
	MGT 3325	Operations Management
	MKT 3305	Principles of Marketing

their mission states, "Many of the skills below are developed, to some extent, in any course in Social Sciences, Arts, or Sciences; the skills relating to Business Studies are relevant in any organizational context and will be developed through work experience and training." The university features functional skills but does so in ways that supports student learning in using them rather than relying on instructional based understanding (see Table 3.3) and appears to attempt integrated liberal/business education in their curriculum in ways that make the liberal learning relevant to the business course.

Table 3.3: University of Edinburgh Skills and Knowledge Education

Proficiency in the use of the techniques of description, analysis, and synthesis designed to encourage students to address problems through systematic, flexible, adaptable, innovative and judgmental approaches to business problems
Presentation and reasoning skills developed through participation in tutorials and seminars, and in writing through the preparation of course work and a dissertation.
Critical judgment Learned by evaluating arguments, to make independent assessments on the basis of evidence sought and to support your case against counter arguments from others. In addition, the ability to examine data and evidence critically.
Team work Gained on team on projects by allocating tasks, managing others and integrating results.
Communication skills Expressed complex ideas clearly, accurately and intelligibly in writing and in oral presentations.

The Said School of Management at Oxford (2003) reflects a similar bias as the Edinburgh program, as reported on their business web page:

> "Our undergraduate programmes are not intended to turn you into effective managers - only experience can do that. Instead, the programmes are designed to give you a thorough grounding in the theory of management studies and the intellectual skills of the social sciences. You will be challenged to question conventional wisdom and your own assumptions, and encouraged to develop and express your own ideas. We think that this background - especially when combined with study of another discipline such as Economics, Engineering and Materials Science - gives students a huge advantage in whatever they do later."

The outcomes in all these examples remain technical with focus on "what to do" business skills. Also, the European program's cultural exploration focuses on the European Market and pays scant attention to emerging markets.

Business Major Program: The A.U.B.G. Business Curriculum

The intent of the A.U.B.G. business curriculum was to provide students with an ability to make profound changes in any environment in which they chose to work. The business curriculum was assumed to be a social science discipline rather than a science one. The business curriculum at the American University in Bulgaria (A.U.B.G.) in the years 1994-95 provides an example of business learning situated in a liberal education. Integrated into several of the courses was the study, analysis, and application of basic cultural values and logic skills of Bulgarian and other national value systems. The curriculum (Table 3.4) reflected the four-year program by semesters. Note that there was a mix of business courses, core courses, and general education courses throughout the four-year cycle, permitting parallel learning of business and life skills.

The general education categories (see Table 3.5) reflect both analytical skills and specific knowledge in fields other than business. To further broaden the student's experience base, the business curriculum added elective courses from other social science disciplines.

The curriculum was designed to create a basic paradigm shift from a producer-consumer paradigm to a customer-supplier paradigm (Reeves-Ellington, 1994). It fit into a framework that prepared students for further graduate study, employment in global organizations, or local Bulgarian ones. Preparation required a shift in faculty and student attitudes from businesses being independent realities to being interdependent ones. Accomplishing this attitudinal shift required the business curriculum to have (1) faculty meld theory, analysis, and action; (2) students demonstrate an ability to work with ongoing problems and institutions located within and outside Bulgaria; and (3) faculty and students work together in ways that develop leadership and motivational skills. These innovations created a learning organization with the business curriculum – an organization in which all participants were teacher and student. In an effort to expand the traditional liberal education components, other disciplines taught many of the elective courses. These included organizational behavior and human relationships by psychologists, organizational development and group interactions by sociologists, advertising by journalists, and speech by theater people. Traditional business faculty then integrated this learning into their course work. The business faculty believed that teaching the craft of business education was a worthy goal but insufficient. They operated on the assumption that business education could help graduates make profound changes, but only if that education was situated in a broad education including geography, politics, and history.

Table 3.4: A.U.B.G. Business Program (1994-95)

Required Courses - Four Year Program	**Business Electives**
First Semester Macro-Economics University Skills Computer Applications General Education (2)	**First Semester** none
Second Semester E.U./U.S. Business Law English Composition General Education Course	**Second Semester** none
Third Semester Financial Accounting General Education (4)	**Third Semester** none
Fourth Semester Statistics (Applied) General Education or Elective (4)	**Fourth Semester** Management Information Systems
Fifth Semester Marketing Managing in a Market Economy General Education or Elective (3)	**Fifth Semester** Money and Banking
Sixth Semester Managerial Accounting Human Resource Development General Education or Elective (3)	**Sixth Semester** Complex Organizations Organizational Behavior
Seventh Semester Financial Institutions General Education or Elective (4)	**Seventh Semester** Managerial Marketing Advertising Price and Forecasting Market Persuasion
Eighth Semester International Strategic Mgmt. General Education or Elective (4)	**Eighth Semester** Small Business Enterprise Business Special Studies

Professional Education

Twenty-two universities in the sample had statements of purpose (the others had none) that included what they expected of students graduating from their programs. The 22 were consistent with what they promised – business skills for employment. For example, Zicklan School of Management states,

"Our programs are designed to provide students with the specialized knowledge they need for entry into the work force along with the analytical and communication skills requisite for a successful career." Baylor (2003)

Table 3.5: General Education Requirements

Courses	Number of Courses Required
Literary Analysis	2
Historical Analysis	2
Quantitative Reasoning	2
Social Analysis	2
Moral Reasoning	1
Natural Science	1
Philosophical Inquiry	1
Multicultural Studies	1
Fine Arts	1
Statistical Analysis	1
Total	**14**

aspires to be a leader amongst business schools, requiring an examination of other programs to identify exactly what they want to accomplish. Kogod School of Management succinctly states that the focus of business education is professionalism. Babson College (2002) challenges people that love business to attend and learn how to do business. California State (2003) expresses the same hope:

> "Programs in the College of Business and Economics at California State University, Los Angeles are designed to equip students with the concepts and the professional skills they need to assume responsible positions in business, industry, education, government, and social organizations."

The University of Edinburgh (2003) clearly states, "During your studies at University you have the opportunity to develop a number of skills which are considered valuable by employers, in addition to acquiring concrete subject knowledge of business processes, methods, activities and behaviour, accounting, economics and law." The A.U.B.G. business program had the broadest professional scope in that it wanted to have business student graduates who could make an impact in whatever endeavors they chose to pursue after college.

Teamwork

Within the sample of forty business schools, 21 make no official mention of teamwork, ten list it as a part of their business program but with no details as to how teamwork is taught or practiced, and the remaining nine have a more expanded description of what their teamwork activities are. Of those that make no mention of teamwork efforts in their programs, their mission statements and purposes emphasize individual success in business. Baylor (2003) states in their catalogue that they want to develop objective analysis and rationality in their students. Binghamton University requires team work in all upper level business courses, but offers no formal training as to how to achieve competency when working in teams. The remaining programs that acknowledge the importance of team work fail to offer formal education in it, with the exception of Boston College. As stated on Boston College's (2003) website, "Teamwork is critical to success in business today. We help you leverage it." They offer a four year development program in team building and teamwork understanding and practice. Babson's (2003) business page makes claim to excel in leadership, creativity, collaboration, and shared learning, without offering specific courses or clearly defined programs in which students learn these skills. The University of Tulsa (2003) features an emphasis on teamwork on their web page – "We emphasize teamwork and technology" -- but fail to list a course in teaching teamwork skills. Within my sample, the most used text for teamwork and team building, *The Fifth Discipline* (Senge, 1990), is rarely assigned to undergraduates for understanding, and I could find no case where it was used as a workbook for student use in team activity learning and practice.

Teamwork at A.U.B.G. was predicated on students being exposed to human interaction and dynamics in the first two years of the program. These skills were reviewed in the third year, based on *The Fifth Discipline Fieldbook* (Senge, 1994). The fourth year strategy course served as the capstone to team building and teamwork understanding and application. The application areas included small and large business organizations, charities, and team building across cultures.

In summary, the sample business school curricula have the primary purpose of providing future employees to large companies, preferable those that participate in the global economy as predicted by Cavusgil (1993) and Town and Nigh (1999). As Toyne and Nigh (1999) suggest, the drive of these business programs appears to be to disseminate an A.A.C.S.B. approved "body of knowledge" that is based on academic research and approved by peers. Some schools do acknowledge the importance of teamwork but, with one exception, offer no formal education in the subject. El-Ahraf, Levine, and Alkhafaji (1995) argue that this business education model is inappropriate for those coming from much different educational systems, cultural backgrounds, and markets. Certainly this would include emerging markets. The A.U.B.G. program, being situated in an emerging market and having a bulk of its students coming from emerging market environments, realized the importance of individual and collective social and cultural understanding and the ability to use that understanding in concrete ways.

Socio-Cultural Learning in B.S. Programs

In the business school sample, the traditional mental skill usage focuses on quantitative and analytic skills. When referenced in my sample, social analysis, social reasoning, and social judgment, and understanding and use (as exemplified in Jackell's (1988) Moral Mazes) are assumed to have been taught in the first two years of university education and not in the purview of business school education. Cultural understanding offerings, when found, were centered on Adler (1997) or Brisslan, et. al. (1986). No apparent cultural learning and applications strategies were apparent, rather cultural and social understandings appear to be marginal to business education at the sampled schools. Even international programs were more economics and trade focused rather than culturally directed.

Socio-Cultural Learning Models Used at A.U.B.G.

The following cultural models were adopted in all Reeves-Ellington's (1996) business classes during his tenure at A.U.B.G. with about a third of the faculty. Their design was meant to encompass all the socio-cultural skills outlined in Table 3.1 and provide rationale that facilitated student understanding, their ability to third-party teach cultural understanding, and their ability to learn about themselves and others who were not indigenous to their own culture.

Cultural Encounters

Reeves-Ellington (1996) found that students benefited from thinking about cultural encounters in terms of an interplay between three kinds of cultural elements: (1) the normative values that together can be seen to form the cohesive cultural logic; (2) prescriptive social ethics, the social knowledge of insiders who guide and interpret their actions in accordance with this logic; and (3) the most visible part of the cultural set, artifacts, which are comprised of outward physical and symbolic manifestations such as dress, architecture, office layout, seating arrangements, and other visible parts of the context. To act appropriately, newcomers to an environment must become aware of all three orientations. Cultural logic, social knowledge, and artifacts provide direction to the cultural context, ethic, and reflection of a peoples' particular view of the world. In order for students to systemically learn and apply cultural and social knowledge, an understanding cultural paradigm was developed and used at the team level within the total class and in internships and volunteer work associated with classes.

In a cross-cultural encounter, whether between subcultures of different organizations or between the cultures of two similar organizations from different countries, these elements will most often be accessible in the order illustrated in Figure 3.1.

The understanding culture model shows levels of orienting data for people who must deal with other partners across cultural boundaries. The model makes the user aware of possible differing interpretations of visible symbols and behaviors and of reactions to one's own behavior in the encounter. This model assumes initial transcultural contact at the level of the most obvious and visible difference, the outward artifacts.

Using the model in the classroom, students at A.U.B.G. gained a social interpretation for better comprehending those artifacts by empirically inquiring through practice and feedback in actual situations. After discussion of personal experiences and comparisons of outcomes, they gained an understanding about the cultural logic that forms a basis for the more

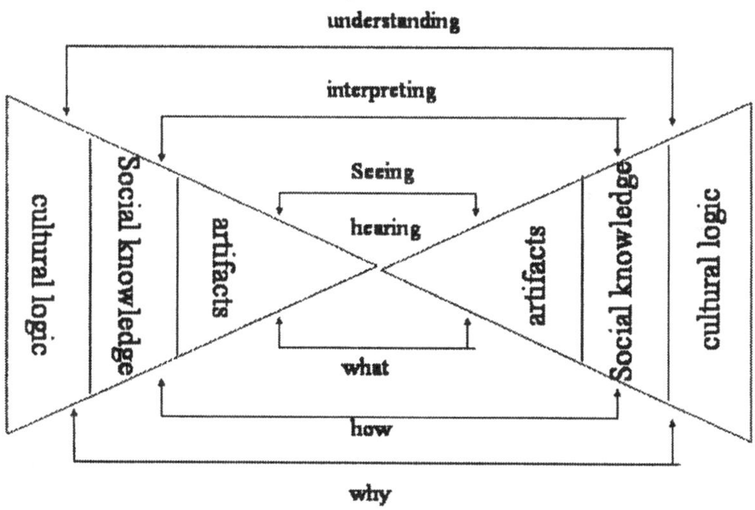

Figure 3.1: Understanding Cultures

superficial expectations and appearances. This cultural learning model thus offered a progressive learning sequence. The model permitted students to become more conscious of their own culture as well as the cultures of others. They discussed their understandings as individuals, then members of a team, and finally in internships and case creations.

The importance of viewing all three kinds of cultural elements in practice cannot be overstated. While cultural logic answers the journalistic "why" about underlying group assumptions of people, human nature, human relations, and our relationship to the environment, alone it will not give much information for day-to-day respectful and knowledgeable interaction. Elements of social knowledge, on the other hand, are subject to continual reinterpretation and change; this is why they are not easily obtained through consulting cultural "cookbooks" of behavior, no matter how popular these have become. While cultural logic usually changes less quickly, no specific actions flow from it. Its normative values orientations are ideological and treated as absolute.

Constructs for Cultural Encounters

Using the three heuristics of culture – cultural logic, social behavior, and artifacts – as outlined above and adopting the role of participant observer, students discover central cultural value orientations in both familiar and unfamiliar settings. The key modality for students to gain information was through the role of participant observer. Effective P.O. required a combination of direct observation and questioning techniques. This allowed students to systematically and continuously acquire information about what was important to people. Gaining this needed information about others also required active listening, with two main objectives. The first is to hear what is meant by listening for the vocabulary chosen and voice inflections used. The second is to "listen" with senses other than hearing for nonverbal messages. Student participant observers were required to formulate specific plans for action that moved them from that which is easily known to that which is normally concealed.

To assist students, Reeves-Ellington (1993) conceptualized the learning process by linking three categories — cultural logic, social knowledge, and artifacts (see Figure 3.2.) In this form, the model provided semantic cues for the lay user regarding appropriate kinds of information to seek in cultural encounters (what, how, who) as well as how the information is likely to be acquired and processed (i.e., seeing, hearing, interpreting, understanding). The categories of Figure 3.2 provide orienting assumptions for members of a transcultural organization. They permit the user to gain information about basic assumptions of others to interpret concrete behavior from the perspective of other cultural frames. Visually and intellectually, the model assumes initial transcultural contacts with outward artifacts, then the acquisition of social interpretive knowledge for better comprehending those artifacts, and finally, if possible, an understanding regarding the cultural logic that forms the basis for all of the more superficial expectations and appearances.

Through teamwork, off-site internships, and case creations, students assumed the perspective of an ethnological field researcher as reflected in the culture model described by Figure 3.2. The student participant observer experienced being in the center of a given cultural milieu, with all three types of cultural information bombarding the student simultaneously. I required the student to enter this situation with a clear understanding of the problems at hand, and they began to address interpretations reflectively and systematically. A plan-do-check-act cycle, illustrated here on the outer ring of Figure 3.2, gave cues for continual reflective practice in members' ethnographies. After each encounter, the participant observer made notes about the observed and entered data into the appropriate database (artifacts, social knowledge, and cultural logic). This process allowed students to understand what is culturally important in their team, at their university, or in other workplaces.

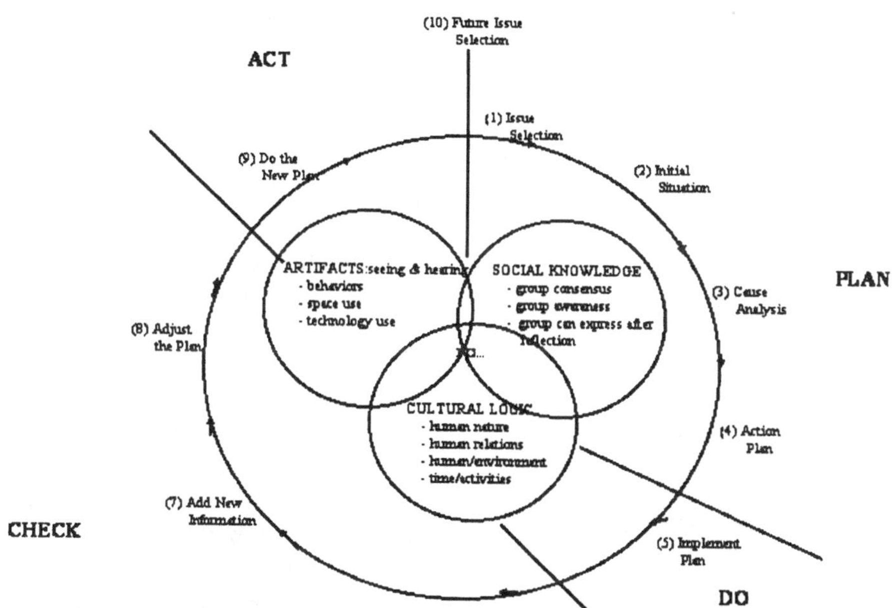

Figure 3.2: Understanding and Predicting Culture

With iterative self-study and feedback, students and student teams developed a shared cultural set. These included (1) its intensity (the strength of the ethic), (2) the norm of the values (i.e., what principles members ought to follow), (3) choice and differential allocation of effort (a set of situational priorities), (4) deeds (to demonstrate the strength of the value and ethic), (5) relative importance within the entire cultural set (how a particular ethical dimension is ranked compared to other dimensions in the social knowledge set), and (6) its evaluation in interactive.

CONCLUSION

As Hanna has aptly observed, "every organization is perfectly designed to get the results it gets" (1988). Business education, as noted, is designed to support large Western organizational needs – not those of emerging markets. The nature and self-defined missions of modern business education discourages holistic integration of business and more general living skills. They assume a general understanding of underlying mores and culture. Programs are designed to deliver business skills at the expense of all others. Achieving the purest rational management to maximize overall business return means studiously avoiding the more ambiguous and compromising considerations of human interactions that are based on shared power and some level of equality. The pure-business paradigm of most business curricula is solidified in the mass-production era of industrialism, is one of producers and consumers, not customers and suppliers (Reeves-Ellington, 1995). It relies on an I – It paradigm to avoid social entanglements. We (the producers) of education provide knowledge for *them* (the consumers), who we do not care to know personally. This is not the type of education needed in emerging markets, however. A more commercial orientation is desired and needed.

In contrast to purer conceptions of business, the idea of commerce is older. It predates the rise of Western capitalism. It is bundled with additional meanings because it had been merged institutionally and embedded in earlier social forms and contexts of exchange. Commerce's meanings still linger in its contemporary connotations. It can never be morally neutral because of the active presence of persons who are continually responding with interpretations and decisions. More than just economic exchange takes place in commerce. It is closer to the ground, involving not only goods, currencies, and instruments, but also contextual and tangential information and all kinds of social contact. It is social traffic in things valued and cannot long exist without an I and a Thou.

A commercial education was the aim of the A.U.B.G. business program: integration of the business and commerce in ways that made graduates successful in whatever endeavors they undertook. We wanted graduates to be commercial actors and not business functionaries. As commercial actors, A.U.B.G. graduates occupied themselves with opportunities, not problems. They interacted continuously and pragmatically in the present, always with an eye to maximizing future choices and benefits. They necessarily mediated and interpreted between systemic levels and often resisted, avoided, or reinterpreted mandates and limitations imposed by governing and outlying systems. They knew that if they cannot avoid imposed constraints, as successful commercial actors, they must creatively reinterpret and avoid overt dissonance with their larger systems. I believe a commercial education in which all participants learn to do business, develop a wide range of thinking skills, and can interpret and use cultural constructs in ways that make commercial actors is of great value to all emerging markets.

REFERENCES

A.A.C.S.B. (2003). Accreditation standards. http://www.aacsb.edu/accreditation/Accreditation. (Found on 17 July 2003).

Adler, N. (1997). *International dimensions of organizational behavior.* Cincinnati: Southwestern Press.

American University. (2003). *Kogod business school. http://kogod.american.edu/ArtPage.cfm?ItemID=221. (Found on 17 July 2003).*

Ashkanasy, N.M., Wilderrom, C.P.M., & Peterson, M.F. (Eds.). (2000). *Handbook of organizational culture and climate.* Thousand Oaks: Sage Press.

Arpan, J.S., & Kwok, C.Y. (2001). *Internationalizing the business school: global survey of institutions of higher learning in the year 2000.* Columbia, SC: The Academy of International Business.

Ashley, T.G. (1999). Globalization and education: a critical view of post-secondary education for the millennium. (Doctorial Dissertation. Simon Fraser University, 1999). First Search: Dissertation Online. Acquisition Number: AAIMQ51288.

Austin, B. (2000). *Capitalizing knowledge: essays on the history of business education in Canada.* Toronto: University of Toronto Press.

Babson College. (2003). *Welcome.* http://www3.babson.edu/ug/. (Found on 17 July 2003).

Baruch College. (2003). *Undergraduate programs.* http://bus.baruch.cuny.edu/programs/undergrad/undergrad.html. (Found on 17 July 2003).

Baylor University. (2003). *Undergraduate Curriculum.* http://business.baylor.edu/undergrad/default.aspx?pageID=389. (Found on 17 July 2003).

Baylor University. (2003). *University Bulletin.* http://www3.baylor.edu/learn_rsrc/publications/Undergrad_Cat/UndergradCatalog.pdf. (Found on 20 July 2003, 144).

Boothman, B. E.C. (2000). The development of business education in Canada. In B. Austin (Ed.). *Capitalizing knowledge: essays on the history of business education in Canada* (11-86). Toronto: University of Toronto Press.

Boyd, R., & Richerson, P. (1985). *Culture and the evolutionary process.* Chicago: University of Chicago Press.

Boston College. (2003). *Team Building.* http://management.bu.edu/smg. (Found on 20 July 2003).

Brigham Young University. (2003). *Required Courses.* http://marriottschool.byu.edu/bsmgt/. (Found on 17 July 2003).

Brislin, R., Kenneth, C., Craig, C., & Young, M. (1986). *Intercultural interactions: a practical guide.* Beverley Hills: Sage.

Cal State L.A. (2003). *College of Business and Economics.* http://cbe.calstatela.edu/mission.htm. (Found on 17 July 2003).

Cameron, D.. S. (1980). A study of program relevance and student reparation in business education. (Doctorial Dissertation. University of North Carolina at Greensboro, 1980). First Search: Dissertation Online. Acquisition Number: AAG8021769.

Carevale, A.P. (2000). *Community colleges and career qualifications*. Washington, DC: American Association of Community Colleges.

Cavusgil, S. (Ed.). (1993). *Internationalizing business education: meeting the challenge*. East Lansing: Michigan State University.

Christ Church. *Business Education*. (2003). http://www.cce.ac.nz/info/sob/. (Found on 17 July 2003).

Doeriat, A.W. (1990). Does management education make a difference? A case study of a management training program in Indonesia. (Doctorial Dissertation, Harvard University. 1990). First Search: Dissertation Online. Acquisition Number: AAG9032426.

El-Ahraf, A., Levine, G.R., & Alkhafaji, A. (Eds.). (1995). *Internationalizing the university curriculum: strategies and opportunities*. Dominguez Hills, CA: California State University.

Edinburgh University. *Current students: Undergraduates*. http://www.managementschool.ed.ac.uk/study/current_undergrad/skillsandknowledge.html. (Found on 17July 2003).

Excelsior College. (2003). Excelsior college curriculum review. Albany: Author.

Gordon, G., Haddad, K. M., Chow, C.W., Hwang, R. N-C., We, A. (1996). Cross-national differences in corporate cultures and the culture-performance relationship: a two country comparison. ***CIBER** Working Paper Series*. San Diego: San Diego State University.

Greenwalt, M.B. (1999). Fostering student's critical thinking skills. In J. Hommes, P.K. Keizer, M/ Pettigrew, & J. Troy (Eds.). *Educational innovation in economics and business IV* (pp. 239-253). Boston: Kluwer Academic Publishers.

Grendler, P.F. (1989). *Schooling in renaissance Italy's literacy and learning – 1300-1600*. Baltimore: Johns Hopkins University Press.

Hale, J. (1993). *The civilization of Europe and the Renaissance*. London: Fontana Press.

Henning, A. M. (1980). History and problems of cross-cultural university education: a case study of Norwegian students and their academic performance at the University of Colorado. (Doctorial Dissertation. University of Colorado, 1980). First Search: Dissertation Online. Acquisition Number: AAG8113966.

Hofstede, G. (1980). *Culture's consequences: International differences in work-related values*. Beverly Hills: Sage Publications.

Hommes, J., Keizer, P.K., Pettigrew, M., & J. Troy (Eds.). (1999). *Educational innovation in economics and business IV*. Boston: Kluwer Academic Publishers.

Horswell, M. (1996). Time and control in a Mexican maquiladora: a case study. Occasional Paper #82. College Park: College of Business and Management, University of Maryland.

Hudson, S. A. (1998). Tteamwork skills and group dynamics training in computer applications and computer programming courses in community colleges and universities. (Doctorial Dissertation. Southern Illinois University, 1998). First Search: Dissertation Online. Acquisition Number: AAG9902722.

Hugstad, P.S. (1983). *The business school in the 1980s*. New York: Praeger.

Iqra University. (2003). *BS in Business Education*. http://www.iqraisb.edu.pk/academics/bba.htm. (Found on 17 July 2003).

Isbell, K.G. (1999). Developing a student's sense of self: A constructivist evaluation of the first four years of the International School of the Americas. (Doctorial Dissertation. Texas A&M University, 1999). First Search: Dissertation Online. Acquisition Number: AAI9957454.

Jackell, R. (1988). *Moral mazes*. New York: Oxford University Press.

Jensen, D. F. N. (2000). The relationship between philosophy and practice at the University of Alberta: An analysis of stakeholders' metaphors. (Doctorial Dissertation. University of Alberta, 2000). First Search: Dissertation Online. Acquisition Number: AAINQ59977.

Keizer, P. K. (1999). How to prepare graduates for the changing workplace? In J. Hommes, P.K. Keizer, Pettigrew, & J. Troy (Eds.). *Educational Innovation in Economics and Business IV* (pp. 14-27). Boston: Kluwer Academic Publishers.

Kristeller, P. (1980). The modern system of the arts. *Renaissance Thought,* 2, 12-31.

Locke, R. R. (1999). International management education in Western Europe, the United States and Japan. In B. Toyne, & D. Night (Eds.). *International business: Institutions and the dissemination of knowledge* (pp. 25-43). Columbia, SC: University of South Caroline Press.

London School of Economics. (2003). *Degree Structure.* http://www.ebslondon.ac.uk/programmes.asp. (Found on 19 July 2003).

McLean, P., & Tatnall, A. (2000). *Studying Business at University.* St. Leonards, NSW: Allen & Unwin.

Matveev, A. V., & Serpilin, A. B. (1999). Business education in Russia needs change. In J. Hommes, P.K. Keizer, M. Pettigrew, & J. Troy (Eds.). *Educational Innovation in Economics and Business IV* (pp. 29-47). Boston: Kluwer Academic Publishers.

Mole, J. (1991). *When in Rome-A business guide to cultures and customs in 12 European nations.* New York: AMCOM.

Munday, D.R. (2002). Effects of learning strategy awareness on learning, learners, and instructors. (Doctorial Dissertation. Oklahoma State University, 2002). First Search: Dissertation Online. Acquisition Number: AAI3057290.

Nehrt, L.C. (1993). Business school curriculum and faculty: Historical perspectives and future imperatives. In S. Cavusgil (Ed.). *Internationalizing business education: Meeting the challenge* (pp. 31-44). East Lansing: Michigan State University. pp 31-44.

Oblinger, D.G., & Verville, A.L. (1998). *What business wants from higher education.* Phoenix: Oryx Press.

Ohio State University. (2003). *Business Curriculum.* http://fisher.osu.edu/regionals/curriculum/guidelines.htm. (Found on 19 July 2003).

Ojeda Diaz, E. J. (1999). Identifying knowledge, skills, and abilities (KSA'S) required by human resources managers to face twenty-first century challenges: The case of Venezuela. (Doctorial Dissertation. University of Sarasota, 1999). First Search: Dissertation Acquisitions Number, AAG9919804.

Onyefulu, C. N. (2001). An evaluation study of the business education programs in the University of Technology, Jamaica. (Doctorial Dissertation. The University of Technology, Jamaica, 2001). First Search: Dissertation Acquisitions Number, AAINQ60330.

Oxford. (2003). *Undergraduate Program.* http://www.sbs.ox.ac.uk/html/undergrad_main.asp. (Found on 19 July 2003).

Pedersen, V. (1996). Living a job, learning a culture: A study of international business students in a semester abroad program. (Doctorial Dissertation. University of North Dakota, 2001). First Search: Dissertation Acquisitions Number, AAG9721217.

Pupo, N. J. (1985). Educational promises and efficiency ideals: The development of management education in Ontario. (Doctorial Dissertation. University of Ontario, 1985). First Search: Dissertation Acquisitions Number, AAG0556659.

Rao, M., & Sylvester S. (2000). Business and education in transition: Why new partnerships are essential to student success in the in the new economy. *AAHE Bulletin,* 52(8), 11-13.

Redding, G. (1996). Thickening civil society: The impact of multinationals in China. *Perspectives on business, economic growth and civil society, CDE.* Johannesburg, SA.

Reeves-Ellington, R.H. (1993).Using cultural skills for cooperative advantage in Japan. *Human Organization*, Vol 52(2), 203-216.

Reeves-Ellington, R. H. (1996). Liberal arts business education in Bulgaria: A vehicle for change. *International Education,* vol 25 (2), 5-33.

Reeves-Ellington R. H., & Anderson, A. (1997). *Beyond agenda: culture, commerce and social responsibility.* Lewiston, NY: Edwin Mellon Press.

Reeves-Ellington, R. H. (1998). A mix of cultures, values, and people: An organizational case study. *Human Organization*, Vol 57(1), 94-107.

Reeves-Ellington, R. H. (1999). From command to demand economies: Bulgarian organizational value orientations. *Practicing Anthropology*, Vol 21 (4), 5-13.

Rosenbloom, A. A. (1995). Grounded theory of knowledge utilization in undergraduate management majors. (Doctorial Dissertation. Loyola University of Chicago, 1995). First Search: Dissertation Acquisitions Number, AAI9517199.

Searle, J.R. (1996). The case of traditional liberal education. *The Journal of Blacks in Education.* 10(13), 91-98.

Segal, N. (2000). Business schools in a developing economy: The new challenges. Inaugural Lecture, New Series No. 218, University of Cape Town Department of Communications.

Senge, P.M. (1990). *The fifth discipline.* New York: Doubleday.

Senge, P.M. (1994). *The fifth discipline fieldbook.* New York: Doubleday.

Tulsa. (2003). *Undergraduate business programs.* http://www.cba.utulsa.edu/programs. (Found on 20 July 2003).

Toyne, B., & Night, D. (1999). *International Business: Institutions and the Dissemination of Knowledge.* Columbia, SC: University of South Carolina Press.

Weatherhead. (2003). *Undergraduate education.* http://weatherhead.cwru.edu/undergraduate/majors.htm. (Found on 17 July 2003).

Wharton. (2003). *Undergraduate Curriculum.* http://www.wharton.upenn.edu/undergrad/curriculum/outline.html. (Found on 19 July 2003).

Wharton. (2003). *Ethics Center.* http://ethics.wharton.upenn.edu/. (Found on 19 July 2003).

Yahoo. (2003). *College essentials: Advice about business schools.* http://dir.yahoo.com/Education/By_Subject/Business_and_Economy/. (retrieved on 17 July 2003).

Zakaria, F. (2003). *The future of freedom: Illiberal democracy at home and abroad.* New York: W.W. Norton.

Chapter 4
University Educational Reform in Transition Economies: The Case of China

Richard Fey
Trinity College

Alan Zimmerman
City University of New York – College of Staten Island

INTRODUCTION

The World Bank includes educational reform on its list of critical tasks facing transition economies (World Bank, 1996). This despite the fact that the quality and availability of basic education are among the great successes of central planning. Obviously the curriculum must be revised to include the core disciplines of economics, mathematics, and behavioral science. Beyond that language, management sciences, psychology, and law are essential. On the other hand, education in planned economies emphasized conformity as much as specialized skills with the result that the performance of students in the application of knowledge, especially to unanticipated circumstances, was considerably below that of their counterparts in established market economies (World Bank, 1996). This suggests that changes in curriculum to add market oriented subject matter may not be sufficient to meet the needs of a market economy. This paper examines a typical business curriculum and addresses the question whether additional skills are needed by university graduates in the Peoples Republic of China.

Following the death of Deng in 1997, the government of the P.R.C. has remained strongly committed to creating a "socialist market economy" which includes support for the development of new market oriented business as well as selling, merging, or closing the vast majority of state-owned enterprises (S.O.E.s) inasmuch as more than half of these are inefficient and reporting losses (State Department, 1999). China's gradual approach to reform and privatization achieved record rates of growth from the outset. Per capita income quadrupled between 1978 and 1995. While Russia and other East European emerging economies faced the loss of safety nets coupled with sharply lower living standards as a result of rapidly declining real G.D.P. and high inflation, the inflationary pressures in China in the early years of reform were kept within manageable levels and G.D.P. grew rapidly. Moreover, the improvement in living standards resulted in a dramatic reduction in poverty in China from 270 million, or 28% of the population, in 1978 to about 97 million, or less than 10% of the population, by 1985 (Graham, 1994).

According to the Chinese government, at the end of 1998 there were 1.2 million private businesses in China and 31.2 million people self-employed. The number of people employed by private businesses or self-employed rose by more than 5.5 million in 1998 (China Embassy, 1999). The Chinese government reported at the end of 1997 that state-owned enterprises contributed about 29% of the country's industrial output, collective economic forces 44%, and non-public ownership about 31%. The latter compares with only 13% contributed by non-public firms in 1992. An official Chinese website cites Chinese economist Ma Hong as saying that "China can keep improving its economic structure and efficiency only by developing an economy on market demands." (sic.) (China Embassy, 1997). In the aftermath of the Southeast Asia financial crisis, the growth of the Chinese economy slowed somewhat, with real GDP increasing only 7.6% per year from 1997 to 2000.

A consequence of the gradual approach to economic reform is that much of the work of transition remains to be done. Despite rapid expansion in new market-oriented business, primarily township and village enterprises (T.V.E.), there was virtually no privatization of state-owned enterprises (S.O.E.) until the mid 1990's. Even then most mid-sized and large S.O.E.s were allowed to continue in business. Of the 300,000 S.O.E.s that remain, only 10,000 are required to operate according to plans devised by the state. The remainder are required to meet production according to market demands, and success is measured by profitability (China Embassy, 1997). The overhanging burden of S.O.E. transformation is driving the need for comprehensive change in the education of Chinese managers. Writing in 1992 for U.N.C.T.A.D., Perkins states that "making enterprise decision makers behave according to the rules of the market has proved to be the most difficult challenge" (1992). Harvie cites four major areas where the influence of markets on the economy must be strengthened (1999). One of these is to change S.O.E.s into modern corporations with independent managers. Despite phenomenal growth from new market oriented enterprise, S.O.E.s remain a significant and largely unprofitable component of the Chinese economy. According to official estimates, bad loans to the S.O.E. sector may total as high as 20% of G.D.P. (Stiglitz, 1998). Success for China's economy moving forward will depend critically on its ability to extend economic reform to the S.O.E. sector.

EDUCATIONAL REFORM IN THE MID 1980'S

Prior to economic reforms, urban workers were assigned by the government to an enterprise where they remained for life, while rural workers were assigned to agricultural communes. Urban wages exhibited little differential between skilled workers, unskilled workers, or professionals (Maurer-Fazio, 1999). The advent of economic reform brought managerial contracts that linked manager's pay to profit and sales performance (Chen, 2000). In return, managers demanded more control over hiring, firing, and monetary incentives tied to productivity. In addition, for the collective T.V.E.s, decentralization granted the local government authority to fire managers for nonperformance. One case study found that the town government changed the managing director of a factory three times between 1984 and 1987 while another changed its director twelve times between 1957 and 1992 (Wong, Ma, and Yang, 1995). Reform also brought a labor market to China where workers could choose where they wished to work and compete for employment on the basis of education and experience.

The reforms also had a profound effect on the education system. By 1992, 40% of university students were admitted as "commissioned" students, that is, they were admitted on the basis of contracts between universities and enterprises. A further 25% were admitted as private fee payers (Maurer-Fazio, 1999). In response the education system was reformed in the mid-1980's to focus on economic development and on raising the return on investments in education.

Levels of educational attainment in China received high marks from the World Bank. However most education systems in planned economies were designed to teach fixed, specialized bodies of knowledge to be applied in narrowly defined jobs. The resulting rigidity of socialist education was quite inadequate for a market economy in which workers and managers were free to choose and change their jobs (World Bank, 1996).

Given the goals of education reform, a number of studies examined the rate of return to education in China, both before and after the reforms of the education system. The benchmark study based on data from 1981 established the rate of return to education before economic reform at 2.5% (Meng and Kidd, 1997). Other studies based on data from 1981, 1985, and 1986 reported returns that their authors characterized as very low (Byron and Manaloto, 1990; Jamison and Van Der Gaag, 1987; Gregory and Meng, 1995). However, the study by Knight and Song singled out university education as having an extraordinarily low value in the market economy (1991). Their estimated impacts for different levels of educational attainment, converted to rates of return by Maurer-Fazio, revealed a rate of return for primary education of 2.9% and for university education of only 0.5% (1999). After educational reform, the returns to education showed some improvement but remained low in comparison to most other countries (Maurer-Fazio, 1999;

Psacharopoulos, 1993; Anand, 1983; Johnson and Chow, 1997).

The data in Table 4.1 is consistent with the frequently reported anecdotal evidence of the extreme importance of education in China as seen in the high levels of average years of schooling (Maurer-Fazio, 1999, Table 9). On the other hand, serious questions are raised concerning the effectiveness of that education in support of a market economy by the rate of return data. The market continues to assign an economic rate of return to education in China that is quite low in comparison to the other countries reported. The potential negative consequences for the future of China's economic reform have been well documented (World Bank, 1996). Based on these data, we determined that if educational reform is to succeed, additional research is needed to examine the specific needs of the market economy that are not being met and to propose curriculum enhancements to address those needs. In light of the Knight and Song results, it appears that the greatest need for additional reform is at the university level.

Table 4.1: Rates of Return to Education

Country	Rate of Return (%)	Years of Schooling (sample mean)
China (males, 1991)	3.7	11.4
China (females 1991)	4.9	11.3
China (rural 1988)	4.0	6.0
Hong Kong	6.1	9.1
Japan	6.5	11.1
South Korea	10.6	8.0
Taiwan	6.0	9.0
Indonesia	17.0	5.0
Malaysia	14.0	7.3
Pakistan	9.7	8.6
Philippines	8.6	9.0
Sri Lanka	7.0	4.5
Thailand	10.4	4.1

ADAPTING UNDERGRADUATE EDUCATION TO A MARKET ECONOMY

We begin with a conceptual framework drawn from the efforts to internationalize undergraduate and graduate business education in the U.S. over the past few years. The effort to internationalize is in fact an effort to prepare graduates with the skills needed in a market economy that extends across national boundaries. This process exhibits many striking parallels to the problems facing transition economies. Both internationalization and the change to market-based economics pervade every aspect of commerce: "trade, investment and ownership, manufacturing and sourcing, markets and customers, finance and technology and R & D" (Cavusgil, 1993). Because of the pervasive nature of internationalizing or marketizing the curriculum, major changes must be undertaken in every aspect of the university. For this project we have taken as a starting point the idea that the approach to adapting undergraduate education to a market economy mirrors that recommended by Cavusgil for internationalizing business education. The model shown below (Figure 4.1) is adapted from his. The feedback loop has been added to specifically call attention to the critical nature of this aspect of program development, assessment, and refinement that was implied but not specifically depicted in Cavusgil's original model. It is this aspect of the model that is examined here.

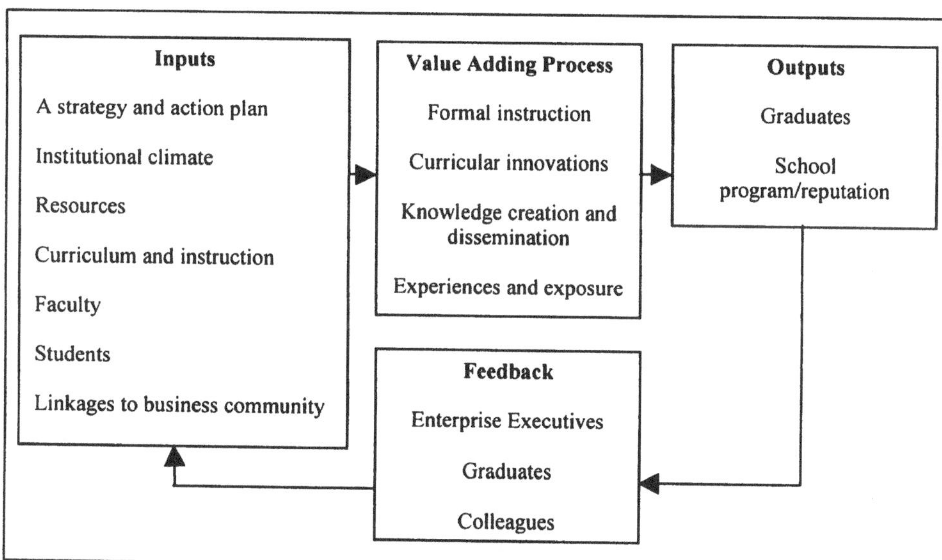

Figure 4.1: Adapting Undergraduate Education to a Market Economy.

SHANGHAI UNIVERSITY PROGRAM

As part of the national program of educational reform, the College of International Business of Shanghai University developed a comprehensive program to train managers for the market economy. This curriculum includes major commitments to English, economics, mathematics, and computer skills as well as courses in finance, management, marketing, and international business. The curriculum is attached as Appendix 1.

As we examined the curriculum (see Appendices 1 and 2), it appears that the reforms in terms of content are strong on language skills as well as the core disciplines of economics and mathematics, but there is little emphasis on behavioral science compared to similar universities in the U.S. However this difference in emphasis on content alone seems unlikely to have generated the extraordinarily low returns to education in China. More important, despite the large proportion of "commissioned" students, there was no feedback loop to enable the university to assess the effectiveness of their programs and identify additional knowledge and/or skills that were needed in their graduates.

Based on the parallels described above for using internationalization as a model, we identified critical discussion areas which would point toward possible improvements in the college's current program. We believed the College had passed through the awareness and understanding phases identified by Arpan and that competence, which Arpan says provides specific skills, was to be tested (1993). Reflecting the work of Kolb (1984), Allen and Young recommend multiple methods of instruction, especially focusing on experiential learning, rather than concentrating on a narrow range of training techniques (1997). Cavusgil makes the point that there is an acute need to promote real-world problem solving (1993). The focus on problem solving is also mentioned by Kam, and he adds the need for independent thinking as an important goal of a university education (1988). Schertzer, Schuster, and Zimmerman identify 15 activities for internationalization including guest speakers, cases, computer simulations, hypothetical projects, internships, and development of a business plan (1994). Beck identifies common complaints about MBA graduates: the inability to work properly within a team and to think strategically (1994). Leitch and Harrison recommend "reciprocal integration" of cognitive learning provided by the university and practical skills provided by a business organization (1999). Their thoughts echo Raelin's assertion that the professional education model and action learning approach each offer important contributions to the training of managers (1994). Cavusgil recommends periodic re-examination of the curriculum (1993). The observations of all these researchers were incorporated into the in-depth research project discussed below.

RESEARCH PROJECT

To test the effectiveness of the current curriculum at the College of International Business of Shanghai University, a research project was developed. This project is one of many undertaken through the ongoing City University of New York - Shanghai University cooperative program. Two faculty members from City University of New York - College of Staten Island and two faculty members from Shanghai University were chosen to develop and execute this research. The goal of the project was to develop an enhancement program for Shanghai University's international business faculty.

Based upon the examination of the curriculum in light of our model and the needs of the Chinese economy, a guide for in-depth discussions with Chinese business managers was developed. The objective of this discussion guide was to discover the perceptions of Chinese employers toward university graduates in general, and toward Shanghai University graduates in particular, and to develop their assessments of the importance of specific skills in undergraduates and their recommendations for improvements in the curriculum. This discussion guide was translated into Mandarin, and all discussions were held in Mandarin. Both China and U.S.-based faculty attended each of the in-depth interviews.

The research question posed was as follows: What skills do non-S.O.E. employers in the P.R.C. see as most important in new college graduates? Respondents represented joint ventures, Chinese entrepreneurs, industrial development zone management, the Shanghai Stock Exchange, a Japanese-based firm, a bank, and an insurance company.

RESEARCH RESULTS

Respondents were asked to select the skills which are most important for a new graduate being considered for employment by his or her company. There was universal agreement among all that business English, the ability to think analytically, and real work experience are the most important skills potential employers want graduates to possess. Also important is the ability to work in teams. Knowledge of marketing and strategic planning capability were chosen by far fewer managers. The ability to select and motivate employees was not considered by any manager as an important skill (see Table 4.2).

Table 4.2: Importance of Specific Skills

Importance of Specific Skills	
Skill	**Proportion Choosing Most Important**
Business English language capability	100%
Ability to think analytically	100%
Real work experience	100%
Ability to work in teams	75%
Knowledge of marketing	38%
Strategic planning capability	25%
Ability to select and motivate employees	0%

Participating managers were then asked to assess the competency of graduates they had recently hired in each of the skill areas. They were most dissatisfied with the real world experience of graduates and their ability to work in teams as well as to think analytically.

When asked how the university can improve the skills of graduates in specific areas, respondents focused on undergraduates' analytical thinking with several suggesting that the students be provided more non-classroom activities and team activities. One respondent suggested the establishment of a small business which students could run. The managers interviewed also suggested the university provide multiple internships and other opportunities to work in the real world.

When asked for specific recommendations for the Shanghai University business faculty, the management respondents suggested establishing relationships with foreign universities as well as with Shanghai companies and improving theoretical instruction by using more up-to-date materials. When answering the final question, which requested any other suggestions, the managers recommended an emphasis on creative thinking, approved of the idea of a company computer simulation, and recommended the university focus on increased computer knowledge, extensive use of case studies, and increased study-abroad opportunities.

CONCLUSION

The results of these interviews are consistent with econometric results showing that the market economy in China places a relatively low value on current university education. They also support the modification to the standard model to include a feedback loop in the process of assessing and improving the curriculum The value of conducting a limited number of in-depth interviews allowed ample opportunity for follow-up questions, clarifying questions, and an assessment of the intensity of the respondents' concern about the issues discussed.

The results of the in-depth discussions closely mirror the suggestions adapted from the literature related to internationalization of education. Most managers interviewed want graduates to be able to think analytically and to solve problems in the real world just as Cavusgil and Kam recommended. As a corollary, they emphasize the need for real work experience.

Business English is seen as very important by nearly all managers interviewed. Despite the fact that at Shanghai University students spend 36 semester hours over two years learning English, many Chinese employers feel their capabilities remain inadequate for everyday commerce.

The need for independent thinking cited by Kam remains a need. Respondents' perception of the need for analytical thinking reflects their desire for new graduates to use their own minds in solving problems. The methods of instruction used throughout the P.R.C. at the university level appear to have a major impact on students' inability to think creatively and independently, but this discussion is outside the scope of this project.

Feedback from potential employers is a new concept to Shanghai University, yet continuing to measure the relevance of the program is critical to its success, reflecting Cavusgil's recommendation for periodic re-examination.

Based on this research project, the team has recommended several actions to be taken by the College of International Business at Shanghai University:

- Regular feedback from employers and graduates to close the feedback loop.
- Development of a faculty team committed to a review of the curriculum and charged with developing goals for the program and recommending needed changes to the faculty at large.
- Greater stress on business English in the curriculum.
- Writing of original cases based on Chinese firms, conditions, and possibilities.
- Use of teams to analyze, present, and discuss these cases.
- Use of computer-simulation "games" with a team approach.
- Encouragement and financial support for students in local or foreign business internships or study-abroad programs.
- Encouragement and financial support for faculty business experiences or foreign exchange programs.

One must always be cautious in generalizing from a specific and nonrandom sample. Still Shanghai is a major commercial and financial center in the P.R.C. with extensive contact with the global economy. Nonetheless, the broad issues facing university educators in transition economies are sufficiently similar that the model and results presented here should be instructive.

The need to train many managers in new approaches is a critical priority for universities where an economy is in transition from planned to market orientation. Even more critical is the development of cases and other materials that train students to solve problems they have not seen before. These materials must use local business situations, accounting, and law if they are to be effective. This is arguably the most important difference between planned economy education on the one hand and market oriented education on the other. While this need has been implied, little specific attention has been given to the process.

The conceptual framework using the internationalization approach appears to be validated by the Chinese experience. This suggests the suitability of using the internationalization model for educating managers in transition economies in other regions as well. We believe this finding should be useful to others faced with this challenge. Future research testing other aspects of the model (inputs and the value-adding process) may give further evidence of the parallels of these educational transitions or expose differences.

Finally, the intensity with which these concerns were expressed by successful market-oriented business managers underscores the importance which must be attached to educational reforms that specifically address the needs of the market economy in all transition economies to insure their long term viability.

Appendix 4.1

Table A: Curriculum for International Business

Type	Title	First Year			Second Year			Third Year			Fourth Year		
		1	2	3	1	2	3	1	2	3	1	2	3
Basic Compulsory Courses	College English	6	6	6	6	6	6						
	Economics	3	4	4									
	Principles of Laws	3											
	History of Chinese Revolution	3											
	Philosophy				6								
	Theories of Deng Xiaoping	3			3								
	P.E.	1	1	1	1	1	1						
	Mathematics	6	4	4									
	Linear Algebra					3							
	Probability Theory & Mathematical Statistics				5								
	Computer Culture	3	3	4									
	Moral Education				3								
	Business Correspondence				3	3							
	Principles of Accounting		4	4									

Table B: Curriculum for International Business

Type	Title	First Year			Second Year			Third Year			Fourth Year		
		1	2	3	1	2	3	1	2	3	1	2	3
Major Compulsory Courses	Financial Accounting					4							
	Corporation Finance						4						
	Programming							5					
	Fundamentals of Management								4				
	Statistics								5				
	Business Law							4					
	Money and Banking							4					
	Marketing								4				
	Taxation									4			
	Theory of International Trade									4			
	International Finance										4		
	International Cooperation											4	
	Feasibility Analysis of Investment Project											4	
	Business Correspondence in English									3	3		
	Social practice (one month)									4			

Appendix 4.2

Table A: Curriculum for International Business

Type	Title	First Year			Second Year			Third Year			Fourth Year		
		1	2	3	1	2	3	1	2	3	1	2	3
Major Selective Courses	Import & Export Practice								4				
	International Business Law								4				
	International Marketing										4		
	International Settlement								2				
	International Credit								2				
	Insurance								4				
	English for International Finance (Trade)								3	3			
	Geography for International Trade								3				
	International Service Trade									2			
	World Economics								2				
	Organizational Behavior										3		
	International Taxation										3		
	Managerial Accounting									4			

Table B: Curriculum for International Business

Type	Title	First Year			Second Year			Third Year			Fourth Year		
		1	2	3	1	2	3	1	2	3	1	2	3
Other Selective Courses	Modern Commercial Photograph												
	Appreciation of Movies and Video Arts												
	Science of Literature and Art												
	Music Appreciation												
	Etiquette in Foreign Affairs												
	Human Resources Management												
	The Spirit of Entrepreneurs and their Pioneering												
	Public Relations												
	Hot Topics for World Economy												
	Windows 95												
	Excel 5.0 for Windows												

REFERENCES

Allen, D. B. & Young, M. (1997). Globalizing the executive MBA program: linking class and field experience. *Journal of Teaching in International Business*, *9*(2), 49-68.

Anand, S. (1983). *Inequality and poverty in Malaysia: Measurement and decomposition.* New

York: Oxford University Press for the World Bank.

Arpan, J. (1993). Curricular and administrative considerations - the cheshire cat parable. In S. Tamer Cavusgil (ed.), *Internationalizing Business Education: Meeting the Challenge* (pp. 15-30). Michigan State University Press.

Beck, J. E. (1994). The new paradigm of management education: revolution and counter-revolution. *Management Leaning, 25*(2), 231-247.

Byron, R. P. & Manaloto, E. Q. (1990). Returns to education in china. *Economic Development and Cultural Change. 38*(4), 783-796.

Cavanaugh, J. P. (1999). C is for capitalist. *Johns Hopkins Magazine. 51*(4), 40-46.

Cavusgil, T. S. (1993). Internationalization of business education: defining the challenge. In T. S. Cavusgil (ed.), *Internationalization Business' Education: Meeting the Challenge* (pp. 1-13, 323-327). Michigan State University Press.

Chen, H. (2000). *The Institutional Transition Of China's Township And Village Enterprises*. Brookfield, Vermont: Ashgate Publishing.

China Achieving Progress in Market Economy. (1997). Retrieved from http://www.China-embassy.org/cgi-bin.

Eckholm, E. (1999, September 6). China puts more power in pockets of the people. *New York Times.*

Gregory, R. G. & Meng, X. (1995). Wage determination and occupational attainment in the rural industrial sector of China. *Journal of Comparative Economics, 21*(3), 353-374.

Harvie, C. (1999). Economic transition: what can be learned from China's experience. *International Journal of Social Economics, 26*(7/8/9/), 1091-1119.

Jamison, D. T. & Van Der Gaag, J. (1987). Education and earnings in the People's Republic of China. *Economic Education Review, 6*(2), 161-166.

Johnson, E. & Chow, G. (1997). Rates of return to schooling in China. *Pacific Economic Review, 2*(2), 101-113.

Knight, J. & Song, L. (1991). The determination of urban income inequality in China. *Oxford Bulletin of Economics and Statistics, 53*(2), 123-154.

Kolb, D. A. (1984). *Experiential learning: experience as the source of learning and development*. Englewood Cliffs, NJ: Prentice-Hall.

Kam, H. (1988). China's need to train more personnel in business English. *Bulletin of the Association for Business Communication, 51*(3), 27-30.

Leitch, C. M. & Harrison, R. T. (1999). A process model for entrepreneurship education and development. *International Journal of Entrepreneurial Behaviour and Research, 5*(4), 40-46.

Maurer-Fazio, M. (1999). Earnings and education in China's transition to a market economy survey evidence from 1989 and 1992. *China Economic Review, 10*, 17-40.

Meng, X. & Kidd, M. (1997). Labor market reform and the changing structure of wage determination in China's state sector during the 1980s. *Journal of Comparative Economics, 25(3*), 403-421.

Perkins, D. H (1992). China's gradual approach to market reforms. *United Nations Conference on Trade and Development. No 52*. Geneva: UNCTAD.

Private Businesses Playing Bigger Role in China. (1999). http://www.China-embassy.org/cgi-bin.

Psacharopoulis, G. (1993). Returns to investment in education: a global update. *World Bank Policy Research Working Papers: Education and Employment.*

Raelin, J. A. (1994). Whither management education? Professional education, action learning and beyond. *Management Learning, 25*(2), 301-317.

Schertzer, C. B., Schuster, C. P., & Zimmerman, R.O. (1994). A typology of leaning activities for international business education. *Conference Presentation: Thirteenth Annual EMU Conference on Language and Communications for World Business and the Professions*. Eastern Michigan University.

Shirley, M. & Xu, L.C. (1997). Empirical effects of performance contracts: evidence from China. *World Bank Development Research Group, Working Paper.*

http://www.worldbank.org/research.

Singh, A. (1993). The plan, the market and evolutionary economic reform in China. *United Nations Conference on Trade and Development, No. 76.* Geneva: UNCTAD.

Stiglitz, J. (1998, July 20). Address. Second-generation strategies for reform in China presented at Beijing University. http://www.worldbank.org/html/extme/speech.html.

U.S. Department of State. Bureau of East Asian and Pacific Affairs. (1999). *Background notes: China.*

Wong, J., Ma, R., & Yang, M. (eds.). (1995). *China's rural entrepreneurs.* Singapore: Times Academic Press.

World Bank. (1996). *From plan tomMarket.* New York: Oxford University Press.

Chapter 5

Challenges for Executive Education in Latin America

David C. Bruce
Institute of International Business

João Marcelo Sombra
Institute of International Business

Pedro Carrillo
Institute of International Business

INTRODUCTION: THE EDUCATIONAL SCENE IN LATIN AMERICA

Latin America has fallen behind much of Asia in the most basic measures of educational performance. Many worry that this has been a major contributor to less success in economic development as well. Asian success certainly contributed greatly to the economic policy reform movement in Latin America during the 1990s, also known as applying the "Washington Consensus." That model involved — among several thrusts — trade liberalization, tying funding to performance, downsizing, and privatizing. The latter two raise the question: How can you spend less and still improve education? Also, if you do not improve education in ways that provide appropriate performance measures, will the efforts to reform the political economy of Latin American countries not fall short in terms of long-term economic performance?

Proposals to improve education involve a series of trade-offs. Primary/secondary education versus tertiary education is the most basic issue. Within the field of post-secondary education, there are additional trade-offs between general higher education and technical training, teaching and scholarship, liberal and professional education, graduate professional versus academic programs, degree programs and non-degree offerings, and public versus private institutions. A broad view of the educational challenges in the region can be found in *El gran eslabón*, a study for the U.N. Economic Commission for Latin America and the Caribbean (Hopenhayn and Ottone, 2000). Based on this background, and looking for a guide to determining the importance of executive education for business competitiveness, this paper examines each of these sets of trade-offs as they may affect the choice of offering more extensive and appropriate executive education.

EDUCATIONAL REFORM AND INNOVATION IN THE CONTEXT OF GLOBALIZATION AND NEO-LIBERALISM IN PUBLIC POLICY

In Latin America, education must be considered in the context of several challenges. One is in terms of covering the basics. How do students perform on some standardized measures in reading, math, etc.? As crucial as this is, we must also ask about timeliness and relevance. In these areas, the universal impact of globalization comes into play. On top of the general effects of globalization, Latin American countries have been reforming their economies based on the neo-liberal model. This approach, which opens economies more to the world, accelerates and intensifies the impact of globalization on countries that were economically protected in the past. Have student been prepared to address the consequences?

Thomas Friedman characterizes globalization as the democratization of finance, technology, and information (2000). In terms of business, this has come to mean an increase in global markets and global production. Democratization means, at a minimum, significant complications in the formation and implementation of public policy. These processes result in tremendous pressures on societies to open more to the world, great cost in obsolescence if one does not, and extreme internal tension if one does.

In Latin America, major reforms were made in the 1990s under what has become known as the Washington Consensus. This was a response to expert analysis about sound economic policy for any era, lessons learned from Asia's growth in the 1970s and 1980s, and consensus on how best to address the realities of globalization. The conclusion was to focus on what works to generate macroeconomic stability through the control of public sector deficits, reduce the role of the state in the productive process through major privatizations and deregulation programs, and emphasize the importance of opening the external sector to foreign competition.

The need to address these questions can be seen in country comparisons. World Bank research tried to determine why some developing countries enjoy the highest growth rates in the world while others struggle.

> The World Bank set out to answer this question by comparing four developing nations - China, India, Pakistan, and Bangladesh - that have grown at strikingly different rates. Though these countries were equally under-developed at the beginning of the 1990s, China's economy has since soared, while India and Bangladesh have grown moderately, and

> Pakistan not at all. As David Dollar, Director of Development Policy at the World Bank, explains, the World Bank's survey suggests that trade liberalization must be complemented by a sound investment climate if developing countries are to achieve high growth rates. Institutions, policies, and regulations play integral roles in encouraging foreign investment. However, Dollar says, highly bureaucratic and corrupt governments or unreliable financial services will prevent firms from receiving the services they need. Such conditions make it difficult to persuade entrepreneurs to invest in potential export opportunities since their returns will be low and uncertain (Dollar, 2003, 1).

In the case of Latin America, the reforms of the 1990s were aimed at applying the lessons learned in Asia. Achievement was very uneven across countries and across time.

> By the measures of sustained economic growth, greater equity and employment, the record has been discouraging. Unfortunately, there is little consensus about the reasons why. Some reforms have been incompletely or inefficiently implemented. Often, corruption has clouded the picture; the fruits of privatization, for example, went into private bank accounts rather than facilitating the transition of the workforce to new private-sector jobs. (Bruce, 2003a, 6).

The idea of "incompletely or inefficiently implemented" has been classified as the need for second-generation reforms. These include maintaining prudent macroeconomic policy, effectively managing capital flows, reducing poverty and inequality, increasing domestic savings rates, and strengthening institutional foundations. The institutional need has been great as regulatory agencies (as well as legislatures, courts, nongovernmental watchdog groups, and universities) were often not prepared to deal with the newly privatized industries and other new demands of more open economies.

Looking back on the Asian case, one could say that limited, quality government intervention has been the most successful strategy (see World Bank, 1993). Specifically in reference to education, William Ratliff adds that "one critical factor in Asia's success has been its universal, increasingly high-quality education systems, particularly at the primary and secondary levels, that have enabled most people to promote their own well-being and contribute to national development" (Ratliff, iii). This, then, returns us to the dilemma of how to improve education to deal with globalization when the emphasis has also been on downsizing government and reducing deficit spending. In other words, government generally, and education in particular, have had to focus on defining what should be considered "the basics" and thus most deserving of public support.

Chile has had some success in educational reform. Its approach to expanding coverage and increasing quality has including "improving teaching, enforcing standards, reducing bureaucracy, and decentralizing administrative control" (Ratliff, 2003, 11). On the other hand, despite significant progress, even Chile has not approached Asian achievements in the basics of mathematics and reading.

Just as the amount of support for public education is under great strain, new questions must be asked not only about what the most crucial areas of education are, but also what should be the content in those areas. The Asian success linked basic education at the elementary school level with the needs of industrialization and the export of manufactured goods. Is this now the right formula for Latin America in a period of globalization, neo-liberal public policy, and the information/service era?

TRADE-OFF BETWEEN PRIMARY AND TERTIARY EDUCATION

Regularly there are campaigns to refocus educational spending. For example, President Lula in Brazil has emphasized the importance of the primary school level. Critics have suggested that Brazil spends too much of its education budget on higher education. This issue has come up throughout the region as it is argued that "...biases in per student spending towards the tertiary level have weakened the potential of education to offset socioeconomic and geographic inequalities" (Castro/Verdisco, 2002, 5). The concern involves both equity and effectiveness. In many countries public universities are free of tuition, indicating a commitment to access for all social levels of society. Yet given limited teaching resources, admissions may be based on test scores as is the case in Brazil. Consequently, middle and upper class children have disproportionately gained access in part because many are prepared for the tests by private elementary and secondary schools.

GENERAL HIGHER EDUCATION AND TECHNICAL TRAINING

In some Latin American countries, there have been conflicting pressures regarding post-secondary educational options. Universities can make the case that job creation will flow from the training of potential business leaders, managers, and entrepreneurs. Technical training at vocational schools can provide the prepared workforce if jobs are created (see Castro and Garcia, 2003). In the era of import substitution industrialization and state-directed growth, jobs were generated either by industries protected from foreign competition or by government investment. If economies open and the state is downsized, what will be the source of job creation? Either the traditional family owned firms, foreign investors, or new entrepreneurs must step up to the plate. The former lack the motivation while the latter lack the skills. Thus, to not be too dependent on foreign investors, these countries need to increase entrepreneurial activity, yet, business schools have not been strong in this area.

TEACHING AND SCHOLARSHIP

The question of teaching versus research is a contentious issue in Latin America as it is in other parts of the world. On average, it may be fair to say that historically the majority of Latin American universities have been primarily undergraduate teaching institutions. Furthermore, in many cases, the majority of the professors have taught part-time.

In a number of countries, this has changed substantially, and research has been given a greater emphasis. Many academics now publish in both local and international scholarly journals. A growing number have been trained in North American or European institutions. In addition, some — especially in the case of business schools — have begun to gain accreditation in the United States and Europe (see Castro and Levy, 2000). Often meeting accreditation criteria includes the need for both research and graduate programs. The latter provide both research manpower and the training of future scholars/teachers.

LIBERAL VERSUS PROFESSIONAL EDUCATION

Traditionally Latin American universities were a collection of professional schools. European traditions and perhaps the key role of part-time instructors have contributed to this thrust. In many fields (e.g., law and medicine), students enter the professional schools directly from high school. There has not been a strong tradition similar to the idea of the liberal arts degree that is so common in the United States. This approach was viable for training elites given that the limited number of university students came to the university from high quality private high schools.

Several downside conditions now affect this educational model. As university enrollment expanded, more students entered the universities without a strong "liberal education" from high school. Also, students must select a career at an early age. Once in a professional school (yet undergraduate program), switching fields often requires starting over at the freshman year. In disciplines where job opportunities have been limited, the graduates have to use a transferable-skills approach to finding a job. On this basis, Castro and Levy characterize the "de-professionalization" of certain fields and indicate that some professional schools are, in essence, offering what perhaps should be a more general higher education degree that would better prepare students for new, currently undefined opportunities (Castro and Levy, 2000).

GRADUATE PROFESSIONAL VERSUS GRADUATE ACADEMIC

As explained above, many undergraduate programs in Latin American universities are professional programs. With the addition of distinct graduate degrees, perhaps new distinctions have emerged. This can be seen especially in business. In some countries, the flagship or terminal degree is the Masters. Like M.A.s and M.S.s in the United States, these may involve a thesis. On the other hand, for example in the Brazilian case, M.B.A.s are specialist programs (e.g., M.B.A.-Finance, M.B.A.-Retailing). In the Brazilian situation, with an M.B.A. too specialized and a Masters too academic, the missing element may be the professional, general management degree characterized by the M.B.A. in the United States. The case of a Professional Masters as offered by the Federal University of Bahia may be moving toward the U.S. emphasis (Fischer and Andrade, 2003). This would also apply to the growing number of Executive M.B.A. programs.

DEGREE PROGRAMS VERSUS NON-DEGREE OFFERINGS

There has been a tendency in the United States to view extension courses as a bit like auto mechanics: not of high level or rigorous academic quality. Even though "life-long learning" has become a popular slogan, many academics may still think of extension activities as not too serious. Somehow a lecture to 300 freshmen represents teaching, and a two-day seminar for business people just involves "training." Professional fields such as law, medicine, engineering, and business have led the way in upgrading the offerings and meeting the needs of mid-career professionals.

Nowadays, career advisors tell young people that they may have several careers over their lifetime. Transferable skills will be increasingly important along with an ability to adjust to new demands of new professions. Non-degree, executive programs are a key, viable alternative to costly and time-consuming returns to campus for additional degrees. In Latin America, this may be central to moving quickly in response to globalization, neo-liberalism, and the information age.

Delivery may take one of several forms. Programs open to a variety of participants can take place on-campus or in community locations. This applies as well for company-specific programs that can also be offered on-site. Alternatively, a number of companies have developed their own in-house training programs (see Da Costa, 2001).

PUBLIC VERSUS PRIVATE INSTITUTIONS

In the late 19th century, the anti-clerical movement was linked to the campaign for universal public education. The Church had been the key institution in the field of education. In some cases, such as Argentina, private universities were closed and did not operate again until the 1960s (see Rock, 1987). Within this context we can clearly say that the debate about public versus private education has been a most serious business in Latin America.

Today, private institutions are a major component in higher education. Furthermore, in some cases, the concept of free university studies has come under challenge. The private–school advantage for admissions was mentioned above (also see Fischman, 2001). Some countries have tried to address funding problems — and perhaps competition from private institutions — by turning to tuition and fees. In Chile, for example, "the higher education system draws so heavily on tuition, sales, and contracts that it depends on the government for only one-third of its income" (Castro and Levy, 2000, 73; see also Viola and Castro).

Beyond student access and equity issues, public funding also must be considered in terms of public support for the externalities of research. Private schools often are so dependent on tuition income that more expensive endeavors such as research may not get much attention. In light of this, tuition funding for public universities may be crucial as a way to free up resources to support research.

In the Asia case, funding has made a major contribution to educational success. Compared to Latin American countries, many Asian countries have applied flatter funding across levels. Beyond the resulting resources for primary and secondary schools, Asian success has also involved effective centralization, discipline, and differences in pedagogy (time on task) along with high stakes and aspirations for students and parents. For continuity, education was taken off the political agenda. Given that these latter characteristics do not depend on spending, we are reminded that funding, although very important, is only one element in successful educational programs.

BRAZILIAN EDUCATIONAL ISSUES: A CASE STUDY

The Funding Trade-Off

There has been a significant debate in Brazil regarding the focus and effectiveness of educational spending. Central to the debate is whether a greater proportion of students should attend the primary or tertiary level. Table 5.1 below shows that "Superior Education" receives over half of education spending. Such greater investments at the higher level of education has been successful in moving federal universities to a high standard of quality, and moreover, are a benchmark for academic research and faculty development. It is important to reflect on the reasons for this educational policy and its effect over time.

Table 5.1: Brazilian Educational Spending

Maintaining Expenses and Education Development	Actual Provisions	Executed Expenses	%
			Thousand RS
	(C)	(D)	(D/C)
Planning and Budgeting	4,800	4,275	89.06%
General Administration	53,509	52,795	98.67%
Information Technology	52,305	49,943	95.48%
Human Resources Development	71,857	46,597	64.85%
Recipe Administration	1,950	1,430	73.33%
Community Assistance	87	76	87.36%
Hospital and On site Assistance	140,889	54,010	38.34%
Elementary Education	1,721,839	1,262,170	73.30%
Secondary Education	617,254	600,777	97.33%
Professional Education	938,140	858,233	91.48%
Superior Education	6,562,345	6,297,026	95.96%
Child Education	35,633	6,823	19.15%
Education for Young and Adults	453,566	432,544	95.37%
Special Education	48,914	35,695	72.98%
Culture Dissemination	458	94	20.52%
Poor Indigenous Assistance	300	61	20.33%
Scientific Development	24,197	11,394	47.09%
Dissemination of Scientific Knowledge and Technology	206	191	92.72%
Transferences	474,816	474,816	100.00%
Total Expenses	11,203,065	10,188,950	90.95%

Source: www.tcu.gov.br

The reasons for an existing disparity between primary and tertiary education may flow from a strategic positioning philosophy of the Federal Government. The concept has been that an emerging nation will thrive in part due to its intellectual capacity and in fact proportionally to its knowledge equity. The justification is the conclusion that a nation has to promote its intellectual capital rather than just focusing on natural resources and agricultural products. A major concern, though, develops when the government's educational budget cannot adequately support both primary and tertiary education. This is a common reality for most emerging countries. Societal strains intensify in the short-run as the gap between the lower and higher social classes tends to increase, especially given that education is closely correlated with income levels. In Brazil, to have access to the best universities, most students have to study their entire lives in private schools that offer the best educational preparation. Some of the best universities are the public ones that offer free tuition. Yet, those who can take advantage of this probably could afford to finance their own education. The system thus makes it even more difficult for the lower class to have access to better quality education at any level.

These reasons and effects have been at the center of innumerous debates and have led to some level of consensus in Brazilian society on the necessity to give a higher priority to primary education. The unfortunate trade-off is that with tight budgets, funds for the federal universities must be reduced. On the other hand, proposals of this variety unleash resistance from vested interests among the academic community.

Evaluation and Supervision

The more investments are made to improve education in South American countries, the more evaluation and supervision is required to assure efficiency as well as correction of deficiencies. In Brazil, the Ministry of Education has established Fundação de Coordenação de Aperfeicoamento de Pessoal de Nivel Superior (C.A.P.E.S.), a foundation that is in charge of evaluating and supervising post-graduate programs. The criteria used to evaluate these programs are based on a multidimensional analysis involving seven characteristics. Each characteristic varies in terms of the intrinsic issues concerning every aspect of the discipline. The weight given to these key criteria are: Faculty 20%, Research 10%, Graduate Teaching Activity 10%, Alumni Relations 10%, Masters Theses and Doctoral Dissertations 20%, and Intellectual Production 30%.

Most academic research in Brazil takes place at the federal universities. Partnerships with foreign universities have become a crucial aspect for researchers in all fields of knowledge and an important aspect of the post-graduate faculty strategies. In particular, the Federal Government has been using scholarships and other resources to encourage faculty to go abroad. However, due to the political pressure for higher levels of investments in primary level education, resources have been suffering drastic cuts lately. For example, scholarships for doctoral degrees are available only in specific areas where graduate training is not available in Brazil. On the other hand, according to the specific criteria of business school's faculty evaluation, each program can get a better evaluation for diversity of faculty preparation. This means that the faculty members are motivated to add foreign degrees to their credentials.

Another major issue is time, which currently includes a triennial period for the evaluation and supervision process. There are some discussions about whether or not this period should be extended, mainly because there is a substantial gap between intellectual production and publication and consideration of the time required to complete masters and doctoral programs. Furthermore, time is increased because taking both masters and doctorates from the same institution is discouraged.

Rankings do matter. Moving up on evaluations of post-graduate programs can substantially increase the chances of more resources for a department from the Ministry of Education. In fact, most of the programs struggle for better evaluations, and some of them act strategically under each of the evaluation criteria in order to improve and, as a result, develop better conditions for both research and teaching. This means that each of the criteria utilized by C.A.P.E.S. is carefully and strategically considered by the deans and by faculty boards of directors.

Alternative Models for Business Education: University Extension and Corporate Education

Brazilian business schools have been quite entrepreneurial. As the M.B.A. "brand" became popular worldwide, many new Brazilian products came on the market. The traditional, more academic masters remained the flagship for many universities. Yet at the same time, new programs were offered including Executive M.B.A.s, Professional Masters, and specialist M.B.A.s. The offerings from private institutions particularly expanded business education. Motivations certainly included meeting the needs of the business community. At the same time, other motivations also came into play. For example, since the public universities cannot charge tuition for degrees, the non-degree programs provide desperately needed extra revenue for faculty and departments as well. Innovation in these areas has been possible since they fall outside of the traditional evaluation and accreditation systems. On the other hand, quality control issues are significant.

A gap of availability or relevance may be indicated by the growth of education offered in-house by corporations. Yet much growth could still take place in this area. For Dianne Miester, a corporative education consultant and author of *Corporative Education*, corporations can serve as the gateway within a company through which all education takes place (1999). This means the company itself becomes the organization's strategic hub for educating employees, customers, and suppliers as corporate universities link an organization's strategies to the learning goals of its audiences.

To break traditional concepts and implement new ideas — as well as filling some deficient gaps in the traditional educational system — corporate universities have been developed and strengthened. Companies such as ACCOR, Oracle, Xerox, Motorola, and McDonald's are leading the implementation of corporate universities in Brazil (Costa, 2001). Some were identified as the best companies to work for, and this gives them a competitive advantage in terms of being experts in knowledge management.

On the other hand, big corporations are not the norm. Small and medium sized businesses make up 97.8% of the G.D.P. These smaller firms usually lack the resources to develop their own in-house universities (Franco, 2003). These companies do not have a history of strong investment in training their human resources or any interest in establishing corporate university programs. In reality, corporate universities in Brazil involve no more than 40 companies of which 80% are from foreign countries. According to Martius Vicente Rodriguez y Rodriguez, manager of Petrobras University, the corporate university should help organizations move to the new knowledge society; however, this will not be a simple or fast process. In Petrobras, the largest Brazilian oil company with total revenues around U.S.$33 billion for the year 2002, using training by its corporate university is strictly related to the overall strategic vision of the organization.

Executive Education Options for Latin America

Executive education does not get much attention in the broader debate about educational challenges and reform in Latin America. Nevertheless, it plays a crucial role in the overall education scenario. Particularly in business, leaders must constantly address timely, relevant issues. The evolution of M.B.A. programs and other business degrees indicates that academic institutions are sensitive to the changing needs of the business community. Is the current portfolio of executive programs in business up to the task? Do the movements toward globalization and free trade keep moving the goal posts further away?

We sought ways to get a snapshot of the current state-of-the-art. As a starting point, we decided to examine the programs of the 35 top ranked business schools in the region. For this purpose we used the rankings from *América Economica* (2003). This, of course, leaves out many programs offered by the much larger pool of business schools in the region. It also does not cover programs offered in the region by institutions from other parts of the world without local university involvement. Nevertheless, looking at the portfolios of the major business schools does help in appreciating the priorities that top schools and their clients have emphasized.

We identified executive programs from the websites of the top schools. Six hundred programs, a wide range of which were short courses covering various topics, were identified. Table 5.2 shows the general classification of topics and the percentage of courses in each category. Around 60% fall under the categories of human resources, finance and accounting, strategy and negotiations, and marketing.

Table 5.2: Executive Topics

Topics	Total	Percentage
Human Resources	122	20.33%
Finance and Accounting	101	16.83%
Strategy and Negotiation	74	12.33%
Marketing	62	10.33%
Management	58	9.67%
Technology	41	6.83%
Logistics and Operations	39	6.50%
Product Management	19	3.17%
Economics	18	3.00%
Control	13	2.17%
Entrepreneurship	11	1.83%
Public Management	10	1.67%
Project Management	9	1.50%
International Business	9	1.50%
Business Law	6	1.00%
English	4	0.67%
Services Management	4	0.67%
Total	**600**	**100.00%**

Clearly, none of the executive programs specified globalization, trade-liberalization, or free trade as the primary topic. However, these topics may well be addressed within the framework of the specific disciplines of the courses. Faculty presenters may also greatly utilize international cases and address international challenges within the programs.

In terms of experience, many faculty members of the top schools obtained their professional training in European and United States universities. Major U.S. schools have a much larger percentage of professors from a variety of countries. On the other hand, whether American born or not, U.S. professors completed their academic training at U.S. universities.

Another way to evaluate potential for international relevance in curricula would be to consider the international linkages of the institutions. For the top business schools in Latin America, Figure 5.1 indicates the regional base of major international partners for exchanges and joint programs. Clearly, the strengths are with U.S. and European universities. Latin American institutions are particularly weak in terms of ties to Asia and especially to Africa.

Table 5.3: Strategic Alliances of Latin American Business Schools

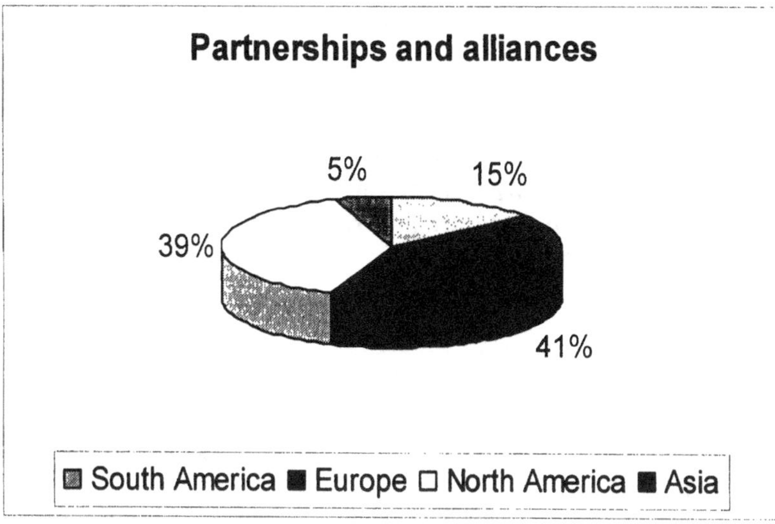

Figure 5.1: Strategic Alliances of Latin American Business Schools

Are executive programs getting attention by the academic and administrative leadership of the Latin American universities? For a quick view, we looked at the latest meeting of C.L.A.D.E.A. (Latin American Council of Business Schools). Out of 125 research sessions and plenary meetings, if one were to stretch the definition of "executive education concerns" to include entrepreneurial and corporate linkage, there were a maximum of ten sessions in the executive domain. A similar ratio applies when looking at the programs of B.A.L.A.S., the Business Association of Latin American Studies. On the other hand, paging through Latin American newspapers these days, one will certainly see a good number of executive programs being advertised.

CONCLUSION

Economic development models in Latin America are discussed by cab drivers and as part of dinner table conversation. This perennial state of affairs is currently in a period of increased intensity. Given the crucial role of education, it is also receiving intense scrutiny. The issues run the gamut from spending on primary schools to the application of research measures in the promotion of professors. Executive education can fall within this large area of public policy concerns, yet it does not fit cleanly into the education or the economic development agendas.

Executive education will be receiving more attention as a source of revenue for both private and public institutions. At the same time, criteria for evaluation remains illusive. How can learning be measured when executives catch a quick course and head back to their day jobs? What criteria of relevance should be applied?

At a minimum we can say that executive training holds the potential to exist on the cutting edge more easily, be it in delivery (e.g., distance learning) or in terms of topics. Collaboration with academic institutions in other parts of the world will probably increase. Activities related to Africa and especially Asia would certainly add relevance if the concern is business opportunities and competitive threats.

REFERENCES

Aguilar, U. (2003). *Relatorio e Pareceres Previos sobre as Contas do Governo da Republica- exercicio 200.* Brasilia: Brazil. www.tcu.gov.br.

América Economia, Edição Brasil. (2003).

Bruce, D. (2003a). Pact rests on a field of untested assumptions. *A World Paper White Paper.*

Castro, C. and Garcia, N. (2003). *Community colleges: a model for Latin America?* Washington, D.C.: Inter-American Development Bank.

Castro, C. and Levy, D. (2000). *Myth, reality, and reform: higher education policy in Latin America.* Washington, D.C.: Inter-American Development Bank and the Johns Hopkins University Press.

Castro, C. and Verdisco, A (eds.). (2002). *Latin American ideas and Asian results.* Washington, D.C.: Inter-American Development Bank.

Da Costa, A. (2001). *Educação Corporativa.* Rio de Janeiro, Brazil: QualityMark Editora.

Didou Aupetit, S. (2000). Globalización, Integración Macroregional y Políticas de internacionalización en el Sistema Mexicano de Educación Superior. *Education Policy Analysis Archives, 8*(11).

Dollar, D. (2003). Why does one country draw more investment than another? Y*aleGlobal.*

Education in Latin America: cramming them in. (2002). *The Economist.*

Espinola, V. and Castro,C. (2003). *La economía política de la reforma educacional en Chile.* Washington, D.C.: Inter-American Development Bank.

Favero, M. (1999). Autonomia Universitária no Brasil: Uma Utopia? *Education Policy Analysis Archives, 7*(24).

Fischer, T. and Andrade, C. (2003). Opportunities and risks in training managers - a narrative of the Brazilian experience with professional masters programs. Federal University of Bahia.

Fischmen, G. E. (2001). Globalization, consumers, citizens, and the 'private school advantage' in Argentina (1985-1999). *Education Policy Analysis Archives,* 9(31).

Franco, D. (2003). *Mito ou Realidade* http://carreiras.empregos.com.br/comunidades/rh/fique _por_dentro/050902-td_ educação_corporativa2.shtm]. www.empregos .com.br.

Friedman, T. (2000). *The Lexus and the olive tree: understanding globalization*, revised edition. New York: Farrar, Straus, and Giroux.

Gorostiaga, J. M., Acedo, C., and Xifra, S. E. (2003). Secondary education in Argentina during the 1990s: the limits of a comprehensive reform effort. *Education Policy Analysis Archives, 11*(17).

Guerra Ortiz, V. Open and distance education programs in Latin America.

Hilbert, M. and Katz, J. (2002). *Building an information society: a Latin American and Caribbean perspective*. Santiago, Chile: Economic Commission for Latin America and the Caribbean.

Hopenhayn, M. and Ottone, E. (2000). El gran eslabón: Educación y desarrollo en el umbral del siglo XXI. Buenos Aires: Fondo de Cultura Economica.

Infante, V. S. (1999). O Perfil da Universidade para o próximo milênio. *Education Policy Analysis Archives* 7(32).

Internationalization of a region, the. (2003b). *Georgia Leaders Shaping Atlanta's Global Future*. Atlanta: GlobalAtlanta/Agio Press.

Levy, D. (2002, March 8). Latin America's tertiary education: accelerating pluralism. *Seminar on Higher Education and Science and Technology in Latin America and the Caribbean: Responding to Expansion and Diversification*. Presented in Fortaleza, Brazil.

Meister, J. C. (1999). *Educação Corporativa*. Sao Paulo: Makron Books do Brasil Ltda.

Micklenthwait, J. and Wooldridge, A. (2000). *A future perfect: the challenge and hidden promise of globalization*. New York: Times Books.

Postrel, Virginia. 2002. Globalism and the Liberal Model, *New York Times*, January 31, 2002.

Organization of American States. (2003). Education: a hemispheric priority. www.oas.org/XXXIIGA.

Quacquarelli, N. (ed.). (2003). *The MBA career guide*. London: TopCareers.

Ratliff, W. (2003). *Doing it wrong and doing it right: education in Latin America and Asia*. alo Alto: Hoover Press.

Regions as global competitors. (1995). *The Economic Review, 10*.

Rocha, C. H. and Granemann, S. R. (2003). *Gestão de Institutições Privada de Ensino Superior*. Sao Paulo, Brazil: Editora Atlas.

Rock, D. (1987). *Argentina 1516-1987: from Spanish colonization to Alfonsin*. Berkeley: University of California Press.

Rosenberg, T. (2002, August 18). The free-trade fix. *New York Times*.

Tachizawa, T. and Bernardes de Andrade, R. O. (2001). *Gestão de Instituições de Ensino. Segunda Edição Revista*. Rio de Janeiro, Brazil: FGV Editora.

VISION. (2000). Vision – July/August. *Corporate Universities: An interview with Jeanne Meister*. http://ts.mivu.org/default.asp?show=article&id=785].

World Bank. (1993). The East Asian miracle: economic growth and public policy. *A World Bank Policy Research Report*. New York: Oxford University Press.

Chapter 6

Business Education in Brazil: Hybridism and Tensions

Thomaz Wood Jr.
Escola de Administração de Empresas de São Paulo

Ana Paula Paes de Paula
Escola de Administração de Empresas de São Paulo

INTRODUCTION

In this chapter, we present and discuss the phenomenon of Brazilian M.P.A. programs (Professional Master in Business Administration), a small group of programs offered by renowned Brazilian institutions. Despite being generically classified by the local business media, students and firms of M.B.A.s, these programs sport peculiar features that set them apart from the American model. In addition, by attempting to align with the regional social and economic context, each program follows its own route. We believe that the experience this article describes, although occurring in a developing country, may raise reflections that go beyond the local context and can make a contribution to the current debate over management education.

Our field work involved document analysis and in-depth interviews with ten coordinators and key-persons involved in six Brazilian M.P.A. programs developed by five different institutions in four different states. Interviews were carried out between March and August 2002.

The remainder of the chapter is structured as follows: the next section seeks to go over the main points of the international debate on M.B.A. programs, thus providing a background to introduce the phenomenon in focus; the following section summaries the recent evolution of business administration courses in Brazil and draws an outline of Brazilian M.P.A. programs; the next section discusses the M.P.A.s' paradoxes and speculate about the factors that conditioned their development; and the final section relates the M.P.A. development with the importation of managerial expertise.

THE REDEMPTION DISCOURSE AND THE CRITICAL DISCOURSE

Although the debate about the M.B.A. model is nothing new, criticism gained fresh momentum in the 1990s. One can say that the debate is polarized between two positions -- redemption discourse and critical discourse.

Redemption Discourse in the Business Media

Redemption discourse can be seen in the business media in the United States, Europe, and also in Brazil; M.B.A. programs are often depicted as a remedy for professional troubles and a safe route to a successful career (Jacomino, 2001, 2000, 1999; Gomes, 1997; Sganzerla, 1995). In the Brazilian media, redemption discourse first considered American and European M.B.A.s. In a typical article published by the business magazine *Exame*, the most important in the country, the journalist points out:

> Few dreams are more present in the managers' imaginary than that of an MBA degree. The Master in Business Administration is a promise for fast track careers, high salaries and, the dream of dreams, the possibility to become the CEO of an important company. (Gomes, 1997, 112)

If one takes the add pages of *Você S.A* (2001, 2000), another popular Brazilian business magazine, or the British magazine *The Economist* (2002a, 2002b), one can find several advertisements that appeal to the courses' impact on one's career and professional life:

- "Make a difference in the world of business: Executives for the 21st century" – F.A.A.P.
- "F.G.V. -- Management: always close to those who wants to exceed" – F.G.V.
- "The doorway to a new professional world" – I.N.P.G.
- "You will be transformed" – Chicago G.S.B.
- "You have the potential: Lift your career beyond expectations" – I.N.S.E.A.D.
- "Global approach: See with your eyes what very few have the privilege of seeing" – I.E.S.E.

On the other hand, the critical discourse, which coalesced in the 1990s, can be divided into two main groups: first, the critical trend led by Henry Mintzberg and his collaborators, which challenges the effectiveness of M.B.A. programs meant to prepare managers; and second, the criticism of the contents and pedagogy of the programs as expressed by researchers involved in Critical Management Studies (C.M.S.).

The Critical Discourse: Criticism of Effectiveness

Henry Mintzberg is certainly one of the most consistent (and persistent) voices to criticize the M.B.A. programs in their capacity to develop managers. He is also concerned with the impact M.B.A. graduates can have on firms. He argues that management schools insist on promoting a disastrous approach; many M.B.A. graduates will skip from one firm to another without ever truly realizing how things work, acting as if they were still in a learning environment. Mintzberg argues that managers can no longer continue to be trained by means of fragmentary case studies and disconnected theories. His central point: M.B.A. programs do not train managers, they only make one believe they do. They teach managerial rhetoric and cause students to believe they are able to control situations and solve complex problems overnight (see Mintzberg and Gosling, 2002; Mintzberg and Lampel, 2001).

Complementary, Warner argues that business schools fail to meet the needs of firms because they adopt a generalist discourse but focus on functional areas of expertise without giving proper attention to the cross-disciplinary character of today's business environment (2000).

The Critical Discourse: Criticism in the CMS domain

The criticism of M.B.A. programs in the 1990s also relates to the emergence of Critical Management Studies – C.M.S. (see Alvesson and Deetz, 1996; Alvesson and Willmott, 1993, 1992). Authors affiliated with these studies point out the following problems concerning management education (Antonacopoulou, 1999; Gold, Holman, and Thorpe, 1999; Reynolds, 1997; Boje, 1996; Dehler, Grey, and French, 1996; Grey, Knights, and Willmott, 1996; Robert, 1996; Willmott, 1994):

- management education is undergoing a "commoditization" process, one that privileges "'mass-production' instead of individualization," "commerce instead of education," and "image instead of substance,"
- most business schools are embedded with and promote the "management culture," a set of values and assumptions that overemphasizes financial success and short term results;
- business schools present a strong tendency toward "instrumentalism," with the use of ready-made prescriptions that lead students to learn how to reproduce techniques instead of performing adequate diagnoses;

- traditional management concepts and visions taught in business schools are increasingly inappropriate because of excessive reduction of the complexity of management to simplistic models;
- most business schools use a poor repertoire of learning methods – focus is on teaching instead of being on learning; and
- students are being regarded as mere spectators, or clients, of the teaching process – there is almost no encouragement of autonomy and self-development.

As regards M.B.A.s, criticism of "commoditization" is foremost among CMS authors. Inspired by Ritzer (1993), Parker and Jary (1995) point to a progressive "macdonaldization" of British universities, with the appearance of an elite that specializes in standardizing higher-education (see also Prichard and Willmott, 1997). Analyzing the case of Malaysia, Sturdy and Gabriel conclude that management education is becoming a commercial asset and that Western schools are increasingly engaged in competition for lucrative opportunities and foreign students ("consumers") in emerging markets (2000). In this context, M.B.A. programs are a standardized commodity with a high symbolic value, as they theoretically imply status, prestige, and power.

M.B.A. PROGRAMS MADE IN BRAZIL

Origins and the Current Situation

In Brazil, as in other countries, the development of business administration as a teaching and research field can be related with the industrialization process. The turning point was in the 1940s when the economy was no longer essentially agrarian and the expansion of the industrial and services sectors began (Martins, 1989).

The first undergraduate course totally focused on business administration was created in 1954 at Fundação Getúlio Vargas (F.G.V.): the Escola de Administração de Empresas de São Paulo (E.A.E.S.P.). A group formed by Michigan State University faculty members took part in the design of the academic programs. As part of the project, Brazilian professors received training in the U.S. After F.G.V.-E.A.E.S.P., other business schools were created in Rio Grande do Sul (E.A.-U.F.R.G.S.), Rio de Janeiro (F.G.V.-E.B.A.P.E. and P.U.C.-R.J.) and Bahia (E.A.-U.F.B.A.).

In the 1960s, F.G.V. created its graduate courses in the fields of public administration and business administration and started to regularly offer master's courses. This enabled the institution to train professors for other business schools.

In the 1990s, management education underwent considerable expansion and diversification. In the year 2000, there were, according to the Ministry of Education, 969 undergraduate programs, 28 master's programs, and ten doctorate programs in Brazil. In August 2002, the number of undergraduate programs had grown to an astonishing 2,687! The number of graduate programs, by their turn, grew at more modest rates.

Concerning practice-oriented graduate programs, between the second half of the 1990s and the early 2000s, three types of programs were consolidated:

- first, about ten elite programs, called M.P.A.s (Professional Master in Business Administration), offered by major public universities and traditional autonomous schools;
- second, close to fifty executive M.B.A.s. These are *lato sensu* graduate programs with a minimum 360-hour duration, generally offered in two modes: (1) general management programs, and (2) special purpose programs, dedicated alternatively to human resources, marketing, finances, information technology, and other specializations;
- third, an expressive, hard to estimate number of executive education programs – including in-company and corporate university programs – with varied durations that use the M.B.A. brand name with great liberty.

M.P.A.s: the Brazilian M.B.A.s?

The M.P.A.s were officially authorized by the Brazilian Ministry of Education in 1998 and accredited in 2001. The only exception is F.G.V.-E.A.E.S.P.'s program, which was created five years before the other programs. Appendix 1 offers information on the six programs analyzed in our field research. It is worth noting that in 2002, four more programs were created. These were not considered in the present survey.

In general, M.P.A.s sport many differences from their American and European counterparts. Based on the data from Appendix 1, the following information must be emphasized:

- As regards the general characteristics of the courses and their relation to student profiles, we point out that M.P.A.s are part-time programs; therefore students attend them at night and/or on Fridays and Saturdays, without giving up their jobs.
- Still regarding student profiles, their average age is greater than that found in international M.B.A. programs: Brazilians, except for F.G.V.-E.A.E.S.P. students, seem to seek out M.P.A.s at a later point in life than their foreign colleagues. Consistently,

Table 6.1: Characteristics of the M.P.A. Programs.

Program		*IBMEC-RJ*	*FGV-EAESP*	*FGV-EBAPE*	*PUC-RJ*	*EA-UFBA*	*EA-UFRGS*
Created in		2000	1993	1999	2001	1999	1998
Students origin	Large firms	30%	60%	40%	40%	60%	30%
	Medium firms	40%	30%	30%	30%	10%	25%
	Small firms and others	30%	10%	30%	30%	30% (includes NGOs, private found., and Gov.)	45%
Tuition	Total (US$)	10000	16000	6500	10000	7000	11000
	Paid by	38% employer 40% emp./stdt. 20% student 2% grants	20% employer 40% emp./ student 40% student	50% employer 30% emp./stdt. 20% student	60% employer 20% emp./stdt. 20% student	10% employer 70% employer / student 10% student 10% grants	5% employer 15% emp./stdt. 80% student
Classes and methods	Attendants per class	30	50	25 to 30	30	35 to 40	25 to 30
	General course structure	6 required disciplines +3 electives	22 required disciplines+ 6 electives; frgn. double degree option	10 required disciplines + 2 electives	18 required disciplines + 3 electives	10 required disciplines + 2 electives	15 required disciplines + one req. international seminar
	Lectures	45%	60%	70%	50%	60%	65%
	Case studies	35%	20%	20%	20%	20%	20%
	Group-based dynamics	20%	20%	10%	30%	20%	15%
Faculty profile	PhD or equivalent holders	95%	100%	100%	100%	90%	100%
	Professors with business activities	100%	100%	100%	50%	70%	100%
Attendant Profile	Average age	36 years	28-32 years	40 years	35 years	35-45 years	35-40 years
	Women	17 %	14-17 %	15-20 %	30 %	30 %	10-12 %
	Top-mngmt.	20%	20%	40%	30%	10%	45%
	Middle mngmt.	40%	40%	40%	40%	70%	30%
	Other	40% (non-mngrs, consultants, auditors, entrepreneurs)	40% (non-mngrs, entrepreneurs)	20% (non-mngrs, professors, entrepreneurs)	30% (non-mngrs, entrepreneurs)	20% (non-mngrs, entrepreneurs, recent retirees)	25% (non-mngrs entrepreneurs, consultants)

they also hold relatively higher hierarchic positions.

- As for tuition, M.P.A.s are a low-cost alternative as compared to foreign M.B.A.s. Of course, one needs to consider the purchase parity power, which makes M.P.A.s comparatively expensive regarding other local alternatives. In addition, we emphasize that these are part-time courses and are often paid (partially or fully) by the students' employers.
- As for classes and methods, the small size of classes draws attention. This is justified, in part, by teaching requirements and, in part, by the level of dedication the courses demand, which limits the number of interested candidates.
- As for faculty member profiles, there is the remarkable fact that although almost all professors are Ph.D. holders, most of them perform extra-academia activities, be it as executives at public and private companies or as consultants.

In addition to the characteristics mentioned above, three other aspects are noteworthy:

- First, we noticed that institutions regard the programs as important showcases as they enable closer ties with the corporate community. This led to significant investment in facilities and teaching resources. Consequently, M.P.A. programs also stand for renewal projects for the institutions providing them.
- Second, Brazilian students probably seek out M.P.A. programs for the same reasons their foreign peers look for M.B.A. programs: professional improvement and career advancement. But a significant number of professionals regard the M.P.A. programs as an opportunity to build either a new or a parallel career as professors or entrepreneurs. We can hypothesize that this may reflect the changes in the labor market, characterized by large restructuring and downsizing processes in the 1990s and the poor performance of the Brazilian economy in the same period. A complementary reason is that many professionals are simply disgusted or annoyed with corporate life and want something new.
- Third, it is worth mentioning the search for a new pedagogical approach. Among other initiatives, we found high flexibility in the design of courses, seeking to adapt to each class' profile; a management and creativity lab that uses theatre techniques; stimulus to exchange experiences between the public sector, the private sector, and the third sector; and the promotion of a "multi-functional, cross-disciplinary" perspective, crossing the borders of traditional areas of knowledge.

Different Paths

Besides their differences from their American and European counterparts, M.P.A. programs are also different among themselves, having developed identities aligned with the history and culture of their respective host-institutions.

F.G.V.-E.A.E.S.P. enjoys a strong tradition as a business school, is located in Brazil's leading economic and financial center, and has always had close ties with international institutions. It has also pioneered the implementation of the new model. F.G.V.-E.A.E.S.P.'s M.P.A. is marked by great student expectations related with career advance and by a spirit of peer competitiveness remindful of the culture of some American M.B.A.s. In addition, its students come primarily from the cadres of large multinational and local corporations. These factors appear to be crucial for the definition of the format and conduction of the program, which is, arguably, the closest to the original American model. P.U.C.-R.J. and I.B.M.E.C.-R.J.'s programs, albeit being created recently, followed approximately the same path.

At F.G.V.-E.B.A.P.E., the program was implemented as part of a shift in the institution that focused exclusively on public administration and wished to become more private sector-oriented. At E.A.-U.F.B.A., the previous relationship with local not-for-profit organizations seems to have influenced the design of the program. At both E.A.-U.F.B.A. and E.A.-U.F.R.G.S., the implementation of the program related also to the context of financial and budgetary crises at Federal public universities.

The prevalent reasoning at Brazilian public universities, the history of the institutions involved, and the teaching vision of those responsible for implementation all had a strong influence on the characteristics of the programs, leading to experimentation and innovation. Although they have drawn closer to the business community, these programs were strongly influenced by a more critical vision of management and of the role that firms play in society (similar, in many instances, to that of the C.M.S. authors, mentioned in the previous section).

DISCUSSION

M.B.A.: To Be or Not To Be?

As we mentioned before, the term M.B.A. is used without constraint in Brazil; the acronym can be applied to designate executive *stricto sensu* graduate programs, executive *lato sensu* graduate programs, and also assorted specialization programs, including long-duration in-company courses.

In our research, we observed that the program coordinators consciously rejected the general label M.B.A. to designate the M.P.A.s. This rejection, however, is not free from contradictions. Indeed, in the course of interviews, and despite prior rejections, the term M.B.A. at times arose spontaneously in the discourse of interviewees to designate their M.P.A. programs. Although the term is insistently denied, they accept reference to the programs as M.B.A.s at the ranking published annually by the magazine *Você S.A.*, the leading local reference for executive programs. In fact, even after almost a decade, the term M.P.A. is still restricted to academic circles, since the business media, students, and firms often refer to these programs as M.B.A.s.

One may relate the use of the acronym M.B.A. to a marketing requirement; for many potential clients it (still) seems to be a valuable and consolidated brand. On the other hand, its rejection and the adoption of the acronym M.P.A. has to do with the wish to differentiate these programs from the dozens of alternatives offered in the management education market. One might forward the hypothesis that, given the inability to state "those are not M.B.A.s" (in reference to other competing models), M.P.A.s' coordinators started to claim: "our program is not an M.B.A.s".

Brazilian M.P.A.s are, in truth, a hybrid model: they do not completely embrace the tradition of American M.B.A.s, but neither are they adaptations of the more academic oriented master's programs that preceded (and also influenced) them.

As such a hybrid, the model (or models, in view of the fact that each institution took its own route) is afflicted by several tensions and ambiguities, some of which are hard to overcome. Among these, we noticed the presence of professors and coordinators that align themselves with the critical discourse *versus* the instrumental expectations of students; the dedication requirements posed by the programs *versus* students' constraints, since the courses are part-time; and the business practice-oriented content *versus* some students' demand for professorial education.

On the other hand, Brazilian M.P.A.s have some traits in common with the "International Masters Program in Practicing Management" (Mintzberg and Gosling, 2002): the cross-disciplinary approach found in some of the addressed programs; student profiles regarding professional experience; the fact that students maintain their professional engagements for the duration of the program; the international experience provided by exchange programs with foriegn institutions; and the small classes, enabling greater interaction among students and between students and professors.

In addition, the awareness of the local context revealed by the interviewees suggests a tendency to resist importing foreign models to generate changes in business education, one of the main factors indicated by Chanlat (1996) and commented upon by Sturdy and Gabriel (2000).

Factors that Contributed for the Development of the MPA Programs

At this point in the paper, after portraying the M.P.A.s, it is worth discussing the "input factors" and the "conditioning factors" that contribute to the development of these programs and their actual characteristics. We define input factors as the primary components of the programs and conditioning factors as those components that restrain or stimulate certain traits in the programs.

The first input factor relates to the process through which the M.P.A.s were created and to the influence of foreign models. Before developing their programs, Brazilian business schools carefully studied American and European M.B.A.s. Top ten programs were commonly used as references and provided insights for the Brazilian future counterparts. We estimate that this first input factor influenced all aspects of the programs: the overall design, structure, contents, and pedagogy.

The second input factor relates to the existing organizational and individual resources and competences. The creation of M.P.A. programs usually succeeded the creation of undergraduate and master's programs. One may therefore hypothesize that these resources and competences conditioned the design given to M.P.A. programs in terms of workload, syllabus, contents, and pedagogy. There is, consequently, a reproducibility or inertia component at the creation of the M.P.A. programs. This second input factor may also be responsible for the following traits in the programs: attention to reflection, recognition of the importance of critical thinking, strong focus on theory and theorizing, and, on the other hand, a certain complacence with out-of-date contents and teaching methods.

The first conditioning factor relates to the influence of local context, at both national and regional levels. The programs we analyzed certainly reflect their social and economic environment, which differs enormously among regions in Brazil. This first conditioning factor may be responsible for different orientations, in terms of content, in the programs: orientation to the reality of small and medium size companies in some programs (E.A.-U.F.R.G.S.), orientation to the reality of not-for-profit organizations in certain programs (E.A.-U.F.B.A.), and orientation to the reality of large size, industrial, and service firms in other programs (I.B.M.E.C.-R.J. and F.G.V.-E.A.E.S.P.). As a result, the programs have acquired different outlines in terms of contents and structure, drifting away one from another.

The second conditioning factor relates to the adoption of imported references – handbooks, papers, and theoretical models. In general, we noticed a massive use of foreign references in the analyzed programs, including, in some cases, guru-authored books and self-help books, which we came to classify as "pop-management literature." We must observe that the tradition of using foreign books, a well as the limited availability of high quality domestic materials for graduate programs, acts as a vector in favor of the continued status of administration as an "imported field." On the other hand, we noticed differences among the programs: while some programs where more influenced by the sociological perspective and adopted, to some extent, French philosophers' books and C.M.S.' texts, others chose to espouse American handbooks, the same used in foreign M.B.A.s. This second conditioning factor certainly influenced the content of the programs. We can also relate these choices to the general approach of the programs (more critical versus more instrumental).

The third conditioning factor has to do with students being unavailable for total dedication as is common in the U.S. This obviously reduces focus and commitment to studies but also favors interaction between management practice and theory, decisively changing the course dynamics and opening new routes for reflection. On the other hand, one might also infer that this factor raises the pressure for instrumentalism, since many students will instinctively look for solutions for their immediate work problems. This third conditioning factor also impacts the programs in terms of work-load and pedagogy.

The forth conditioning factor relates to the presence of internal and external competition with the M.P.A. programs. Internal competition is represented by other courses offered by the same institution and with the same target-audience. With a few exceptions, the business schools we included in our field research offer, besides the M.P.A. programs, executive M.B.A. programs and other diverse executive programs. External competition is represented by other business schools, both local and foreign, that also target the same audience. Indeed, foreign business schools are increasingly present in Brazil, as they form join-ventures with local partners. This context causes M.P.A. programs to develop "competitive strategies," attempting to develop strong brands and to offer "attractive," differentiated solutions to potential candidates. To quote one interviewee, there is a "seduction" component to the relationship between the course and its attendance. This "seduction" component may also be a conditioning vector for content choices and pedagogic alternatives. For instance among students some professors are treated as celebrities, less for their teaching skills and their knowledge of the subjects being taught than for their ability to retain attention and to entertain the pupils.

The fifth conditioning factor relates to direct demand from students to interfere in the design of the programs. At formal and informal evaluation processes, as well as in their direct interaction with professors and coordinators, Brazilian students usually convey their needs and expectations. Even when these are not highly elaborate, they have an influence on the programs. In this sense, the pressure for "novelties" and "practical solutions" can steer the course towards up-to-date contents which is positive, or to an exceedingly instrumental and low-consistency path, which is harmful. Like the "seduction" component mentioned previously, this demand can also be a conditioning vector for content and pedagogy choices.

The sixth conditioning factor relates to demands from firms. This influence doesn't appear to be directly exerted, but there is a clear intent to train professionals that meet the needs of the market and of companies in the analyzed programs. In this sense, coordinators' and professors' interpretation of these needs can also influence both content and pedagogic design. We may also hypothesize that this sixth conditioning factor also raises the pressure for instrumentalism.

Table 1 presents the eight factors, organized into three categories: impact on the program's general strategy, impact on contents, and impact on pedagogy. One should observe that some conditioning factors have impact in more than one category. Another point noted in this comparison is that some factors add contradictory forces to the development of the programs. As we mentioned before, these programs are absolutely not free of tensions and contradictions.

As a result of both input factors and conditioning factors, Brazilian M.P.A.s may resemble, in certain aspects, American M.B.A.s, but differences are conspicuous. In fact, the American model had an undeniable influence on Brazilian programs, but local conditions and coloring were added.

CONCLUSION

The development of Brazilian M.P.A.s may be also be analyzed as a phenomenon of importation of managerial knowledge and expertise and its adoption in an emerging country. Based upon field surveys conducted in Brazil, Wood and Caldas identified three reactions to the adoption of imported managerial expertise: unreasoned adoption, ceremonial behavior, and managerial anthropophagy, (this last named after an old Native South-American ritual in which warriors devoured the defeated to retain their courage and energy) (2002).

The first reaction – unreasoned adoption – occurs when organizations tend to embrace the imported managerial expertise even when it doesn't fit its needs. The result is frequently frustrating.

The second reaction – ceremonial behavior – occurs in the presence of elevated institutional and/or political pressures to adopt legitimated foreign managerial practices when no substantive need would justify it.

The third reaction – managerial anthropophagy – occurs when the organization assesses and adapts the new managerial expertise to its own reality. This third reaction seems to be the case with the M.P.A. programs. Brazilian business schools neither pretended to adopt a foreign managerial model in which it didn't see answers for its

Table 6.2: Factors that Impacted the Development of the M.P.A. Programs.

Factor	*Impact in the general structure and strategy of the program*	*Impact in the content of the program*	*Impact in the pedagogy of the program*
Input factor #1 Benchmarking with foreign MBA programs	Overall design: target-audience, gen. pedagogic obj., gen. structure of programs	Focus on a gen. approach Use of trad. div. of knowledge based on expertise: finances, human resources, etc.	Use of case method
Input factor #2 Use of existing resources and competences	Reproducibility or inertia in relation to previous programs offered in the same institution	Strong focus on theory and theorizing Complacence with out-of-date contents Recognition of import. of critical thinking	Strong focus on theory and theorizing Complacence with out-of-date teaching methods Attention to reflection Recognition of import of critical thinking
Conditioning factor # 1 Local context – national and regional	Contents, structure oriented to firm's reality, profile in different regions Differentiation among programs	Contents, structure oriented to firm's reality in different regions	
Factor	*Impact in the gen. str., strategy of prog.*	*Impact in the content of the program*	*Impact in the pedagogy of the program*
Conditioning factor # 2 Adoption of imported references	Cont. status of business admin. as "imported"	Adoption of "pop-management" books stimulating instrumentalism Adoption of French philosophers' books, CMS' texts stimulating critical thinking	
Conditioning factor # 3 Students being unavailable for full-time dedication		Stimulus for instrumentalism	Stimulus for reflection over mngmt. exp. Stimulus for interaction between mngmt. practice, mngmt. theory Constraints for work-load Limited focus on academic activities
Conditioning factor # 4 Presence of internal and external competition	Attempt to develop brand and niche strategies Attempt to align with supposed market expectations	Stimulus to "seduce" students with appealing contents	Stimulus to "seduce" students with appealing pedagogy (celebrity-professors)
Conditioning factor # 5 Demands from students		Pressure for "novelties" and "practical solutions" leading to either up-to-dateness or fad-orientation	Stimulus for professors to act as entertainers
Conditioning factor # 6 Indirect demands from firms		Pressure for "novelties" and "practical solutions" lead to either up-to-dateness or fad-orientation Stimulus for instrumentalism	

challenges, nor did it simply reject it. What took place was a re-reading of the model, taking into account local reality and aiming to comply with local context and goals. M.P.A.s are thus an example of a "reasonable strategy": the development and implementation of small-sized programs that attempt to meet the market's demands by articulating the basis of existing resources and accumulated experience.

NOTES

1) This research was funded by N.P.P./F.G.V.-E.A.E.S.P. This paper is part of a three year project begun in 2001 with focus on studying the management field in Brazil. The study involves four subjects: the business media, business administration schools, consulting firms, and gurus and the organizational theatre.
2) The authors wish to thank all of the interviewees, who assisted the researchers and talked openly about their ideas concerning management education.

REFERENCES

Alvesson, M., & Deetz, S. (1996). Critical theory and postmodernism approaches to organizational studies. In: Clegg, S., Hardy, C., & Nord, W. R. (Eds.) *Handbook of Organization Studies*. London: Sage.

Alvesson, M., & Willmott, H. (Eds.) (1993). *Making Sense of Management: A Critical Analysis*. London: Sage.

Alvesson, M., & Willmott, H. (1992). *Critical Management Studies*. London: Sage.

Antonacopoulou, E. P. (1999). Teaching 'critical thinking' to M.B.A.s. Proceedings of the 1st International Critical Management Studies Conference. UMIST, Manchester.

Boje, D. M. (1996). Management education as a panoptic cage. In: French, R. & Grey, C. (Eds.) *Rethinking Management Education*. Sage: London, 172-195.

Chanlat, J. F. (1996). From cultural imperialism to independence. In: Clegg, S. R. & Palmer, G. (Eds.) *The Politics of Management Knowledge*. London: Sage, 121-140.

Dehler, G., Welsh, M. A., & Lewis, M. W. (1999). Critical pedagogy in the "new paradigm": raising complicated understanding in management learning. *Proceedings of the 1st International Critical Management Studies Conference*. UMIST, Manchester.

The Economist. (2002a, December 14th – 20), 79-83.

The Economist. (2002b, December 21st – January 3), 124-137.

Gold, J., Holman, D., & Thorpe, R. (1999). The manager as a critical reflective practitioner: uncovering arguments at work. *Proceedings of the 1st International Critical Management Studies Conference*. UMIST, Manchester.

Gomes, M. T. (1997). M.B.A. ajuda? *Exame*, 23 de outubro: 47-54.

Grey, C., & French, R. (1996). Rethinking management education: an introduction. In: French, R., & Grey, C. (Eds.) *Rethinking management education*. Sage: London, 1-17.

Grey, C., Knights, D. & Willmott, H. (1996). Is a critical pedagogy of management possible? In: French, R. & Grey, C. (Eds.) *Rethinking management education*. Sage: London, 94-110.

Jacomino, D. (1999). A Meta é um M.B.A.. *Você S.A*, *12*, 100-103.

Jacomino, D. (2000). Quem são os Brasileiros que Fazem M.B.A. lá Fora. *Você S.A*, *21*, 17.

Jacomino, D. (2001). Os Melhores M.B.A.s do Planeta. *Você S.A*, *32*, 24.

Martins, C. B. (1989). Surgimento e Expansão dos Cursos de Administração no Brasil (1952-1983). *Ciência e Cultura, 41*(7), 663-676.

Mintzberg, H., & Gosling, J. (2002). Educating managers beyond borders. *Academy of Management Learning & Education, 1*(1), 64-76.

Mintzberg, H., & Lampel, J. (2001, February 19). M.B.A.s as C.E.O.s. *Fortune*.

Parker, M., & Jary, D. (1995). The McUniversity: organizations, management, and academic subjectivity. *Organization, 2*(2), 319-338.

Prichard, C., & Willmott, H. (1997). Just how managed is the MacUniversity? *Organization Studies, 18*(2), 287-316.

Reynolds, M. (1997). Towards a critical management pedagogy. In: Burgoyne, J., & Reynolds, M. (Eds.) *Management learning: integrating perspectives in theory and practice*. London: Sage, 312-338.

Ritzer, G. (1993). *The MacDonaldization of society*. Newbury Park, CA: Pinge Fonge Press.

Robert, J. (1996). Management education and the limits of technical rationality: the conditions and consequences of management. In: French, R. & Grey, C. (Eds.) *Rethinking management education*. Sage: London, 54-75.

Sganzerla, V. (1995). Vale a pena fazer um M.B.A. lá fora? *Exame*, 6 de dezembro, 108-110.

Sturdy, A., & Gabriel, Y. (2000). Missionaries, mercenaries or car salesmen? M.B.A. teaching in Malaysia. *Journal of Management Studies, 37*(7), 979-1002.

Voce S.A. (2000). Os melhores MBAs do Brasil. Edição Especial.

Voce S.A. (2001). Os melhores MBAs do Brasil. Edição Especial.

Warner, A. (1990). Where business school fails to meet business needs. *Personnel Management, 22*(7), 52-46.

Willmott, H. (1994). Management education: provocations to a debate. *Management Learning, 25*(1), 105-136.

Wood JR., T., & Caldas, M. P. (2002). Adopting imported managerial expertise in developing countries: the Brazilian experience. *The Academy of Management Executive, 16*(2), 18-32.

II. Curricular and Course Content Innovations

Chapter 7

Replicating Business Education Programs in Emerging Countries

Virginia Yonkers
Siena College

INTRODUCTION

In 1990, the State University of New York's Office of International Programs, with funding from the United States Agency for International Development (U.S.A.I.D.), created a Management Training program for Hungary. The initial plan was to work with universities to establish western style schools of business in the newly democratized East European country. However, by the middle of the first year, it was obvious that this would not work, and another approach would need to be used.

However, the question arises, why was the replication of American style business programs difficult to set-up? What are the factors that influence the curricular and instructional design for projects or activities in business institutions in emerging countries? Which of these factors can be controlled through curricular and instructional design, and which ones will make replication difficult? This paper will look at research on international business education, presenting a framework for analyzing the needs and necessary modifications for business programs in emerging countries.

Programs can analyze the needs of any cooperating institution in an emerging country. In order to do this, they will need to consider: 1) what is the theoretical basis of knowledge for that educational system; 2) what is the perceived role of the teacher; 3) what are the expected responsibilities of the student in the learning process; 4) what is the perception of "business education" within the educational system; 5) what knowledge base can be expected; and 6) the institutional constraints (language, student selection, business resources).

METHODOLOGY AND ASSUMPTIONS

This study looked at research from international and American authors in the fields of comparative psychology, cross-cultural psychology, education, educational policy, and business education in order to get a broad perspective of the literature. While there was an effort to look at equal amounts of research from each continent, it was difficult to get academic quality information about Africa. Case studies and educational reports from official sources such as the ministries of education, the United Nations, and U.N.E.S.C.O. supplemented published research.

The research can be divided into three categories: education system categories and tertiary education systems; instructional design for higher education and foreign classrooms; and instructional design for business education. All three categories, when reviewed together, are the basis for identifying factors that affect business education in emerging countries.

Tertiary education used here is based on the U.N.E.S.C.O. definition that classifies it as "third level education for which completion of secondary school or its equivalent is necessary" (Eurich, ix). This can include universities, colleges, technical colleges, vocational training, polytechnic institutions, open universities, junior colleges, and training centers. (Eurich and Loo, 2002; McLean,1995; Simon ,1983; Squires, 1989; and Tindade, 2000;).

Business education is more difficult to define since the study of business depends on the educational philosophy of a given country. In the U.S., this would include Associate, Bachelor, and Master degrees in the fields of Marketing, Management, Accounting, Finance, Business Administration, and all of their subspecialties (i.e. Healthcare Management, Financial Planning, etc.). However, the definition varied internationally. Therefore, the definition for business education in this paper is the study of business with some formal instruction in an educational setting to prepare entry into the business world (which could include civil servants) at a professional level. This level will require the professional to make decisions and apply theory to business situations.

The definition allows for a much broader venue for business education to include vocational education and apprenticeships, as long as there is some instruction outside of the workplace. This paper also excludes business education below the tertiary education level (human capital development or literacy and skills programs for workers) and workplace training programs with no outside instruction.

OVERVIEW OF THE LITERATURE

There was very little literature on comparative business education and instructional design for business education. This could be because business as a field of study, especially in higher education, is relatively young (MacFarlane and Ottewill, 2001).

Most of the research on emerging countries was in the form of case studies (Brown and Masten, 1998; Contreras and Ruff, 2002; Guilar, 2001). While this limits the quantitative information available, it gives important insights into the state of business education in various countries with emerging markets.

INTERNATIONAL EDUCATIONAL FACTORS

Birgit Brock-Utne, in reviewing educational research for the last three decades, discusses three issues for "Developing" or "Third World" countries: language of instruction, educational funding sources (and their influence on the educational system), and ethno-centricism vs. globalism in education (2002). These findings for business education is supported by researchers from developing countries -- namely Brazil, (Clovis de Azevedo, 2000), French Guinea (Renault-Lescure, 2000), and the Arab countries (Ali and Camp, 1995; Yavas, 1999). Each of these authors identified these three factors as influencing instructional design for business education programs. Renault-Lescure, for example, described a model program that used both the indigenous language and the official languages with the goal of bridging a traditional educational system with the outside business world. Lupton and Braunstein describe a similar situation with a Slovakian university in which Americans teach at least half of business courses, in English (2002). Even when business courses are taught in the native language, texts and reading materials are only available in a second language (Ali and Camp, 1995; Brock-Utne, 2002; Robinson, 1995).

The problem that many emerging countries have is a lack of expertise and/or resources to develop relevant teaching materials, curriculum, and instructors for their own country in the field of business. Universities will turn to resources outside of their country, which may not be relevant to their circumstances. For example, both Brown and Masten (1998) and Guilar (2001) indicate that business and economics faculty in Africa have heavy teaching loads and must support themselves with outside consulting due to low teaching salaries. These faculty members are unwilling (and unable, due to other commitments) to develop country specific texts, cases, or research which can be used in teaching business in the native language.

Both Ali and Camp (1995) and Yavas (1999) question the relevance of predominately American management techniques in the Arab cultural context. Likewise, Luthans, Stajikovic, and Ibrayeva identify a different cultural context for the educational needs of entrepreneurs in the former republics of the Soviet Union (2000). Like S.U.N.Y.'s program in Hungary, these newly emerging economies, with a backdrop of apparently arbitrary political and economic changes, still must contend with strong, centrally controlled governments, a shortage of financial resources, and lack of managers and potential entrepreneurs with the confidence to try innovative, western business techniques. As a result, part of business education's role is to create efficacy for students in these emerging countries. Utsch, Rauch, Rothfufs, and Frese, describe the average East German manager after the fall of communism as risk adversive, with a high locus of control (1999). Therefore, students from emerging countries would be less likely to use the American or western management techniques they have learned in school, due either to cultural resistence or systemic barriers. There may need to be cultural modifications made to management texts in order to make business education relevant.

David Watkins points out that there is a complex relationship between the school and educational system, the learner, the teacher, society as a whole, culture, and even the world at large (2000). Changes in one of these factors will have an effect on the other elements. Both this research and Smith's (2001), along with Osborn (2001) and Hill (2000), indicate that culture alone does not affect the learning environment.

This idea can be expanded to include the relationship of education to business. The role of business education depends on the educational philosophy of a country. In some cases, business and education are completely separate, so a person does not require any education to start, own, or manage a business (Ahwireeng-Obeng, 1999). In other instances, only those with a specialized business degree will be able to gain entry into the business world (Yavas, 1999). Finally, many countries have a dual system with entry depending on work experience and education combinations (PÜtz, 2002).

Taking all of these factors into consideration when trying to replicate a program in an emerging country can be overwhelming. As a result, there needs to be a systematic approach to analyzing business education in emerging countries.

FRAMEWORK FOR COMPARING EDUCATIONAL SYSTEMS

Comparative education researchers have used various methods to categorize education systems in other countries. These categories help to identify and explain factors influencing instructional design and curriculum for business education between countries. This is useful in making sense of the variables when replicating instructional design, content, and tasks outside of the U.S.

McLean's model of comparative educational systems is the most useful in creating a framework to identify basic educational philosophies that will influence the approach a business program should take when establishing itself in an emerging country (1995). McLean identified five systems of education based on educational values. These groups include Humanism, Rationalism, Naturalism, Universal and Comprehensive Naturalism, and Confucianism. The remainder of the paper will look at how the definition of knowledge in each of these categories lays the foundation for the educational system for higher education, business education, and instructional and curriculum design. I will then discuss the implications for replicating a program for each of these categories, giving actual examples from emerging countries.

HUMANISM

Those countries that have humanism as their basis believe that "a student would appreciate moral lessons by intuitive, indeed empathic, interaction with the material. And behind much of this assumption of learning was the social elitism that only the best and brightest would have that intuitive insight." (McLean, 1995, 29). Humanism looks at the individual and their moral development rather than "the structure of the physical universe" (McLean, 1995, 23). This is similar to the classic European model of higher education where the teacher, a specialist in their field, helps guide students to fulfill their potential, both morally and intellectually. The English educational system is an example of Humanism, which means countries that are part of the Commonwealth or former British colonies will probably fall into this category.

A Humanist higher business education system focuses on developing the individual through tutorials in a linear fashion, building on previous learning to come to a deeper understanding of the field (Squires, 1989). Within this system is an elite that specializes in the theory of business (Oxford, Cambridge), with less prestigious schools developing the "professional." The professional still specializes in a field and develops life long learning skills through interaction with a tutor (Squires, 1989). Even within the secondary schools and vocational education, the teachers are specialists within a given field (Osborn, 2001; Squires, 1989).

The educational goals in the Humanist system include "behavioural and moral norms" (Osborn, 2001, 271). Osborne goes on to identify some factors that would affect instructional design. This includes a stressful balance between academic achievement and social acceptance. Osborn also determined that learning was more practical and experimental in the Humanist school system (2001). This would tie into McLean's discussion of intuitive interaction with the course material. At the other end of the educational process, managers were found to have a much more intuitive style of decision-making, which was attributed, in part, to the Humanist educational system (Hill, 2000).

The results of Smith's study between Chinese learners from Malaysia, Hong Kong, and Singapore indicate that tension between academic achievement and social acceptance may still exist at the university level (2001). Students from Hong Kong were found to be more anxious and less analytical (thus more intuitive) learners. This could be the influence of the British educational system when Hong Kong was a colony.

Finally, the role of the tutor in the Humanist system is very important to the learning process. The design of curriculum and instruction is one in which the teacher and student have an equally important role in the learning process. A tutor scaffolds the student's learning, giving direction through choice of reading, discussion of the subject area, and question and answer. This system is not dependent on the expert imparting their knowledge to the novice, but rather on the student developing their own learning and outcomes (McLean, 1995). Students in humanist systems are encouraged to find their own solutions and learn by discovery. The teacher's role is to motivate students and provide a comfortable learning environment (Planel, 1997). This fits the description not only of the British learner (McLean, 1995; Osborn, 2001), but also of Ghana's higher education system (Brown and Masten, 1998), a former British colony.

INSTRUCTIONAL APPROACHES TO HUMANISTS SYSTEMS

Looking at the research by Armstrong (2000), Hill (2000), McLean (1995), Osborn (2001), and Planel (1997) indicates that pertinent factors to consider in replicating business education in a Humanist system would include the teacher-student relationship, the role of morals and ethics, the emphasis on experimentation, sequencing of material, time needed to learn prerequisite skills, specialization within an academic discipline, and social interaction in the learning process. In addition, business experience and the study of business tend to be distinctive between the work world and the academic world. Business curriculum is based on the study of business, developing an individual's skill rather than contributing to the world of business (Brown and Masten, 1998; Smith, 2000).

Brown and Masten indicate that any activity or program would need to work with each of the business fields of study separately (Marketing, Management, Information Systems, Accounting, Finance, Business Law, or

Human Resources) due to the academic specialization (1998). Because of the close relationship between the professor and student, there would need to be sufficient guidance and background material available to the professor, but any activity would have to have student choice built into it. Case analysis with guidance from the tutor, for example, would work well in this system. This would be one way to bring some sense of real world into the classroom.

Because researchers (Armstrong, 2000; Osborn, 2001; Planel, 1997) indicated the focus of instruction is on developing the potential of the individual, I feel a large group activity with the focus on group consensus probably would not work. The same researchers did indicate, however, that there is interaction with the teacher and classmates. Therefore, learning is not done in isolation. This is why simulations, small group work with students working on different parts of a problem to be assimilated at the end of the project, and directed learning, such as case studies and on-line discussions, work best in humanist business education systems.

RATIONALISM

Educational systems that are based on rationalism hold to the tenant that the purpose of education is to transfer knowledge to the student. McLean describes this knowledge as:

> Capacities for logic, deduction and abstraction together with systematization and synthesis should be developed to make sense of this universe and ultimately to change it ... But worthwhile knowledge is also external and standardized and the student should cover the encyclopedic kaleidoscope of all legitimate areas for as long as possible. The private and irrational are rigorously excluded (1995, 30).

Planel describes the French system, the classic example of rationalism, as one that is based on order and structure with the intention of imposing "order on the chaos of nature" (1997, 6). In other words, the goal of education should be to give all students, regardless of their ability or background, the knowledge that will enable them to understand and be part of the world. That knowledge will allow them to manipulate their environment and contribute to society as a whole.

Another aspect of Rationalism is a rigid educational structure controlled centrally by an elite who are the highest achievers in the educational system. There are four distinct groups that make up the educational system, each group having their own set of responsibilities. The first group provides the research and theoretical knowledge that will be the basis of the curriculum. The curriculum is based on research, usually conducted outside of the educational system. In the case of business, the curriculum is based on theories and abstract ideas that have been proven or disproved by research institutes based on the scientific method of inquiry (McLean, 1995).

The second group functions as the designer of the curriculum. This is done centrally, either by the government or the governing body of the university. These designers decide what each student must know before they can go to the next level of education. The central governing body also creates assessment tools, which are often standardized exams, to assess learning (Contreras and Ruff, 2002; Cova, Kassis, and Lanoux, 1993; Lupton and Braunstien, 2002; McLean; Osborn, 2001; Planel, 1997; Sharpe, 1997; Trindade, 2000).

Sharp explains the values that are the basis of the French school have its roots in the Catholic Church (1997). He compares the structures of the Catholic Church with his qualitative research in French classrooms. The values common to both systems include obedience, free will, and self-discipline. These same basic values can be applied to the private and more traditional universities of Latin America (Contreras and Ruff, 2002; Serles, 1970; Trindade, 2000) and Eastern Europe (McClean, 1995; Hill, 2000). This is not surprising given that the Catholic Church established many of the institutes of higher education in these regions.

In all of these systems, students are expected to learn the educational doctrine verbatim. To accomplish this, students must listen to their teachers and work hard (self-discipline). However, it is not the teacher's role to motivate a student to learn, but rather the responsibility of the student to learn what knowledge the teacher will impart to them (Osborn, 2001; Planel, 1997). Therefore, most teaching comes in the form of lecture and didactics.

The research of both Osborn and Planel demonstrate that while teacher-centered, there is still interaction between the teacher and student at the primary and secondary level. This interaction, however, is initiated by the teacher to insure that students understand the material. At the university level, there is very little interaction between the knowledgeable specialist (Cova and Lanoux, 1993) and the lecture hall of students (McLean, 1995). Student achievement is the total responsibility of the student; their failure (in the form of standardized exams) is due to their lack of effort rather than poor teaching (Planel, 1997).

Hill's research on cognitive styles of Polish managers indicates that the results of business education in the Rationalism tradition is a manager that prefers more information for decision making, not trusting their past experience but rather others data (2000). Hill found this surprising and attributed this to Poland's changing economic and political structure. However, based on the research by Cova and Lanoux (1993), Osborn (2001), Planel (1997), and Sharpe (1997), it is more likely students from the Rationalist tradition would look to theoretical models more than personal experience.

INSTRUCTIONAL APPROACHES TO RATIONALIST SYSTEMS

Any program used in a Rationalist system would need to be very structured, especially in the initial stages, with sufficient resource information to support teacher direction. As Planel writes, "... teachers favoured pupils learning by system and method and placed more emphasis on developing thinking skills in general and abstract thinking skills in particular" (1997, 6). Students in a Rationalist based system perceive the instructor as "access to the syllabus and the educational system" (1997, 6). Therefore, it would be important to have as much structure and supporting information available to the instructor as possible. The available supporting information would need to include the theoretical basis for the activity or program.

This was the case with S.U.N.Y.'s Hungary program. University faculty were much more receptive to new business and economic theories such as T.Q.M. rather than new ways to do business. Once an established program (in the form of T.Q.M. Centers) based on theory was developed (rather than individual courses on various business concepts), it was easier to get Hungarian partners.

Related to this is the need for any new programs in a Rationalist educational system to begin with the central curriculum designers. This was the problem with S.U.N.Y.'s management training program. In the beginning, they worked with professors that were open to new management methods. However, without the support of the Rectors or their "faculties," no program could be developed. Using accredited curriculums or standards from A.A.C.S.B. or the European equivalent (European Quality Improvement System or E.Q.U.I.S.) gives credibility that the centralized curriculum planners would be looking for.

THE NATURALIST AND THE UNIVERSAL AND COMPREHENSIVE NATURALIST EDUCATION SYSTEMS

McLean differentiated between the naturalist and universal and comprehensive naturalist education systems (1995). However, when reviewing the research, it is difficult to differentiate between these two categories. As a result, I will discuss both categories as if they were a continuum between the Naturalist system at one end and the Universal and Comprehensive Naturalist system at the other end.

According to McLean, the Naturalist system looks internally to create knowledge for the learner, as opposed to the Humanist and Rationalist, which look externally for universal truths. Naturalism has many variations, and "one [variation] focuses upon the physiological and psychological drives of the person. Another [variation] assumes that the natural world is that of small-scale organic communities" (McLean, 1995, 36).

This is the direction in which Mongolian schools are headed (Robinson, 1995). Students stay with the same teacher throughout primary and secondary school so that the teacher knows their needs, both within and outside of school. In this system, "teachers, generally, felt free to interpret the national curriculum framework in a way that supported the needs of their pupils by introducing themes that had a direct relevance to their lives outside of school" (Osborn, 2001, 272).

Clovis de Azevedo describes a program in Brazil that fits McClean's second variation (2000). Brazil's national goal of education is to prepare its citizens to participate in the democratic process politically, economically, and socially. The community of Porto Algre developed the curriculum and instructional design for its public school system. All parties, parents, children, administration, teachers, the business community, and the community at large participated in a series of workshops that resulted in the school curriculum. This program emphasized the individual's role in society with education being an instrument of change. Therefore, business and business education is not necessarily distinct from society, the whole educational process, and cultural values. This is also the direction that many South Africans have called for (Henderson as cited in Ahwireng-Obeng, 1999) in their economics education.

Universal and Comprehensive Naturalism, on the other hand, is based on the common school developed in the U.S. during the nineteenth century.

> Knowledge was viewed pragmatically. Existing knowledge was treated promiscuously. It was drawn upon where necessary to help to solve problems. But the learners sought solutions by starting from the problems and not from the acquisition of bodies of pre-packaged knowledge. A curriculum could not predetermine what knowledge was needed. (McLean, 1995, 40).

This pragmatic approach, according to McLean, starts with the premise that all students can learn. However, because of limited resources within a society, students at the level of higher education are responsible for funding their own education. Tertiary education is comprised of a universal core of knowledge, necessary for the student to contribute to society by being flexible in their profession with additional course work or structured experience to meet the student's personal goals (Etis, 2002). There is also a strong component of socialization through sports and extra-curricular activities. This system can be found in the U.S., Australia, and Canada (Etis, 2002; Kyvik and Tvede, 1998; MacFarlane, 2001; McLean, 1995; Roach and Byrne, 2001; Simon, 1983).

Because of the student centeredness of Naturalism, those systems that fall into to this category will tend to focus on learning environments and affective factors in learning. Even though Naturalism is student centered, the teacher plays an important role in motivating and facilitating student learning. Therefore, this should be the focus in business teacher training for programs trying to replicate an American Business School model (Guilar, 2001).

The one factor that distinguishes pure Naturalist and the Universal and Comprehensive Naturalist approaches is the role of education in society and business. According to McLean, Naturalism perceives education as learning for the sake of learning (1995). It may take a long time for a student to fulfill their potential. Therefore, the educational system needs to support the best students until they are mature enough to reach their optimum level. There is no set curriculum since it is the individual's definition of knowledge that is important (Kvyik and Tvede, 1998). A Naturalist system in countries such as Brazil or many of the African countries identify an "elite," through testing and educational tracking, who will be able to study at any institute of higher education for any period of time. The elite will leave the university to enter positions of leadership (civil service, political, or economic), thus contributing to society in exchange for their fully paid education. Those that are not part of the elite will be trained more pragmatically in vocational education programs that combine classroom and on-the-job instruction (Kyvik and Tvede, 1998; McLean, 1995; Nassif, Rama, and Tedesco, 1984; PÜtz, 2002; Squiress, 1989). Most Marxist (socialist) systems would be considered pure Naturalists.

The Universal and Comprehensive Naturalists, on the other hand, work on the premise that all people have the potential to succeed in higher education. The goals of the institutes of higher education in countries such as Mexico, Argentina, Costa Rica, and Venezuela are to make as many modes of study available to the greatest number of students, regardless of the students' learning styles and abilities. However, student choice and direction requires the student to be responsible for funding their own education and finding employment after completing school (Kyvik and Tvede, 1998; McLean, 1995). As a result, many in the universal and comprehensive naturalist system work and go to school at the same time (Squires, 1989). Unlike the naturalists, where work and study are two distinct learning environments that do not necessarily overlap, the universal and comprehensive naturalists try to make connections between work and school (Simon, 1983).

INSTRUCTIONAL APPROACHES TO NATURALIST SYSTEMS AND UNIVERSAL AND COMPREHENSIVE NATURALIST EDUCATION

In designing for the Naturalist and Universal and Comprehensive Naturalist systems, the focus should be on creating learning environments that are relevant to the student. The learning landscapes include "the school context, the family environment, the workspace as a space of learning, specific training settings or even entire areas like organizational learning" (Visser and Berg, 1999, 102). Visser and Berg conducted a series of case analyses in which they identified the factors that were necessary in successful instructional design for naturalist systems. The design needs to have flexibility to meet the student's needs, both in terms of time (weekend, night, or in-house courses) and content. Guilar also commented that there was a need to work with Senegalese instructors, from a Rationalist system, in developing more interactive activities for the purpose of creating a more Naturalist business education system (i.e. American business school) (2001).

For both the Naturalist and Universal and Comprehensive Naturalist systems, there would need to be a strong business-university component. In the case of the Universal and Comprehensive Naturalist systems, this would have to be very pragmatic, e.g. internships, case studies, business based research, and student projects for local businesses.

Simulations, on-line discussion groups, problem-solving activities, and group projects give the flexibility needed for students to construct their own knowledge and relationship with the outside world. However, working with the indefinite time frame of the Naturalist system would be difficult. Therefore, there also needs to be a flexible time frame for any program, in which participants could move in and out of the program without interrupting the learning process. The curriculum for the Naturalists would need to have input from the community (Clovis de Azevedo, 2000; Contreras and Ruff, 2002; Renault-Lescure, 2000). There would probably be more demand for joint business-academic projects.

Since many of the programs based on the American business school are based on the Naturalist system, it would be important to make sure that all participants in the program understood the underlying philosophy of any American partnership.

CONFUCIANISM

Like the Naturalists, educational systems based on the values of Confucianism do have variations, often with influences from countries that had colonized them in the 18th and 19th centuries (Kember and Sivan, 1995;

Smith 2001; Watkins 2001). The basic values common to all include the definition of knowledge and the role of the teacher (Hiebert and Stigler, 2001; McLean, 1995; Neuliep, 1997; Smith; Ukai, 1997; Watkins). McLean's description of this system of Confucianism is weak. Fortunately, there are other authors that, through their research, helped to define the educational values in systems based on Confucianism.

Knowledge, in a Confucian system, is acquired over a long period of time from a much more knowledgeable master (Smith, 2001; Stevenson and Lee, 1997; Watkins, 2001). As Watkins concludes from his research on Chinese learners, "whereas the Western students saw understanding as usually a process of sudden insight, the Chinese students typically thought of understanding as a long process that required considerable mental effort" (Role of Repetition section, para. 2). This requires repetition of the material in which the student finds a deeper understanding in the material each time. Smith and Kember and Sivan (1995) support Watkins' conclusions with Smith's study of the learning styles of ethnic Chinese from Malaysia, Hong Kong, and Singapore, and Kember and Sivan's study of Polytechnic students in Hong Kong. The study groups self-reported that deep learning, interrelating ideas, and use of evidence was important to their learning. Stevenson's observation of classrooms in Japan and China also reinforces Watkins' conclusions. Teachers often had students repeat information in different ways, through questioning and readings. They also spent multiple classes on the same topic. While some instructors outside of this system may perceive this as rote learning, those researchers familiar with Confucian systems, such as Smith, Stevenson and Lee (1997), and Watkins, have documented that deeper learning occurs.

Both Hiebert and Stigler (2001) and Stevenson and Lee (1997) observed a teacher-student relationship similar to a rationalist system. They focused on the Japanese system where there was a teacher-centered approach. Like the Rationalist system, Japanese teachers are required to transfer their knowledge to the student. Also like the Rationalist system, Confucian systems begin with the premise that success in school is dependent on student effort and not an innate intelligence (Osborn, 2001; Watkins, 2001).

However, there are two main differences between Rationalism and Confucianism. Unlike Rationalism, where the individual is responsible for learning the curriculum interpreted by the teacher, yet designed by a central authority, in Confucianism the curriculum is determined at the local level by teachers, administrators, and the community (Hiebert and Stigler, 2001; Stevenson and Lee, 1997). The teachers have a great deal more accountability to the community, therefore. If a student fails, it is not only the student's responsibility, but also the parents, teachers, and peers.

The second difference is related to this responsibility for learning. The value of cooperation and community in Confucianism is very important (Hiebert and Stigler, 2001; Smith, 2001; Watkins, 2001). The teacher has a moral obligation to impart his or her knowledge to the student, and the student has a moral obligation to his or her family and society to learn. If a student cannot keep up, he or she owes it to the class to get extra help, so as not to slow the learning process for everyone (Ukai Russel, 1997).

Cooperation and community are also the foundations of teacher planning and coordination. Japanese teachers, for example, spend almost as much time planning their classes with colleagues as they do teaching in the classrooms (Hiebert and Stigler, 2001; Stevenson and Lee, 1997). This planning includes anticipating student questions (so as to maintain the role of master prepared to answer any question), group development within the class, and planning the sequence of introducing and practicing new material. Watkins (2001) also noted the Chinese teacher should "have deep knowledge, be able to answer questions, and be a good moral model" (The Good Teacher section, para. 1). Watkins interpreted this moral model as the teacher setting a good example in society, thus linking school with the community. Thompson's study of Chinese M.B.A. students indicates that the students would rather use cases based on well-known local companies (2000). This could be because they can then make the connection with the community.

INSTRUCTIONAL APPROACHES TO CONFUCIANISM

The role of questions in the Confusion system is to deepen knowledge, not to fill in gaps of missing information, according to Watkins (2001). This would indicate that any discussion or problem-solving activity must come after students have had time to study and master the material. The curriculum should allow for the same themes to be repeated with additions to the material at each level. Also, due to Confucianism's emphasis on cooperative learning, the goal of any interactive activity (case study, simulation, projects, or problem solving) would also be to provide learning opportunities for group members and to create a community for learning.

Any program, therefore, would need to include time to plan on close collaboration with teachers in Confucian education systems (Hiebert and Stigler, 2001; Kembler and Siven, 1995; Steveson and Lee, 1997, Watkins, 2001). Since the teacher and community seem vital to curriculum and instruction, and instruction is usually planned collaboratively, it would be important to include a systematic design process as part of the program.

CONCLUSION

Many researchers discussed the educational systems of economies in transition (Ahwireeng-Obeng, 1999; Ali and Camp, 1995; Brown and Masten, 1998; Contreras and Ruff, 2002; Evans and Birsch, 1995; Hill, 2000; Luthans,

Stajkovic, and Ibrayeva, 2000; Morrison, 2000; Renault-Lescure, 2000; Rauch, Rothfufs, and Frese, 1999). The assumption was that educational institutions in these countries would welcome programs that would support the countries' changes. However, this did not prove to be the case. For example, Ahwireeng-Obeng and Luthans, Stajkovic, and Ibrayeva describe the national debate on the vision of economic and educational structure of South Africa and the former Soviet Republics, respectively. While public opinion supports a transition from a centrally governed economy and school system, the countries' structures are slow to change.

As a result, foreign assistance will either take a long time to influence any substantial change or will have to work outside the traditional structures. S.U.N.Y. began by establishing its own Center (working outside the traditional structures) while developing long term programs with major universities (affecting change over a long time period). The results of the research have a number of programmatic implications. Before establishing a program in an emerging country, a school should look at those factors discussed in this paper. Specifically, they should look at indigenous resources, the language of instruction, the educational basis for business education, and the relationship between business school stakeholders (students, teachers, administrators, businesses, society, and culture). Once these factors are understood, a successful customized program that fulfills all participants' needs can be developed.

REFERENCES

Ahwireeng-Obeng, F. (1999). Internationalizing economics education in South Africa. *Competitiveness Review*, *9*(1), 30-39. Retrieved February 22, 2003 from Proquest Database.

Ali, A. & Camp, R. (1995). Teaching management in the Arab world. *The International Journal of Educational Management*, *9*(3). Retrieved September 17, 2002 from Proquest Database.

Armstrong, S. (2000). The influence of individual cognitive style on performance in management education. *Educational Psychology*, *20*(3), 323-340. Retrieved October 29, 2002 from Academic Search Premier.

Brock-Utne, B. (2002). Education and development: a developing theme. *International Review of Education*, *48*, 45-66.

Brown, S. & Masten, J. (1998). The role of a business school in an emerging country -- the case of Ghana. *Journal of Education for Business*, *73*(5), 308-13. Retrieved February 22, 2003 from Wilsonweb Database.

Clovis de Azevedo, J. (2000). L'Ecole Citoyenne: L'expérience de Porto Alegre [Community School: the Porto Algre Experience]. In Blanquer, J.M. & Trindade, H. (Eds), *Les défis de l'éducation en Amérique latine* [Educational Challenges in Latin America] (pp. 203-215). Paris: Institut des hautes études de l'Amérique latine (IHEAL).

Contreras, J. & Ruff, E. (2002). MBA education in Latin America: the case of Chile. *Journal of Education for Business*, *78*(1), 51-55. Retrieved February 22, 2003 from Proquest Database.

Cova, B., Kassis, J. & Lanoux, V. (1993). Back to pedagogy: the EAP's 20 years of European experience. *Management Education and Development, 24*(1). Retrieved September 17, 2002 from Proquest Database.

Eurich, N. (1981). *Systems of higher education in twelve countries: a comparative view*. New York, N.Y.: Praeger.

Etis, K. (2002). Global trends, implication for vocational training and lifelong learning: response of the university sector. In Burke, G. & Reuling, J. (Eds.) *Vocational Training and Life Long Learning in Australia and German: Australia Centre Series (*pp. 73-90). Leabrook, Australia: National Centre for Vocational Education Research.

Evans, F. & Birsch, N. (1995). Business education and change in Russia and Eastern Europe. *Journal of Education for Business, 70*(3), 166-172. Retrieved November 11, 2002 from Academic Search Premier database.

Gulliar, J. (2001). Founding an American university campus in West Africa: success factors and challenges for Suffolk University's Dakar campus. *International Education, 3*(1), 24-37. Retrieved February 22, 2003 from Wilsonweb Database.

Hiebert, J. & Stigler, J. (2001). Proposal for improving classroom teaching: lessons from the TIMSS video study. *Elementary School Journal, 101*(1), 3-22. Retrieved October 11, 2002 from EDBSCOHost Academic Database.

Hill, J. (2000). Cognitive style and socialisation: an exploration of learned sources of style in Finland, Poland and the UK. *Educational Psychology, 20*(3), 285-306. Retrieved October 21, 2002 from EBSCOHost Research Databases.

Kember, D. & Sivan, A. (1995). An analysis of the learning process of business students at Hong Kong Polytechnic. *Journal of Education for Business, 70*(3), 172-179. Retrieved November 11, 2002 from Academic Search Premier database.

Kyvik, S. & Tvede, O. (1998). The doctorate in the Nordic countries. *Comparative Education, 34*(1), 9-26. Retrieved November 23, 2002 from Academic Search Premier database.

Loo, R. (2002). A meta-analytic examination of Kolb's learning style preferences among business majors. *Journal of Education for Business, 77*(5), 252-257. Retrieved October 23, 2002 from Proquest Database.

Luthans, F. Stajkovic, A., & Ibrayeva, E. (2000). Environmental and psychological challenges facing entrepreneurial development on transitional economies. *The Journal of World Business, 35*(1), 95-110.

Lupton, R. & Braunstein, L. (2002). Measuring business teachers' educational philosophies: an exploratory, cross-national study. *Business Education Forum*, Washington, DC, *56*(4), 24-27.

MacFarlane, B. & Ottewill, R. (2001). Traditions and tensions. *Effective Learning & Teaching in Business & Management*: London: Kogan Page.

McLean, M. (1995). *Educational Traditions Compared: Content, Teaching and Learning in Industrialised Countries.* London: D. Fulton.

Morrison, A. (2000). Entrepreneurship: what triggers it? *International Journal of Entrepreneurial Behaviour & Research,* 6(2). Retreived January 8, 2003 from Proquest database.

Nassif, R., Rama, G., & Tedesco, J. (1984). *Sistema Educativo en América Latina* [Education System in Latin America]. Buenos Aires :UNESCO-CEPAL-PNUD.

Neuliep, J. (1997). A cross-cultural comparison of teacher immediacy in American and Japanese college classrooms. (Special Issue on Communication in the Global Community) *Communication Research, 24*(4), 431-452. Retrieved October 11, 2002 from Expanded Academic ASAP database.

Osborn, M. (2001). Constants and contexts in pupil experience of learning and schooling: comparing learners in England, France and Denmark. *Comparative Education, 37*(3), 267-278. Retrieved October 20, 2002 from EbscoHost Database.

Planel, C. (1997). National cultural values and their role in learning: a comparative ethnographic study of state primary schooling in England and France. *Comparative Education, 33*(3), 349-374. Retrieved November 11, 2002 from Academic Search Premier.

PÜtz, H. (2002). The international economy, changing employment and lifelong learning: response of the vocational training sector in Germany. In Burke, G. & Reuling, J. (Eds.) *Vocational Training and Life Long Learning in Australia and German: Australia Centre Series (*pp. 63-71). Leabrook, Australia: National Centre for Vocational Education Research.

Renault-Lescure, O. (2000). L'Enseignment Bilingue en Guyane Française: Une Situation Particuliere en Amérique du Sud [Bilingual Teaching in French Guiana: a Unique Situation in South America] In Blanquer, J. M. & Trindade, H. (Eds), *Les Défis de L'éducation en Amérique Latine* [Educational Challenges in Latin America], (pp.231-246), Paris: Institut des hautes études de l'Amérique latine (IHEAL).

Roach, D. & Byrne, P. (2001). A cross-cultural comparison of instructor communication in American and German classrooms. *Communication Education*, Annandale, *50*(1), 1-14. Retrieved November 13, 2002 from Proquest Database.

Robinson, B. (1995). Mongolia in transition: a role for distance education? *Open Learning, 10*(3), 3-15.

Searles, J. (with Jorkasky, B. & Schultz, C.). (1970). *Verbal Styles of Teachers in a Latin American Society.* University Park: Pennsylvania State University.

Sharpe, K. (1997). The protestant ethic and the spirit of Catholicism: ideological and institutional constraints on system change in English and French primary schooling. *Comparative Education, 33*(3), 329-349.

Simon, R. (1983). But who will let you do it?: counter-hegemonic possibilities for work education. *Journal of Education, 165*(3), 235-257.

Smith, S. (2001). Approaches to study of three Chinese national groups. *British Journal of Psychological Society, 71*, 429-441.

Squires, G. (with Furth, D.). (1989). *Pathways for Learning: Education and Training from 16 to 19.* Paris :Washington, D.C.: Organization for Economic Co-operation and Development.

Stevenson, H.& Lee, S. (1997). The East Asian version of whole-class teaching. In Cummings, William K & Altbach, Philip G (Eds.). *The Challenge of Eastern AsianEeducation : Implications for America.* (pp. 33-49). Albany: State University of New York Press.

Thompson, E. (2000). Are teaching cases appropriate in a mainland Chinese context? Evidence from Beijing MBA students. *Journal of Education for Business, 76*(2), 108-112. Retrieved February 22, 2003 from Proquest Database.

Trindade, H. (2000). Esquisse D'une Histoire De L'Université en Amérique Latine. [Outline of the History of the Latin American University]. In Blanquer, J. M. & Trindade, H. (Eds), *Les Défis de L'éducation en Amérique Latine* [Educational Challenges in Latin America] (pp. 15-28), Paris: Institut des hautes études de l'Amérique latine (IHEAL).

Ukai Russell, N. (1997). Lessons from Japanese cram schools . In Cummings, William K & Altbach, Philip G (Eds.). *The Challenge of Eastern Asian Education: Implications for America,* (pp. 153-170). Albany: State University of New York Press.

Utsch, A, Rauch, A., Rothfufs, R., and Frese, M. (1999). Who becomes a small scale entrepreneur in a post-socialist environment : on the differences between entrepreneurs and managers in East Germany. *Journal of Small Business Management, 37*(3), 31-42. Retreived January 8, 2003 from Proquest Database.

Visser, J. & Berg, D. (1999). Learning without frontiers: building integrated responses to diverse learning needs. *Educational Technology Research and Development, 47*(3), 102-114. Retrieved November 11, 2002 from Ebscohost Research database.

Watkins,D. (2001). Learning and teaching: a cross-cultural perspective. *School Leadership & Management, 20*, 161-174. Retrieved October 22, 2002, from Proquest database.

Yavas, U. (1999). Training needs in Saudi Arabia — a survey of managers. *Journal of Education for Business, 75*(2), 117-121. Retrieved February 22, 2003 from Proquest Database.

Chapter 8
Linguistic Competency, Cultural Understanding, and Business Education in Ukraine

Lyudmila Bordyuk
Lviv Polytechnic National University, Ukraine

Richard E. Lee
State University of New York, Oneonta

INTRODUCTION: "UKRAINE IS NOT RUSSIA!"

Because most people outside Ukraine[1] erroneously believe that Ukraine is a part of Russia, Ukrainians often resort to this phrase in their conversations with foreigners. Visitors to Ukraine can perhaps be forgiven their oversimplification of a very complex socio-cultural situation; the history of the two nations is inextricably interwoven as both trace their roots back to the great state of *Kyivan Rus* that emerged in the 9th century. Further, although the Russian and Ukrainian languages are distinct linguistic entities, they are similar in some respects. But a conflation of Ukraine as "part of Russia" is a substantial — and potentially problematic — mistake. Ukraine's history of colonization by Russia, Austria-Hungary, Poland, and the Soviets means that it is inappropriate to uncritically link Ukraine and Russia; the linkage also calls to Ukrainian minds the deliberate famine engineered by Stalin to destroy the nation (Conquest, 1987). Calling a Ukrainian a "Russian" is an example of a signal — if understandable — cultural misunderstanding, one that flows from a shallow understanding of a foreign culture.

A related knowledge-base derives from what most visitors and business people *do* know about Ukraine: that it is well-known as the breadbasket of the former Soviet Union and the site of the world's most horrible nuclear accident — Chernobyl. Unfortunately, the latter's negative image is so vivid internationally that the Euro Disney Resort complex in France was metaphorically dubbed "a cultural Chernobyl" as a way of illustrating the depths of misunderstanding that exist between American business people and some of their potential French customers (Euro Disney, 1993). The iconography of Ukraine is thus oversimplified into a binary: it is positive (farmland, nurturing) yet negative (nuclear disaster), and this binary understanding is too-often subsumed into a categorical sense that Ukraine "equals" Russia.

The relative obscurity of Ukraine as a distinct cultural entity is part of the reason for the common visitor's tendency to understand one nation and culture (Ukraine) only insofar as it resembles a larger and better-known one (Russia). An American expert on the Soviet Union and the Ukraine claims "the paucity of information available on Ukraine is striking and most often Ukraine is relegated to the back sections of books on Russia" (Dalton, 2000, 11). In fact, although there is increasing critical attention, when one seeks information on Ukraine, one is often referred to "Russia" as an indexical location (Gesteland, 1999; Mole, 1991; materials of the annual C.I.B.E.R. — Center for International Business Education and Research — conferences on Language, Culture and Global Management, and others). There are few primary sources of information on doing business in Ukraine or with Ukrainians: the Internet (www.thepost.kiev.ua), U.S.-Ukraine Foundation materials, and occasional publications in international periodicals (*The Economist*, *The Financial Times*, *The Wall Street Journal*). The few available books are difficult to find. Those worth the search include Jolly and Kettanch's *Doing Business in Ukraine* (1998) and Dalton's *Culture Shock! Ukraine* (2000). Dalton addresses her book to all those who accept the challenge of living and working in Ukraine and dedicates it to a better Ukraine and a better life for Ukrainians. Dalton's perceptions come from her expertise in the Soviet Union; her perspective is particularly interesting as her heritage includes no Slavic blood. As an American — and not a Ukrainian expatriate — her work is relatively free of the ideological (and cultural) biases that mark commentaries by those with affiliations to Ukraine.[2]

Although present-day Ukraine is the largest country in Europe,[3] its population of 47.6 million is at risk due to two major factors: a declining birth-rate and massive worker emigration to Italy, Spain, Portugal, the U.S. and Russia. To the east and northeast of Ukraine is Russia. To the west are Poland, Slovakia, Hungary, and Romania. Ukraine's strategic geographical position has meant that it has a very long history as a crossroads between eastern and western Europe. The development of a market economy should serve to elevate Ukraine to a position of economic influence commensurate with its geographical location.

After the collapse of the Soviet Union, Ukraine proclaimed its independence in 1991. Like other members of the former Soviet Union, Ukraine is in a period of painful transition. Recently, the hypothesis has been developed that the radical changes from communism (communist / socialist values) to capitalism (Western values) have caused a collective cultural shock within a society which is similar to individual culture shock, but which lasts much longer (Fink, 2000). This hypothesis is one which is mirrored in the linguistic differences between low-context and high-context cultures first promulgated by the anthropologist Edward Hall in *Beyond Culture* (1976), and later incorporated into other disciplinary studies.[4] The complicated process of Ukraine's integration into European and world institutions strongly supports the above hypothesis. More to the point, social and linguistic conventions are at the heart of the challenges that face anyone who wishes to conduct business in Ukraine.

CURRENT CHALLENGES FACING TEACHERS OF BUSINESS ENGLISH IN UKRAINE

Globalization has come to mean that individuals operate in a highly charged political environment, one in which a tension exists between national (and cultural) identification and cross-cultural homogenization. The issue of "identification" is perhaps particularly strong in countries which have only recently been allowed to govern themselves. However individuals negotiate this socio-political issue, the Ukrainian consensus seems to be an overwhelming desire for international involvement and understanding. The present political and economic climates present attractive opportunities to today's Ukrainian university graduates. But to better equip Ukrainian students to meet the challenges of the 21st century, a university education needs to develop in ways that will meet the changes implicit in the culture as a whole by emphasizing internationalization, integrating foreign language and culture competence, developing social / communicative skills, and providing an entrepreneurial orientation. There is a great demand for economic and business professionals in Ukraine. Additionally, a growing number of students majoring in applied linguistics are seeking employment outside of the educational system as translators / interpreters or office managers with international companies and joint ventures: the multinationals (Coca- Cola, Pepsi, Kodak, Procter & Gamble, and McDonald's) have arrived in Ukraine. In major Ukrainian cities there are networks of business people engaged in U.S.-Ukrainian business relationships (Peace Corps business consultants, Business Incubator, Consortium for Enhancement of Ukrainian Management Education / C.E.U.M.E., and others). The net effect of these various networks and educational frameworks has been that future business leaders need to be trained not only in "business," but in the less-straightforward areas of language and cultural adaptation. The globalization process has had a strong impact on the conceptual and pragmatic needs of Business English and Business Communication curricula in countries with transition economies. Ukraine is no exception.

Ways of bringing an international and, thus, an intercultural perspective into business-language education in Ukraine will be discussed in this paper. The lead author's experience as an English lecturer at the School of Economics and Management and the Department of Applied Linguistics at Lviv Polytechnic National University, West Ukraine, a school with a good reputation in research and training students, as well as her intercultural experience in American and European exchange programs and joint projects, is central to this discussion.[5]

Today's business world requires strong linguistic skills and communicative competence — covering grammatical, discursive, and strategic aspects (Canale and Swain, 1980) — as crucial factors for advanced professional performance. A sociolinguistic perspective on language as a powerful means of communication may be found in Lemke: "When we think of power in the social world, we imagine power to do things: to buy and sell, to command obedience, to reward and punish, to do good to others or do them harm, both physically and emotionally. In all of these, language can and often does play a critical role" (1995, 1).

All business activities (leading, motivating, decision-making, dealing with colleagues, customers, and suppliers) involve communication in the variety of its forms: verbal, non-verbal, internal / external, operational, and personal (Adler, 1977; Lesikar, 1996; Locker, 1995). Managers are professional communicators by definition, and communication is a major part of their work.

Foreign-language(s) proficiency is a valuable asset for those searching for competitive international job opportunities. English is the most powerful member of the "language ecology" (McArthur, 2002). American English is internationally accepted as the language of business and technology. But business communication requires more than the standard vocabulary and trade jargon. The goal of language education is not to learn the target language-code only, but to develop a cross-cultural perception of similarities and differences and to arrive at a shared meaning.[6] Cultural strategies are an integral part of business communication and business transactions. Foreign learners acquire various aspects of American culture via the target language — English. Scollon and Scollon, experts in intercultural communication, claim that "many aspects of western culture, especially western patterns of discourse are carried within English" (1995, 4).

INCORPORATING CULTURE INTO THE BUSINESS ENGLISH CURRICULUM: BACKGROUNDS AND A PROGRAM FOR CHANGE

Culture, in a broad sense, is viewed as a process, that is, a way of perceiving, interpreting, feeling, and being in the world (Robinson, 1991). Nimgade maintains that "for all its faults and weaknesses . . . American business still forms a key model for much of the world" and "an important force in disseminating the American style of management is the role of the U.S. as the world's largest manufacturer of contemporary culture" (1989,

299).[7] Numerous studies on what makes America "American" (Adler, 1999; Hofstede, 1994; Thiederman, 1991; Trompenaars, 1993) emphasize the most valued traits in American culture: individualism, success-orientation, pragmatism, progress, efficient use of time, action, assertiveness, perseverance, mobility, hope, optimism, and opportunity. Thiederman claims that American culture is almost unique in its belief that change is always equated with growth, improvement, and progress (1991).[8]

It is a central assumption of intercultural education that cultural issues of values, beliefs, and attitudes are the most difficult to teach (Allwood, 1990).

The U.S. is a low-context culture, that is, an individualistic, pragmatic society (Victor, 1992); Ukraine, a former collective, is closer to a high-context culture. Victor, extending the theories of Hall (1976) and others, points out that high- and low-context cultures privilege different kinds of information and have different attitudes towards oral and written communication channels. In high-context cultures (such as Japan, China, and Arab countries), most information is inferred from the context of a message, little is explicitly stated. Conversely, low-context cultures (such as America, Germany, and Scandinavian countries) prefer explicitly conveyed information. Thus, high-context cultures favour indirectness and ambiguity; low-context cultures favor directness and clarity (Victor, 1992; Locker, 1995). People in Slavic societies employ different linguistic codes and culturally predetermined strategies to achieve their communicative goals, using different "conceptual filters" (Gudykunst and Kim, 1984) in the process of perceiving and interpreting reality. Naturally, they have different assumptions, expectations, and employ different patterns of social behaviour. As a result, Ukrainian and American businesses develop and operate in discrete cultural frameworks. Dalton dubs the preferred Ukrainian framework one of "contacts, not contracts" — privileging interpersonal networks rather than legal requirements (2000).[9] Wierzbicka claims that representatives of different cultures are "different" people not only because they speak different languages but because they think differently, feel differently, and relate differently to other people (1999).

The general tendency of Ukraine and other post-Soviet states has been to elide the systematic study of culture within the framework of language courses. The teachers' own experiences of Western cultures were usually rather limited. Like other professional groups within the Soviet Union, teachers lived and worked in an isolated society, separated from the rest of the world by an Iron Curtain. Thus, cultural instruction covered some sporadic facts on monuments, cities, festivals, traditions, literary characters, and national heroes, but there was no coherent focus on patterns of Western values, beliefs, and attitudes. Such a conventional approach has been strongly criticized by Kramsch: "Culture is commonly seen as making the study of a foreign language more attractive and as providing a welcome relief from grammar and vocabulary exercises. Learning about a foreign culture is not expected to require any intellectual effort since it is generally conceived only as the tourist's view of the foreign ways of life" (1991, 221).

Bridging the gap between language and culture is very important for those who plan to be engaged in global competitive activities. Cross-cultural competence implies an awareness of one's own cultural heritage and a thorough understanding of the target culture in addition to knowledge of the language. In other words, cultural self-awareness — a willingness to examine the presuppositions of one's own culture — is a prerequisite for truly understanding the culture of another.

The Business English course designed by the Ukrainian Academy of Banking (I.A.T.E.F.L.-UKRAINE, 2003) emphasizes the need to develop general language knowledge as well as oral and written professional communication skills. It is sketched (one sentence only), but not specified, in the course description that "cultural awareness is also developed throughout the course" (22). In the English Business Communication course description developed at the Thunderbird School of Management (Uber Grosse, 1999), promoting cross-cultural understanding and developing cross-cultural communication skills are central. So there is a slowly dawning recognition of the need to understand "language" within a framework of culture — and as a prerequisite for business interaction.

To make Ukrainian business students successful and effective in their future careers, an insight into the culture of the target language should be emphasized in the re-designed model of the Business English curriculum. Cross-cultural training would provide a necessary scaffold for understanding international business realities. The socio-economic content of Business English classes provides opportunities for linguistic and cross-cultural guided exploration and discoveries. An updated Ukrainian interdisciplinary Business English curriculum should integrate the target language (English), an international perspective, and cross-cultural professional content. To accomplish this task, it is necessary to: 1) elaborate an efficient strategy for integrating language study and cultural instruction; 2) select appropriate cultural content; and 3) apply effective methods and techniques of bringing the real business world into the classroom.

The strategy of cross-cultural instruction is to make business students linguistically and culturally competent. To comprehend culture-specific differences in English and Ukrainian business contexts, a comparative-contrastive analysis is efficient, combined with the following methods and techniques: a balanced integration of cognitive and communicative approaches, a content-based approach with the focus on acquiring the target information via a foreign language, discourse-patterns analysis, role-playing, brainstorming, and case studies.

ACQUIRING CULTURE VIA LANGUAGE

"Ability to speak a foreign language is often mistaken for ability to function in a speech community, but speaking ability can be a mechanical skill devoid of cultural competence" (Richard Swiderski).

Lexical Competency

Culture can be effectively taught when practicing new vocabulary, grammar, and discourse patterns. It should be emphasized that the interlocutors should know not only about a lexical equivalent of a certain semantic formula, but also be aware of its functional and contextual appropriateness. So, when a Ukrainian speaker says "May I take your pen?" he / she means "May I borrow your pen?" Teaching idiomatic usage is always a problematic affair; in this case, *take* and *borrow* are not synonymous.

A group of business words of Latin origin (for example, *affair, execute, execution*) have strong negative connotations in Ukrainian, meaning, respectively, *fraud* and *lawful killing as a punishment.* The prevalence of terms such as *executive board, executive director,* and *exec* in Business English discourse means that students learning only vocabulary will regularly trip over connotative misunderstandings. Another standard term in the English business lexicon, *manufacture / manufacturer*, retains its Latin transliteration in Ukrainian but is regarded as archaic (it was in use in the 17th-19th centuries).

Similarly, semantic, pragmatic, and culture-specific functions of the attribute *aggressive* in American and Ukrainian discourse combine to provide a dramatic example of language and culture interaction — and potential misunderstanding. In Ukrainian, the adjective *aggressive* and everything related to it is viewed in various negative ways as "belligerent" (an understanding that flows from the etymological root of the Latin, *aggressio*). A somewhat different situation is characteristic of an American socio-linguistic context which reflects the peculiarities of the national spirit and culture. In the above list of American national traits (Thiederman, 1991), a special emphasis is laid on *assertiveness.* Considerable illustrative data have been accumulated to argue that the adjective *aggressive* can function as a synonym of the adjective *assertive* in business-related and general contexts, thus implying a positive connotation. For example: "I.B.M.: Is this an ethical issue or just *good, aggressive* accounting? (Pearce, 1994, 515). *Aggressive candidates* in an American interpretation mean *self-starters* (Nimgade, 1989), i.e. ambitious and proactive people. *The Oxford Dictionary for the Business World* (1993) defines *aggressive* not only as *hostile, forceful,* but also as *self-assertive. The Longman Dictionary of English Language and Culture* (1998) defines the adjective *aggressive* as follows: "1) in a derogatory way as always ready to quarrel or attack, *belligerent: an aggressive manner* 2) appreciatively as *not afraid of opposition; determined and forceful, assertive: an aggressive marketing campaign.*" (emphasis added throughout).

Analyzing an intercultural aspect of assertiveness, Dodd maintains that in Western, low-context, direct cultures, "assertiveness is defined as the ability to state clearly what you expect or want and to work toward achieving that goal" (1995, 259). In his observations of the American character, Nimgade concludes that sometimes "there may be more bark than bite to American aggressiveness" (1989, 298).

Numerous business terms and concepts contain the attribute *aggressive* as a component of their semantic structure, e.g.: *aggressive bank management; aggressive dividend policy; aggressive investment policy; aggressively trained managers;* etc. Most of these terms in a transliterated Ukrainian version are currently registered in Ukrainian professional business discourse as well. But in different patterns of general Ukrainian discourse, the adjective *aggressive* is used with a strong negative connotation only.

Frequently used concepts such as *aggressive management* and *aggressive marketing* — denoting *dramatic publicity, successful encouragement,* and *extensive self-promotion* — are central strategies of the Walt Disney Company, evidenced by three examples: "Nothing was left to chance at Disney theme parks. Standards of service, park design and operating details, and human resource policies and practices were integrated to ensure the Disney 'play' would be flawlessly performed every day in and out at each location. Known for its *aggressive management of operational details*, Disney's stated goal was to exceed its customers' expectations every day" (Euro Disney, 4).

"At the same time Disney *aggressively cross-trained* managers_and supervisors to ensure service quality. Prior to opening, 270 managers were crossed-trained in the Disney methods at the company's other parks to work at Euro Disney" (Euro Disney, 12).

"Euro Disney was *aggressively marketed* by Disney as well as other firms. Disney *successfully* encouraged dozens of articles on the complex in magazines throughout Europe. Prior to the opening it sent a model of the Sleeping Beauty Castle around Europe to the opening celebration, which was broadcasted live across Europe. In addition, Swiss food giant Nestle sponsored extensive cross-promotions of Euro Disney at its own expense" (12). (Emphasis was added throughout.)

Another vivid example of positive semantic modification and culture-specific functioning of the adjective *aggressive* is a letter of sympathy from a U.S. colleague, a professor of economics, as a response to the terrible air-crash at the military air-field at Sknyliv-Lviv, Western Ukraine, which killed or crippled over 200 people during a military air-show on July 27, 2002. It reads: ". . . so many reasons to cry — we must search *more aggressively* for more reasons to smile and protect our families and friends."

Cross-cultural sensitivity and awareness may equip students with an appropriate understanding and interpretation of "American aggressiveness" in professional and general contexts. Dodd argues that "beyond using language, the study of intercultural communication recognizes how culture pervades what we are, how we act, how we think. . . ." (1995, 3).

Idiomatic expressions (similes, metaphors, proverbs, sayings, jargon, slang, and phrasal verbs) are notoriously untranslatable. They should be treated with a special care in order to transact business effectively. The author of "Biz Talk I" argues that "without an understanding of this type of lingo, any non-native speaker conducting business in America is at a grave disadvantage, especially during important meetings and negotiations where it is common to hear expressions like: 'to have the floor, to stone-wall, to brainstorm, to table a discussion'" (Burke, 1993, vii).

Grammar and Usage

Culture-specific differences between English and Ukrainian speakers in their inborn attitude to privacy, private property, and quality service can be grammatically traced in the following examples:

American-English Usage	**Ukrainian Usage**
(1) *The manager's office* (a possessive attribute is emphasized)	*The office of the manager* (the owner is de-emphasized)
(2) *He changed his mind* (a possessive pronoun is the norm)	*He changed mind* (ownership, is de-emphasized)
(3) *I want my car repaired* (the customer's passive role is explicit)	*I want to repair my car* (the passive role is implied)
(4) *Every student may use the Internet at his/her convenience* (the gender aspect is explicit)	*Every student may use the Internet at his convenience* (the gender aspect is ignored)

Discourse Patterns

Clyne maintains that variation in discourse and pragmatics results from differences in pragmatic formulae and ways of structuring information (1994). Culture-specific patterns of business discourse, both written and oral, can be effectively analyzed in various genres: presentations, meetings, negotiations, getting through an interview, business letters, résumé writing, etc. The résumé genre may serve as a vivid illustration of specific cultural assumptions. There is little research available on how résumés function across cultures; Semenova compares North American, Japanese, and Russian samples of résumés and concludes that they differ in the choice of layout, content, and language (2000).

The samples of Ukrainian résumés submitted by M.B.A. students at Lviv Management Institute (Ukraine) in 2000 are less persuasive and self-promotional than American ones. This does not seem to be merely a manner of "choice," but a condition which is registered in content and language: superlative forms of adjectives are rare; the range of dynamic words (such as *provide, increase, improve, implement, design, promote, develop*, etc) is much broader in American than in Ukrainian samples. The pragmatic goal of the résumé — to promote, "to sell one's self" — is much less explicit in Ukrainian than in English, which reflects Ukrainians' national peculiarities and attitudes. This is in keeping with a general understanding of Ukraine as a high-context culture — at least in comparison to America. It is worth mentioning that cover letters are never employed in Ukraine. A certain amount of diffidence (and self-consciousness?) attaches to the concept of "selling one's self" in Ukraine.

Sources of Cultural Content

The criteria for selecting "authentic texts"[10] (Galloway, 1998) for cross-cultural analysis depend on pragmatic learning-goals. Allens maintains that linguistic communication is always carried on in a context which is in large parts culturally constituted (1990). Appropriate cultural content *may* be found in prominent business publications (Trompenaars, 1993; Adler, 1997; Hofstede, 1991; Locker, 1995, which have become available in Ukraine partly due to donations from the Sabre Foundation / the U.S. /), business periodicals (*Harvard Business Review, The Wall Street Journal, Business Week, The Economist*, etc), mass media, and practical business classes providing a wide range of issues: money and banking, corporate culture, brand management, interview skills, etc. The three fundamental business-skills-based activities (presentations, meetings, and negotiations) are specifically designed to instruct students to act and react properly in realistic situations. They are "the finest American blend" of business matter, language, and specific cultural behavior and promote the ability to speak fluently and accurately, which is often the secret of success.

The process of teaching Business English at top Ukrainian business schools has become much more effective in recent years due to communicative[11] methods of teaching and updated materials: *Business English Class* (Cotton, D., and Robbins, S., Thomas and Sons, 1998); *Effective Socializing* (Comfort, J., Oxford University Press, 2002); *New Insights into Business* (Tullis, G., and Trappe, T., Pearson Education, 2000); *Longman Business English Usage* (Strutt, P., Longman, 1995); *Business Across Cultures: Effective Communication Strategies* (English, M., and Lynn,

S., Longman, 1995) and excellent comprehensive dictionaries on business, finance and commerce.

CULTURAL AND HISTORICAL DIMENSIONS OF AMERICAN BUSINESS PRACTICES AND VALUES IN A UKRAINIAN BUSINESS-ENGLISH CLASS

"What is it you Americans want out of life?'
Well, I suppose you might say we want success — in the North at all events"
(John Galsworthy, *The Silver Spoon*)

In his novelistic examination of European and American values and expectations, John Galsworthy's *The Silver Spoon* (the second book in a trilogy entitled *A Modern Comedy*, itself a part of the multi-volume *Forsyte Saga*) recounts the cultural mis-steps and stereotypical assumptions of those who venture out of their native cultures. Not surprisingly, one source for English stereotypes of Americans in this novel (and of American and English stereotypes of English, Austrian, and other characters) are other novels, other narratives. The idea that novels and literary texts can supply cultural "truth" is well founded in the Western literary tradition.[12]

Wood argues that as useful as professional business materials are, it is important to provide a broad cultural and historical dimension of business practices as part of national identity (1998). The vocational nature of the Business English course can be given a new perspective by adding appropriate literary texts to the core program. Cognitive and aesthetic benefits of the compatibility of business and literature in the educational process result in contextualization and reinforcement of the business lexicon, an engagement of students' cultural background and a concomitant broadening of their outlooks. For our purposes, literature can be seen as contextualizing patterns of social behavior. When reading and analyzing literary texts, students explore, diachronically and synchronically, various business issues and practices and gain cultural insights. Carter and Long argue that students will be better motivated to read a literary text if they can relate it to their own ideas, feelings, opinions, and perceptions (1991). Unlike professional materials, literature provides texts that have something to do with us and our problems. In other words, literature asks questions about what it means to be human — questions that are unquantifiable, but no less important than statistical measurements and other scientific, analytical methods. As G. K. Chesterton once pointed out, "we can learn a good deal about entomology without being insects, but if we want to understand humanity, we have to be human ourselves and project our understanding from inside" (cited in Hunt, 1991, 2).

Business students are not to become experts in literature, but they need to be knowledgeable about the world, various cultures, interpersonal relations, and human experience. There is no point in educating a businessperson who is nothing but a businessperson. Interweaving literature in the Business Language course might enrich the learning process and augment an increasingly absent sense of the world — a sense that only literature can convey.

There are many examples of times when business people, in creative ways, need to employ their knowledge of literature, vivid literary characters, metaphors, and quotations to cross the boundaries of shoptalk, and, when necessary, to treat professional issues from a fresh perspective. Describing the American style of management as viewed by international professionals, Nimgade, vice president of Genesis Technology Group (Cambridge, Mass.) and a research associate at Harvard Business School, opens his analytical paper by quoting Robert Burns, then uses Gustave Flaubert's observation on human nature for support of his ideas (1989). Finally, he cites Oscar Wilde's comments on the materialistic and utilitarian bent of the American character. He could also have quoted Wilde's aphorism that "Life imitates Art far more than Art imitates Life."

When analyzing the concepts of brand image and brand management outlined in an article in *The Economist*, 24 out of 25 business students and 65 out of 93 applied linguistics students at Lviv Polytechnic National University "did not hear" the paraphrase of Shakespeare's memorable verses from *Romeo and Juliet* –

"What's in a name? That which we call a rose /
By any other name would smell as sweet" –

in the following sentences: "Brands add value by making customers loyal and, often willing to pay more for the things branded. *Roses by another name might smell as sweet* but they would no longer fetch $30 a dozen" (emphasis added). It is essential to mention that there are excellent Russian and Ukrainian translations of major Shakespearean works which are part of a standard Ukrainian high-school world literature syllabus. Ignorance of a foreign culture's literary tradition is insufficient excuse, at least in this case, for not recognizing a cultural touchstone — and the metaphoric and allusive possibilities of the usage.

Compiling an American Literature Supplement for Use in Ukrainian Business-English Class

"This books can do –
Not only this alone: they give
New views to life, and
Teach us how to live."
(George Crabbe)

To diversify the vocational nature of the Business English class, an American Literature Supplement to the Business English course is being compiled and introduced at the Department of Applied Linguistics at Lviv National Polytechnic University. The goal of this project is to introduce an interdisciplinary program in language and culture for business. The use of the Supplement is intended to demonstrate how American cultural values have been embedded in business practices.

Galloway argues that "the culture of a people cannot be boxed, exported or delivered in a class-room. The real-life story of intricate connections, integrating perspectives and internal sense-making cannot be told. It must be entered and experienced with respect for its own validity and regard for its own integrity" (1998, 140). In the case of Ukrainian students, the very limited possibilities for live communication with native speakers make the use of print and audio-visual materials a necessity. Galloway maintains that "a visit to an authentic text is much like a visit to the country itself" (1998, 134).[13]

The functional theory of language is based on the assumption that all language use is textual and, thus, is realized in real-life contexts.[14] The Supplement under design offers a thrilling journey to the world of American business to serious explorers, not tourists.

Selection of Appropriate Literary Passages

The American Literature Supplement to the Business English course is a collection of passages from novels, short stories, and essays chosen to appeal to readers and involve them emotionally. Krashen argues that "when second language acquirers read for pleasure they develop the competence they need to move from the beginning 'ordinary conversational' level to a level where they can use the second language for a more demanding purpose, such as the serious study of literature, business, so on" (1993, 84).

Writers represented include texts such as Margaret Mitchell (*Gone with the Wind*), Jack London (*Martin Eden*), Theodore Dreiser (*The Financier, Stoic, Titan*), F. Scott Fitzgerald (*The Great Gatsby*), O. Henry (*The Selected Stories*) and contemporary authors such as William Saroyan (*Short Stories*), Arthur Hailey (*Airport, Hotel*) Randall Jarrell (*A Sad Heart at the Supermarket*), Margaret Mead (*Sex and Achievement*), John Grisham (*The Firm*), Sidney Sheldon (*The Stars Shine Down, Master of the Game*), Barbara Bradford (*To Be the Best*) and others. Selection criteria included availability and prior student knowledge. Many works of American literature are available at Ukrainian academic libraries, both in English and excellent Russian and (occasionally) Ukrainian translations. The issue of student familiarity was taken seriously. 130 students at the Business English class were surveyed: *all* of the students had read Jack London, 63 (all female students) had read Margaret Mitchell, 55 students had read O. Henry, 16 students had read Theodore Dreiser, and one student had read F. Scott Fitzgerald.

Students have also demonstrated a special interest in contemporary American literature as a means of learning more about contemporary American life, especially the language people speak today (both formal and informal registers). Unfortunately, there is less contemporary literature to choose from. Usually, such texts are brought by American visiting professors, Peace Corps volunteers, or are made available through the Sabre Foundation.

The selected passages — a few paragraphs or a page long — are arranged thematically and explore a relevant professional issue of the Business English course: Presentations, Negotiations, Meetings, Entrepreneurship, Brand Management, Corporate Culture, Advertising, Intercultural Communication, Women in Business, etc.

How can new knowledge be squeezed into an already overcrowded curriculum? It should be incorporated into Business English studies and become an integral part of learning **the target matter** (business) via **the target language** (English) and **the target culture** (American).

The Business English course in Ukrainian universities is usually taken over one or two semesters. It appears reasonable to conclude each topic of the Business English syllabus with the relevant unit from the American Literature Supplement.

Key Features of the Supplement

The business-oriented literary Supplement is activity-based and student-centered. It

- offers insights into a wide range of business issues;
- reinforces business terms and concepts in contexts which provide a panorama of business and social life as well as cultural traditions of various American historical periods;
- represents human experience and interpersonal relations;
- involves students in such activities as analytical thinking, discussion, and generalization.

The Supplement is designed to (1) reinforce the business lexicon in a literary context and to (2) develop cross-cultural competence. It is essential, as Wood maintains in negotiating literature in the Business French Class, "to establish a constant and predictable pedagogical framework so that students have a clear set of expectations as they read and consider each work." (1999, 163). Reading is one of the four basic communicative skills; appropriate reading strategies may determine language acquisition. Knowing how to read is essential for the dynamic interplay between a reader and a text. Reading involves the cognitive processing of language and discourse structure, text construction as well as socio-cultural contexts and cultural and literary conventions.

A set of exercises ranging in their pragmatic objectives requires students to review the content of the passages to better understand and retain the plot and characters and to recognize some factual, business-related issues. Along with vocabulary and grammar exercises, comprehension and discussion questions in a pre-reading section and post-reading activities enhance learners' analytical and critical thinking abilities.

An essential benefit of integrating business and literature in the Business English class is that the passages under analysis can be considered **specific case studies** due to their realism, practicality, and human experience. Pearce and Robinson maintain that case analysis is both a proven educational method that adds realism and excitement to the business course and an excellent opportunity to develop and refine analytical skills (1994). Thus, in the case of *Euro Disney: The First 100 Days*, prepared by The Harvard Business School, "little things like the attitude of different nationalities with respect to disposing of trash are noticeable" (1993, 4). A vivid example, below, of the early days when there was "no extended street cleaning service" in the U.S. and how garbage collecting turned into a very profitable business is described by Theodore Dreiser:

One man in particular had grown strong in his estimation as having some subtle political connection not visible on the surface, and this was Edward Malia Butler. Butler was a contractor, undertaking the construction of sewers, water-mains, foundations for buildings, street-paving and the like. In the early days, long before Cowperwood had known him, he had been a garbage-contractor on his own account. The city at that time had no extended street-cleaning service, particularly in its outlying sections and some of the older, poorer regions. Edward Butler, then a poor young Irishman, had begun by collecting and hauling away the garbage free of charge, and feeding it to his pigs and cattle. Later he discovered that people were willing to pay a small charge for this service. Then a local political character, a councilman friend of his — they were both Catholics — saw a new point in the whole thing. Butler could be made official garbage collector. The council could vote an annual appropriation for this service. Butler could employ more wagons than he did now — dozens of them, scores. Not only that, but no other garbage collector would be allowed. There were others, but the official contract awarded him would also, officially, be the end of the life of any and every disturbing rival. A certain amount of the profitable proceeds would have to be set aside to assuage the feelings of those who were not contractors. Funds would to be loaned at election time to certain individuals and organizations — but no matter. The amount would be small. So Butler and Patrick Gavin Comiskey, the councilman (the latter silently) entered into business relations. Butler gave up driving a wagon himself. He hired a young man, a smart Irish boy of his neighborhood, Jimmy Sheehan, to be his assistant, superintendent, stableman, bookkeeper, and what not. Since he soon began to make between four and five thousand a year, where before he made two thousand, he moved into a brick house in an outlying section of the south side, and sent his children to school. Mrs. Butler gave upmaking soap and feeding pigs. And since then times had been exceedingly good with Edward Butler. (Dreiser. *The Financier*. Moscow: Foreign Language Publishing House, 1954, 9-10).

The professional, linguistic, and cultural aspects of the topic "Women in Business" may be reinforced by passages and their analyses from a number of contemporary novels. However, "the hardness and endurance" as well as "the shrewd trading instinct" of Scarlett O'Hara (*Gone with the Wind)* who "had the aggressiveness and intended to use it," who "was conducting her affairs in a masculine way," who "ventured out into the rough world of men, competing with them, rubbing shoulders with them" (when the public opinion was that "a woman had no business even knowing what a mortgage was") make Scarlett O'Hara a particularly vivid — and useful — female character. Her characterization can be used to shed light on qualities that are favored in the business world (and on the problems women face within that sphere). Of course, the danger is overgeneralization and oversimplification: Scarlett could just as easily be seen as a shallow narcissist so focused on her own needs that even tragedies such as the American Civil War and chattel slavery are mere backdrops to her personal desires. The use of texts such as *Gone With The Wind* can help Ukrainian students see — in the very broadest strokes — how metaphor, characterization, dialogue, and idiom in a once-popular American novel provide a limited insight into a culture they presume to understand because of basic language study and the ubiquity of the American pop-culture presence.

The pages of *Gone with the Wind* boast a collection of quotations which mirror the business world and that provide a focus for students:

"Deaths and taxes and childbirth! There's never any convenient time for any of them!"

"There's just as much money to be made in the wreck of a civilization as in the upbuilding of one. . . There's still plenty of money to be made by anyone who isn't afraid to work – or to grab."[15]

The lead author of this essay was reproached by some American colleagues for employing such literature as "out-dated material" to explore business matters. But literature is known for exposing readers to common human values, problems, and joys. Literature's ability to ask difficult questions is not necessarily time-bound. An additional argument for the use of American fiction in a Ukrainian Business English class comes from an American: O. Henry's humorous — but apt — words are engraved in the Consular Section for American citizens at the U.S. Embassy in Ukraine, and visitors can make as much sense of them today as they could have 100 years ago: *"You can't appreciate home 'til you've left it, . . . nor old glory 'til you see it hanging on a broomstick on the shanty of a consul in a foreign town."*

Parallel examples (found in business editions and fiction) are abundant and can foster a high level of personal involvement and student response. As Rusterholz reasonably argues, "We can never prepare our students adequately for the variety of working situations in which they may eventually find themselves, but by teaching them to be skillful readers, we can give them the tools to continue to teach themselves" (1987, 433).

UKRANIAN STUDENTS AND INTERNATIONALIZATION

The most viable ways to acquire international, professional, and intercultural experiences are through credit transfer practices, internships, university joint projects, and exchange programs. Credit transfers across national boundaries are part of established practice in many Western countries; in Ukraine it is still under discussion.

In the wake of the Soviet Union's collapse in the early 1990s, young people from countries just regaining their sense of national identity found themselves in the dramatic situation of having to navigate between nationalism and internationalism. Exchange programs offer outstanding opportunities for students to implement people-to-people democracy and enhance their academic competence, although the price some students will pay — psychically — is sometimes high. This price, and the relationship between such programs and the use of American literature in business-English classes, will make sense after a short overview.

The goal of student-exchange programs is to promote mutual understanding and cooperation among nations. It is not only a valuable educational experience but also an excellent opportunity for personal and professional development. Exchange programs provide students with the opportunity to become professionally competitive in a global context, to shape or deepen awareness of shared human values and interests, and to increase their sensitivity to cultural differences and similarities.

The term *exchange student* refers to students on a study program abroad, even if the student's natural family is not hosting a foreign student.

There are several types of short-term (one-to-three months) and long-term (six-to-twelve months) exchange programs in Ukraine: those administered by governmental structures (e.g. the Freedom Support Act Undergraduate Program or the Edmund Muskie Graduate Fellowship Program) as well as programs supported by various foundations and private organizations (e.g. Central European University Graduate and Undergraduate programs, International Renaissance Foundation, Canada-Ukraine Parliament Foundation in Toronto, European University Center for Peace Studies, among others). The U.S., Germany, the Netherlands, Austria and Switzerland are leading participants.

Recent statistical data processed by the American Consular office in Lviv, Western Ukraine (Table 8.1), reflect the strong interest of Ukrainian students in academic exchange programs:

Table 8.1: Ukrainian Student Interest in Academic Exchange Programs

2000 – 2001	2001 - 2002
Edmund Muskie Graduate Fellowship Program • Applicants: 1,053 • Semi-finalists: 337 • Finalists: 106	**Edmund Muskie Graduate Fellowship Program** • Applicants: 1,092 • Semi-finalists: 323 • Finalists: 120
Freedom Support Act Undergraduate Program • Applicants: 1,471 • Semi-finalists: 483 • Finalists: 128	**Freedom Support Act Undergraduate Program** • Applicants: 2,300 • Semi-finalists: 473 • Finalists: 128

All international programs are highly competitive; prospective exchange students need to demonstrate the following characteristics along with academic excellence: adaptability, leadership potential, high motivation, responsibility, interpersonal and communication skills, and proficiency in a foreign language (English in particular).

Applying to student-exchange programs and, if chosen, participating in them, can be exciting and challenging. It can also, at times, be disappointing or frustrating trying to fit into a foreign environment. On entering a different cultural milieu, students are more knowledgeable about its explicit, "surface" manifestations and less knowledgeable about its implicit, "deeper" aspects. It is essential to emphasize that "intercultural education involves a way of thinking, including a philosophical perspective, a set of decision-making criteria and a specific value orientation" (Lasonen, 2003, 2). The process of adaptation to a new academic and cultural environment may be, and usually is, different for students from different countries. It is much easier for students from Germany, Austria, the Netherlands, and Belgium to adjust to American culture than for students from Ukraine. The primary issue is that the former countries are culturally more compatible with the U.S. because their status as low-context cultures means that they share habits of mind and discursive tendencies.[16]

An exchange program typically occurs in the following stages: applying and then undergoing a pre-departure orientation, entering the host's cultural and academic community, living and studying abroad, returning home. The application process includes filing a résumé, writing an essay, and participating in an interview. Résumés are interesting examples of specific cultural assumptions. To successfully negotiate an interview, Westerners know that they generally need to present themselves with confidence, maximizing their strengths and creating a positive effect. Western candidates demonstrate their assertiveness (or "aggressiveness" in an American context) to prove that they are the right candidates. Such a direct approach is not characteristic of a Ukrainian mentality oriented — or rather, formerly oriented — toward collectivism and the indirect presentation of information.

Ukrainian and American applicants also employ different cultural strategies in essay writing: the former prefer inductive discourse patterns while the latter lay emphasis on introducing the most essential information through deductive discourse patterns. Scollon and Scollon have observed that cultures such as Ukraine's tend to avoid discursive strategies that are overt and direct, preferring writing strategies that defer important, detailed information until quite late (by American standards) in the presentation (1995). Neglecting such culture-specific aspects may be a serious strategic drawback.

The importance of training students for the culturally bound expectations of a successful application process as well as for a pre-departure orientation increases dramatically in short-term programs: the period of experiential and cognitive learning about a new cultural environment is rather limited. The concept of the interdependence of communicative skills, intercultural competence, and professional performance has been successfully implemented by the U.S. in a new paradigm of foreign language education in interdisciplinary Foreign Language, Culture and Business Studies by the Centers for International Business Education and Research / C.I.B.E.R.s (Voght 1999). This kind of educational innovation could be of great practical benefit for Ukrainian universities as they internationalize their curricula, making students competitive in a global context and better equipping them as new leaders for the 21st century.

The feedback loop created by student-exchange programs has had a dramatic effect in Ukraine. The new knowledge gained by exchange students is shared and spread throughout many social and economic national projects. On their return home, professionally trained, cross-culturally minded and globally oriented exchange-students are able to affect Ukrainian society. Additionally, these students — who have been exposed at first hand to a different cultural context — become voices that help to educate the next generation of Ukrainians. Their experiences, coupled with curricular development plans such as that supported by the English Supplement under discussion here, can bring about an easier interface between radically different cultures — and easier integration equals more opportunities for economic interaction. American and European countries seeking joint venture or other business relationships with Ukraine seek out those students who exhibit bi-cultural competence, creating a symbiosis between educational activity and economic opportunity.

Culture Shock: Before or After?

In recent years, the Ukrainian understanding of the concept of "culture shock" has begun to change. More and more exchange students claim that the culture shock they experience on entering a foreign country is less than that they experience on returning home. Such cultural pioneers pay a psychic "price," one that is a serious social phenomenon requiring special consideration by Ukrainian politicians, economists, and sociologists. One of the reasons — according to exchange students and researchers — is the striking difference in patterns of attitudes, social life, accommodation of cultural diversity, and high standards of customer service. The "non-service" mentality typical of Ukrainian businesses and service circles hinders the development of a more competitive market economy and may partially account for the Ukraine's painful transition. The importance of linking cultural and linguistic competence is thus tied to a longer-term goal: the incorporation of rationalist techniques (including the ability to bridge low- and high-context cultural differences) that will aid the development of a market economy and a subsequent increase in the standard of loving for all Ukrainians.

CONCLUSION

In this paper, we have attempted to give an outline of some of the ways in which business language education in Ukraine could be reconsidered from an intercultural perspective. Current challenges of teaching and learning Business English in Ukrainian schools of business have been addressed, since broadening an international understanding is critical for Ukraine. The shaping of intercultural competence as part of effective business practice has been mostly absent from university business-language curricula. An updated, interdisciplinary, Business-English curriculum in Ukrainian schools of business should integrate the target language (English), an international perspective, and cross-cultural professional content. Some practical suggestions for acquiring culture via language (vocabulary, grammar, and discourse patterns) have been made.

Sources of cultural content, appropriate from the point of view of effective business performance, have been considered. Special emphasis has been laid upon diversifying the vocational nature of the Business English course and compiling an American Literature Supplement which mirrors the cultural and historical dimensions of American business practices and values.

The benefits of involving Ukrainian university students in the international educational community through exchange programs was demonstrated. As a result, the phenomenon of culture shock in a Ukrainian context needs further political, economic, and sociological consideration.

Implementing the principles of cross-cultural sensitivity in foreign-languages business education is sure to contribute to the emergence of a strong cadre of future Ukrainian business leaders.

NOTES

[1]The absence of the definite article "the" when referring to "Ukraine" is purposeful. It is a political sore point with Ukrainians — one which is tied to the concept of socio-linguistic assumptions that this paper addresses.

[2]That Dalton has her own bias is inevitable; her ideological filter, however, is not the issue here. What is of interest, though, is that the sort of cultural oversimplification that is described in the foregoing paragraphs also occurs when foreign readers consume narratives dealing with America — the antithesis of a "culturally invisible" society. The *reductio ad absurdum* that essentializes America (and perhaps other low-context cultures as well) into a one-dimensional, un-nuanced caricature is a function of the same engine of understanding, actually an engine of misunderstanding, that is discussed relative to Ukraine. The present essay acknowledges the deeper waters involved in the use of texts "out of culture," but suggests that the *careful* use of

foreign-language texts has positive benefits in a business education context that *can* outweigh the negative effects of oversimplifying cultural complexity.

[3]Technically, Russia is the largest of the former Soviet states; however, its land area is not entirely in Europe, but crosses over into Central Asia.

[4]Gudykunst (1984, 1996), Victor (1992), and others extend Hall's (1976) rubric; this "transportation" of anthropological theory into other fields of inquiry seems to support the contention that language-training, acculturation, and cross-cultural interaction are never as simple as learning the superficial structure of a language as a means to the end of "doing business." Such interdisciplinary — and, thus, intercultural — interaction is normal, of course; Hall was building upon prior anthropological, ethnographic, psychological, and linguistic research.

[5]Additional anecdotal information on intercultural issues related to the intersection of business-English education, Ukrainian-American interaction, and knowledge transference can be found in reportage such as that related in Gerlach (1999).

[6]The issue of how one conceives *of* language is precisely the point. Those who attach only a functional value to language use (thinking, for example, of language as a tool outside of themselves to be used without regard for cultural consequence) are opposed by linguists and philosophers of language in the West who see language as integrated with culture — inseparable from users and pre-existent to tool-users' functional desires. In this latter sense, language competency is a precondition for thought itself. Useful overviews and summaries of the arcs and intersections of neurobiology, linguistics, and cultural formation include Pinker's (1994) explanations and extensions of Chomsky's conceptualization of transformational grammar and collections such as Martinich, 1990. See also notes 11 and 14, below.

[7]Communication theorists differ on just what it is one means when one refers to "culture." A useful discussion of the "system of competence" that is a generally agreed-upon conception of the term "culture" is undertaken by a well-published researcher in the field, Gudykunst, W. B. (Cultural variability in communication. *Communication Research 24* (July-August, 1997: 327-49). In a different article (1996), Gudykunst refers to Keesing (1974) by stating that "culture provides its members with an implicit theory about how to behave in different situations" (512). He continues with a useful summation of the connection between low-context (individualistic) and high-context (collectivistic) cultures insofar as their respective cultures shape values and behaviors, having already made the point that these are not mutually exclusive contexts:

> As members of individualistic cultures are socialized into their culture, they learn the major values of their culture (e.g., independence, achievement) and acquire preferred ways for how members of the culture are expected to view themselves (e.g., as unique persons). Members of collectivistic cultures learn different major values (e.g., harmony, solidarity) and acquire different preferred ways to conceive of themselves (e.g., as interconnected with others). Members of individualistic and collectivistic cultures, however, do not just learn one set of values or just one way to conceive of themselves. Because individualism and collectivism exist in all cultures, members of individualistic cultures learn some collectivistic values and vice versa (Gudykunst, Matsumoto, et al., 512-13).

The most useful treatments of the high- and low-context paradigm recognize it as a spectrum, not a binary; cultures are high- or low-context only in relation to other cultures, and cultures do not fall comfortably into categories, but present tendencies that lean toward one or the other pole.

[8]Although Thiederman states that America's belief in the telic nature of progress is "almost unique," most historians and cultural theorists would agree that "cultural modernism" (or simply Modernism) is defined by its adherence to a model where change, secularization, rationalization, scientific inquiry, urbanization, individualism, and universal education lead to "progress." Modernism dates from roughly the 17th through the 20th centuries in the West. As a cultural concept, Modernism supplants "traditional" societal patterns (agriculturally based, respect for religion and other forms of hierarchical authority, superstition rather than science,

stability preferred to change, etc.) and is itself generally supplanted by "postmodernism." See, among many others, Stromberg (1994, pp. 8-13).

[9]The examinations of anthropologist / economist Duran Bell and of social psychologist Michael Bond in their discussions of the Chinese concept of *guanxi* seem relevant here. See, for example, Bond, M. (1992). *Beyond the Chinese Face: Insights from Psychology*. (Oxford University Press); and Bell, D., & Avernarius, C. (1999). Guanxi, bribery and ideological hegemony. (http://orion.uci.edu/~dbell/).

[10]The issue of what constitutes an "authentic text" is the subject for a book length, not an essay-length, discussion. Discussions of the aesthetic distinctions to be made between, for example, Jack London and Sidney Sheldon — while amusing and interesting — are not relevant here. A too-easy attachment to the idea that "texts reflect culture — the implication of using literary texts to "teach" culture — is very problematic, and a discussion of this very problematic is at the heart of much American poststructuralist literary theory. It is a tangent in the current discussion, but a useful start for the philosophically inclined can be found in Lamarque and Olsen's *Truth, Fiction, and Literature: A Philosophical Perspective* (Oxford: Clarendon Press, 1994). The concept of "mimesis" — the artistic reflection of the real — goes back at least as far as Plato. Competing theories of the relationship(s) between art (texts), authors, and the world — and the reflexive and representational possibilities and assumptions that underlie those theories — are well represented in such works as Lentricchia and McLaughlin's *Critical Terms for Literary Study* (University of Chicago Press, 1995); Greenblatt and Gunn's *Redrawing the Boundaries: The Transformation of English and American Studies* (M.L.A. of America, 1995); or any of a number of introductions to literary theory, such as *Introducing Literary Studies* by Richard Bradford, (Prentice Hall, 1996). Aesthetic engagements with the "reality effect" of literature abound. Notable texts include Auerbach, E., *Mimesis* (Princeton University Press, 1953); Levin, H., *The Gates of Horn: A Study of Five French Realists* (Oxford University Press, 1964); and Lukács, G., *The Historical Novel* (translated by Hannah and Stanley Mitchell, University of Nebraska Press, 1983 [originally published—Boston: Merlin Press, 1962]).

[11]The "communicative" method — conversationally oriented — replaced the "grammar-translation" method, which focused on the interlinear translation of foreign texts and was favored in the former Soviet Union until the early 1990s. Today in Ukraine, university teachers with some experience of international projects and exchange programs with European and American partners employ a "lecture-seminar" format rather than a formal lecture. One wonders if the osmotic influence of American educational methodology will result in a Ukrainian classroom which exhibits behaviors such as those witnessed by a Ukrainian teacher who visited America: "In my opinion, American teachers are more like friends to students than an authority you have to obey. . . the atmosphere of friendliness. . . allows students to easily express themselves. But sometimes the teachers cannot tell the truth to their students about the real state of things — their abilities, their talents, their behaviors, and their attitude to their studies. . . They can't say they aren't pleased with the students' work. They have to praise and find diplomatic phrases so as not to offend students. They have to be very democratic, and thus they become victims of democracy" (Olena Tarasova, in Gerlach, 1999, p. 126). There is an interesting paradox in the image of low-context American teachers forced into euphemistic deference to students to whom self-esteem has overwhelmed accomplishment. Or, in the words of an American teacher who spent two weeks in Ukrainian classrooms, students in Ukraine "place a great deal of emphasis on scholastic achievement," and "share most the burden of their own education" (Kathy Megyeri, in Gerlach, 1999, 127).

[12]There is an equally long tradition, since at least *Don Quixote* (1605), which warns of the dangers of believing the cultural denotations and connotations of novelistic texts. Such works as *Quixote*, Flaubert's *Madame Bovary* (1857), and many others concern themselves with the sad fate that awaits those who believe that what they read in novels is a valid reflection of the world. See also note 10, above, on mimesis. Of course, expecting Ukrainian students to understand American business culture based solely upon a selection of narratives is akin to expecting American students to "understand" the nature of pre-emancipation Russia from a

reading of Gogol's *Dead Souls*. The American Literature Supplement being used in this Ukrainian business-English class is an adjunct to study, not the study itself. As such, it provides a way of getting at some of the more nuanced realities of American culture embedded in American business practice — and it contributes to a level of understanding that a shallow knowledge of business English does not usually allow.

[13]See note 10, above.

[14]*The Encyclopedia of Language & Linguistics* (Pergamon Press) offers this explanation of the "functional theory of language": "Systemic, or Systemic-Functional, theory has its origins in the main intellectual tradition of European linguistics that developed following the work of Saussure. Like other such theories, both those from the mid-20th century (e.g. Prague school, French functionalism) and more recent work in the same tradition (e.g. that of Hagège), it is functional and semantic rather than formal and syntactic in orientation, takes the text rather than the sentence as its object, and defines its scope by reference to usage rather than grammaticality. Its primary source was the work of J.R. Firth and his colleagues in London; as well as other schools of thought in Europe such as glossematics it also draws on American anthropological linguistics, and on traditional and modern linguistics as developed in China." In brief, this theory locates the proper object of linguistic study as what language *does* and how language works — in context, in the real — rather than on theoretical models of abstract possible behavior.

[15]The ideological baggage which is carried by texts such as *Gone with the Wind* when taught in an American context — not just the existence of slavery, but racial, class and gender stereotyping, historical mythologizing, et al. — is elided here. This elision, and the invisibility of such issues to many foreign readers of "classic" American texts, is a sub-theme inextricably tied to the use of textual materials in "other" cultures. Ultimately, the collaborative nature of the present essay is itself an exploration of the interaction of high(er)- and low(er)- context cultures. The discursive and explanatory structures of the lead author — a pedagogical specialist operating within Ukrainian social sciences — needed to meld with the comparative literary expertise of her American co-author. The process has been one that would lend itself to a pragmatic analysis of the cross-cultural *aporia* inherent in any "transfer" of cultural information: the co-authors collaborated across the boundaries of language, culture and discipline.

[16]See notes 4 and 7, above.

REFERENCES

Adler, N. (1997). *International dimensions of organizational behavior.* Cincinnati, Ohio: South-Western College Publishing.

Allwood, A. (1990). On the role of cultural content and cultural context in language instruction. *Gothenburg Papers in Theoretical Linguistics, 60*, University of Götheborg, Dept. of Linguistics, 1-11.

Anthony, R. (1993). Euro Disney: The first 100 days. Unpublished case study prepared for Harvard Business School.

Asante, M., & Gudykunst, W. (Eds.). (1989). *Handbook of international and intercultural communication.* London: Sage Publications.

Bain, B. (Ed.). (1983) *The sociogenesis of language and human conduct.* New York and London: Plenum Press.

Burke, D. (1993). *Biz talk-1: American business jargon.* Optima Books.

Canale, M., & Swain, M. (1980). Theoretical bases of communicative approach to second language teaching and testing. *Applied Linguistics, 1*, 1-47.

Carter, R., & Long, M. (1991). *Teaching literature.* New York: Longman Press.

Clyne, M. (1994). *Intercultural communication at work: Cultural values in discourse.* Cambridge University Press.

Conquest, R. (1987). *Harvest of Sorrow: Soviet Collectivization and Terror-Famine.* Cambridge: Oxford University Press.

Dalton, M. (2000). *Culture shock! Ukraine*. Portland, Ore.: Graphic Arts Center Publishing.

Dodd, C. (1985). *Dynamics of intercultural communication.* Brown & Benchmark.

Fink, G. (2002). *Intercultural knowledge research and intercultural knowledge management (InterKnow).* Research Institute for European Affairs.

Galloway, V. (1998). Constructing cultural realities: "Facts" and frameworks of association. In *The coming age of the profession: Issues and emerging ideas for the teaching of foreign languages* (129-140). Heinle & Heinle Publishers.

Gerlach, J. (Ed.). (1999, September). International English (teaching English in the Ukraine). *English Journal, 89*, 125-28.

Gesteland, R. (1996). *Cross-cultural business behavior: Marketing, negotiating and managing across cultures.* Copenhagen Business School Press.

Gudykunst, W., & Kim, Y (1984). *Communicating with strangers: An approach to intercultural communication.* New York: Random House.

Gudykunst, W., Matsumoto, Y., Ting-Loomey, S., et. al. (1996, June). The influence of cultural individualism-collectivism, self construals, and individual values on communication styles across cultures." *Human Communications Research, 22,* 510-543.

Hall, E. (1976). *Beyond culture.* New York: Anchor Books.

Hofstede, G. (1994). *Cultures and organizations: Software of the mind.* London: Harper Collins.

Hunt, D. (1986). *The Dolphin Reader.* Houghton Mifflin.

I.A.T.E.F.L.-Ukraine Newsletter 2003. British Council. Kyiv.

Jolly, A., & Kettanch, N. (1998). *Doing business in Ukraine.* London: Kogan Page.

Keesing, R. (1974). Theories of culture. *Annual Review of Anthropology, 3*, 73-97.

Kramsch, C. (1991). Culture in language learning: A view from the United States." *Foreign Language Research in Cross-Cultural Perspectives* (217-239). Amsterdam & Philadelphia: John Benjamin Publishing.

Lasonen, J. (2003, June 15-18). U.N.E.S.C.O. Conference of Intercultural Education: Teaching and Learning for Intercultural Understanding, Human Rights and a Culture of Peace. Opening Address.

Lemke, J. (1995). *Textual politics: discourse and social dynamics (critical perspectives on literacy and education).* London: Francis & Taylor.

Lesikar, J., Petit, J. Jr., & Flatley, M. (1996). *Basic business communication.* McGraw Hill.

Locker, K. (1995). *Business and administrative communication.* Chicago: Irwin Press.

Martinich, A. (Ed.). (1990). *The philosophy of language.* New York & Oxford: Oxford University Press.

McArthur, T (Ed.). (2002). *Oxford guide to world English.* Cambridge: Oxford University Press.

Mole, J. (1991). When in Rome... a business guide to culture and customs in 12 European nations. Amacon, American Management Association.

Nimgade, A. (1989). American management as viewed by international professionals. *Business Horizons,* November-December, 293-300.

Pearce, R., & Robinson, R. (1994). *Cases in strategic management.* New York: McGraw Hill.

Pinker, S., (1994). *The Language Instinct.* William Morrow.

Robinson, G. (1991). Second language acquisition, linguistics and language pedagogy: The state of the art. *Proceedings of the Georgetown roundtable on languages & linguistics* (114-122). Washington, D.C.: Georgetown University Press.

Rusterholtz, B. (1987). Reading strategies for the business foreign class." *Foreign Language Annals, 20*, 427-433.

Scollon, R., & Wong Scollon, S. (1995). *Intercultural communication: A discourse approach.* Cambridge: Blackwell Publishers.

Semenova, D. (2000). Résumés as a genre: Crossing cultural boundaries. *Materials of A.A.A.L.-2000: Crossing the Boundaries*. Vancouver, Canada.

Stromberg, S. (1994). *European intellectual history since 1789* (6th ed., rev.). Englewood Cliffs, New Jersey: Prentice Hall.

Swiderski, R. (1993). *Teaching language, learning culture*. Westport, Conn.: Bergin & Garvey.

Thiederman, S. (1991). *Profiting in America's multicultural marketplace: How to do business across cultural lines*. New York: Lexington Books.

Trompenaars, F. (1993). *Riding the waves of culture: Understanding cultural diversity in business*. London: Economist Books.

Victor, D. (1992). *Intercultural business communication*. New York: Harper Collins.

Voght, G. (1999). New paradigms for U.S. higher education in the 21st century. Keynote address at the 17th Annual Conference on Languages and Communication for World Business and Professions. Ypsilanti: Eastern Michigan University.

Wierzbicka, A. (1999). *Emotions across languages and cultures: Diversity and universals*. Cambridge University Press.

Wood, A. (1998). Negotiating literature in the business French class." In S. Loughrin-Sacco & J. Arbate (Eds.), *Making business French work: Models, materials, methodologies* (161-186). S..D.S.U. C.I.B.E.R. Press. San Diego University Press.

Chapter 9

Case-Based Teaching in Business Education in the Arab Middle East and North Africa

Kate Gillespie
University of Texas, Austin

Liesl Riddle
George Washington University

INTRODUCTION

Managers in today's Arab Middle East and North Africa region (M.E.N.A.)[1] face a business environment that is dramatically different from the recent past (Al-Shamali and Denton, 2000). These changes have not generated an increase in economic prosperity in the region. Although in the 1970s most M.E.N.A. countries benefited from increased oil prices and substantial inflows of worker remittances, trade, and capital, in the latter part of the twentieth century, the economic condition of the region deteriorated. During the 1990s, M.E.N.A. average annual G.N.P. growth was a mere 1.3 percent — compared to an annual average of four percent for all developing countries (Abed and Davoodi, 2003). Trade liberalization has not generated substantial increased employment opportunities in the region (Dasgupta, Nabli, Pissarides, and Varoudakis, 2003), and labor productivity has gradually declined since the 1990s (Gardner, 2003).

Middle East business leaders often complain that the M.E.N.A. workforce is ill-prepared for today's business environment. Many have called for educational reform because of an overemphasis on rote learning and memorization pedagogy common throughout all levels of education in the region (Rugh 2002). Educational reform has moved slowly in M.E.N.A. countries (UNESCO, 2002). Rugh notes that at a 2002 international conference on Arab higher education "a leading Arab businessman stated that the Middle East would not achieve its full economic potential 'unless we revolutionize our educational system and adopt a total change in our mindset'" (2002, 406-407). A recent World Bank report on Arab education argues that this educational revolution must "impart skills enabling workers to be flexible, to analyze problems, and to synthesize information gained in different contexts" (World Bank, 1998, 18). This sentiment also has been echoed by educational academics (e.g., Cassidy, 2003).

We argue that the case method can provide students with an opportunity to exercise problem-solving and decision-making skills, which are crucial to coping with the changing business environment that M.E.N.A. managers face. But how should the case method be used in the M.E.N.A. classroom? Specifically, how well suited is the case method to the M.E.N.A. classroom experience? What case resources are available for business education in M.E.N.A. countries? What are the obstacles for developing cases in the region? We address each of these issues in turn in this paper.

SUITABILITY OF THE CASE METHOD FOR THE MENA CONTEXT

As institutions, educational entities are embedded in the local cultural context. They are both affected by and affect change within local culture. To be effective, pedagogy must have a connection with local cultural values and norms. How suitable, then, is case-based teaching for the M.E.N.A. classroom?

In business education, the case method is employed to develop and hone students' analytical skills. A business case is a description of a real business situation including a particular set of problems where the protagonist is most commonly a manager (Shapiro, 1984). In the case method, students are called upon to analyze the situation and decide on a plan of action. The case study acts as a vehicle to practice analytical skills as well as a base from which to generalize managerial lessons. The case method is experiential learning in which students are encouraged to learn from semi-structured experiences. While utilizing a common core of generally validated concepts, students construct individual interpretations of the case (Bonoma, 1989), thus resulting in the oft-mentioned lack of "right" answers to case studies.

The seminal work on the case method was written by Charles Gragg and published by the *Harvard Alumni Bulletin* in 1940. Entitled "Because Wisdom Can't be Told," this essay is available today as a note through Harvard Business School Publishing (H.B.S., 9-451-005). Gragg argues that the case method opens "the way for students to make positive contributions to thought ... and to prepare themselves for action" (1940, 1). To Gragg, the case method generates "democracy in the classroom" since "no longer is the situation that of teacher on the one hand and a body of students on the other" (1940, 5). Gragg also notes that students learning via the case method pass through discernible phases.

> The second phase is that of *accepting easily and without fear the need for cooperative help*. . . . The third and final phase toward

> maturity . . . [is] *the recognition that the instructors do not always or necessarily know the "best" answers*, and, even when they do seem to know them, *that each student is free to present and hold to his own views* (1940, 5).

The statements above suggest several potential flashpoints when bringing case learning to M.E.N.A. countries. Roles and norms in the M.E.N.A. classroom differ from their Western counterparts. In M.E.N.A. countries

> the classroom is basically controlled by the teacher, who as a rule lectures constantly to the students. The students are to copy, memorize, and when asked, recite these lectures ... This style of classroom instruction does not leave much room for creativity or for problem-solving behavior on the part of students (Massialas and Jarrar, 1991, 34).

Rote learning and memorization exercises are the primary pedagogy employed throughout the educational system — including tertiary education — in the M.E.N.A. region (U.N.E.S.C.O., 2002). There is little emphasis placed on higher-order cognitive skills such as flexibility, problem solving, theory application, and decision-making (World Bank, 1998). Large class sizes and overcrowding make teacher-student and peer-to-peer interaction often impossible (Rugh, 2002; Cassidy, 2003). Interaction is further constrained by hierarchy norms, impeding not only teacher-student interaction but also peer-to-peer interaction (Massialas and Jarrar, 1991).

The case method puts the student front and center. This upsets the hierarchal education system described above where instructors profess and students listen subserviently. A look at the Hofstede measures of culture for Arab countries (scores for separate countries are not available) suggests that M.E.N.A. society reinforces this style of learning (1980). Arab countries are hierarchal, scoring 80 (versus 40 in the United States) on power distance, the degree to which unequal power distribution in society is expected and accepted. Arab countries also score 68 on uncertainty avoidance versus only 46 in the United States. Teachers in uncertainty-avoidant cultures are expected always to have the answers. Uncertainty-avoidant cultures do not like ambiguity; events should be clearly understandable and predictable. So the problem is not just that the instructor does not have the correct answer, but that there is no correct answer.

The collectivist nature of Arab culture also poses other difficulties for the case method. Arab countries score 38 on the Hofstede measure of individualism (the opposite of collectivism) versus 91 for the United States. Collectivism reflects the degree to which individuals are integrated into strong, cohesive in-groups. Case studies require that students assume the role of the manager protagonist — to get inside the skin of the person facing the decision. This is arguably easier for students from the United States, where recreating oneself is a national pastime. But individuals from collectivist cultures, which are characterized by their worldview of in-groups and out-groups, may find it more difficult to play this role unless the protagonist closely resembles members of the student's in-group. Otherwise, they may continue to look in from the outside, mere observers of the protagonist and the situation he or she faces. This would inhibit the nature of the learning experience which is the goal of case experiential learning, one that Bonoma describes as "powerful, intimate, and personal" (1989, 3). Collectivism may also present a challenge to the ability of students to learn from one another — if the others are not from one's in-group. Trust is not easily given to outsiders in collectivist societies. Will students listen to and learn from other students if they inherently distrust them?

A final obstacle to the case method in the M.E.N.A. region may lie in its democratic vision. Some have argued that Arab states may be reticent to pursue radical changes to existing education curriculum and pedagogy since educational institutions often historically have been hotbeds of revolutionary activity (Mojab, 2000). In case learning, critical thinking is hard to contain. Will all Arab leaders truly welcome learning environments that encourage students to act as *"adult members of a democratic community?"* Bernard Lewis contends that the spread of education in the Middle East today imposes limits on the autocracy of rulers (2002). Azar Nafisi's autobiographical novel, *Reading Lolita in Tehran* (2003), chronicles the contentious relationship between an autocratic government and its university students in neighboring Iran — an antagonism that has even resulted in government forces firing on students. Nafasi reflects upon how even the study of literature — another form of experiential learning — threatened this totalitarian regime. In the past, revolutions have either begun in university classrooms or have received their momentum there. A number of current regimes attempt to be sure new revolutions receive no such nurturing. To this end, large lecture classes with enrollments in the many hundreds would suit their agenda.

Of course, the problems outlined above are also the promise of the case method. It encourages students to practice analytical thought, to take charge of their own thinking, and to include others beyond their in-group in the task of solving problems. Not only do managers in a global world require these skills, but these skills are also necessary to foster a strong civil society in the M.E.N.A. region.

American-style education remains immensely popular in the M.E.N.A. region. But most consumers and would-be consumers of American education remain uninformed as to what it actually entails. Commenting on the new American schools proliferating in the M.E.N.A. region, John Waterbury notes that many in the region "may have little real knowledge of what American higher education is all about ... This audience ... recognizes English as the key to technology and business ... and their ... ladder to success. They do not know much or care about the real keys to this success

— flexibility and choice, critical thinking and problem solving, [and] academic freedom ..." (2003, 65-66).

USING CASES IN BUSINESS COURSES IN THE MENA REGION

The case method places students in the role of a business decision-maker. Business cases force students to develop analytic and problem-solving skills to navigate the uncertain waters of the problems posed in the case scenario. This experience can be valuable for M.E.N.A. managers, but the implementation of the case method may need to be amended to leverage the full benefits of the technique in the M.E.N.A. environment.

Because the case method strongly differs from the educational experience of M.E.N.A. students, instructors wishing to utilize the case method in their classrooms must recognize that students will need to be socialized into the norms of the case-based learning experience. In situations where the case method will be employed throughout a university's curriculum, university and program administrators also may be involved in the socialization process. Expectations for teachers and students regarding preparation and roles during case discussions should be clearly communicated and explained to students. Offering students a "dry run" with the method, such as allowing students to sit in on a class employing the case method, watching a video of a case-method class discussion, or executing a small, quick, initial in-class case discussion, will demonstrate the roles and norms related to the case method. Some institutions may find it helpful to offer mini-courses on case analysis and discussion, making case preparation techniques, teacher-student roles during case discussions, in-class note taking during case discussions, and other case-related activities explicit and transparent to students.

Successful use of the case method in the M.E.N.A. classroom may require a reduction in the number of students in each class. Increasing the homogeneity of participants (particularly in terms of gender and age) also may decrease the discussion-inhibiting effects of power distance and hierarchy. This may be particularly important for executive-level education, where classrooms may contain a wide array of management status levels, from first-tier management to C.E.O.s. In situations where such class homogeneity is impossible, it may be advisable to first place students in small homogeneous teams to discuss various aspects about the case then share their conclusions with the broader group, beginning first with the lower-status groups.

Still, how to address issues of collectivism during case discussions is problematic. Arguably, collectivist mindsets could pose obstacles in the case classroom. Collectivism is associated with a strong adherence to established group norms or views and is a cultural aspect associated with M.E.N.A. economies. One might conclude that students in a collectivist culture would work well in groups, accepting easily and without fear the need of cooperative help. But one must wonder when Gragg noted his observations (1940) if he was not envisaging that working together was to the end of discovering a new idea, a new truth — and not working together to restrict individual thought and to enforce established ideas and behaviors. Furthermore, the cooperative help that Gragg alludes to is a reflection of an individualistic society in which persons with no prior relationship come together to get a job done, a phenomenon that Fukuyama calls "spontaneous sociability" (1995). Collectivist societies lack this spontaneous sociability. Group membership is not self-defined but is pre-defined by the society. The distrust of the outsider found in collectivist societies may prove to be a formidable challenge in a global economy where interacting with and trusting outsiders is unavoidable.

MENA CASE RESOURCES

Instructors in M.E.N.A. countries choosing to incorporate cases into their curriculum have two options: utilizing existing, published cases or researching and developing their own.

Utilizing Existing Cases

With a few exceptions, business texts used in M.E.N.A. university classes are primarily mere translations of American textbooks; little local content is incorporated in terms of examples or theory (Ali and Camp, 1995). The suitability of these materials for the M.E.N.A. context has been questioned, as critics cite a disconnect between the cultural and economic environment of the United States and the M.E.N.A. region (Ali and Camp, 1995; Rugh, 2002). For reasons outlined below, few cases have been written in Arabic.

Even when classes are taught in English, business cases written in English but dealing with the Arab World are difficult to find. A search of case offerings on Harvard Business School Online for Educators reveals only 12 cases focusing on the Arab World. In comparison, a similar search revealed 11 cases for Turkey alone. A word search on the site returned 78 hits for Mexico, 40 for Brazil, 35 for Argentina, 33 for Taiwan, 21 for Thailand, and even 42 for Russia. Of the 12 cases focusing on the Arab World, only seven involve Arab protagonists — and of these, three are Arabs who have returned to their homelands after sojourns in the West. A relative spurt in case writing (seven cases) appears between 1995 and 1999, with only four cases written in the 2000-2003 period.

This poses a problem as to case materials that are appropriate to the Arab World. An argument could be made that emerging markets have issues in common, and instructors could use cases from these other countries in classes for Arab participants. However, clear differences in culture and history are apparent when cases outside the Arab World are examined. Management scholars have observed that the Arab cultural milieu gives rise to management values and behaviors that are different than in other parts of the world (e.g., Hofstede, 1980; Weir, 2002). The few available cases based on Arab cultural settings provide limited opportunity for students to examine the impact of these managerial practices on business activities.

Developing New Cases

Ali and Camp suggest that developing local cases in Arab countries accomplishes two purposes: it "sensitize[s] students to the reality of management in the Arab environment and sensitize[s] students to the cultural relativity of foreign management theories" (1995, 15). Recently, an Internet survey of members of the Academy of International Business and the Middle East Studies Association, who have conducted qualitative data collection in the M.E.N.A. region on business-, economic-, or trade-related topics, was administered to investigate their research experiences in M.E.N.A. countries.[2] Follow-up interviews were also conducted with several sample volunteers. Study results reveal three major challenges to qualitative data collection in the M.E.N.A. region that could affect casewriters' efforts as well as explain why there are so few extant cases from this region. These challenges comprise government involvement in the research process, respondent reticence to participate in research, and the impact of local culture on data-collection activities.

Government Involvement

Many cases written on firms in emerging economies have been written by academics at the Western business schools that value and employ the case-study method. However, unlike most governments in Asia, Eastern Europe, or Latin America, governments in the Arab World are often hostile to outside researchers. When queried by an open-ended question about the distinctive characteristics of the M.E.N.A. research environment, about one-fifth of survey respondents (21 percent) cited government involvement as an important characteristic. Included in these responses were phrases such as "political constraints" on the researcher (three mentions), necessary "research visas" (two mentions), and "registration requirements" (one mention). One-third of the survey respondents mentioned that government involvement was the greatest obstacle that they had personally faced while collecting data in the M.E.N.A. region. Ten survey respondents (42 percent) claimed to have sought formal permission from a M.E.N.A. government authority before commencing a research project.

In some M.E.N.A. countries, foreign researchers are compelled to acquire a specific research visa. In many countries, casewriters staying beyond the duration of a tourist or business visa — which can be as short as 15 days or as long as four months — may have to submit a description of his/her research project in order to acquire a residence permit. In others, a local sponsor (e.g., Saudi Arabia) or a letter of invitation (e.g., Yemen) must be presented to a government authority before a visa (tourist or business) will be granted to the researcher. Sponsors and those offering letters of invitation to research visitors often are held accountable for researchers' actions and therefore may seek official government approval for the researcher's project before the visa is granted. Casewriters may need to apply for research permission from a country's Ministry of Education or some other agency before beginning a research project.

In some cases, governments may restrict the data collection methods that the casewriter (particularly foreign casewriters) may employ. For example, one survey respondent explained that the Egyptian Ministry of Education had told him that he could "only use archival materials or interview government officials" as he conducted research in Egypt, but he was specifically "forbidden from conducting fieldwork."

Some countries may not have a formal process by which researchers seek government permission for their activities, but government approval — or at least awareness of the researcher and his/her project — may still be necessary and sought on an informal basis. Informal permission may be necessary for both foreign and local researchers. One interview respondent told a story of what happened when she failed to seek informal government approval in Jordan, a country that does not formally require researchers seek data collection permission. After a couple of weeks of conducting in-depth interviews, she was intercepted on the street by the *muhabbarat*, the secret police, prevalent in many M.E.N.A. countries, and was interviewed for several days about her research. Several times during the inquisition, the researcher was asked "for proof that [she] had acquired formal permission from government authorities to conduct [her] research project." They could not accept that she had proceeded with the project without receiving some type of approval to conduct the interviews.

Without government approval, researchers may be more prone to research material sabotage or confiscation by local security, particularly if the research topic is of a politically or economically sensitive nature. For example, one in-depth interview respondent who conducts research in the West Bank and Gaza Strip claimed that "it is absolute hell getting in and out of the airport in Israel [for me]. Everything is taken out. They go through my notes, my computer. My computer has been deliberately broken. Sometimes stuff just disappears." Another in-depth interview participant told a story of how a box of her data (interview transcripts, notes, etc.) was taken by Yemeni authorities at the airport as she prepared to leave the country. Months later the box was returned to her U.S. residence. In it she found copies of her original materials (the originals were never returned) along with duplicates of some materials belonging to other researchers.

Government involvement in researchers' activities may extend beyond up-front approval. M.E.N.A. governments also may monitor researchers' activities. Seventeen percent of the survey respondents mentioned government surveillance as the greatest obstacle that they faced when conducting research in M.E.N.A. countries. One of the survey respondents claimed, "I was aware that they were monitoring my activities and probably tapping my phone." Another described how "the government checked up" on her informants. In some countries, such as Yemen, researchers are assigned an official "mentor" to, as one in-depth respondent put it, "keep an eye on what they are doing." Some mentors have been known to keep track of a researcher's publications after they have left the field. One in-depth interview respondent mentioned that her mentor had attended a presentation she made at an academic conference in the United States.

Difficulties related to possible government involvement in the case-writing process may be alleviated by the use of a local co-author. Local co-authors may not be subject to the same level of scrutiny as outsiders, and they may have personal contacts within the government and the business community that may be useful. Most importantly, local co-authors provide keen insight into the cultural, economic, political, and legal environment in M.E.N.A. countries. It may be difficult to identify local co-authors with interest and/or experience in case writing. Rugh has noted that faculty research production in Arab universities is low because faculty are "hampered by top-down bureaucracies" or have left the Arab World for "more conducive research environments" (2002, 410). Business academics often must supplement low salaries with consulting. While this consulting can lead to possible case leads, the remuneration for case writing is essentially non-existent; as such research seldom is required by Arab universities and rarely results in higher pay.

Reticence to Participate in Research

Bonoma suggests three reasons why companies/managers cooperate in the creation of real-life case studies (1989). Managers can gain insight into their situation from the casewriter, who, like a consultant, has experience with similar situations in other firms. Managers may feel a debt to the process of management education. Finally, they can observe intelligent students engaging in a discussion of their company and its issues, consequently providing new insights.

However, 21 percent of the scholars surveyed cited the reluctance of potential respondents to participate in research as a defining characteristic of the M.E.N.A. research environment. Three respondents stated that it is often difficult to gain "accessibility to individuals." Two others commented that they often observe a reticence to participate in research in M.E.N.A. societies because they "fear how the research will be used" and are "not willing to be interviewed."

Three of the in-depth interview respondents mentioned that foreign researchers in M.E.N.A. countries are often assumed to be undercover spies. "You get used to it," explained one respondent. "After a while, once people get to know you, these accusations tend to go away." But in her dissertation about the Egyptian tourism industry, Lisa Wynn relates that this suspicion may not fully dissipate over time:

> My [Egyptian] friends joked about [me being a spy] often, and once, finally, I asked a close friend if he really thought I was working for the CIA. "Look," he said, "I don't really think that you are, but I don't know for sure. Let's say I think there's a 90 percent chance that you're not working for the CIA. But there's still that 10 percent chance that you are, so I would be a fool not to keep it in mind. But even if you're not actually working for them, your research will still be used by the CIA and other U.S. government organizations to compile information on Egypt. (2003, 27)

Uncertainty about the researcher's intent and how collected data will be used means that when people in M.E.N.A. countries participate in a research study, they often are very careful with what they say. Dealing with participant self-censorship and fear was mentioned by one-fourth of the survey respondents as the greatest obstacle that they had faced while in the field in a M.E.N.A. country. Researchers complain of an "absence of free flow of information," a "fear to give a judgment that might be used against them," and a "reluctance of participants to comment on relevant issues." In some cases, the stakes of participation may be very high for individuals, particularly in M.E.N.A. political contexts where government control and monitoring are strong, and the nature of the research questions is politically sensitive. In such cases, protecting the anonymity of sources assumes paramount importance for researchers in M.E.N.A. countries. One in-depth interview respondent explained, "you have to remember that you are going into an area where people are at risk ... people will put themselves at risk to help you. But you don't want to put your sources at risk."

In addition, managers in the M.E.N.A. region often believe that knowledge is market power and are likely to be reluctant to share company information with the casewriter, especially if it contains any information useful to a competitor. Most business are not publicly owned, and giving anyone (including investors) information is an alien concept. Business owners and executives also may be wary of information that could be used against them by either the government or the press. While the option of disguising the case exists, in these markets where everybody knows everybody else, it can be difficult to disguise a case adequately. Furthermore, appealing to managers to support case education may not fall on sympathetic ears. In Arab hierarchal societies, managers may not enjoy the thought of students discussing — and criticizing — their actions.

Impact of Culture on Data Collection Activities

Thirty-three percent of respondents mentioned "cultural differences," "need for cultural sensitivity," or "cultural issues" as distinctive characteristics of data collection in M.E.N.A. countries. As noted above, cross-cultural studies of management values and practice have sought to isolate the key cultural characteristics of the M.E.N.A. region, and several studies have observed a marked dissimilarity between the M.E.N.A. region and the West, particularly in terms of individualism/collectivism and power distance (e.g., Hofstede, 1980; Kabasakal and Bodur, 2002). Although researchers' nationality was not oollected in the Internet survey of scholars with M.E.N.A. data-collection experience, the majority of the sampling frame — members of the Academy of International Business and the Middle East Studies Association of North America — originate from Western countries and/or have been socialized by Western educational institutions. Most of the survey and interview respondents' comments regarding the role of culture in the data-collection process focus on the ways in which high collectivism and high power distance affect data-collection activities.

Forty percent of the survey respondents mentioned "introductions" or "networking" as essential for access to respondents and gaining detailed and valid responses from them. In-depth interview discussions reveal that in M.E.N.A. countries, introduction by merely a single individual is often insufficient to establish initial trust. One interview respondent explained, "your contact just gets you in the door. The first meeting usually consists of informal conversation about this-and-that, but all the while they are name-dropping, and you are expected to name-drop. This is where you set the context of who you are." Another respondent, commenting on the distinctive character of data collection in the M.E.N.A. region mentioned, "most of this [research] centers on the personal aspects, knowing the researcher, and how well-known the researcher is."

Once embedded in a network and identified as such, a casewriter may discover that his/her social network may actually restrict his /her access and ability to acquire detailed and valid data. An interview respondent observed that

> The elites [in the M.E.N.A. region] have known each other since childhood. They see themselves as related. There are multiple networks. If you get too closely related to the group, you get branded as 'you belong to them.' Networks can cut both ways.

The M.E.N.A. collectivist and power-distance worldview can affect how individuals within the firm participate in conversation and who within the firm is willing to talk to the casewriter. Case writing rarely involves interviewing only one person. Instead, many individuals in a firm are contacted to develop a larger corporate memory of an event and to receive input from a variety of persons involved. In the M.E.N.A. context, however, it is not uncommon for a request to speak to others to be dismissed by the higher manager. Talking to others would suggest that the higher manager could be wrong – or at best not omniscient. This can be difficult to accept in M.E.N.A. culture. For example, during a reported focus group of several M.E.N.A. industrialists, participants typically waited for the powerfully connected individual to speak first and then agreed with whatever he had to say. If called upon to speak before the powerfully connected person, weaker connected people demonstrated their discomfort non-verbally, looking to the more powerfully connected person and offering a non-committal answer.

There are several steps that a casewriter can take to minimize the obstacles involved in data collection in M.E.N.A. countries. First, casewriters should investigate the formal and informal government approvals that may be needed in the country they intend to visit. Whereas embassies and consulate offices may provide information about any required formal approvals for foreign researchers, casewriters may need to consult the advice of colleagues with data-collection experience in their country of interest to learn about requisite — or suggested — informal approvals. In some cases, foreign researchers with data-collection experience in the country may be better sources of this information than local researchers because local academics may be unfamiliar with the government's perspective and procedures related to foreign research.

Before leaving for the field, casewriters should develop a familiarity of local journalism in the country of interest. Analysis of news reports — and the company, family, and individual names mentioned within them — may provide the casewriter with a better understanding of power and hierarchy within the society. In most M.E.N.A. countries some — if not all — national newspapers are owned and operated by the state. Positive or negative portrayals of firms and/or individuals within state-owned newspapers may reveal information about business-government relations within the country.

Casewriters seeking to conduct research in M.E.N.A. countries should recognize the importance of developing a large and diverse social network comprised of individuals with strong ties to the region. Fellow academics are a good place to begin. Although there are few members in the Academy of International Business with research interests in the Middle East and North

Africa (37 researchers listed in the A.I.B. database specifying M.E.N.A. as a geographic specialty), many social scientists, including anthropologists, economists, political scientists, and sociologists, conduct research related to business, industry, and/or trade in the M.E.N.A. region and may be extremely valuable contacts. Many are members of the Middle East Studies Association. While in the field, some casewriters may choose to visit one of the six American Overseas Research Centers in the M.E.N.A. region (Egypt, Jordan, Morocco, Tunisia, West Bank, or Yemen). These non-governmental institutions can be good places to meet fellow foreign academics engaged in field research in the region. Western-trained business academics, firm or N.G.O. managers, and government officials also are useful resources since many may be familiar with the case-study method. M.E.N.A. students, particularly executive M.B.A. students, may also serve to be helpful social network contacts.

Local casewriting should also be encouraged in the region. M.E.N.A. academics and/or businesspeople may find that co-authoring with experienced casewriters may help to shorten the case-writing learning curve. Arab business schools that aspire to be elite should take the initiative to write cases. In some situations, powerful business supporters could provide funding to support this initiative. Local M.B.A. programs, particularly those that are executive-oriented, should make case researching and writing an integral part of their curriculum. Some programs may offer awards or some other form of recognition for quality case publications.

CONCLUSION

Instructors seeking to utilize cases in M.E.N.A. educational institutions should be aware of how differences in M.E.N.A. culture and classroom norms might impact case-based learning in this region. In particular, high collectivism, uncertainty avoidance, and power distance associated with the M.E.N.A. cultural milieu give rise to a learning environment that is divergent from the Western classroom context, where the case method was born and developed. Case method socialization and classroom-composition or process adaptations may be necessary to better fit the case method to local cultural values and norms.

There is tremendous opportunity to contribute to a greater understanding of M.E.N.A. management challenges by adding to the small, existing corpus of available M.E.N.A. business cases. Casewriters face several challenges when conducting research in M.E.N.A. countries, including government intervention, respondent reticence to participate in research, and cultural adaptations in the data-collection process. But these obstacles can be mitigated by sufficient and careful casewriter preparation.

There is a need for case-based business education in the M.E.N.A. region. The case method simulates the real-world business environment, placing students in the position of the managerial decision-maker. Case-based learning experiences can help prepare M.E.N.A. students for the challenges that await them in a global economy, enabling them to better navigate uncertainty by employing analytic and problem-solving skills to seek solutions to complicated business problems.

NOTES

[1]Here we employ the term Middle East and North Africa (M.E.N.A.) region as it is referred to by the International Monetary Fund: the Arab states of Algeria, Bahrain, Djibouti, Egypt, Iraq, Jordan, Kuwait, Lebanon, Libya, Mauritania, Morocco, Oman, Qatar, and Saudi Arabia.
[2]The sample frame consisted of two components. First, the email addresses of scholars listed in the Academy of International Business' (A.I.B.) membership directory with the research field "Country/Area study: Africa and Middle East" were included in the sampling frame. A total of 37 A.I.B. members were associated with this research field. The 315 social scientists with email addresses listed in the Middle East Studies Association's membership directory were also included. Filter quests were employed in the survey to identify respondents who had collected data concerning business-, economic-, and/or trade-related issues in M.E.N.A. countries. Surveys were mailed to the 324 addresses on January 28, 2003, and a reminder email was sent two weeks later. Fifty-three total responses were received (19 percent response rate). Twenty-four surveys were returned from researchers with qualitative data collection experience in M.E.N.A. countries on business, economic, and/or trade issues. Since most case-based research requires the use of in-depth interviews, observation, focus-groups, and other qualitative methods, the results described in this paper reflect the responses of these 24 scholars.

REFERENCES

Abed, George T. & Davoodi, Hamid R. (2003). *Challenges of growth and globalization in the Middle East and North Africa.* Washington, DC: International Monetary Fund.

Al-Shamali, A. & Denton, J. (Eds.) (2000). *Arab business: the globalization imperative.* Bristol, England: Kogan Page.

Ali, A. J. & Camp, R. C. (1995). Teaching management in the Arab world: confronting illusions. *International Journal of Educational Management, 9*(2), 10-17.

Bonoma, T. V. (1989). *Learning with cases.* Note 9-589-080, Cambridge, MA: Harvard Business School Publishing.

Cassidy, T. J. (2003). Education in the Arab States: preparing to compete in the global economy. In Klaus Schwab & Peter Cornelius (Eds.), *The Arab World competitiveness report* (pp. 218-234). Geneva: World Economic Forum.

Dasgupta, D.; Nabli, M. K.; Pissarides, C.; & Varoudakis, A. (2002). *Making trade work for jobs: international evidence and lessons for MENA.* Washington DC: The World Bank.

Fukuyama, F. (1995). *Trust: The social virtues and the creation of prosperity.* New York: Free Press.

Gardner, E. (2003). *Creating employment in the Middle East and North Africa.* Washington, DC: The International Monetary Fund.

Gragg, C. I. (1940.) Because wisdom can't be told. *Harvard Alumni Bulletin*, October 19. Reprinted as Note 9-451-005, Cambridge, MA: Harvard Business School Publishing.

Hofstede, G. (1980). *Cultures and organizations: software of the mind*. NY: McGraw-Hill.

Hunt, D. M., & At-Twaijri, M. I. (1996). Values and the Saudi manager: an empirical investigation. *The Journal of Management Development, 15*(5), 48-55.

Kabasakal, H. & Bodur, M. (2002). Arabic cluster: a bridge between East and West. *Journal of World Business, 105*, 1-25.

Lewis, B. (2002). *What went wrong*? Oxford, England: Oxford University Press.

Massialas, B. G. & Jarrar, S. A. (1991). *Arab education in transition: a source book*. NY: Garland Publishing.

Mojab, S. (2000). Adult education in the Middle East: etatism, patriarchy, and civil society. *Convergence, 33*(3), 9-15.

Nafisi, A. (2003). *Reading Lolita in Tehran*. NY: Random House.

Rugh, W. A. (2002). Arab education: tradition, growth, and reform. *The Middle East Journal, 56*(3), 396-414.

Shapiro, B. P. (1984). *An introduction to cases*. Note 9-584-097. Cambridge, MA: Harvard Business School Publishing.

U.N.E.S.C.O. (2002). *Arab states: regional report*. Montreal, Canada: U.N.E.S.C.O. Institute for Statistics.

Waterbury, J. (2003). Hate your policies, love your institutions. *Foreign Affairs, 82*(1), 58-68.

Weir, D. (2002) Management in the Arab world: a fourth paradigm? In Ali Al-Shamali and John Denton (Eds.). *Arab Business: the globalization imperative*. Bristol, England: Kogan Page.

World Bank. (1998). *Education in the Middle East and North Africa: a strategy towards learning for development*, Washington DC: The World Bank.

Wynn, L. (2003). From the pyramids to pyramid road: an ethnography of the idea of Egypt. (Doctoral dissertation, University of Michigan, 2003). *Dissertation Abstracts International* (UMI No. 3078644).

Chapter 10

Graduate Certificate for Students with Undergraduate Degrees from Foreign Universities: Implications for Students and Schools in Emerging Markets

C. McInnis-Bowers
Rollins College

E. Byron Chew
Birmingham-Southern College

Michael R. Bowers
Rollins College

INTRODUCTION

A challenge for management education is to prepare business practitioners to succeed in the global marketplace (A.A.C.S.B., 2003; Shetty and Rudell, 2002; Porter and McKibbin, 1988). Curricular buzz words -- "think globally," "value diversity," "cross-cultural perspectives," and the like -- have been readily written into text books and course syllabi to denote the international context of current business education. If reading and thinking about international and cross cultural contexts were successful pedagogological methods, then the continued and ongoing demand to internationalize business curricula would be lessening rather than continuing to gain momentum.

Thus, the challenge is to prepare American students to see and experience issues from historical, economic, and socio-cultural perspectives other than their own and to prepare students from foreign markets to experience and understand an "Americanized" way of doing business and test their own perceptions of what Americans are like. After September 11, 2001, students are indicating that they perceive the need and value for educational exchange programs to enhance their learning (Kerr, 2002; Marcus, 2002).

Schools are continuing to report dissatisfaction with the internationalization of their programs (Kwok and Arpan, 2002). Higher education is looking for better, more cost-effective ways to enable internationalized business education, particularly for students from emerging markets where economies may not be stable and where the political and cultural environments have historically been internally focused. Failure to meet the challenge would suggest management education lacks relevance for stakeholders other than business schools and students.

There are a number of approaches to meeting this challenge (Ahmed and Krohn, 1994; Nash, 1997; Pitt, Berthon, and Robson, 1997). To succeed requires students to recognize the relationship of the world community to their organizations, to think beyond their own cultural context, thus taking into consideration the cultural, legal, and political values of others. Concerns exist regarding the numbers of students graduating from college who lack the sufficient international business knowledge to manage the requisite responsibilities inherent in these complex settings (Webb, Mayer, Pioche, and Allen, 1999).

"Out-of country experiences are particularly effective ways to heighten students' understanding concerning the complexities of international business" (Kwok and Arpan, 2002, 577). Augmenting management education with opportunities for student exchange programs better meets the challenge of providing management education with international perspectives (Kedia and Cornwell, 1994). Therefore, graduate management programs must enable students to genuinely experience international perspectives by collaborating with people who themselves embody a variety of international perspectives. This can be accomplished by collaboration in an educational setting, i.e. classroom, web based degree program, internship, and/or living in foreign communities (Johnson and Mader, 1992; Fugate and Jefferson, 2001). "Differences of opinion and critical thinking in the classroom environment should be encouraged. Adding some international students from abroad to an American classroom brings a new kind of thinking and an appreciation for how things are different" (Nash, 1997, 83).

As noted by Shetty and Rudell, it is challenging for small schools to offer international programs (2002). This article will discuss how a small, private, liberal arts college with a graduate management program designed a curriculum for students with undergraduate degrees from foreign universities to attract international students and develop an internationalized program for its domestic students. The structural elements of the program are first described. Features and benefits of the program are then identified. A discussion of the issues in starting and maintaining the program suggest why the program is appropriate when working with students from emerging markets. The paper concludes with a description of core success factors to facilitate the replication of the program elsewhere.

DESCRIPTION OF THE STRUCTURAL ELEMENTS OF THE PROGRAM

A key mission directive of this graduate management program is to foster the development of managers capable of adapting to a changing world, who can provide organizations with leadership and vision for the future, to lead, and indeed to become leaders, in complex situations. The international contexts inherent in "doing business" can best be defined as complex. To responsibly educate practicing managers in the international contexts of business requires more than course work. It requires both content and context. Context can be best understood through experience. Relevant experience, for students, is derived from in-class collaboration and cultural immersion through living in a community.

The Certificate program for the graduate program is necessary to enable domestic graduate students to meet and work with people from around the world and to enable foreign national students to experience business practices and study leadership and management theory from an American perspective. The foreign students bring much to the classroom, and for their part, they seek out a quality education, along with exposure to the American culture and business environment. The first student to have completed the Certificate program was from the emerging market of India. Furthermore, using the framework of the Certificate program, the college has been able to partner with a school in an industrialized country overseas to create a study-exchange program for working professionals studying in the college's two-year graduate management program. Domestic students in the college's graduate program are, thereby, able to attend classes and live from one week to up to one month in an overseas international community.

Curriculum Elements

The Certificate program differs from the traditional part-time graduate management program in that it is a one-year program for a small number of professionals with degrees earned outside the United States and with a mandated paid internship as a key part of the learning experience. The curriculum is organized around three core courses, up to four elective courses, and the internship, which integrates the student into the American business community.

Students in the Certificate program take two academic courses in the college's graduate management program during each regular term and complete a three-term internship. The curricular design ensures that no more than two and one-third (2 1/3) courses are carried in any one term, thus enabling the students to participate more fully in activities in the community and at the internship site. Core courses are Perspectives on Management, Ethics, and Internship. Examples of electives from which the students can choose are: Leadership, Decision Analysis, Public Policy Process, Organizational Behavior, International Business, Contemporary Economic Policy, and topical issues, such as civil rights/human rights. Being located in an urban setting in the southeastern United States provides the opportunity to offer a focus on civil rights.

The Certificate program is completed in one calendar year. International students begin the program with an in-coming class of graduate management students in the fall, spring, or summer terms. They attend a weekend seminar/experiential program where the international students can interact with about half of the graduate management student body. Other than the introductory Perspectives on Management course, which is offered over three weekends during the year, the international students are enrolled in two classes, each meeting one night per week, as part of the regular graduate management program.

Administrative Elements

Administratively, the Certificate program is integrated into the roles and responsibilities of existing staff. However, the enrollment of international students requires certain tasks to be revised and new tasks undertaken.

Administrative tasks needing adjustment include the process of admission, class scheduling, recruitment, and evaluating internship placements. Additional administrative responsibilities include working with international legal counsel to ascertain and address potential issues raised by the Immigration and Naturalization Service (I.N.S.), developing financial support, assisting with social security and income tax issues, and coordinating the students' on and off-campus experiences, including the provision of housing and transportation.

DISCUSSION OF THE PROGRAM'S FEATURES AND BENEFITS

Features

The Certificate program offers foreign students a broad perspective of management issues from an American vantage point of private business, not for profit organizations, and governmental agencies. Particularly important features of the Certificate program that provide these broad perspectives are the curriculum, the paid internship, cultural immersion programming, and support of the local business community through the college's advisory boards.

The internship placements, which include a market value stipend, are a distinctive feature of the program. "The use of international internships tremendously increases the student's abilities" and "allows students to apply their academic knowledge in real-world decision-making situations" (White and Griffith, 1998, 4). This participation in an American organization enables the students to experience business practices and collaborate with working professionals in organizational settings. The internship and its sponsoring company have played an important role in the assimilation of foreign students into "real" American life. To facilitate the students' working experiences, a mentor from within the company is assigned. The mentor's responsibilities include encouraging productive work relationships and overseeing an appropriate scope of work in the internship. The mentor and the students meet regularly with the faculty to discuss the students' observations, feelings, and perspectives about their day-to-day experience. The learning, which occurs through the internship, has been valuable for all involved: the companies, faculty and students. Placements have been with organizations that would utilize the talents and perspectives that international students possess, such as sensitivity to diverse customer needs in a heterogeneous market place.

Programming to facilitate cultural immersion is critical to the success of the Certificate program. In addition to orientations to the school and community, incoming foreign graduate students can begin their program with an American home-stay of up to one week. College faculty and staff who have worked with international students and are sensitive to their needs volunteer to host the students. It has been suggested that the role of the faculty should focus on enabling "international students in adapting to the U.S. education culture rather than to bring about, or even encourage, their assimilation" (Ladd and Ruby, 1999, 365). Yet, using faculty in the role of cultural interpreters has enabled open dialogue on topics, such as appropriate business/business casual attire, cultural differences in the role meal times play in social vs. business settings, the subtle display of deference to those in authority in business settings, gender issues in the workplace, sexual harassment criteria, cultural expectations of patriotism and nationalism, and differing viewpoints on world events. One of the nine learning objectives that underpin the college's Certificate program is global/cultural understanding. These open dialogues are a key component to meeting this learning objective by all the college's graduate management students.

The home-stay provides each student with a personal family type experience; throughout their time in the program, students have continued to cultivate the relationships with these families, thus expanding their social network in a new country. After the home-stay, housing for students is provided in a local residential community rather than on-campus dormitories. Automobiles are provided for transportation. Living off-campus and commuting to work and class further assures complete cultural immersion in U.S. life by the international student.

The college has a network of advisory committees whose mission is "meeting students' needs." Two of these committees have added oversight of the Certificate program to their scope of work. Members of the advisory committees support the program by securing paid internships for the students, securing housing and transportation, hosting industry tours to widen the students' views of business activities, and providing social/cultural excursions, such as attending sporting events.

Benefits of the Program

The Certificate program for students with undergraduate degrees from foreign universities benefits the graduate management program, foreign students, the local business community, and the college's relationship with external stakeholders in the business community. Quality graduate management education must enable students to both learn about and experience the implications of "doing business" from an international standpoint. As others have suggested, this part-time graduate management program should be more effective in providing internationalized business education because the Certificate program provides a continuous conduit of students from various parts of the world to enrich class discussions, collaborate on team projects, and exhibit the richness of diversity (White and Griffith, 1998).

This blending is valuable from both domestic students' and international students' perspectives. Through in class and out of class interactions, students learn from each other's accumulated knowledge and experiences about topics like the role of governmental regulations on business, the cultural norms of minorities and women in professional settings, cultural norms of business interactions in formal and informal settings, cultural differences in valuing time, organizational hierarchy, and perspectives on leadership.

The need for internship placements in local business settings makes the business community an important stakeholder. Recruiting talented business students from overseas is paramount to sustaining the support of the business community. It is important that local business leaders believe a tangible benefit will result from hosting a foreign student in their organizations as an intern. Prior to the start of the internship, faculty work with the selected mentor from the sponsoring organization to identify projects or responsibilities that fit with the background of the student, thus enabling a good fit and increasing the likelihood of the internship providing a clearly identifiable value outcome. Business people who sponsor internships report that their organizations benefit in a number of ways, including helping the businesses enhance employee sensitivity regarding changing demographics in local markets, and, specifically, how to more effectively reach an increasingly culturally diverse customer base. Another benefit expressed by representatives of the host companies stems from having the interns integrated into the workflow, which produced natural dialogues and cross cultural sensitivities throughout their organizations. Interns have also enhanced Internet B2B initiatives because of their developed skills in the use of technology.

Although not stated as an educational outcome goal, the people to people relationships that have developed as a result of this program are significant not only to the individuals themselves, but also to the larger communities in which these people live. Bridging across borders is accomplished through human dynamics and the relationships that are built and sustained. The continued connections that have been maintained between foreign students with their domestic colleagues, foreign students with professors, and internship sponsors with foreign students are important. The nature of these continued relationships seems to emphasize the personal domain rather than business; but, understanding that business is fueled by, stimulated, and transacted at personal levels, it is probable that these connections will lay the foundation to future global business connections. As pointed out by Nash, "a foreign student hopes that by attending a U.S. college, he or she will have an opportunity to make many new friends. They tend to recognize, more than American students do, the future business relationships that might accrue from these relationships" (1997, 79).

ISSUES IN STARTING AND MAINTAINING THE PROGRAM

One of the first challenges was developing a written articulation for the Certificate program that successfully addressed the United States government's requirements as administered by the Immigration and Naturalization Service (I.N.S.). The complicating factor in the Certificate program is the paid internship for foreign nationals in combination with traditional academic course- work. The design phase required assistance from legal counsel with expertise in international and immigration law. It is important to offer the internship to meet a clear educational need from the foreign student's perspective. These complexities added the better part of an academic year to the development of the Certificate program.

A continuing issue is the recruitment of suitable students into the Certificate program. There are three components to this problem. First, it is difficult to make institutions of higher education, particularly in emerging markets, aware of the program. Because of limited financial resources for marketing the Certificate program, the primary way potential partners, or individual students, learn about the program is by word of mouth; secondary means of program identification is through internet searches. Second, some assurance must be communicated to foreign institutions that a quality educational experience will be provided to their students. Finally, the cost of study must be kept low and the means to cover the cost for the foreign students identified. The next section describes the steps taken to address the problem.

ADAPTING THE CERTIFICATE PROGRAM INTO A PLATFORM FOR INSTITUTIONAL EXCHANGE

The Certificate program is a cost effective and flexible curricular platform for institutional exchange of students. Joining with foreign universities, rather than recruiting individual students, addresses a number of the challenges such a program faces First, a formalized exchange relationship with another educational institution provided an ongoing process of student recruitment and selection that is the responsibility of the foreign exchange partner, thus ensuring representation of foreign nationals in the Certificate program. Therefore, the goal of providing an enriched student body that combines foreign students with domestic students on a regular basis is achieved.

Second, the ability to benefit from an international business education is made more affordable to the students, both domestic and foreign. Students continue to pay their home institutions the normal tuition charges; hence, the college receives tuition from its graduate students when they are studying at a partner institution overseas. The institutions can negotiate on other charged items, such as lodging, thus further reducing the cost to the students.

Third, through an exchange partnership, each school is able to provide curricular offerings from their strengths while drawing upon the strengths of another school to shore up weaknesses in faculty expertise or course content. For example, by partnering with universities abroad, the domestic students are able to study with faculty who can more effectively address how international business is conducted in the geographic area and cultural milieu wherein their school is located.

A specific benefit of partnering is the ability to negotiate courses offered in a timeframe that allows for participation of the majority of the domestic graduate management students. In this particular Certificate program, the domestic graduate students are also working professionals with jobs of their own. They have received an international educational experience, flexibly offered for one week to one month, because of this

Certificate program. Courses are taken at the partner institution overseas and are taught in English, totaling thirty-five hours of instruction per week. The partnering foreign institution is also able to deliver specific cultural immersion experiences, such as living accommodations in the local community rather than on campus, evening meals with groups of international students, and attendance at cultural events.

Fourth, the Certificate program lends itself to being adopted into a foreign school's curriculum in whole or part. Partner institutions articulate a transfer of credit agreement prior to the students' arrival on campus. Students are then able to select courses at the foreign university that their home institutions do not offer but will accept for course credit, such as ethical decision making discussed in the context of American business.

Assurances of quality are being made through several sources. The graduate management program is A.A.C.S.B. International accredited. Recent efforts by A.A.C.S.B. to become the international leader in accrediting business programs should globalize the brand. The graduate management program should benefit as institutions around the world come to understand the quality inherent in the A.A.C.S.B. brand. The Certificate program has been in existence for several years and may now lay claim to testimonials from students who have matriculated as well as other stakeholders such as internship sponsors. It is also possible to track the career paths of students completing the program.

The paid internship helps to defray the cost of the educational experience for the foreign students. However, when students were first admitted to the program, it became clear that it is necessary to coordinate with the human resources department at each of the sponsoring businesses to handle issues related to reporting and filing taxes and applying for social security numbers. These tax issues are common (Burbach and Fisher, 1996). The procedures are now codified within the administration of the Certificate program.

CONCLUSION: FACTORS ALLOWING FOR SUCCESSFUL REPLICATION WITH SCHOOLS IN EMERGING MARKETS

The international Certificate program, with the associated institutional exchange, was designed and is run by a small college with limited financial and faculty resources. Other partnering institutions may replicate factors contributing to the success of the program. The model is particularly appropriate for students and their universities in emerging markets.

The design of curricular platforms that enable flexibility in partnering with foreign institutions does not require extensive infrastructure. Schools, particularly in emerging markets that may not have significant resources to develop and market programs, can design customized offerings that are tailored to the program needs of one or two American institutions during an academic year. These customized programs can be "exchanged" for the ability of placing their students into courses and business internships in the U.S., thus enabling schools, domestic and foreign, to work together to enhance international business education. The benefit to small schools in the United States is that by partnering in an ongoing relationship, there is a continuous process of infusion of foreign students into the program, and offerings can be tailored to specific needs of the students regarding language, timeframe, cultural immersion, etc.

The institutional exchange model presented does not need a large number of students to "make classes" or to develop internship placements. The program may be run with one or two students visiting the host institution. The small number of students needed to mount a program makes it attractive to universities that may not have large number of students able to participate but still desire to offer an international experience. Because of the small number of students participating, the institutional exchange would not grow significantly out of balance.

The faculty and administrative costs to each institution are relatively low in comparison to establishing separate administrative units to recruit business internships or offer educational/cultural immersion endeavors. An institutional exchange of one term that includes an immersion experience with a paid internship lowers the cost to the student and requires less time away from home. The lower cost and shorter duration of time may be attractive to students from emerging markets. Some students may also be attracted to the personable and individual approach to cultural immersion offered by such a program.

There are four structural elements that need to be in place to replicate the program at other colleges and universities. First is a faculty that is willing to accept and embrace foreign students into their classes and their homes. Second is the active support of the local business community. Business leaders must see a benefit to hosting and helping the foreign student. This Certificate program is housed in a college with a large and active business advisory council. Third, it is important to have a knowledgeable legal advisor with specific expertise in international and immigration law to work with I.N.S. issues. Finally, the program will need an advisor on tax and human resource issues to work with the companies hosting the internships.

Business students from emerging markets need and want a complete international experience working with a company and living in a country with a developed economy. Cost, time, and cultural unfamiliarity may be obstacles to their international experience. The Certificate program described in this paper offers a lower cost option, with a flexible time commitment and a cultural immersion which is personable, almost familial. The domestic host school receives the same benefits for its students with the additional benefit of providing domestic students with the opportunity to study in a growing, challenging, emerging market.

REFERENCES

A.A.C.S.B. International -- The Association to Advance Collegiate Schools of Business. (2003). *Eligibility Procedures and Standards for Business Accreditation,* (3), St. Louis MO.

Ahmed, Z. V. & Krohn, F. B. (1994). The symbiosis of liberal arts and international business. *Journal of Education for Business, 69*(4).

Burbach, J. & Fisher, A. L. (1996). The deductibility of traveling expenses for foreign nationals on U.S. internships. *The Tax Adviser,* New York.

Fugate, D.L. & Jefferson, R. W. (2001). Preparing for globalization — do we need structural change for our academic programs? *Journal of Education for Business, 76*(3).

Johnson, D. M., & Mater, D. D. (1992). Internationalizing your marketing course: the foreign study tour alternative. *Journal of Marketing Education,* (Summer), 26-33.

Kedia, B.L., & Cornwell, T. B. (1994). Mission based strategies for internationalizing U.S. business schools. *Journal of Teaching in International Business, 5*(3), 11-29.

Kerr, A. Z. (2002). An education for them, a bargain for us. *International Educator, 11*(2).

Kwok, C.Y. & Arpan, J.S. (2002). Internationalizing the business school: a global survey in 2000. *Journal of International Business Studies, 33*(3), 571-581.

Ladd, P. D. &and Ruby, Jr. R. (1999). Learning style and adjustment issues of international students. *Journal of Education for Business, 74*(6), 363-367.

Marcus, J. (2002, September 13). Exchanges move up agenda after terrorism. *The Times Higher Education Supplement,* No. 1555.

Nash, B. (1997). Internationalizing the business school-responding to the customer's needs. *Journal of Teaching in International Business, 9*(1), 73-84.

Nehrt, L.C. (1993). Business school curriculum and faculty: historical perspectives and future imperatives. In S. T. Cavusgil (Ed.), *Internationalizing Business Education: Meeting the Challenge* (pp. 31-44). East Lansing: Michigan State University Press.

Pitt, L., Berthon, P., & Robson, M. (1997). The internationalization of management knowledge dissemination: a dialectic. *Journal of World Business, 32*(4).

Porter, L.W., & McKibbin, L.E. (1998). *Management Education and Development.* New York: McGraw Hill.

Shetty, F. and Rudell, F. (2002). Internationalizing the business program -- a perspective of a small school. *Journal of Education for Business,* November/December), 103-110.

Webb, M. S., Mayer, K.R., Pioche, V., & Allen, L. C. (1999). Internationalization of American business education. *Management International Review, 39*(4), 379-379.

White, S. D., & Griffith, D. A., (1998). Graduate international business education in the United States — comparisons and suggestions. *Journal of Education for Business, 74*(2), 103-113.

Chapter 11
Training Heritage Students for Managing in Emerging Markets: The Case of Business in Israel in the United States

Daniel Laufer[1]
University of Cincinnati

INTRODUCTION

In January 2003, approximately 2,000 non-resident Indians living in industrialized countries attended a conference organized by the Indian government. The purpose of the conference was to strengthen ties between India and its successful diaspora[2] in the industrialized world. Indians living in the United States, for example, have a median income 50% higher than the national average for the United States (Waldman, 2003). The Indian government, eager to attract these successful emigrants back to India, announced during the conference that legislation would be introduced to grant dual citizenship to people of Indian origin living in industrialized countries (Waldman, 2003).

Interest by members of diasporas to return to their former homelands, and foreign governments' efforts to attract them, are by no means unique to India. In fact, Gillespie, et. al. suggest that "as international migration and market liberalization expand globally, homeland investment by diaspora businesses and entrepreneurs may become a significant category of foreign investment" (1999).

A significant challenge facing diaspora members interested in returning to their former homelands is reacquainting themselves with the business environment in their former countries. It is worth noting that despite sharing a common heritage, many diaspora members are generations removed from their former homelands. This creates an opportunity for universities in developing courses that educate heritage students about business in emerging markets ("heritage courses"). These heritage courses could potentially attract students from ethnic groups in the United States and Europe, such as Indians, Koreans, Turks, Chinese, Mexicans, and Cubans, who wish to learn more about the business environment in their former homelands. This opportunity is particularly attractive to universities with large ethnic student populations. For example, universities with large Hispanic student populations could benefit from offering courses on business in Mexico or Cuba.

This paper describes my experience teaching a heritage course, "The Business Environment of Israel" ("Israel course"), at the University of Texas at Austin over a five-year period from 1996-2001. During biblical times, Israel was the homeland of the Jewish people, and, after being occupied multiple times over the centuries, was reestablished as a Jewish state in 1948. Despite the creation of a Jewish state in 1948, the majority of Jews still live outside of Israel. The Israeli government, eager to increase the country's population, encourages immigration through the granting of citizenship and financial assistance to Jews that decide to relocate to Israel.

University educators can learn from my experience teaching the Israel course in creating heritage courses for other emerging markets. This paper provides guidance in developing course content for heritage courses, promoting the courses, and collaborating with government and industry. The success of the Israel course at the University of Texas at Austin suggests that heritage courses targeting other emerging markets can also be successfully implemented.

TARGET AUDIENCE FOR THE COURSE

During the five years I taught the Israel course at the University of Texas at Austin, the three credit hour course was offered as a seminar on both undergraduate and graduate levels. The courses were taught either once a week as a 3-hour session or twice a week as two 90-minute sessions. As an undergraduate course it was listed as an upper level course, restricted to juniors and seniors. The class size was limited in order to facilitate class discussion, and the number of students varied depending on whether it was offered as a graduate or undergraduate course. On a graduate level the class size was between five to ten students, and the undergraduate course varied between 15 to 20 students.

The primary target audience for the course was business majors, however students from other disciplines were targeted as well. The course was therefore cross-listed in both the business school and in the Middle Eastern studies department at the university. As previously mentioned, diaspora communities are groups potentially interested in learning more about their former homelands, and individuals from these groups could be interested in registering for this type of course despite not being enrolled in the business school. This in fact was reflected in registration for my Israel course. The overwhelming majority of students in my Israel course were Jewish. I also estimate that during the period I taught the Israel course, over 30% of the students were non-business majors. The non-business majors included students from Middle Eastern studies, Judaic studies, economics, political science, history, and engineering. These students were highly motivated and brought an interesting perspective to the classroom discussion. The non-business majors were typically more knowledgeable than the business majors in the discussion of qualitative issues such as cultural differences and the impact of geographical and historical factors on the business environment. On the other hand, in the more quantitative areas of the course, such as profitability analysis and discussions of tax and accounting issues, the non-business majors had to work harder than the business majors to grasp the concepts. Despite this obstacle, the high motivation levels of the non-business majors enabled them to make up for their lack of formal training in these areas. It is worth noting, however, that these differences in skill levels between the business and nonbusiness majors creates a more challenging environment for the instructor to manage. My experience suggests that this situation can be handled effectively by spending more time with non-business majors during office hours and perhaps scheduling an extra class session to review topics such as profitability analysis.

COURSE CONTENT

The two stated objectives of the Israel course were to build an understanding of the business environment in Israel and to learn about the major factors driving foreign investment in Israel. The course was divided into two main sections: the Israeli economy and the business environment in Israel. The section on the Israeli economy focused on macro-level topics such as the political system, an overview of the Israeli Economy, the banking system, and privatization. The section on the business environment in Israel, on the other hand, focused more on firm-level issues such as business entities, accounting and tax issues, and investment incentives (see Appendix 11.1 for course syllabus). Many of these topics are equally relevant for other emerging markets, however, it is worth noting that certain topics can be unique to a particular country. In the case of Israel, the Peace Process and the Arab Boycott of Israel are two notable examples.

In order to teach the various topics incorporated in the course, a number of teaching methods were utilized to achieve the learning objectives. Incorporating multiple teaching methods in a course has been shown to be more effective in educating students (Kolb, 1984). Methods used in teaching the Israel course included lectures, case analysis, student projects, and guest speakers.

Lecturing was the method used most often in the Israel course. Prior to lecturing on a particular topic, readings were assigned to the students to provide them with the necessary background to understand the lecture content. It is worth noting that despite the passive nature of this teaching method (Benjamin, 1991), the students were actively involved in the learning process, participating in discussing the important issues pertaining the topic of the lecture. This was greatly facilitated by the small class size. For example in the section of the Israel course covering the Arab Boycott of Israel, the students were required to discuss the implications of an American company receiving a request to comply with the boycott of Israel. The discussion took place after reading the material from the reading packet as well as listening to the lecture on the topic.

A challenging aspect of organizing the Israel course was putting together a reading packet. Unlike courses such as International Business or International Marketing, courses on specific emerging markets are unlikely to have textbooks that an instructor can use in the course. My experience suggests that a reading packet is the most effective way to aggregate the material for the course. The reading packet can include information from book chapters, academic studies, newspaper articles, government publications, and materials provided by multinationals, accounting firms, and law firms. In addition, including in the reading packet a list of useful websites related the business environment in the specific emerging market is also highly recommended. Sample items from my reading packet include the academic study "Corporate Governance in an Emerging Market: The Case of Israel" (Blass et al, 1998); the newspaper article "West's Slump and Intifada Hit Israel's Pocketbook" (Orme, 2001); the Israeli government publication "The Israeli Economy at a Glance - 1999" (2000); and the U.S. government publication "Country Commercial Guide for Israel FY 1999."

In addition to lectures, case studies were incorporated in my course to facilitate the learning process. The case study method effectively complements the class lectures by connecting in-class learning with the reality outside the classroom (Silverman and Welty, 1990). Despite the availability of case studies at outlets such as E.C.C.H. at Babson, Harvard Publications, and Ivey Publishing, it may be difficult to find good cases for certain countries. This was my experience when organizing the Israel course. An alternative, however, to relying on other cases is for instructors to develop their own cases (for a good resource on the topic, see Leenders, et. al., 2001). Whereas writing a case can be very time consuming, it can be extremely effective as a teaching tool because it is developed specifically with the course in mind. I developed two case studies that I incorporated in my Israel course. In the first case study, "Country-Specific Mutual Fund: The Growth Fund of Israel" (Laufer, 1997), students analyzed how the economic and political situation in Israel impacted the sales of an Israeli Mutual Fund sold in the United States. In the second case study, "Caniel: An Israeli Company in Jordan" (Laufer, 1998), students were required to analyze how an Israeli company's operations would change as a result of expanding their operations into Jordan in the aftermath of the signing of a peace treaty between Israel and Jordan. This case facilitated learning about the potential for collaboration between Israeli and Jordanian companies and fit nicely with the lecture topic of regional trade prospects. My experience with teaching these case studies suggests that they are effective in stimulating discussion and greatly enhance the learning experience of the students.

Similar to case analysis, student projects involve connecting in-class learning with the reality outside the classroom. The student project assigned in the Israel course involved the preparation of a business plan for selling a product or service in Israel. Some of the issues the students were required to address in the business plan included an analysis of the potential market, the proposed location of operations in Israel, the type of business entity to operate as, the type of government incentives to apply for (if any), and tax implications of their decisions.

In the business plan projects, the students chose to focus on business ventures that were of interest to them. One student, hired to work for a multinational tobacco company, wrote a business plan about selling cigarettes in Israel. Another student, interested in the automobile industry, wrote about establishing an automobile dealership in Israel. The student was subsequently hired by the Israeli affiliate of a large American car manufacturer as a marketing manager. Finally a non-business major wrote a business plan about setting up a microbrewery in Israel. His plan generated the interest of an American investor who was contemplating an investment in Israel. My experience with incorporating a business plan project in the course has been very positive. Not only did it reinforce concepts learned throughout the course, but it also helped students in their future careers by enabling them to think about projects relating to their future jobs.

Finally, integrating guest speakers can also be very effective in the transfer of knowledge to students about various aspects of the business environment in emerging markets. I incorporated a number of guest speakers in my Israel course from both industry and government. These included senior executives from multinationals such as Motorola, Amoco, Bell South, and K.P.M.G. as well as senior government officials such as the Israeli Economic Minister to North America, the Israeli Consul General for the Southwest region of the United States, the Egyptian Consul in Houston, Texas, and the former U.S. Ambassador to Israel and Syria. The success in attracting well-known speakers to the Israel course is partially due to a successful promotional effort (see following section), however finding effective guest speakers for these types of courses does not have to be overly cumbersome and time consuming. The big accounting and law firms are great potential sources for guest speakers. These firms have clients worldwide so they are very knowledgeable about issues pertaining to conducting business in emerging markets. In addition, it is fairly easy to find local companies with operations in emerging markets who are willing to share their experience in an academic setting. Finally, videoconferencing is a great way to have guest speakers, situated in distant geographical areas, share their knowledge with the students in the course if it is not feasible to bring them into the classroom.

In addition to speakers from industry, government diplomats and trade officials can also be effective guest speakers for a heritage course. It is important, however, to keep in mind that the learning objective of the course can differ from the information conveyed by government officials whose role is to encourage trade and investment in the emerging market. The role of the instructor, on the other hand, is to educate the students about the business environment in the emerging market in an objective and impartial manner. For example, whereas Israeli government officials tend to downplay the risk associated with foreign investment in Israel, the role of the instructor, on the other hand, is to fully discuss these risks and their implications on existing and potential foreign investors. Despite these potential conflicts, incorporating government officials as guest speakers can still be beneficial if the students are aware of the different agendas of the various guest speakers. This can be conveyed through classroom discussions both before and after the guest speakers' presentations.

Despite the potential benefit in using guest speakers in a course on an emerging market, it is important to clearly specify the topics to be covered in the guest speaker's presentation in advance. For example, in my courses I have asked multinational corporations to talk about topics such as the impact of cultural differences on their operations in Israel as well as their experience applying for investment incentives, both of which are directly related to the course's learning objectives. I also have asked Israeli government officials to talk about topics such as the political system in Israel as well as privatization. If the invited guest speaker does not focus on the agreed upon topic, valuable course time is wasted. In order to prevent this digression from occurring, the instructor should ask questions that will redirect the guest speaker to the agreed upon topic. In my experience with over 15 guest speakers in my Israel courses, this is rarely necessary if the guest speaker knows in advance the topic he or she is scheduled to discuss.

PROMOTING THE COURSE

In addition to developing the course material, it is important to develop a strategy to promote the course. A number of audiences have to be targeted in promoting the course including students, companies, and government officials.

Students are an important group to target in promoting the course. This is particularly important when the course is initially launched because positive word of mouth has not yet been generated. The development of a course website, presentations in other strategically important courses, and writing articles in student newspapers can create awareness and generate student demand for the course.

The development of a course website is an effective way to promote a new course. A course website should include information about learning objectives, teaching material, guest speakers, and background information about the instructor. Once the course website is developed, instructors of courses in strategically important areas should be contacted and informed of the course website. These instructors should also be encouraged to inform their students of the course website. In the case of my Israel course, I informed instructors in the areas of International Business, Middle Eastern Studies, and Judaic Studies.

In addition to the website, presentations in strategically important classes such as international business courses can generate demand for the course. The best time for the presentations is a couple of days before student registration. For example, I was a guest speaker in a Business in Emerging Markets course, and a number of students decided to register for the course after listening to my presentation.

Finally, offering to write an article in the student newspaper is another effective way of generating demand for the course. I wrote an article in the student newspaper about privatization in Israel (Laufer, 1997). In addition to the article, the newspaper provided information about the course which was helpful in informing students about the course.

In addition to students, companies are another important audience to target in promoting the course. Companies can potentially provide support in a number of ways including sponsoring the course, sending guest speakers, providing material for the reading packet, and occasionally providing job opportunities for students.

In organizing my Israel course, I approached multinational corporations as well as accounting firms with operations in Israel. These companies were a logical source for support since they had the most to contribute in terms of country-specific knowledge. Their experience operating in Israel was a rich source of information to incorporate both in terms of written material for the reading packet as well as guest speakers. In addition, they had much to gain in contributing to the development of the Israel course because of their need for graduates with the type of expertise the course provides to students. In organizing my Israel course I compiled a list of 20 multinationals with investments in Israel, and four agreed to sponsor the course, provide material for the reading packet, and send guest speakers to the course.

In order to successfully attract companies to sponsor this type of course, a number of factors play an important role. First, once a well-known company agrees to participate as a sponsor in the course, other well-known companies are likely to follow suit. Therefore the biggest challenge is to find the first corporate sponsor. Here university officials and alumni can help facilitate making contacts with the appropriate decision makers in the corporation.

Another factor improving the chances of finding corporate sponsors is press coverage. When a company sees that a course is receiving favorable press coverage, it increases the likelihood of participation. Due to the unique nature of heritage courses, there is a high likelihood that local, overseas, and heritage press outlets will be interested in writing stories. My Israel course was featured in various press outlets in the United States ranging from the local ABC News TV affiliate in Houston, Texas to the Journal of Accountancy (Koreto, 1999). In addition to coverage in the United States, major newspapers in Israel also expressed interest in the course (Dagoni, 1996; Handwerker, 1996). Finally, Jewish newspapers in the United States wrote articles about the course as well, including the largest Jewish newspaper in the United States, the *New York Jewish Week* (Brown, 1996).

The last factor that assists in recruiting corporate sponsors is acknowledging the support of existing corporate sponsors. This may seem obvious, but unfortunately it is often overlooked. Acknowledging the participation of corporate sponsors on the course website and in press articles is a good way to thank companies for their contribution to the course and also signals to other potential corporate sponsors that their contribution to the course is recognized and valued.

The last audience to target in promoting the course is government officials who can be found in embassies, consulates, and trade missions throughout the United States and Europe. Similar to companies, government officials are a valuable source for reading packet material and guest speakers for the course. It is worth noting that based on my experience, government officials are typically more receptive to providing assistance than companies. As previously mentioned, governments are interested in encouraging investment in their countries, and they probably believe that a heritage course can assist in achieving that objective. Companies, on the other hand, may be more hesitant to cooperate because of concerns regarding the sharing of proprietary information outside of the company.

An effective way to enlist the support of government officials is to inform them about the course through the distribution of the course syllabus and previous articles about the course, as well as sending them information about the course website. As was the case with corporate sponsors, acknowledging the participation of government officials on the course website and in articles is a good way to ensure continued cooperation.

It is worth noting that government officials do not necessarily have to be exclusively from the emerging market of interest. In the case of my Israel course in addition to Israeli government officials, non-Israeli government officials also participated as guest speakers in the course. For example, the former U.S. Ambassador to Israel and Syria spoke about the impact of the peace process on the Israeli economy, and the Egyptian Consul spoke about the prospects for regional trade. The main criterion driving the selection of guest speakers is whether they contribute to achieving the learning objectives of the course.

JOB OPPORTUNITIES FOR STUDENTS

The unique nature of a business in emerging markets course can create job opportunities for students. The skills students gain from taking the course is beneficial to both industry as well as government employers. Multinationals with existing operations in an emerging market or with an interest to expand into those markets are frequently looking for graduates who can assist them with dealing with the challenges of operating in those countries. Over the years, I have witnessed this happen on numerous occasions. For example a multinational participating in my course expressed interested in hiring a student into their international internal audit group which was responsible for reviewing the company's overseas operations that included Israel. Another example was a major accounting firm with a presence in Israel expressing interest in hiring another student into their audit practice.

Job opportunities available to students are by no means limited to industry. The Israeli government has hired three of my former students in their diplomatic missions in the United States, and they have contacted me on numerous occasions to find qualified students for other job openings as well. I believe that courses focusing on other emerging markets can assist students in finding job opportunities in both industry and government as well.

CONCLUSION

Heritage courses can play an important role in preparing students for future careers as managers and entrepreneurs in emerging markets. These students need to familiarize themselves with the business environment in their former homelands, which in many cases they have not lived in. Universities, through the development of heritage courses, can play an important role in helping students achieve this goal.

Cooperation with both industry and government plays an important role in the success of a heritage course. These parties provide valuable resources such as material for reading packets as well as guest speakers. In addition, industry and government provide unique job opportunities for students successfully completing these types of courses. Promotional activities such as the design of course websites and public relations greatly assist in enlisting the support of industry and government.

The demand for heritage courses will continue to increase in the future. Governments will follow the example of India and Israel and provide incentives to members of diasporas, particularly in industrialized countries, to return to their homelands. In addition, economic growth in these countries will also draw members of diasporas back to their former homelands. Universities should capitalize on these trends and play a role in the development of future business leaders in emerging markets.

APPENDIX 11.1

Appendix 11.1: Sample "Business Environment in Israel" Syllabus, the University of Texas at Austin

Lecturer: Daniel Laufer

Course Description: The objectives of the course are as follows:

- Building an understanding of the business environment in Israel
- Learning about the major factors driving foreign investment in Israel

The course will be divided into two main sections: an overview of the Israeli Economy and the Business Environment in Israel.

Credit: Three Credit Hours

Target Audience: The course is designed for undergraduate students. The primary interest would be for Business Majors and Middle Eastern Studies students, however the following students may also be interested in the course as an elective:

- Economics
- Liberal Arts
- Political Science
- Engineering

Grading: The grading for the course is as follows:

1. Exam I -- 20%
2. Exam II -- 20%
3. Case Analysis (2) -- 20%
4. Business Plan Project -- 30%
5. Class Participation -- 10%

Office Hours: CBA 5.334 BB: Tues/Thurs 8:30-9:15
danlaufer@aol.com

Course Website: http://menic.utexas.edu/menic/cmes/laufer/bio.html

Readings: The reading materials include the following:

- Reading Packet which includes Israeli Government Publications, articles about the business environment in Israel, and other documents relating to the Israeli Economy and Business Environment in Israel.
- Handouts
- K.P.M.G. "Investment in Israel" Publication

All readings should be completed before topics are covered in class, and students should be prepared to discuss the issues addressed in the articles/readings.

Case Analysis: This assignment is an individual project and involves writing an analysis of the cases "Country Specific Mutual Fund: Growth Fund of Israel" (due on October 4, 2001) and "Caniel: An Israeli Company in Jordan" (due on November 15, 2001). The assignment is due at the beginning of class. Assignments submitted late will not be accepted.

Limit your case analysis to a maximum of five pages per case. You may include appendices in addition to your analysis. The appendices could include detailed analyses or tables and graphs. Please limit the appendices to three pages.

List of Topics for Business Environment in Israel Course

Date	Topic
8/29	Introduction K.P.M.G.: pages 11, 14-17
9/4	Peace Process Arab Boycott
9/6-9/11	Political System in Israel *Guest Speaker: Dr. Tzion Evrony - Israel's Consul General in the Southwest* K.P.M.G: pages 12-13
9/13-10/2	Israeli Economy: *Guest Speaker: Alan Weinkrantz - President of Public Relations Firm Specializing in Israeli High Tech Companies*
9/18	No Class – Rosh Hashana
9/27	No Class – Yom Kippur K.P.M.G: pages 38-40

10/4	Case Study: "Country Specific Mutual Fund: Growth Fund of Israel" Assignment: Case analysis due at the beginning of class
10/9-10/11	Tel Aviv Stock Exchange Israeli Companies on Wall Street K.P.M.G: pages 124-126
10/16-10/18	Banking System in Israel Currency Foreign Investment in Israel K.P.M.G: pages 119-124, 36-37, 129-134
10/23	Business Entities in Israel Privatization of Government Owned Companies K.P.M.G: pages 45-51
10/25	Exam I
10/30-11/6	Business Practices and Accounting Principles in Israel Tax System in Israel *Guest Speaker: Jerry Borowick, KPMG Partner* K.P.M.G: pages 63-107
11/8-11/13	Investment Incentives *Guest Speaker: Dara Rosenkranz, Israel Economic Mission – Los Angeles* K.P.M.G: pages 19-36
11/15-11/27	Regional Trade Prospects Israeli Companies in Jordan Case Study: "Caniel: An Israeli Company in Jordan" Assignment: Case analysis due at the beginning of class on 11/15
11/23	No Class – Thanksgiving Break
11/29-12/4	Labor Relations and Working Conditions in Israel Immigration of Soviet Jews to Israel Import and Export Regulations K.P.M.G: pages 109-117, 41-43
12/6	Exam II

NOTES

[1]Daniel Laufer is an Assistant Professor of Marketing at the University of Cincinnati. He has conducted research on Israel-related topics and has extensive experience providing consulting services to multinationals in Israel.

[2]Diaspora members maintain a memory, vision, or myth about their original homeland; are committed to the maintenance or restoration of their homeland; and their consciousness and solidarity are importantly defined by this continuing relationship with the homeland (Safran 1991). It is worth noting that not all emigrants are diaspora members. Emigrant communities that attempt to assimilate into their new culture and distance themselves from their country of origin would not be considered diaspora communities (Gillespie, et. al., 1999).

REFERENCES

Benjamin, L. (1991). Personalization and active learning in the large introductory psychology class. *Teaching of Psychology, 18*, 68-74.

Bertrand, T. (1997). Holy land of opportunity: course on doing business in Israel first in nation. *Texas Alcalde* (May/June).

Blass, A., Yafeh, Y., & Yosha, O. (1998). Corporate governance in an emerging market: the case of Israel. *Journal of Applied Corporate Finance, 10*, 78-89.

Brown, E. (1996). Israeli business, Texas style. *The New York Jewish Week* (Oct. 25).

Dagoni, R (1996). First time offered in U.S. university: course on doing business in Israel. *Globes* (Aug. 12).

Gillespie, K., Riddle, R., Sayre, E. & Sturges, D. (1999). Diaspora interest in homeland investment. *Journal of International Business Studies, 30*, 623-634.

Government of Israel – Ministry of Industry & Trade (2000). *The Israeli Economy at a Glance – 1999*. Jerusalem: Israel.

Handwerker, H. (1996). Israeli Economy in Texas. *Haaretz* (Dec 25).

Koreto, R. (1999). It's a small-firm world after all. *The Journal of Accountancy* (May).

Laufer, D. (1997). Privatization of Israel. *Texas Business Weekly* (Jan 4).

Laufer, D. (1997). *Country-Specific Mutual Fund: Growth Fund of Israel*. Boston: E.C.C.H. at Babson College.

Laufer, D. (1998). *Caniel: An Israeli Company in Jordan*. Boston: E.C.C.H. at Babson College.

Leenders, E., Erskine, J., & Mauffette, L. (2001). *Writing Cases* (4th ed.). London, Ontario: University of Western Ontario.

Safran, W. (1991). Diasporas in modern societies: myths of homeland and return. *Diaspora, 1*(1), 83-89.

Orme, W. (2001, June 6). West's slump and Intifada hit Israel's pocketbook. *The New York Times*.

Silverman, R. & Welty, W. (1990). Teaching with cases. *Journal on Excellence in College Teaching, 1*, 88-97.

United States Government – Department of Commerce (1998). *Country commercial guide for Israel FY 1999*. Washington: USA.

Waldman, A. (2003, Jan. 12). India harvests fruits of a diaspora. *The New York Times*.

Chapter 12
Usefulness of Micro-Business Models in Developing Countries

Charles M. Wood
University of Tulsa

INTRODUCTION

The richest and the poorest regions of the world are far apart on a number of key indicators: e.g., life expectancy, gender equity, education levels, economic and political stability, access to markets, health, and general quality of life. Many of these gaps between rich and poor countries are chronic and have been attributed to a lack of access to resources, which in turn causes low levels of individual "capabilities" (Sen, 1999). In recent years, greater attention has been given to differences in access to and use of information technology. This "digital divide" appears to be growing, particularly among the underrepresented (U.N.D.P., 2000).

Many solutions and programs have been proposed to address these problems, but a current trend among agencies such as the United Nations (U.N.) and Non-Governmental Organizations (N.G.O.s) is to emphasize approaches that activate, educate, and empower the individuals living in poverty in ways that allow them to change their own circumstances. For example, a recent United Nations report on urban slums in developing nations states that the most effective programs are those that address the livelihoods of slumdwellers and get the slumdwellers actively involved in identifying their problems and implementing solutions (U.N.-Habitat, 2003). As a result, many programs attempt to develop and stimulate economic and market activity.

THE CASE FOR E-COMMERCE

A number of international aid and development organizations have begun to focus on initiatives for developing nations that include technical education, technical training, e-entrepreneurship, and e-commerce for development. This follows the reasoning of Nobel Prize-winning economist

Amartya Sen, who stated that "it can be argued that poverty is not a matter of low well-being, but of the inability to pursue well-being precisely because of the lack of economic means" (1992, 110). However, providing Internet access to a community does not necessarily mean that it will be used widely or benefit the people. This has been demonstrated in the chronic poor performance of telecenters in rural areas. Users need an economic incentive to learn to use the technology to enhance existing commerce or well-being, or to create new avenues of enterprise.

Attention has been focused in recent years on the potential of the Internet to help remedy some of the problems in developing nations. For example, the United Nations Development Program has stated that "information and communications technology (I.C.T.) has become an indispensable tool in the fight against world poverty" (U.N.D.P., 2000). Because telecommunications and Internet costs tend to be higher in developing nations (due in large part to state telecommunication monopolies), many development programs have emphasized shared computing solutions such as telecenters, Internet kiosks, and community learning centers. Unfortunately, the pattern for these centers is that they often flounder or fail because they require ongoing funding from the government, which over time proves to be inadequate. This highlights the need for profitable commercial applications of Internet technology to be used in these centers because these applications will help to provide revenues to these shared computing centers and keep them open for non-commercial purposes (e.g., education, communication). Necessarily, this also highlights the need for education in micro-business models that involve using the Internet to make a profit and that are appropriate for existing conditions in developing nations.

With this perspective in mind, this chapter describes an example of a successful micro-business model that has been demonstrated in business classrooms with the aid of an experiential pedagogical tool. The purpose is to educate individuals regarding a business model that: 1) can be readily implemented by individuals, and 2) has the potential to improve existing businesses and to launch profitable new ones. In the following sections, the main challenges and opportunities related to commercial development in developing countries will be reviewed, an overview of micro-business models and the proposed pedagogical tool will be presented, and regions of the developing world with the highest potential for successful use of the tool will be highlighted.

GOALS AND CHALLENGES IN DEVELOPING ECONOMIES

Development activities typically focus on building commercial opportunities because development agencies are aware of the direct correlation between level of commercial activity and long-term improvements in areas such as gender equity, access to markets and investment capital, and preservation of local culture. Discussion of these issues follows.

Gender Equity

Women and children are impacted the most by poverty (Sen, 1999). There is evidence that gender equity is directly correlated with the extent of a community's commercial activity. Olson found in Guatemala that women will often achieve economic independence when given the opportunity to participate in commercial activities (1999). Smith found in his study in Northern Kenya that a market-oriented economy tends to give women greater economic autonomy than women in pastoral economies (1998). The data suggest a pattern in which women make economic and social gains when they have control over the sale of products: "What gives them greater economic autonomy in a farming economy geared toward market exchange is that resources women control have become more valuable and that women have a more important role in supplying the household materially" (Smith, 1998, 466).

Access to Markets

Cohen conducted an ethnographic study of an artisan cooperative in the Oaxaca region of Mexico and identified three chronic hindrances to economic development: market access, access to export networks, and poor market knowledge (1998). He stated that "the importance of export market access cannot be emphasized enough" (1988, 80), and "geography, economy and history limit the ability of Santaneros to meet potential buyers" (1988, 76). In the case of this artisan cooperative, it is evident that the primary needs are related to both business education and practice.

Preserving Local Culture

A major concern in non-industrialized nations is the steady erosion of the interests of their people in local values, customs, and traditions, sometimes referred to as a "homogenization" of local cultures, as interaction with western culture increases. The challenge for developing nations is how to increase exchanges with global markets without also causing the abandonment of the roots and richness of local cultures. Researchers have called for studies that are a combination of economics and anthropology and policies that embody both top-down (structured) and bottom-up (participatory) approaches (Hackenburg, 1999; Keare, 2001). An ideal situation would be one in which developing nations find a product that both reinforces local culture and can be leveraged as a competitive advantage in global markets. Many N.G.O.s believe that artisan craft is one such product.

Other Needs

Structural, sociocultural, and political challenges to the adoption and diffusion of the Internet must be overcome: low levels of literacy, political instability, insufficient infrastructure development, socio-cultural factors, overcoming inefficient traditional practices, regulations, and power structures (Samiee, 1998; Klein and Nason, 2001). Clearly, it is also imperative that business education in developing nations keep pace with changes in e-commerce. As these economies begin to move forward to compete in global markets, the core educational needs for topics such as accounting and financial management, strategy, marketing, and operations management will remain. However, a new set of topics are likely to grow in importance: market research, relationship building within channels of distribution, new product development, quality control, and training in Internet technology. If a successful technological leapfrog for business is to occur in these nations, it is vital that small businesses gain access to current research on consumers' tastes and trends. This is particularly true for artisan craft produced in these countries. As stated earlier, effectively breaking into existing channels of distribution and gaining access to markets via intermediaries may be the most important aspect of profitably selling some products. Attention to planning for the production of a steady flow of new products as well as attention to quality control issues remain crucial elements of any successful small business management.

OPPORTUNITIES IN DEVELOPING ECONOMIES

> Network communications have been a tremendous leveling force for small businesses, enabling them to compete - and succeed – in lucrative niches of the global market (U.N.D.P., 1999, 58).

> Communications technology opens new opportunities for small players to enter the global marketplace and political arena.... Now innovative small businesses can find their niche and compete alongside giants (U.N.D.P., 1999, 59-60).

> ...[C]omparative advantage is not a fixed given, but can be created in the information economy (U.N.D.P., 1999, 61).

Developing nations must identify and leverage their "cultural capital" in order to develop unique and competitive uses of Internet technology in keeping with principles of comparative advantage. In addition, several other aspects of Internet-mediated pathways to development deserve recognition.

Preserving Local Culture

The Internet appears to offer more promise as a development tool than first thought. Everett states that

> Increasingly, aid agencies are turning to information technology as a key to promoting development and political reform..... In contrast to previous Orwellian visions of the homogenizing and controlling tendencies of technology, some now argue that technology can contribute to the creation of 'hybrid cultures' and to 'autonomous social expression (1998, 385).

Escobar has stated that "where the 'postmodern condition' is sometimes characterized as a strong force for homogenization of culture and domination by big capital, some local groups are resisting these trends by seeking specific markets for their goods and using their cultural identity as capital to gain competitiveness" (1995, 427-8).

Bypassing the "Middleman"

Alternative Trading Organizations (A.T.O.s) have arranged with small artisan cooperatives to serve as a market intermediary: "Development specialists and communities increasingly see craft production as a vehicle for socio-economic development and empowerment...[y]et they remain captive to exploitation by middlemen" (Page-Reeves, 1998, 92). A.T.O.s such as Pueblo to People, Ten Thousand Villages, PeopLink, and the International Federation of Alternative Trade (I.F.A.T.) provide a much-needed service to artisan groups worldwide in the spirit of "Fair Trade." However, Littrell and Dickson have asked how A.T.O.s will be able to keep prices to consumers low while at the same time paying a fair wage to the craftspeople (1997). Page-Reeves agrees: "While not-for-profit organizations and networks have been crucial clients for most Andean knitting organization, this market remains too small to absorb the amount of knitwear which could be produced by women in need of income" (1998, 85). A basic premise in marketing is that when channels of distribution become too cumbersome or costly, sellers should attempt to take the exchange offer directly to end customers. This is termed "disintermediation," and some have suggested that one of the advantages of the Internet for commercial purposes is its ability to effectively eliminate the costs imposed by multiple channel intermediaries (Benjamin and Wigand, 1995).

Technological "Leapfrog"

A pattern that emerges as technology becomes more inexpensive over time is termed "leapfrogging": "By creating a basic capacity to operate imported technology, countries can progress, climbing the rungs of the ladder, by learning to duplicate, to adapt to their own needs and, finally, to innovate" (U.N.D.P., 1999, 61). The 1998 U.N. Human Development Report also highlighted the advantages of helping developing nations jump ahead technologically. "If poor countries can leapfrog in both consumption patterns and production technologies, they can accelerate consumption growth and human development without the huge costs of environmental damage" (Canada and the World Backgrounder, 2000, 16). Because the costs of learning and operating a business on the Internet have been falling steadily, commercial use of the Internet may now represent a leapfrog opportunity for developing nations.

Adaptive Outcomes

What happens when traditional organizational forms meet new technological and market forces? Organizational theory has examined this interplay from several perspectives: the "swelling middle" between market and hierarchical structure (Zenger and Hesterly, 1997); the rise and dominance of small entrepreneurial firms (Birch, 1987); and technology as an enabler of organizational change and community/trust as an emerging organizational paradigm (Adler, 2001). Often, an organization will adapt itself into a structure that embraces the old and the new, rather than completely abandoning the previous system. Local Javanese woodworkers demonstrated this phenomenon, creating a hybrid of "kinship and contract" which gave them the ability to compete with vertically integrated transnational factories (Alexander and Alexander, 2000). The Japanese integrated Western technology after the Meiji Restoration of 1868, and this combination of systems was symbolized by the slogan "Wa-kon Yo-sai," which means "Japanese spirit and Western ability" (Morishima, 1982, 23).

Cultures affect the nature of change depending on whether they relate their beholders to the past or to the future (Coser and Coser, 1990). Some developing economies have already combined elements of traditionalism and modern technology with their integration into the world economy. Rosser and Rosser have labeled these as the "new traditional" economies, which use modern technology while simultaneously resurrecting or preserving traditional social practices, creating a superior synthesis of the old with the new, the individual with the collective, and the ethical with the practical (1998). In Chiapas, Mexico, a coffee cooperative "... has been successful in finding a strategy for competing in the global economy while reaffirming the cultural identity of its members. The organizational structure adopted to achieve this success is a hybrid form of organization that combines aspects of traditional Mayan Indian community democracy with the characteristics of a modern capitalist corporation – an 'associative corporation'" (Escobar, 1995, 428). In summary, there is a clear need for easy-to-implement, profitable (self-sustaining) business models that leverage the unique resources of developing countries and that can be successfully implemented and conducted within the constraints that currently exist within developing nations. Furthermore, this type of development activity need not lead to cultural homogenization; on the contrary, there is evidence that it can result in heightened cultural identity.

MICRO-BUSINESS MODELS AND BUSINESS EDUCATION

Simply stated, a business model describes the specific methods used to conduct transactions and reveals how profits are generated for the business. A business model accomplishes this in part by specifying where the business is positioned within its industry's value chain. Models can be simple or very complex and require either little or very large amounts of investment and coordination. "Micro" implies the transactions occur at the lowest operational level possible: one individual seller procures and sells a single product via a simple channel of distribution to one individual buyer. Therefore, "micro-business models" are basic in nature, can often be implemented without additional overhead costs, require little investment and coordination, but still provide a profit for the business. Micro-business models are therefore well suited for business educational purposes, as well as serving as an appropriate starting point for individuals in traditional economies that wish to conduct business in market economies.

Practical, hands-on, field-ready instruction is more important in developing nations than in fully industrialized countries. There is a need for an experiential, practical tool using Internet technology that can be used to illustrate a broad range of business topics for instructional purposes and to improve current business practice or launch profitable businesses. Although there are many e-commerce tools and models, the tool that remains the most profitable and is the easiest to learn and to implement is the online auction. Why online auctions? They contain all the elements of the exchanges typically found in business: buyers, sellers, products, distribution, accounting, customer satisfaction, and profits. Additional advantages include: 1) many exchanges can take place in a short timeframe, 2) students can run it as a small business, 3) they tap a huge potential market (regional or global customers), 4) they allow direct sales to end consumers ("disintermediation"), and 5) there is interest in unique products, such as artisan craft from developing countries, at online auctions, which allows a community's cultural capital to be used as a source of competitive advantage. All that is required is access to a digital camera or scanner and access to the Internet.

Overview of the Pedagogical Tool

Online auctions represent an efficient and profitable micro-business model - "a small business" that can be run on its own or used to supplement an existing business. This unique tool is currently being used successfully by thousands of businesses in the U.S., and by instructors to illustrate a variety of business concepts in the classroom. The tool is experiential in nature and demonstrates a business model that can be used "in the field."

Step-By-Step Description of the Teaching Method

A teaching method that focuses on an online business model would include the following goals:

- To demonstrate an online business model that is working effectively for thousands of small and large businesses nationwide;
- To allow students to sell merchandise in an real-world marketplace;
- To apply marketing textbook concepts; and
- To encourage entrepreneurial students to develop their own business by exposing them to a readily available online business model.

In past semesters, excess inventory has been obtained from retailers, or students have been assigned to find their own merchandise. These items are prepared for sale on eBay.com, the largest auction service on the web. According to the eBay website, the auction site has 61.7 million registered members representing over 150 different countries (eBay, 2003a). Beyond its own revenues, eBay's gross merchandise sales – the value of all the goods and services traded on eBay – totaled over $14.8 billion in 2002 (eBay, 2003b). A number of small companies around the country rely on eBay as their primary means of transacting business, and many others have become "bricks and clicks" – using auctions to supplement their existing brick and mortar business. Fortune 500 companies have discovered the advantages of online consumer auctions and are increasing their use of them (Wingfield, 2001).

Project Design and Management

Students complete two written exercises before the items are put up for bid:

- Assignment 1: Each student is required to visit three of the major consumer-to-consumer auction sites (Amazon, eBay, and Yahoo!). Students are to read the guidelines and rules regarding buying and selling then search for items that interest them. They must also record "tips" for sellers given in the Help sections on these sites and make note of auction elements that caught their attention (wording, photos, descriptions, etc.).
- Assignment 2: Once assignment 1 is complete, the merchandise is assigned to two-person teams in class. The instructor keeps the merchandise, so a portion of a class period is devoted to allowing students to become familiar with their assigned item, describe it, and individually photograph it. Students must also research the regular retail price of the item if unknown and set the starting bid price. To make the information easier to upload to eBay, the teams are required to turn in the written part of this assignment on diskette or via email.

Next, the instructor posts a few items each week on eBay using what the students have turned in. All auctions are set up to last seven days, although this may be set between three and ten days. When this tool has been used as a supplement to an existing course, brief updates on the progress of the students' auctions are presented throughout the semester. In some cases, the auction updates are used to underscore a point on topics such as risk perception, satisfaction, brand equity, or pricing theory. Most of the merchandise sells with no problem, and the proceeds either go back to the retailer who supplied the merchandise or to a collective class fund. Students will often set a goal of receiving only positive feedback from all of their "customers."

A number of discussion points are possible when this teaching tool is used, including:

- Business uses of auctions
  - To liquidate inventory
  - To add a "fun" element to an existing company website (e.g. SharperImage.com)
  - To research initial prices of new products
  - Various types of auctions and their uses at the B2B level
  - How the "after-market" market works

- Consumer behavior
    - How do people get carried away at auctions? What is the role of perceived urgency and competitiveness in the bidding process? How does the "winner's curse" occur?
    - What are the main sources of perceived risk in the online environment, and how can sellers reduce it?
    - Describe the various types of bidder strategies
    - How important is brand/site/company loyalty in the online environment?
- Auction research topics – questions, hypotheses, and analysis
    - What is the relationship between number of bids, number of bidders, and the final price received?
    - Identify the factors that are within the control of the seller that are likely to impact the final selling price and the number of bids an item receives (brand name, reputation (feedback score) of seller, starting price, presence of a photo of the item, item description, auction site, and length of auction). Hypothesize the nature of the impact you expect each of these factors will have on the D.V.s (final price and number of bids).
- Business models
    - What is meant by the term "business model?" Why/how does this one work?
    - Suggest improvements or possible extensions to the online auction model
- Marketing mix
    - Brand equity – does a national brand name have an actual value at online auctions? Why or why not?
    - Promotional elements – what seemed to work? – choice of product category, presence of photos, the use of certain words in description, attention getters,
    - Dynamic pricing concepts; and the difficulty of forecasting sales and profits in a negotiated environment
    - What role does an auction service play in the exchange process? Distribution channel? Agent? Broker? Promoter?
- Customer satisfaction
    - The key role of fulfillment in the online environment – payment processing, shipment, responsiveness to inquiries, customer feedback

Research needs are great for those in developing nations wishing to sell to western consumers. The business classroom can include projects that are designed to satisfy these needs. Assigned projects can include the following: consumer preferences and trends, trends in product design, finding consistent sources of high quality goods, tariffs and trends in government regulations, finding artisan cooperatives to participate, and costs of shipping and currency exchange issues.

Technological Developments

Appendix 12.1 is designed to reveal e-commerce development potential in developing countries categorized by continent. The most populous developing nations from each continent are presented. A review of these measures helps answer the question: "In which countries could this micro-business model be most readily applied?" The best candidates will have a moderate and growing Gross Domestic Product (G.D.P.) per capita, a reasonably high technology achievement index (T.A.I.), evidence of innovation as indicated by number of patents filed per million people, moderate levels of education as evidenced by the percent of people living below the poverty level, and adequate I.T. infrastructure as measured by number of Internet Service Providers (I.S.P.s) and number of P.C.s and telephone lines per thousand people. The United States and Canada are included as points of reference.

Based on the metrics provided, there appear to be a number of countries where an investment in education regarding micro business models involving e-commerce is likely to pay good dividends, including:

- Eastern/Central Europe (Russia, Ukraine, Romania, the Czech Republic, Hungary, and Bulgaria)
- Asia (India, Pakistan, Iran, and Uzbekistan)
- Africa (Algeria, Kenya, Egypt, and Morocco)
- Central America/Caribbean (Dominican Republic, Guatemala, and Honduras)
- South America (Chile, Brazil, Ecuador, Peru, and Bolivia).

CONCLUSION

Micro-business models have the advantage of being powerful and relatively easy to understand, teach, and implement in developing nations. It is recommended that international business education include the pedagogical tool presented in this paper, whether the classroom is in developed or developing nations. This practical tool involving online auctions illustrates business concepts while giving students hands-on experience with a business model that has been successfully used by thousands of businesses worldwide. The tool has potential for business education both in the classroom and in the business arena. In the classroom, students are exposed to a variety of key business concepts, they experientially see e-commerce in action via a straightforward micro-business model, and they can develop needed research via class assignments for successful implementation of e-commerce businesses. In the business arena, entrepreneurs in developing nations can use Internet Cafes in their home nation to launch new businesses. They can help artisan cooperatives bypass traditional intermediaries and sell their merchandise online or work with manufacturers, wholesalers, or retailers (as is now being done in the U.S.) to use online auctions as a means of liquidating excess inventory. Students may locate and organize artisans into cooperatives which should help to improve the profitability of sale of individual auctions. If developed up from the grassroots, there is potential for long-term impact on G.D.P., gender equity, and retention of local cultural practices. There is also potential for increasing interactions between professional schools and industry or government agencies as these entities choose to cooperate in classroom projects involving this tool. Limitations to the use of micro-business model and business education in developing nations include language differences, distribution challenges, currency fluctuations, inconsistent supply of products and materials, governmental restrictions, tariffs, shipping costs, and logistics to developed nations, all of which require further research on the part of users and participants.

APPENDIX 12.1

Eastern/Central Europe	Russia	Turkey	Ukraine	Poland	Romania	Yugoslavia	Czech Republic	Belarus	Hungary	Bulgaria
Population (mil.)	145	67	48	39	22	n/a	10	10	10	8
GDP per capita	9,300	7,000	4,500	9,500	7,400	n/a	15,300	8,200	13,300	6,600
GDP % growth	4.2	7.8	4.1	1.3	4.5	n/a	1.5	4.2	3.2	4.8
Income class.	LMC	LMC	LMC	UMC	LMC	n/a	UMC	LMC	UMC	LMC
Exports ($ mil.)	104,600	35,100	18,100	32,400	13,700	n/a	40,800	7,700	31,400	5,300
GDI Rank	56	81	63	35	57	n/a	32	48	36	51
% below poverty	25.0	n/a	29.0	18.4	44.5	n/a	n/a	n/a	n/a	12.6
Patents per mil.	105	n/a	12	26	41	n/a	22	39	30	25
TAI score	n/a	n/a	n/a	0.41	0.37	n/a	0.47	n/a	0.46	0.41
Phone lines /1000	207	290	195	209	169	n/a	377	224	307	418
PCs per 1000	43	37	18	69	32	n/a	122	n/a	86	33
Internet users	18,000,000	2,500,000	750,000	6,400,000	1,000,000	400,000	2,690,000	422,000	1,200,000	585,000
ISPs	35	50	260	19	38	9	301	23	16	200

Asia	India	Pakistan	Iran	Burma	Uzbekistan	Nepal	Iraq	Dem. People's Rep. of Korea	Afghanistan	Sri Lanka
Population (mil.)	1046	148	67	42	26	26	24	22	28	20
GDP per capita	2,540	n/a	7,000	1,660	2,500	1,400	2,400	1,000	700	3,700
GDP % growth	4.3	4.5	6.5	3.3	3.0	-0.6	-3.0	1.0	n/a	3.2
Income class.	LIC	LIC	LMC	LIC	LIC	LIC	LMC	LIC	LIC	LMC
Exports ($ mil.)	44,500	9,800	24,800	2,700	2,800	720	13,000	n/a	1,200	4,600
GDI Rank	103	120	86	n/a	79	119	n/a	n/a	n/a	80
% below poverty	25.0	35.0	40.0	25.0	n/a	35.0	n/a	n/a	n/a	n/a
Patents per mil.	1	n/a	2	n/a	20	n/a	n/a	n/a	n/a	0
TAI score	0.20	0.17	0.26	n/a	n/a	0.08	n/a	n/a	n/a	0.20
Phone lines /1000	26	19	95	6	77	9	28	50	1	25
PCs per 1000	4	4	60	1	n/a	3	n/a	n/a	n/a	7
Internet users	7,000,000	1,200,000	420,000	10,000	100,000	60,000	12,500	n/a	n/a	121,500
ISPs	43	30	8	1	42	6	1	1	1	5

Africa	Nigeria	Egypt	Ethiopia	Congo	South Africa	Tanzania	Sudan	Kenya	Algeria	Morocco
Population (mil.)	130	71	68	55	44	37	37	31	32	31
GDP per capita	875	3,900	750	610	10,000	630	1,420	1,020	5,300	3,900
GDP % growth	3.0	1.7	5.5	3.5	3.0	5.2	5.1	0.8	3.0	3.2
Income class.	LIC	LMC	LIC	LIC	LMC	LIC	LIC	LIC	LMC	LMC
Exports ($ mil.)	17,300	7,000	433	1,200	31,800	863	1,800	2,100	19,500	7,500
GDI Rank	124	99	139	111	90	130	116	115	88	102
% below poverty	60.0	n/a	45.0	n/a	50.0	36.0	n/a	50.0	23.0	19.0
Patents per mil.	n/a	1	0	n/a	0	0	0	n/a	0	0
TAI score	n/a	0.24	n/a	n/a	0.34	0.08	0.07	0.13	0.22	n/a
Phone lines /1000	4	56	3	7	115	3	11	10	71	45
PCs per 1000	6	11	1	0	66	3	3	5	6	11
Internet users	100,000	600,000	20,000	6,000	3,068,000	300,000	56,000	500,000	180,000	400,000
ISPs	11	50	1	2	150	6	2	65	2	8

North America	The United States	Mexico	Canada
Population (mil.)	281	103	32
GDP per capita	37,600	8,897	28,932
GDP % growth	2.5	1.0	3.4
Income class.	HIC	UMC	HIC
Exports ($ mil.)	687,000	158,400	260,500
GDI Rank	5	52	6
% below poverty	12.7	40.0	n/a
Patents per mil.	298	1	44
TAI score	0.73	0.39	0.59
Phone lines /1000	691	119	652
PCs per 1000	574	55	404
Internet users	165,750,000	3,500,000	16,840,000
ISPs	7,000	51	760

Central America/Caribbean	Guatemala	Cuba	Dominican Republic	Haiti	Honduras
Population (mil.)	14	11	9	8	7
GDP per capita	3,700	2,300	6,100	1,700	2,600
GDP % growth	2.0	0.0	4.2	-1.5	2.0
Income class.	LMC	LMC	LMC	LIC	LMC
Exports ($ mil.)	2,700	1,800	5,300	298	1,300
GDI Rank	97	n/a	77	122	96
% below poverty	75.0	n/a	25.0	80.0	n/a
Patents per mil.	n/a	4	n/a	0	1
TAI score	n/a	n/a	n/a	n/a	0.21
Phone lines /1000	n/a	42	81	8	36
PCs per 1000	10	12	n/a	n/a	11
Internet users	200,000	120,000	186,000	30,000	40,000
ISPs	5	5	24	3	8

South America	Brazil	Colombia	Argentina	Peru	Venezuela	Chile	Ecuador	Bolivia	Paraguay	Uruguay
Population (mil.)	176	41	38	28	24	15	13	8	6	3
GDP per capita	7,600	6,500	10,200	4,800	5,500	10,000	3,100	2,500	4,200	7,800
GDP % growth	1.0	2.0	-14.7	4.8	-8.9	1.8	3.3	1.9	-2.5	-10.5
Income class.	UMC	LMC	UMC	LMC	LMC	UMC	LMC	LMC	LMC	UMC
Exports ($ mil.)	59,400	12,900	25,300	7,600	n/a	17,800	4,900	1,300	2,000	2,100
GDI Rank	58	55	34	72	60	43	84	94	69	39
% below poverty	22.0	55.0	37.0	50.0	47.0	21.0	70.0	70.0	36.0	6.0
Patents per mil.	3	n/a	4	n/a	n/a	1	n/a	n/a	n/a	3
TAI score	0.31	0.27	n/a	n/a	n/a	0.36	0.25	0.28	0.25	0.34
Phone lines /1000	97	133	198	64	107	168	83	39	49	274
PCs per 1000	48	37	68	38	45	92	20	17	12	103
Internet users	13,980,000	1,150,000	3,880,000	3,000,000	1,300,000	3,100,000	328,000	78,000	20,000	400,000
ISPs	50	18	33	10	16	7	31	9	4	14

REFERENCES

Alexander, J. & Alexander, P. (2000). From kinship to contract? Production chains in the Javanese woodworking industries. *Human Organization*, 59 (Spring): 106-116.

Benjamin, R. & Wigland, R. (1995). Electronic markets and virtual value chains on the information superhighway. *Sloan Management Review*, 36 (Winter): 72.

Birch, D. L. (1987). *Job Creation in America*. Free Press: New York.

Canada & the World Backgrounder. (2000). *Stacked Deck*, 65 (6): 16-20.

Cohen, J. H. (1998). Craft production and the challenge of the global market: an artisans' cooperative in Oaxaca, Mexico. *Human Organization*, 57 (Spring): 74-82.

Coser, L. A. & Coser, R. (1990). *Time Perspective and Social Structure in the Sociology of Time*. MacMillan: London.

eBay. (2003a). "eBay Inc. Announces Fourth Quarter and Year End 2002 Financial Results." http://www.shareholder.com/ebay/news/20030116-99663.htm.

eBay. (2003b). "Company Overview," http://pages.ebay.com/community/aboutebay/overview/index.html.

Escobar, A. (1995). Anthropology and the future: new technologies and the reinvention of culture. *Futures*, 27 (4): 409-421.

Everett, M. (1998). Latin America on-line: the Internet, development, and democratization. *Human Organization*, 57 (Winter): 385-393.

Hackenberg, R. A. (1999). Victims of globalization: is economics the instrument needed to provide them a share of the wealth? *Human Organization*, 58 (Winter): 439-442.

Keare, D. H. (2001), Learning to clap: Reflections on top-down versus bottom-up development. *Human Organization*, 60 (Summer): 159-165.

Klein, T. A. & Nason, R. W. (2001). Marketing and development: macromarketing perspectives. In *Handbook of Marketing and Society*, eds.Paul N. Bloom and Gregory T. Gundlach. Thousand Oaks, CA: Sage.

Morishima M. (1982). *Why Has Japan 'Succeeded'? Western Technology and the Japanese Ethos*. Cambridge, UK: Cambridge University Press.

Olson, J. M. (1999). Are artesanal cooperatives in Guatemala unraveling? *Human Organization*, 58 (Spring): 54-66.

Page-Reeves, J. (1998). Alpaca sweater design and marketing: problems and prospects for cooperative knitting organizations in Bolivia. *Human Organization*, 57 (Spring): 83-93.

Rosser, J. B. Jr., & Rosser, M. V. (1998). Islamic and Neo-Confucian perspectives on the new traditional economy. *Eastern Economic Journal*, 24 (Spring): 217-227.

Samiee, S. (1998). Exporting and the Internet: a conceptual perspective. *International Marketing Review*, 15 (5): 413-426.

Sen, A. (1999). *Commodities and Capabilities*. Oxford: Oxford University Press.

Smith, K. (1998). Sedentarization and market integration: new opportunities for Rendille and Ariaal women of Northern Kenya. *Human Organization*, 57 (Winter): 459-468.

U.N.C.T.A.D. (2001). *E*-commerce and Development Report; United Nations Conference on Trade and Development, (http://www.unctad.org/en/press/pr0134en.htm). Accessed on August 19, 2002.

U.N.D.P. (1999). Human Development Report, United Nations Development Program; (http://www.undp.org/).

U.N.D.P. (2000). Driving Information and Communications Technology for Development, United Nations Development Program; (http://www.undp.org/)

U.N.-Habitat. (2003). The Challenge of Slums - Global Report on Human Settlements 2003, United Nations Human Settlement Program, (http://www.unhabitat.org/)

Wingfield, N. (2001). Corporate sellers put the online auctioneer on even faster track. *The Wall Street Journal;* June 1, 2001: A1.

Zenger, T. R. & Hesterly, W. S. (1997). The disaggregation of corporations: selective intervention, high-powered incentives, and molecular units. *Organizational Science*, 8 (3): 209-222.

Sources for data in Appendix 12.1

U.N.C.T.A.D. (2001). E-commerce and Development Report; United Nations Conference on Trade and Development, (http://www.unctad.org/en/press/pr0134en.htm). Accessed on August 19, 2002.
U.N.D.P. (1999). *Human Development Report.* United Nations Development Program; (http://www.undp.org/).
www.nationmaster.com
www.cia.gov (World Factbook)
www.geographic.com
www.bartleby.com (World Factbook)
www.worldbank.org (Countries & Regions)
www.undp.org (Human Development Report, 2002)

Chapter 13

Virtually Situated Learning Environments – the Business Educational Model for Developing Countries in a Knowledge Era

Dr Sandra Jones
Royal Melbourne Institute of Technology

Jackie McCann
Royal Melbourne Institute of Technology

INTRODUCTION

The plethora of change facing society as new communication technology leads to the need for a new approach to knowledge is leading to re-assessment of the focus of business. Herzenberg, et. al. state that "communication of knowledge accelerates the achievements of economies of depth....transfer and sharing of knowledge holds considerable untapped potential for performance gains" (Herzenberg, Alic, and Wial, 1998, 91). Zack claims that many organisations are recognising that to remain competitive, they must manage their "intellectual resources and capabilities" (Zack, 1999, 125). Seely Brown states that change requires multiple, intertwining forces of content, context and community (1999). Allee states that change requires a reassessment of the relationship between society, business and the political system (2003).

What this pressure has done has placed knowledge as the new business competitive advantage for the future (Quinn, 1992; Drucker, 1993; Davenport, 1997). This has led to a spate of literature on what is being discussed when we talk of knowledge. Knowledge, it is claimed, can be both explicit (observable) or tacit (within the knowledge of employees), (Leonard-Barton, 1995; Nonaka, 1998; Nonaka and Takeuchi, 1995). It is recognised that the new communication technology is very good at helping collect, collate, and codify explicit knowledge. However, it is less able to access tacit knowledge that lies within the heads of employees, that requires employees to first recognise that they have the knowledge and then to develop a willingness to share it (Nonaka, 1998; Nonaka and Takeuchi, 1995). Nonaka states that "creating new knowledge....depends on tapping the tacit and often highly subjective insights, intuitions, and hunches, of individual employees and making these insights available for testing and use by the company as a whole" (1998, 24). This is not an easy task, indeed Polanyi contends that tacit knowledge is innate intelligence, perception, and capacities for reasoning, rather than memory and knowledge store, and thus difficult, and sometimes impossible, to share (1958, 1962). Thus tacit knowledge underlies any act of communication and is not easily recognisable or able to be separated from other knowledge. This creates particular challenges for managers and employees given the need to first assist employees to understanding and acknowledging the tacit knowledge they possess and then to encourage employees to be motivated to continuously develop and share this tacit knowledge.

As well as this distinction between explicit and tacit knowledge, there is a body of literature that discusses the different dimensions of knowledge. Leonard-Barton identifies four interdependent dimensions – employee knowledge and skills, physical and technical systems, managerial systems, and values and norms (1995). Each of these dimensions requires different strategies for ongoing development. Zack differentiates six types of knowledge – declarative, procedural (know how), causal, conditional relational, and contributional (1999). Allee takes these types of knowledge and relates them to domains that range in degree and type of skills required, from simple data (know what) to more skill-based application that involves more abstract reasoning (know why) (1997). This creates further challenges for business and business educators who have relied more on communicating know-what and know-how than know-why knowledge.

Finally, it is recognised that knowledge can be individual or part of a collective, with different cultures varying in the importance attached to whether knowledge is individual or shared. For example Allee states that Western cultures have traditionally focused on individual rather than collective knowledge development (1997). Encouraging employees to share knowledge, especially tacit knowledge, thus requires moving to a more collective, or team oriented, approach. This, it is argued, is influenced by the ability to physically meet, the intelligent use of electronic networks, levels of I.Q. and emotional intelligence. Goleman argues that the single most important element of group intelligence is emotional intelligence, stating:

> the key to high group harmony is social harmony. It is the ability to harmonise that, all things being equal, will make one group especially talented, productive and successful and another-with members whose talents and skills are equal in other regards – do poorly (1995, 159-160).

UNIVERSITIES IN A KNOWLEDGE ERA

Universities have been traditionally the principle source of graduates with knowledge required for industry. The new emphasis on these different forms of knowledge is forcing universities to reassess their approach to teaching, particularly in the business disciplines. In many countries, the role of universities was founded on a liberal tradition in which knowledge is acquired and disseminated "for its own sake as well as for the benefits that knowledge brings to the whole community" (Miller, 2000, 110). This role was premised on the belief that to have knowledge one must possess rational capacities, that is "capacities that enable not only the acquisition of certain kinds of information, but especially the development of understanding" (Miller, 2000, 158). Coady quotes Newman's (1960) picture of universities as "communities of learning devoted to the pursuit of significant truth, as an end in itself, and, as such, fulfilling a central cultural and ethical role for society at large" (2000, 6).

This liberal tradition of discipline-based "scholarly exchange" has been under pressures over the last decade to move towards a more service model in which academics have more temporary appointments, and the learning environment is more focused on graduating students with professional skill sets. Five years ago, Dudersadt stated of universities:

> although the primary mission of the university –the creation, preservation, integration, transmission, and application of knowledge—is not changing, the particular realization of each of these roles is changing dramatically. So, too, is the nature of the higher education enterprise as it evolves into a global knowledge industry (1998, 1).

Universities are no longer seen as the "custodian of national science and culture," but rather as a commercial enterprise subject to the same rational economics as other such enterprises (McIntyre and Marginson, 2000, 67). In this environment, public funding of universities is seen as a cost rather than an investment, with universities expected to serve national objectives in new ways:

> as a teaching institution engaged in vocational training of a far more direct and systematic nature, as a place of research where the production of knowledge is much more closely linked to practical and commercial uses, and as a business with the potential to generate foreign income (McIntyre and Marginson, 2000, 67)

This creates a dilemma for universities in delivering a business education. At the very time that the knowledge economy needs universities to provide a more liberal business education that develops graduates with advanced skill, systems understanding, and intuition, governments are exhorting universities to adopt a more corporate 'service' approach in which universities respond to industry needs. The potential for this to lead to universities only delivering what industry thinks it needs today, does not augur well for the continuously changing challenges of a knowledge era.

Accompanying this, there is pressure on universities to change the form in which education is delivered to accommodate a more practical approach to learning and a more student-centered emphasis in order to encourage the know-why form of knoweldge. This requires business academics to change their approach from one of content delivery to skill development if students are to graduate with the capabilities required in a knowledge era. Biggs states:

> when the basic bodies of knowledge and knowledge relating to professional practice, are changing as rapidly as they are, it no longer makes sense to teach students all those things they will need to know in their professional careers....Students should be taught how to learn, how to seek new information, how to utlize it and evaluate its importance, how to solve novel, non-textbook, professional problems. They will need metacognitive skills, and an abstract body of theory on which to deploy them, so that they can judge reflectively how successfully they are coping with novel problems, and how they may do better (1999, 90).

This requires the teacher to become a guide, coach, motivator, facilitator, and co-ordinator of learning resources, creating a "context of learning which encourages students actively to engage in subject matter" (Ramsden, 1992, 114; Laurillard, 1994), while the student becomes an active 'doer,' presenting, analysing, questioning, judging, and combining ideas and information against an argument in order to solve problems and construct ways to develop knowledge (Ballard and Clanchy, 1997). Subject matter becomes integrated across a broad range of disciplines, and students work both individually and as a team to collect and assess information to solve problems. Laurillard provides a model of a student-centred teaching model (see Figure 13.1) that recognises the need to integrate the teachers conceptual knowledge with that of the students in a manner that encourages, through experiential learning, discussion, interaction, reflection and adaptation of conceptual knowledge (1994). Gibbons, et. al. described this as a move from Mode 1 to Mode 2 knowledge production (1994).

Figure 13.1

Student-Centred Teaching Model

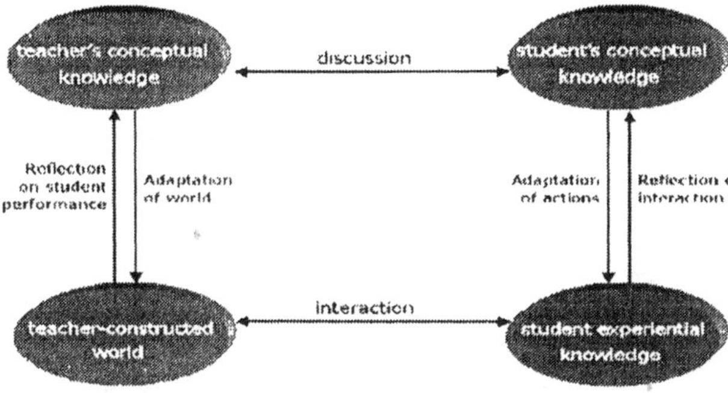

When applying this to the needs of a knowledge era, we need to add the importance of students learning as groups rather than individuals. Student experiences through interaction not only with the teacher but also with students and providing opportunities for students not only to self reflect but also to reflect as a group can thus be important elements of the learning process. In this environment, what then are the consequences for business education in developing countries?

BUSINESS EDUCATION IN DEVELOPING COUNTRIES

Given the confluence of pressures for change outlined above, it is not surprising that teaching business in developing countries presents further challenges, especially as Western universities, forced to become more financially self sufficient, recognise the opportunity to earn substantial income from mass delivering education to developing countries. Many Asian cultures, especially those steeped in a rich Confucian educational heritage, place greater emphasis on a conserving approach rather than an extending approach to knowledge (Biggs, 1999). Ballard and Clanchy state that in Asian cultures "scholarship is traditionally manifested by an extensive and accurate knowledge of the wisdom contained in authoritative texts or the sayings of earlier scholars and sages" (Ballard and Clanchy, 1997, 14). Tyson describes the traditional Asian educational process as based on, and perpetuating, a "culture of dependent learners in a didactic, knowledge-focused classroom...*[rather than]*...collaborative learners organising and managing their own learning processes" (1997, 77). This compares to the Western scientific and philosophical knowledge that is characterised by its "persistent openness to revision and change" (Ballard and Clanchy, 1997, 14). This results in students who are reluctant to express their point of view or question teachers during class; instead they seek clarification at the end of the class (Yap, 1997). It also produces a tendency by these students to memorise and rote-learn statements by eminent scholars in order to produce a 'correct' answer (Kember, 1996; Marton, et. al., 1993). Used to deferring to such authority, these students have difficulty offering their own views, especially if they are seen to be more learned and published. This leads to confusion about what in Western educational tradition is regarded as the 'cardinal sin' of plagiarism (Ballard and Clancy, 1997). In this environment, the easy response from Western universities is to deliver mass education focused on content rich material and to ignore the educational needs of a knowledge economy that seeks to equip students with skills required to either become employed in Western business or to deal with Western businesses styled in a more democratic basis.

On the other hand, universities that aim to genuinely deliver business education that will assist developing countries to compete in a global world market are designing a different educational experience. In so doing, they are heeding the advise by such as Biggs, who argues that the teaching response to these problems should not be to merely accommodate these students by adapting one's teaching towards meeting their preferred approach, but rather, it should be to design cognitive educational experiences that activate student or learning processes as appropriate to the objectives (1999). This can be done by positively encouraging students to critically evaluate information, to vocalise their opinions, and to ask questions (Yap, 1997).

One further advance needs to be taken into account when designing business educational opportunities for developing countries. The technological age has presented universities with the opportunity to use Interactive Communication Technology (I.C.T.) to provide business education to a larger and more geographically spread number of students, and in fact to cohorts of students in significantly different locations simultaneously.

However, use of this technology without thought can simply replicate a content-driven, teacher-centered education. Rose and Ryan argue that on-line delivery cannot be limited to simply the transfer of traditional teaching material to a computer-based learning format, rather it requires new design formats (Rose and Ryan, 1999). From his experience in developing educational delivery through the Internet, Hannah claims that a standard requirement for on-line educational delivery is new forms of expertise in "electronic inquiry and discourse" (1996, 1). This led Jones (forthcoming) to argue that technology should be used to augment, rather than replace, F2F learning environments.

Second, academics-as-business teachers may not have the skills required to provide this new high quality learning environment. Laurillard states that teachers may not have the skills to adapt to a new role as a "facilitator of knowledge preparing, supervising and de-briefing the multimedia assisted learning and providing students with interactive access to large text and audio-based learning" (Laurillard, 1994, 21). Thus, Collings separated the knowledge and skills required for teaching or 'real work' from that required for 'articulation' or "the work involved in negotiating the development and use of information technology infrastructure and designing and organising new ways of teaching" (1999, 5). This led Jones to argue that academics-as-educators must adapt to a more collaborative approach to designing educational experiences (2003). These problems are increased when delivering education on-line. Similarly, Smith argues that the teacher has to have the skills to use the multimedia as "it falls upon the teacher to constantly recreate the instructional process and offer a variety of choices" (1997, 36). Finally, students may not have the skills to use the on-line educational process effectively, and thus the teacher needs skills to guide the learner in the use of this new teaching medium. Laurillard states

> the learner ...cannot be expected to set appropriate goals, or plot a reasonable path, they will under-specify the problem, be distracted by irrelevancies, be unsure how to evaluate the information they find, over generalise from instances, remain unaware of incompleteness, fail to recognise inconsistencies....there is every opportunity to fail to meet the objective (1994, 24).

On the other hand, I.C.T. can be used to present students with learning opportunities that model real world activities and create interactive opportunities for students and to support a two-way dialogue between students and between teacher and students. Laurillard described how computers could be used to provide students with a simulated environment with which to interact and to "simulate the real world and to link students to various audio and visual data bases" (1994, 20). Gerrard explains how the third generation of technology enables communication between students that eradicates the disadvantage of 'social distance' by enabling students to share ideas, knowledge, and experience (2001).

Thus, I.C.T. can be used to design business education opportunities for developing countries that assist the development and sharing of knowledge and do so in a way that maximises a student-centered learning design. The next section presents an example of just such an approach.

DESIGNING A VIRTUAL SITUATED LEARNING APPROACH (V.S.L.E.)

The University of the Royal Melbourne Institute of Technology (Australia) [R.M.I.T.] has developed a suite of interlinked, proprietary software suited to a range of teaching and learning approaches as part of a distributed learning system (D.L.S.). This system enables technology to be used to provide a diversity of educational experiences through online content and interactions with both peers and academics. In 2003 the School of

Management was asked to prepare a business course on Leadership and Management Skills for on-line delivery as part of an M.B.A. program to be delivered in various developing countries, commencing with Vietnam and China.

The Leadership and Management course is the introductory course in the M.B.A. that is delivered generally and in industry specific formats in both Australia and overseas, in a F2F experiential learning environment. The course is designed to maximise experiential group learning opportunities through small and large group interactions designed to encourage students to reflect upon the real-world working environment in which they seek to become leaders and managers of the future. The group learning opportunities forces those students who are more accustomed to working as individuals into collective activities that they will encounter in work life. Each group includes a mix of local and international students and thus assist students from more teaching-oriented backgrounds into more student-centered experiences. What eventuates is that students' experience, and build skills, in the gamut of issues associated with group dynamic.

Given its design, the course provides an important role in embedding the student-centered, group oriented, learning pedagogy that underpins the entire M.B.A. Accordingly, the course is designed as an intensive four-day workshop in which assessment is part of continuous group activities. This presented many challenges for the academic designers of the on-line delivery option for students in developing countries. As well as the challenges outlined above, consideration had to be given to the fact that the local facilitators employed in the developing countries to assist the learning process had little experience of a student-centered educational pedagogy. Further, it was important that the learning experience was designed as a culturally sensitive educational experience appropriate to the particular culture of various developing countries, whilst still providing students with the opportunity to develop knowledge about Western business leadership and management challenges. To summarise, the academic designers of the on-line course recognised that they faced a number of challenges including how to:

- reproduce the group learning process, including how to ensure support and monitoring for the group dynamic learning process,
- assist academic facilitators in the local countries to support students in this learning mode,
- design professional practice activities that have 'real-life' educational value and skill development,
- design assessment activities that will support the group learning process, both verbal and written,
- design professional practice and assessment opportunities with emphasis on reflection as a learning activity,

- assist academic facilitators to understand how and when to add local and culturally specific content,
- design a course with a core content which must be delivered and additional options which can be included or not, depending on the progress of the class as a whole or individual groups (to allow customisation of the experience), and
- assist local academics to deal with a wide variety of work and life experience in the student population.

Following some discussion between the academic and educational designers, it was agreed that the on-line course would incorporate a number of elements. First, the academic content would provide material on the appropriate theories of leadership and management. This material was fairly easily accessible from lecture notes, power point slides, and reference material. It was produced in a static form with assistance from educational designers and with some embedded exercises that could not be tampered with by students or local facilitators. The design, however, did enable local facilitators to add material relevant to the culture and environment in which the learning was occurring, for example topical news items. Following discussion with the multi-media groups assisting the academic designers, the static material was complemented by video 'grabs' of speakers, discussion questions/issues, links to websites of leading exponents of management theories, and links to journals through university library copyright capabilities. This is depicted in graphic form in Appendix 1. In this way it was considered that this would ensure the consistency, integrity, and quality of the material irrespective of where the course was delivered.

Second, and more importantly, as further shown in Appendix 1, the course was designed with a Virtual Situated Learning Environment (V.S.L.E.) that provides the opportunity for professional practice experiential opportunities of management and leadership challenges and the raw material from which student assessment can be designed to extend students' analytical and reflective skills. It provides the opportunity to normalise the experience for students by providing them with a common company to work within which goes some way to both overcome the range of student experience and to provide them with the challenges of a new business environment. Finally, it provides role play opportunities by assigning students to groups and by giving them challenges to act as Leaders in the groups and as virtual leaders in the V.S.L.E. company. This enables students who may never have had the chance to 'act out' a business leadership role to do so in a 'safe' learning environment.

The V.S.L.E. provides the dynamic part of the course and enables cultural sensitivity related to the country in which the course is delivered to become part of the underpinning learning of the course. As mentioned above, it provides students with a 'safe environment' in which they can apply theory, reflect upon the practice, and relate the theory to reality. In so doing, the

V.S.L.E. is designed to assist students to develop knowledge appropriate to the business environment in which they operate. It also enables students to experience different learning environments, and thus caters to a variety of learning styles.

The V.S.L.E. is accessible to students through a virtual company website that adds a degree of authenticity to the exercise. It is designed as a restaurant complex with a history that includes being initially established as a privately-owned restaurant complex in France but was later floated as a public company. It was then purchased by a major American company and is now extending into South East Asia. Multiple divisions have been designed into the company to allow further local development or the sense of a diverse organisation.

This V.S.L.E., and the industry identified for the V.S.L.E., was chosen for the following reasons:

- First, it can be safely assumed that all students have real-life experience of a restaurant (either as customers or employees) of some sort relevant to the country in which they are located. This then enables student to adopt a more realistic approach to the learning environment and participating in role play a more comfortable experience.
- Second, the history of company change and expansion from private to public and from a single country base to a global network provides the opportunity for students to explore leadership and management challenges associated with a knowledge era and multiple cultural challenges.
- Third, the use of a single V.S.L.E. provides the opportunity for all students to have some consistency in their learning experience given that they are working within the same framework rather than extracting information from a variety of locations in the same business or a variety of businesses in the same location. This consistency allows for relatively controlled conditions and assists easier and more consistent assessment whilst still recognising that every response/experience/piece of work will be different. It also allows managers and leaders from a broad range of industries to explore both the similarities and differences they are facing.
- Fourth, the design of the V.S.L.E. as a globally networked company enables students in developing countries to consider their role in the broader global environment.
- Fifth, the V.S.L.E. provides the potential for student networking through virtual interaction and, indeed, for networking students across environments, countries, cultures, in varying stages of development.
- Sixth, the V.S.L.E. provides opportunities to design activities that link various subjects and specialisations as part of an overall business

studies program; for example it can be extended into marketing, logistics, finance and accounting, corporate responsibility, or H.R.M.

- Seventh, the V.S.L.E. provides potential and future managerial executives in developing countries the opportunity to learn how to communicate in an on-line environment and to use the tools that are necessary skills for managers and leaders of business today.
- Eight, it also provides managers/leaders in developing countries the opportunity to undertake post-graduate studies in order to update, and reflect on, their knowledge through formal, practice-based, work-integrated learning opportunities that are self-paced and enable some degree of self-assessment through which they can develop an understanding of academic rigor requirements, and, at the same time, develop realistic expectations of their objectives: real skills development through real learning.
- Finally, the V.S.L.E. provides universities the opportunity to design a business learning environment that accords with a student-centered experiential educational pedagogy that recognises, on the one hand, the importance of practice-based and work-integrated learning, and on the other hand, the need for academic rigour to be associated with a university award. It also provides academics the opportunity to combine their full-time professional teaching experience as authors and facilitators of theoretical knowledge (know what) with the valuable experience of practitioners as supporters and facilitators of practice or skills-based knowledge (know how).

Once the V.S.L.E. was designed and integrated into the content part of the course, attention was given to developing a series of professional practice activities and assessment activities that links the theory to the practice and that requires group interactivity. A number of activities, both assessable and non-assessable were developed. It is in this area that the greatest scope is created for developing business activities appropriate to the country/ culture in which the course is being delivered as well as changing business conditions. The challenges presented are real and reflect what they would find in real life.

While identifying the positive potential of using V.S.L.E. as a tool to assist business education in developing countries, there are some problems that need to be considered to ensure that this form of business education is effective.

First, there is need to ensure that the technology platform available in the developing country, or at least on campus, is sufficient to enable the course design. Associated with this is the need to ensure some degree of equity is available to enable student access and that students (and facilitators) are adequately trained to use the technology.

Second, there is need to ensure that students can access adequate research links through the web. The shortage of readily accessible reference material in many developing countries makes it imperative to ensure that students have access to the latest business research to ensure that the learning process does take account of the rapid changes in business associated with a knowledge era.

Third, there is need to provide, at least initially, adequate F2F learning support as students in developing countries seek to address the challenges not only of a rapidly changing knowledge era, but also of an educational process that requires much greater participation than they are used to in a remembered teacher-centered environment.

Fourth, there is need to ensure that there are open-channels of communication between the academic designers of the course and the users (academic facilitators and students) so that feedback can be used to continually improve the quality of the educational experience.

Fifth, the dynamic nature of the V.S.L.E. means that it requires maintenance and updating to ensure that it remains valid in terms of course objectives, the environment in which it is being delivered, the technology available, student needs, and the commercial environment. This means that there may be an increased cost in course delivery over and above less dynamic course designs.

Sixth, this approach requires a combination of two skill sets (academic and business) in the course development phase. This may also increase the costs of course design and content production. However, this may be offset by the reduction in seniority of the facilitators who will be following guidelines for pre-prepared materials and need only customise the local content and monitor team development rather than be theoretical experts in the field. This means that they may be sessionally employed rather than being fulltime members of staff.

CONCLUSION

In recognising the need of developing countries to quickly enhance the business skills of large number of employees if they are to develop competitive industries in a globally networked business world, this paper set out to present an appropriate educational model that will maximise business skills development of students in a minimum time period. Given recognition of the need to not only teach business content and theories developed in Western countries, but also to design educational experiences that use I.C.T. to provide 'virtual' learning opportunities, and at the same time, adhere to a student-centered learning environment, the authors introduced the concept of V.S.L.E.s and proposed that the educational design include experiential learning opportunities. By using a case study example of a recent development of a V.S.L.E. designed to assist student learning about leadership and management challenges for business, the authors describe an educational approach that is experiential, student-centered, supportive of reflective learning through group processes, and that aims to develop graduates with skills required for a knowledge era. The authors acknowledge the many challenges still confronting implementation of this educational activity, and conclude that further ongoing research is needed to confirm the effectiveness of this learning activity in teaching business in developing countries.

Appendix13. 1:

Module No.	Module Sequence	Case Study	Activity	Assessment
1	Overview/Introduction	Case Study.com	Discussion Forum	
2	Evolution of Management Thoughs		Mngr. Challenges: Readings; Question/Issues; Video grabs of speakers; Links to mngmt. guru sites	Case study mngmt. issue in own org.
3	Management Paradigm		Read; Discuss; Analysis of own org.; Video grabs	Online discussion; reflective paper on comparison of co. characteristics; Analysis of case study
4	Knowledge Management		Read; Discuss: responses in own co.; Video grabs	Analysis of case study in terms of challenges facing mngrs. in a knowledge economy
5	Leadership Theory	Adding/ Interactive (interviews, video grabs, memo's etc)	Read; Exercises/discussion on mngmt vs leadership; Video grabs	Online discussion; reflective paper
6	Summary: Implementing Theory		Read; Discuss; Video grabs	Individual assignments

REFERENCES

Allee, V. (1997). *The Knowledge Evolution*, Butterworth – Heinemann, Newtown, MA.

Allee, V. (2003). *The Future of Knowledge*, Butterworth – Heinemann, Burlington, MA.

Ballard, B. and Clanchy, J. (1997). *Teaching International Students*, IDP Education, Deakin ACT.

Biggs, J. (1999). *Teaching for Quality Learning at University*, Open University Press, Buckingham.

Coady, T. (2000). *Why Universities Matter*, Allen and Unwin, St Leonards, NSW.

Collings, P. (1999). "Sustaining academics' agency in determining work practices in information technology-mediated teaching and learning," *HERDSA Annual Conference Proceedings*, Melbourne, July 12-15.

Davenport, T. (1997). *Information Ecology*, Oxford University, New York, Oxford.

Duderstadt, J. (1998, August). "The future of the university in an age of knowledge," *Journal of Asynchronous Learning Networks*, *1*(2). http://www.aln/alnweb/journal/jaln_Vol1issue2.htm. , accessed 28th September 200.

Drucker P. (1998). "The coming of the new organisation," *Harvard Business Review on Knowledge Management*, Boston, (reprint, first published 1997), 2-23.

Gerrard, C. (2001). "Promoting excellence in distance education – a TQM led approach," *Integrated Management – Proceedings of the 6th International Conference on ISO 9000 and TQM*, Ho, K. & Donnelly, M. (eds.) School of Business –HKBU Paisley Business School & Authors, 578-583

Gibbons, M. (Swedish Research and Planning Council), (1994). *The New Production of Knowledge*, Sage, London.

Goleman, D (1995). *Emotional Intelligence*, Bloomsbury Publishing, London.

Hannah, R. (1996). "An academic perspective of the evolving of internet and employment relations," *Proceedings of the Third Annual World Web Symposium*, Hong Kong, May 7-10, 106-120, http://www.mtsu.edu/~rlhannah/hongkong.html

Herzenberg S.A., Alic J.A., and Wial H. (1998). *New Rules for a New Economy*, ILR, Ithaca, Cornell.

Jones, S. (forthcoming). "Using IT to augment authentic learning environments." Herrington, A. and Herrington, J. *Authentic Learning Environments'*

Jones, S. (2001a). "Collaboration – a threat to academic autonomy?" *Proceedings, ASCILLITE Conference*, Dec.

Kember, D. (1996). "The intention to both memorise and understand: another approach to learning." *Higher Education*, 31, 341-354.

Laurillard, D. (1994). "Multimedia and the changing experience of the learner." *Proceedings: Asia Pacific Information Technology in Training and Education Conference and Exhibition*, 19-25, June

Leonard-Barton D. (1995). *Wellsprings of Knowledge: Building and Sustaining the Sources of Innovation*, Harvard Business School Press, Boston Massachusetts

McIntyre S. and Marginson, S. (2000). "The university and its public." Coady T. *Why Universities Matter*, Allen & Unwin, St Leonards, NSW, 49-71

Marton, F; Dall'Alba G & Tse, L (1993). "The paradox of the Chinese learner." *Occasional Paper 93.1*, Educational Research & Development Unit, RMIT, Melbourne.

Miller S. (2000). "Academic autonomy." in Coady T. *Why Universities Matter*, Allen & Unwin, St Leonards, NSW, 110-131.

Nonaka I. (1998). "The knowledge-creating company." Harvard Business Review on Knowledge Management, *Harvard Business Review*, Boston (reprint, first published 1997), 24-44.

Nonaka, I. and Takeushi, H. (1995). "*The Knowledge-Creating Company,*" Oxford University Press, New York and Oxford.

Polanyi, M. (1958; 1962), *Personal Knowledge: Towards a Post-Critical Philosophy*, Chicago University Press, Chicago.

Quinn, J. (1992). *Intelligent Enterprises*, Free Press, New York.

Ramsden, P. (1992). *Learning to Teach in Higher Education,* Routledge, London.

Rice, J. and Ryan, N. (1999). "World wide web based teaching in industrial relations: potential, pitfalls and challenges for the future." *Proceedings: Annual Conference: Association of Industrial Relations Academics of Australia and New Zealand,* February 3-5, Adelaide

Seely Brown J. (1999). "Foreword," in Ruggles R & Holthouse D (eds.), *The Knowledge Advantage*, Capstone Dover, USA.

Smith, K. (1997). "Preparing faculty for instructional technology: from education to development to creative independence." *Cause and Effect,* 20 (3), 36-7.

Tyson, T. (1997). "Undergraduates in the deep end: first-year students as proactive experiential learners." Ballantyne, R; Bain, J; Packer, J. (eds.), *Reflecting on University Teaching Academics' Stories,* Committee for University Teaching and Staff Development, DEETYA, AGPS, 75-88.

Yap, C. (1997) "Teaching overseas students: the case of introductory accounting." in Ballantyne, R; Bain, J; Packer, J. (eds.). *Reflecting on University Teaching Academics' Stories,* Committee for University Teaching and Staff Development, DEETYA, AGPS, 55-64.

Zack M. (1999). "Developing a knowledge strategy." *California Management Review,* 41(3) Spring,, 125-145

Chapter 14
Using Experiential Exercises to Underscore the Challenges and Opportunities of Emerging Markets

Jonathan P. Doh
Villanova University

Sushil Vachani
Boston University

INTRODUCTION

Experiential exercises are one of the most effective tools for advancing student learning in management and organization. The challenges associated with understanding the complexities of international business (I.B.) environments, negotiating market entry strategies with host governments and potential partners, and the ongoing issues related to managing joint ventures and other types of alliances, are important elements of I.B. education, in general, and courses related to emerging markets, in particular. Cultural differences, development gaps, differing views on the role of the state in economic life, and the recent emergence of concerns about the social and environmental spillovers associated with economic globalization (such as human rights violations by M.N.C.s and environmental degradation in developing countries), all interact to make doing business in emerging economies challenging and difficult. These same factors, however, also generate new opportunities and suggest new business approaches.

In this paper, we describe our experiences with use of experiential exercises to underscore critical I.B. concepts specific to emerging markets. We begin with a brief summary of some of the recent management literature on emerging economies, noting the relative paucity of rigorous pedagogical materials that focus specifically on the challenges and opportunities associated with doing business in emerging markets. We then summarize some of the literature related to the effectiveness of experiential exercises in management education and offer a framework for examining a range of issues associated with I.B. concepts as they related to emerging markets. We provide a short summary of emerging markets exercises developed and used by the authors in courses at various levels and describe two of these exercises in depth.

We suggest that because most students in North America have had less exposure to emerging markets and are therefore less familiar with the particular features of emerging economies, experiential exercises are an especially valuable tool in helping underscore the unique characteristics of these markets and the sometimes unusual situations facing managers operating in these environments. We conclude with a reflection of our experience with use of these materials and describe some of the learning outcomes we expect and have observed related to use of these exercises. We include author contact information for instructors interested in using the exercises we have developed.

INTERNATIONAL BUSINESS AND EMERGING ECONOMIES

Trade, investment, and a range of business relationships between developed and developing counties have grown rapidly over the past two decades. Driven by globalization, economic integration, technological advances, and policy changes in developing countries, multinational corporations (M.N.C.s) from developed economies have become increasingly active in emerging markets, and firms from the developing world have become more active outside of their home countries. As one measure of increased integration and business activity related to emerging markets growth and integration, foreign direct investment (F.D.I.) flows into developing countries grew from $23.7 billion in 1990 to $204.8 billion in 2001 (U.N.C.T.A.D., 2003), a nine-fold increase, helping to contribute to growth in the stock of F.D.I. in developing countries from five percent to 20.5 percent of G.D.P. over this same period (U.N.C.T.A.D., 1999). In telecommunications, electric power, water, and other sectors, developing countries are increasingly turning to private sector investors to help increase availability, improve access, and move toward market-based pricing of resources and services (Kambhato, 1998). These investors are most often large M.N.C.s eager to take advantage of emerging markets opportunities. In addition to infrastructure and capital goods concerns, consumer products and retail companies such as Avon, Amway, Wal-Mart, and Starbucks have also pursued aggressive strategies to bring to the developing world a product, service, or shopping experience that is readily available in the developed world.

There is increasing interest on the part of I.B. researchers in the conditions surrounding foreign entry and competitive advantage in emerging markets (Doh, 2000; Encarnation and Vachani, 1985; Hoskisson, Eden, Lau, and Wright, 2000; Peng, 2001; Vachani, 1990, 1997; Ramamurti, 2000; Zahra, Ireland, Gutierrez, and Hitt, 2000). Building on the work of classic

I.B. perspectives on F.D.I. and business-government relations (Dunning, 1988, 1995; Fagre and Wells, 1992; Vachani, 1995; Vernon, 1971), these researchers have attempted to uncover the factors that influence countries to adopt and implement specific policies. In addition, researchers have studied challenges faced by international companies as they consider the preferred entry modes and governance choices they should pursue in response to these opportunities (Doh, 2000). Some researchers have explored the continuing challenges and risks associated with F.D.I. in emerging markets in particular sectors (Wells and Gleason, 1994; Doh and Ramamurti, 2003).

One research stream has used transactions costs and I.B.-government bargaining approaches to analyze the hazards M.N.C.s face from specific political systems (Henisz and Williamson, 1999; Henisz and Zelner, 2001). The state and its constituent institutions may themselves pose a threat to multinational corporations through policy shifts in taxation or regulation, through outright or *de facto* expropriation, or by permitting opportunistic exploitation of assets by local firms through violations of intellectual property rights, via forced transfer of technology, or other means, and firms seek to mitigate these risks by lowering their exposure. These risks are especially problematic in emerging markets as they have been shown to affect foreign entry mode and governance choices (Doh, Teegen, and Mudambi, 2003). Few researchers have investigated how local firms in emerging economies respond to the challenges of globalization and foreign entry into their home, domestic markets, with some exceptions (Aulakh, Kotabe, and Teegen, 2000).

In addition, there are increasing resources and material available to I.B. faculty seeking to teach about emerging economies. Numerous articles, cases, and at least three volumes have been published related to developing and transition economies (Cavusgil, Ghauri, and Agarwal, 2002; Luo, 2002; Peng, 2000). These works have focused on the unique challenges of doing business in emerging and transition economies, emphasizing the institutional and environmental constraints (Peng, 2000), the impact of emerging market characteristics on foreign entry modes and negotiation strategies (Cavusgil, Ghauri, and Agarwal, 2002), and the experience of M.N.C.s as they operate in emerging economies (Luo, 2002). Despite these recent contributions, there is still a relative dearth of materials available to instructors wishing to teach about management in emerging economies.

In sum, I.B. researchers and teachers have turned increasing attention to emerging markets in their effort to provide resources and educational materials to students from within emerging markets and to those from North American and European countries eager to learn more about the dynamics of the global business environment in which emerging markets figure prominently.

USE OF EXPERIENTIAL EXERCISES IN MANAGEMENT EDUCATION

Simulations and experiential exercises have been shown to be an effective method for studying managerial behavior. In a classic article on the use of experiential exercises, Thornton and Cleveland note, that "unlike direct observations, simulations allow greater control and opportunity for manipulating an event and understanding subsequent behavior" (1990, 191). Experiential exercises provide assessors and participants with the opportunity to evaluate qualitative skills: "Simulations give the individual participant a chance to experience a segment of organizational life in a safe environment and to obtain self-insights" (Thornton and Cleveland, 1990, 191). More specifically, experiential exercises provide a mechanism to accelerate the learning process for both new and experienced managers: "Simulation learning can be more effective because content and ability are tested and practiced in an appropriate venue and integrated into learners' experience" (Mailick and Stumpf, 1988, 24).

Although simulations can have a powerful impact on student learning, in general, and management practice, in particular, simulations should be used in a planned and purposeful manner, moving from less complex to more complex stages. According to Thornton and Cleveland, "reliability of simulation assessment can be enhanced by training observers and making repeated observations of individuals in similar situations" (1990, 195). Simulations can have practical applications in the context of training new employees to the specific tasks and operating procedures associated with a new employment situation or environment. Simulations (such as role plays and in-baskets) encourage careful observations of others and introspection about one's own beliefs and behaviors (House, 1982). Researchers also suggest that specific skills can be learned in isolation in controlled conditions through the use, for example, of one-on-one interview simulation and in-basket simulations (Thornton and Cleveland, 1990).

Keys, Stumpf, and Fulmer (1996) distinguish between two types of simulations. "Simuworlds" are general management games (often computerized) that are based on published industry knowledge and in which participants can analyze cause and effect relationships and overcome the blind spots that develop in the real world. These types of simulations focus on big picture learning. "Microworld" simulations are often in-basket simulations focusing on leadership strategy integration, dynamic interdependencies, and high-risk learning problems. (An in-basket exercise is a simulation in which participants are given a set of materials – sometimes different for each role – that often include memos, letters, requests, data, and other information, and then work through these materials in a manner that requires interaction with others in the organizations through meetings, additional memos, or other exchanges. Such simulations are designed to closely mirror the actual way in which work is often processed in modern organizations.)

Educational researchers caution about the over-use of or over-reliance on simulations: "Simulation techniques are means, not ends" (Mailick and Stumpf, 1998, 43). Educators should choose the type of simulation based on whether a given application uses principles relevant to the intended outcome. They should also ensure that outcome measures properly convey desired managerial skills. They should ensure that the simulation is being used as intended. The user has the responsibility to limit the application to its validated uses (i.e. follow standard procedures by basic testing practice and experimentation). Indeed, for inexperienced managers, large-scale behavioral simulations of organizations may not provide the conditions necessary to foster efficacy (Bandura, 1982). We favor using a combination of case discussion, simulations, role-playing, lectures, and readings to enhance impact and maintain a high level of interest.

USE OF EXPERIENTIAL EXERCISES TO REINFORCE CONCEPTS ASSOCIATED WITH MANAGEMENT IN EMERGING MARKETS

Experiential exercises are an effective tool for advancing student learning in management and organization and, we believe, a particularly useful approach for helping students understand the challenges and complexities of emerging markets. In the last fifteen years, a number of key developments have enhanced the importance of focusing on the study of emerging markets. These issues are important to address in designing programs for sensitizing managers and students to special aspects of the developing-country environment and the management challenges and opportunities they present for multinationals. Below is an illustrative (but not exhaustive) list of these issues:

- Globalization and its impact.
- The transformation of the G.A.T.T. into the W.T.O. and related trade issues such as the political economy of trade protection.
- The inclusion of developing countries in bilateral and regional trade agreements with developed countries; for example, in N.A.F.T.A., the expanded European Union (E.U.) and the proposed Free Trade Area of the Americas (F.T.A.A.).
- Economic liberalization. For example, the fall of the Berlin wall, the opening up of Eastern Europe, and the integration of Eastern and Central European countries into the global economy.
- The importance of market-supporting institutions to buttress economic integration and development in emerging economies.

- The Asian and Latin American financial crises of the late 1990s.
- The rise in consciousness regarding M.N.C.'s social obligations.
- The opening up of the Asian giants, China and India, and the large Latin American emerging markets, Brazil and Mexico. Liberalization in such countries and their role in the W.T.O.
- The reaction of local, indigenous firms to foreign market entry.
- Rise of non-governmental (N.G.O.s) organizations and their impact.

We recommend using a variety of materials that together cover this range of topics, while varying the format from simulation to role-playing to case discussion in order to sustain interest. We have developed a number of experiential exercises (listed in Table 14.1) that focus on various aspects of management and strategy in emerging economies. For each case, we indicate the major topics listed above that are addressed. In addition, the materials are designed to examine issues related to these topics at three important levels of analysis:

1. Supranational level.
2. Country level.
3. Company level.

Illustrative Cases on Emerging Markets

Below are brief descriptions of eight cases and exercises we have developed to underscore the concepts and themes described above. Some of these are more conventional decisions cases, and others include an explicit experiential component. In the next section, we describe two of these in detail.

In or Out: The Corning/Vitro Joint Venture Negotiation Simulation.

This case simulation focuses on the response of two North American firms – Vitro and Corning – to the challenges presented by economic integration and globalization within an emerging markets context – Mexico. Some of the information in the case is drawn from the author's personal experiences as a trade negotiator for the U.S. government. This case addresses issues related to the opening up of large Latin American emerging markets to liberalization, the inclusion of developing countries in bilateral and regional trade agreements, challenges in cross-cultural management and integration, and other related topics.

Table 14.1: Experiential Cases, Topics Covered and Level of Analysis

Topic	Corning Vitro	South Africa & AIDS	US Steel tariffs	Korea 1998	Chile – Trade Strategy	India– The Shackled Giant	McDonald's in the Soviet Union	AES in Merida, Mexico
Supranational lvl.								
Globalization	X	XX		XXX				
W.T.O. & trade issues	X	XXX	XXX		X			
Bilateral & regional trade agreements	XXX		X		XXX			XX
National level								
Economic Liberalization – (E.g., Opening up of Eastern Europe)	XXX				XXX	XXX	XXX	XXX
Financial crises				XXX			X	XX
Market-Supporting institutions			X	XXX	X	XX		
China & India			X			XXX		
Latin American large emerging markets – Brazil and Mexico	XXX	X			XX			XXX
Company level								
Reaction of Indigenous Firms	XX	X	X					X
Multinational social obligations	X	XXX		XX			XXX	XXX
Social responsibility		XXX						XXX
Non-governmental organizations		XXX						XX

(XXX = significant focus; XX = moderate focus; X = low focus)

South Africa and the A.I.D.S. Epidemic and "Storm Warning" Stakeholder Dialogue.

The "South Africa and the A.I.D.S. Epidemic" case, and its brief companion follow-on case, provide information on the severity of the A.I.D.S. epidemic in South Africa. The case outlines the factors that have contributed to the current situations, such as socio-economic disruption related to apartheid, culture, poor infrastructure, government policies, and multinational strategies, and discusses the purpose of intellectual property rights regimes in encouraging innovation and its impact on drug pricing. The companion "Storm Warning" case exercise describes actions taken by the Global Fund, the W.H.O. and the W.T.O., and provides an opportunity for role-playing that helps students understand the managerial implications of multilateral actions.

U.S. Steel Tariffs.

The case focuses on the U.S. government's action of imposing tariffs on steel imports in March 2002, providing an opportunity to discuss the political economy of the contemporary trade environment and the changing dynamics of the W.T.O. It can be used to examine the impact of domestic political agendas on international trade actions, implications for different countries including new players such as China, strategic options for retaliation, and the pros and cons of such action. It also illustrates the asymmetries in the impact of protectionist action resulting from regional and bilateral trade arrangements, such as N.A.F.T.A.

Korea 1998.

This is a short case that can be used for role playing to understand the impact of the Asian financial crisis on different stakeholders such as domestic companies, multinationals, regional governments (such as the Japanese government), and the U.S. government. It describes the causes of the crisis in Korea (such as the exposure resulting from globalization and the inflow of short-term debt, poor transparency, and peculiarities of the business system), the bailout, and the opportunities arising in the aftermath of the crisis.

Chile – Trade Strategy.

An important aspect of the evolution of the trade environment is the rising importance of bilateral and regional trade agreements, the momentum for which has increased with the grant of fast track authority to the U.S.

administration. The Chile – Trade Strategy case describes the perspective of a small but dynamic country that has a notable commitment to free market principles and has aggressively sought to enter into bilateral trade treaties. The case can be used to illustrate how historical context molds country strategy, and how a small nation can be positioned to affect the strategies of large and influential countries such as the U.S. and Brazil, which have significantly different positions with regard to the Free Trade Area of the Americas

India – The Shackled Giant.

The India case is useful for discussing the complexities of economic liberalization that has swept across countries in the 80s and 90s. It demonstrates how the social, political, and economic environment has an impact on the implementation of liberalization and what that means for multinationals.

McDonald's in the Soviet Union.

Business opportunities in liberalizing economies often require careful balancing of risks and benefits, as this case study illustrates. Students can also discuss how companies that decide to take the plunge and enter a risky environment can craft strategies to attenuate risk.

A.E.S. in Merida, Mexico.

In mid 1996, A.E.S. managers decided to bid on the Merida III project in the midst of an atmosphere of optimism over N.A.F.T.A. accompanied by concerns about political upheaval in Mexico. A.E.S. managers viewed Merida III as "subject to a number of risks, including those related to governmental approvals, financing, construction and contract compliance, and there can be no assurance that it will be completed successfully." This case and stakeholder dialogue places students in the role of A.E.S. managers considering how to bring this project to successful fruition and deciding on a broader Latin American strategy in light of the economic challenges in Argentina and withdrawal of investor interest in global power companies in light of Enron's demise.

TWO ILLUSTRATIVE EXPERIENTIAL EXERCISES IN DETAIL

In this section, we describe in detail the use of two of these case simulations. We chose these two because they are among the most well-developed of the group, contain extensive experiential elements, and have provided some of the richest and most lively exchanges in our respective classes. Moreover, we believe our students have drawn valuable lessons from the use of these two cases.

In or Out: The Corning/Vitro Joint Venture Negotiation Simulation

This case simulation focuses on the response of two North American firms -- Vitro and Corning -- to the challenges presented by economic integration and globalization within an emerging markets context - Mexico. Some of the information in the case is drawn from the author's personal experiences as a trade negotiator for the U.S. government. The case is designed for particular emphasis of the following topics:

- The opening up of the large Latin American emerging markets: Brazil and Mexico. Liberalization in such countries, and their role in the W.T.O.
- The inclusion of developing countries in bilateral and regional trade agreements with developed countries; for example, in N.A.F.T.A., the expanded European Union (E.U.) and the proposed Free Trade Area of the Americas (F.T.A.A.).

Case background.

During the N.A.F.T.A. negotiations, many U.S. firms were concerned about the reduction of U.S. tariffs on flat glass, which averaged 20%, and the perceived competitive advantages Mexican glass firms would have in the event these tariffs were removed. In the fall of 1991, in the midst of the N.A.F.T.A. negotiations, Vitro, S.A., the $3 billion Mexican glass maker, signed a tentative $800 million joint venture with Corning Inc. in which two mirror companies were established – Corning-Vitro and Vitro-Corning – with each company taking an equity stake in each of these J.V. firms. In addition, the two parent companies agreed to a series of marketing, sales, and distribution relationships to support the activities of each of the new companies. Just two years later, the joint venture was under distress, with some of the interested parties suggesting that it be dissolved.

Negotiation 1

In this case, students take part in a two-staged negotiation regarding the future of the J.V. In stage 1, students are divided into four groups, two for each company. Groups 1 and 2 are Vitro groups, with 1 generally supporting maintenance of the J.V. and 2 generally opposing its continuation. Similarly, Groups 3 and 4 are Corning groups, with Group 3 generally supporting maintenance of the J.V. and 2 generally opposing its continuation. In the first round of negotiation, these two sets of groups negotiate within each company to develop a common opening position (for each company) to the subsequent inter-company negotiation with the J.V. partner. In effect, groups 1-2 and 3-4 must decide whether each of the companies wants to remain within the J.V. or dissolve it. Each set of groups has 45 minutes to negotiate *within* the respective companies over whether to remain in or dissolve the J.V.

Among the issues groups 1 and 3 are asked to consider are: the logic and original rationale for the J.V.; how that logic may still hold; how the J.V. could be made to work better. Among the issues groups 2 and 4 are asked to consider are: what caused the J.V. relationship to sour; why the partner has not lived up to expectations; what the terms of dissolution should be.

Negotiation 2

Once each company has agreed upon a position to bring forward to the partner (this position need not necessarily be a demand to maintain the joint venture, or dissolve it; rather it could be a contingency laying the conditions for maintenance of the agreement, or demands for how it should be dissolved), at least one representative of each faction (two total) from each company will meet with the counterparts from the other firm. In the subsequent negotiation, designated negotiators (usually 2-4) from each company represent its interests in a bilateral negotiation with counterparts from the other firm. In this negotiation, participants are asked to work toward a resolution or agree on terms of the J.V.'s breakup.

Each company must decide, collectively, through negotiation, whether to remain within the J.V. or dissolve it. The two representatives from each company have 60 minutes to reach some resolution. *They must consult with the other stakeholders within their company throughout the negotiation to ensure support for the outcome.* In considering either resolution, decisions must be addressed regarding:

1. The logic and original rationale for the J.V.
2. How that logic may still hold.
3. How the J.V. could be made to work better.
4. What caused the J.V. relationship to sour.

5. Why the partner has not lived up to expectations.
6. If the J.V. should be terminated, and if so, what the terms of dissolution should be.

The students are advised that in the course of their deliberations, issues 3 and/or 6 must be resolved in one way or another. Areas that could be considered within this mix include, *inter alia*, the relative financial contributions of each firm; marketing, human resources, work, and family policies; marketing cooperation; development of products; and non-competition agreements. Any solution, whether to maintain the J.V., dissolve it, or some hybrid approach, should be comprehensive and address:

1. Financial structure: terms for financing existing or new ventures under the arrangement and/ or payments for dissolution of the relationship.
2. Governance: board, management or other top level changes in ownership and leadership under the present or revised relationship.
3. Marketing: agreements about marketing, distribution, and sales relationships either under the current arrangement or any new structure.
4. Cooperation: changes in the way in which the companies operate in each other's territories and share products and technological information.

Supporting Information and "De-Brief"

In addition to extensive background on the case and literature on emerging markets, students are also provided some brief information on negotiation theory and practice, including cross-cultural negotiation strategies. Once the negotiation simulation is completed – with some outcome – students are provided another "de-brief" document that places the simulation in the broader context of research on alliances and joint ventures between firms from developed and developing economies, including summaries of several additional cases in which J.V.s between developed and emerging economies faced challenges. Participants are given a series of questions to consider regarding the outcome they reached, how it compares to the actual outcome in the Corning-Vitro case (the J.V. was dissolved), and what can be learned about emerging economies from this and other, similar cases. These include:

1. Compare your solution to the J.V.'s problems with the actual outcome. What is different and or/similar to the two approaches?
2. How would you characterize Mexican and U.S. national culture in terms of Hofstede's scheme? In what ways were the cultures similar and in what ways, different?
3. Compare CorningVitro's problems to some of the other I.J.V.s described above (challenges associated with additional U.S.-Latin

American J.V.s are described in the document, such as the Banc One/Bancomer alliance, and the Anheuser - Busch/Modelo alliance). How were they similar, different, and more or less challenging?

4. How have other companies in Mexico and Latin America addressed these conflicts divisions in the recent past? How should they, as they go forward with comprehensive regional Latin American strategies?

Experience With the Case

This case has been used successfully in North America, Europe, and Asia, and at the undergraduate, postgraduate and executive level. The negotiated outcomes have varied considerably, however in all cases, students have reached some kind of specific resolution. In some instances, this has included the complete dissolution of the J.V., which was the actual outcome.

South Africa and the A.I.D.S. Epidemic: "Storm Warning" Stakeholder Dialogue

The "South Africa and the A.I.D.S. Epidemic" case, and its brief companion follow-on case, "Storm Warning," are designed for discussion of the following topics:

- Important changes occurring in the W.T.O., especially with respect to the protection of intellectual property rights (the Agreement on Trade-Related Aspects of Intellectual Property Rights, or the T.R.I.P.S. Agreement).
- Bargaining among multinationals, governments, and non-governmental organizations (N.G.O.s).
- Multinationals' strategies - especially drug pricing, and differential pricing in general.
- Multinationals' social responsibility (and the responsibilities of governments and multilateral institutions).

Case Description

The "South Africa and the A.I.D.S. Epidemic" case provides information on the severity of the A.I.D.S. epidemic in South Africa, where one out of every nine people has H.I.V./A.I.D.S. It goes on to outline the contributing factors to this situation, such as the socio-economic disruption related to apartheid, culture, poor infrastructure, government policies, and multinational strategies. It discusses the purpose of the intellectual property rights regime in encouraging innovation and its impact on drug pricing. The challenges posed by the inability of developing-country A.I.D.S. patients to afford the $10,000 annual treatment cost in the late 90s are discussed against the backdrop of multinationals' strategies, government policies, W.T.O. rules, and the political economy of waiving patents to manufacture generic drugs.

Discussion Items

In the "South Africa and the A.I.D.S. Epidemic" case, which is taught in a regular case discussion format, students are asked to address the difficult question of who is responsible for A.I.D.S. deaths in South Africa (A.I.D.S. claimed 360,000 lives in South Africa in 2001). In doing so, they are forced to wrestle with, and appreciate, the complexities of the situation resulting from the interaction of multinationals' and N.G.O.s' strategies, host- and home-government policies, and the multilateral intellectual property rights regime. The discussion also helps them recognize that the pursuit of legitimate, but narrow, goals by different stakeholders can have serious negative welfare consequences as welfare considerations slip through the cracks.

Students are forced to confront the fact that there are no easy solutions to a crisis that is poised to devastate populous countries of the world, such as China and India, unless curbed with aggressive measures. Multilateral aid action such as the formation of the Global Fund to Fight Aids, Tuberculosis, and Malaria, are heartening, but seem inadequate given the challenges of inadequate infrastructure, poverty, and government bureaucracy. Similarly, recommendations for socially responsible actions by multinationals by differential pricing of A.I.D.S. drugs are tempered by the potential losses in innovation and risks and challenges posed by gray markets.

"Storm Warning" Case

The students are then asked to read "Storm Warning," a short follow-on case that changes the perspective and shines the spotlight on other important stakeholders -- developing-country generic manufacturers. The case describes actions taken by the Global Fund to Fight Aids, Tuberculosis, and Malaria, the W.H.O. and the W.T.O., and how they impact generic manufacturers and multinationals. This provides an opportunity for role-playing that helps students understand the managerial implications of multilateral actions.

Four teams are assigned the roles of C.I.P.L.A. (an Indian generic drug manufacturer), GlaxoSmithKline (a British multinational), Doctors Without Borders (an N.G.O.), and the W.T.O. As the environment shifts, a whole new host of opportunities and challenges seem to crop up for the different players, underlining the need to continually monitor the dynamic global environment.

Experience With the Case.

This case has been used successfully in North America, Europe, and Asia, and at the undergraduate, postgraduate and executive level, and through distribution on list-serves and other dissemination media, has been adopted by a number of instructors around the world. It is also scheduled to be included in a leading international management text. The discussion and role playing in the two cases together take the students all the way from a high-level discussion of the multilateral regime, to the intermediate level of country strategies, and down to the level of organizational strategies for multinationals and N.G.O.s, bringing home the rich complexity of managing in the dynamic emerging market environment.

CONCLUSION: EXPERIENTIAL EXERCISES AND LEARNING OUTCOMES

Experiential exercises can be especially effective in creating an appreciation of developments in global business and political economy, especially those associated with the dramatic transformations underway in emerging markets. While we have described just two specific cases in full, and several others in summary, we believe our approaches – the simulation of managerial decision-making in the challenging emerging markets environment – yields powerful results:

- Students realize, through debate, that there are differences in developing-country and developed-country environments, including differences in institutional development, cultural norms, and political structure, and other key variables, many of which they were previously unaware.
- Recognition of these differences results in a keener appreciation of the complexities of managing in the emerging-market environment.
- In addition, students develop a better understanding of the challenges involved in crafting strategies that are socially responsible while attempting to enhance shareholder value. They often start out with simplistic views that are unrealistic and are forced to adapt them to incorporate perspectives provided by others, and they develop positions that are more in tune with the reality of managing in the emerging-markets environment.
- In general, the heightened understanding of the contemporary emerging-markets environment leads to greater sensitivity and

interest in new developments in international business, and students often continually make connections with these emerging trends and relate insights gleaned from the experiential exercises.

In this article, we have suggested that experiential exercises are an effective tool for advancing student learning in management and organization. We have reviewed management theory and empirical research on the efficacy of simulations, and we have identified salient issues related to emerging markets that should be part of effective exercises and simulations, developing a simple framework to help instructors select materials based on the issues they plan to address and the level of analysis they wish to target. We have briefly described a number of cases and simulations we have developed and presented additional detail on two of these simulations that focus on emerging markets and have been used successfully in various traditional and nontraditional classroom settings in different parts of the world.

Finally, we have described some of the learning outcomes we have observed from our experiences with using these exercises. We hope that this brief article contributes to development of interesting and effective experiential exercises on emerging markets topics, and we encourage instructors to contact us for additional information on the exercises we have developed and used.

REFERENCES

Aulakh, P.S., Kotabe, M., & Teegen, H. (2000). Export strategies and performance of firms from emerging economies: evidence from Brazil, Chile, and Mexico. *Academy of Management Journal, 43*, 342-361.

Bandura, A. (1982). Self-efficacy mechanism in human agency. *American Psychologist, 37*, 122-147.

Cavusgil, T., Ghauri, P.N., Agarwal, M.R. (2002). *Doing Business in Emerging Markets: Entry and Negotiation Strategies.*

Doh, J. P. (2000). Entrepreneurial privatization strategies: order of entry and local partner collaboration as sources of competitive advantage. *Academy of Management Review, 25*, 551-572.

Doh, J.P., & Ramamurti, R. (2003). Reassessing risk in developing country infrastructure. *Long Range Planning, 36*, 337-353.

Doh, J.P., Teegen, H., & Mudambi, R. (2003). Balancing private and government ownership in emerging markets telecommunications infrastructure: country, industry, and firm influences. Working paper.

Dunning, J.H. (1988). The eclectic paradigm of international production: a restatement and some possible extensions. *Journal of International Business Studies, 19*, 1-31.

Dunning, J.H. (1995). Reappraising the eclectic paradigm in an age of alliance capitalism. *Journal of International Business Studies, 26*, 461-491.

Encarnation, D.J., and Vachani, S. (1985). Foreign ownership: when hosts change the rules. *Harvard Business Review*, Sep.- Oct., 152-60.

Fagre, N., and Wells, L.H. (1982). Bargaining power of multinationals and host governments. *Journal of International Business Studies, 13*, 9-23.

Henisz, W.J., and Williamson, O.E. (1999). Comparative economic organization -- within and between countries. *Business and Politics, 1*, 261-277.

Henisz, W.J., and Zelner, B.A. (2001). The institutional environment for telecommunications investment. *Journal of Economics and Management Strategy, 10 (1)*, 123-147.

Hoskisson, R.E., Eden, L., Lau, C.M., and Wright, M. (2000). Strategy in emerging economies. *Academy of Management Journal, 43 (3)*, 249-267.

House, R. S. (1982). Experimental learning: a social learning theory analysis. In R. D. Freedman, C. L. Cooper, & S. A. Stumpf (). *Management Education*: Issues in Theory, Research, and Practice (pp 23-43). New York: Wiley.

Kambhato, P. (1998). The flagship role of telecommunications. In I. Lieberman and C. Kirkness (Eds.), *Privatization and Emerging Equity Markets* (pp. 88-103). Washington, D.C.: The World Bank.

Luo, Y. (2002). *Multinational Enterprises in Emerging Markets*. Copenhagen: Copenhagen Business School Press.

Mailick, S and Stumpf, S (1998). *Learning Theory in the Practice of Management Development*. Westport, CT: Quorum Books.

Peng, M. (2000). *Business Strategies in Transition Economies*. New York: Sage.

Peng, M.W. (2001). How entrepreneurs create wealth in transitions economies. *Academy of Management Executive, 15*, 95-111.

Ramamurti, R. (2000). A multilevel model of privatization in emerging economies. *Academy of Management Review, 25*, 525-550.

Thornton, G., & Cleveland, J. (1990). Developing managerial talent through simulation. *American Psychologist, 45*, 190-199.

Vachani, S. (1990). Strategic responses of multinationals to competition from developing-country cottage firms. *International Marketing Review, 7.1*, August, 31-47.

Vachani, S. (1995). Enhancing the obsolescing bargain theory: a longitudinal study of foreign ownership of U.S. and European multinationals. *Journal of International Business Studies*, first quarter, 159-80.

Vachani, S. (1997). Economic liberalization's effect on sources of competitive advantage of different groups of companies: the case of India. *International Business Review, 6 (2)*, 165-84.

Vernon, R. (1971). *Sovereignty at Bay: The Multinational Spread of U.S. Enterprises*. New York: Basic Books.

Wells, L.T., and Gleason, E. S. (1994). Is foreign infrastructure investment still risky? *Harvard Business Review*, September/October, 44-53.

Zahra, S.A, Ireland, R.D., Gutierrez. I., and Hitt. M.A. (2000). Privatization and entrepreneurial transformation: emerging issues and a future research agenda. *Academy of Management Review, 25*, 509-524.

Keys, B.J., Fulmer, RM., & Stumpf, S.A. (1996). Microworlds and simuworlds: practice fields for the learning organization. *Organizational Dynamics, 14*, 36-49.

United Nations Conference on Trade and Development (U.N.C.T.A.D.) (2003). *World Investment Report*. New York and Geneva: U.N.C.T.A.D..

United Nations Conference on Trade and Development (U.N.C.T.A.D.) (1999). *World Investment Report*. New York and Geneva: U.N.C.T.A.D.

Chapter 15
Experiential Learning in Emerging Markets: Leveraging the Foreign Experience

James P. Johnson
Crummer Graduate School of Business, Rollins College

INTRODUCTION

> *"Most ideas about teaching are not new,*
> *but not everyone knows the old ideas."*
> *-Euclid*

For much of the decade of the 1990s, business schools around the world – and especially in the U.S.A. and Canada – were taking initiatives to internationalize the business curriculum, mainly in response to a directive by the Association for the Advancement of Collegiate Schools of Business (A.A.C.S.B.), the prime international accreditation agency for business schools. A global survey of business schools conducted in 1992 (Arpan, Folks, and Kwok, 1993) found that only a small majority (57%) made specific reference to internationalization in their mission statement, and very few schools had a requirement for a "foreign experience," defined in the survey as a study or an internship experience in another country.

It was evident from this and other studies (see Arpan and Kwok, 2001 for a bibliography) that business schools still faced the major task of (1) infusing international issues into core courses; (2) developing specialized courses in international business (I.B.); (3) internationalizing their faculty; and (4) offering classes and internships overseas. A follow-up survey in 2000 found that schools had made progress in all these areas (Arpan and Kwok, 2001); 65% of bachelors and masters business programs now offered both core courses infused with international issues and specialized I.B. courses, suggesting that business schools were well on the way to meeting the first two objectives of instilling a general awareness in students of the global business environment and developing a basic understanding of I.B. issues in at least one functional field. Significant progress had also been achieved in internationalizing the faculty, with over 90% of schools reporting an increase in this area (Arpan and Kwok, 2001). Furthermore, 52% of bachelors business programs and 48% of masters programs now offered some kind of overseas experience (Arpan and Kwok, 2001), suggesting that business schools were making greater provision for developing students' global expertise by offering them first-hand experiences in other countries. The most commonly offered foreign experience was study tours, followed by study abroad and internships abroad. However, the number of institutions that actually required an overseas experience was still very small -- just 5% of bachelors programs and 11% of masters programs. Data on the number of students who had completed a foreign experience were not available.

The decade of the 1990s also witnessed the rise of emerging markets – nations whose economies were opening to trade and foreign direct investment and were becoming more integrated with those of the richer nations. It was no accident that business schools were increasing their efforts towards internationalization at the same time since it was apparent that emerging markets – especially the "Big Ten" (Garten, 1997)[1] -- were becoming key players in the new global business environment, so an awareness and understanding of the impact of emerging markets on global business was essential. In these markets, the onset of trade liberalization, privatization of state-owned industries, deregulation, the flood of inward foreign direct investment -- and, more recently in some cases economic recession -- have left the business environment in a state of flux. The old ways of doing business are no longer valid as new 'rules of the game' are being written and re-written. In this situation, the challenge of training students for global competence has become even more acute.

The purpose of this paper is to investigate the role of the foreign experience in developing students' global competence in business in emerging markets. Seven types of foreign experience are identified, ranging from classroom-based activities to full-time internships overseas, and their utility is examined through the lens of experiential learning theory. Although a North American perspective is taken here, the concepts, logic, and conclusions presented apply equally to business schools in other developed countries.

EXPERIENTIAL LEARNING

"..there is an intimate and necessary relation between the processes of actual experience and education." Dewey (1938).

John Dewey, American philosopher and educator (1859-1952), was a firm believer and advocate of the importance of individual experiences in education, of "learning by doing." He maintained that it is the teacher's responsibility to structure and organize students' experiences so that these have a positive influence on students' future experiences. Furthermore, writing in the 1930s, he said radical reform was needed of both pedagogical

learning underpin the experiential learning models that developed later in the 20th century (e.g., Joplin, 1981; Kolb, 1984; Priest and Gass, 1997), of which the best known is probably Kolb's (1984) four-stage model:

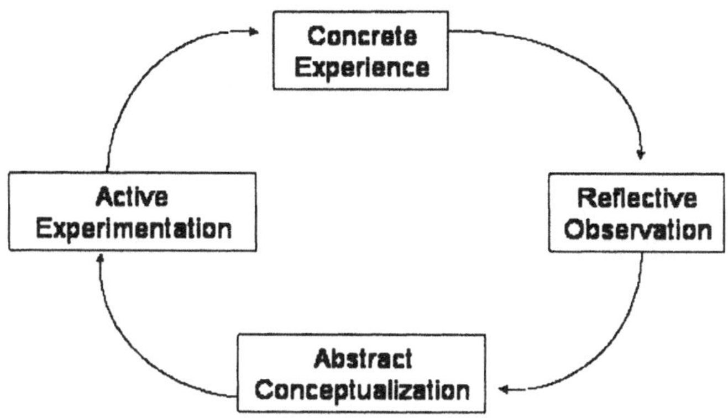

Figure 15.1: Kolb's (1984) Experiential Learning Cycle

Kolb's model breaks down experiential learning into four stages: (1) concrete experience; (2) reflective observation; (3) abstract conceptualization; and (4) active experimentation. The stages of the experiential learning cycle (E.L.C.) are sequential and mutually reinforcing, although there is no pre-ordained starting point. For example, a U.S. businesswoman might go to Mexico on a three day business trip and return unsuccessfully [*concrete experience*]. Reflecting on her experience and why it was unsuccessful, she might confer with colleagues and friends [*reflective observation*] who refer her to one of many publications on doing business in Mexico. She discovers that the Mexican concept of time is very different from that of Anglo North Americans [*abstract conceptualization*], so she develops strategies for dealing with this difference and implements them on her next trip to Mexico [*active experimentation*], continuing the cycle.

In an educational environment, however, the instructor has control over the sequence of the four stages. With a cross-cultural simulation exercise such as *Bafá-Bafá*, widely used in business schools as well as in government and corporate training programs, the sequence could begin with the simulation exercise itself [*concrete experience*] and conclude with active experimentation when the student next finds himself in a cross-cultural environment. Alternatively, it could start with lectures and background readings on cross-cultural differences [*abstract conceptualization*] and conclude with a class debrief and discussion after the simulation [*reflective observation*].

The E.L.C. is a useful model for educators who wish to use experiential activities as part of their pedagogy. The following section examines how the E.L.C. can be applied to different types of foreign experience in business courses[2].

THE FOREIGN EXPERIENCE

To develop global competence, students not only need an awareness and understanding of international business issues, but they must also develop the ability to operate effectively in a foreign environment – that is, they must know how to respond to the social, cultural, economic, and political differences that they might encounter. There are several ways of exposing students to foreign influences, not all of which require travel overseas. They range from in-class activities to short-term trips to long-term work and residence overseas:

1. In-class foreign experience
2. Study Tour
3. Integrated Study Tour
4. Overseas Practicum/Project
5. Foreign Language Training
6. Exchange Program
7. Internship

In-Class Experience

A basic way of enhancing the foreign experience in the classroom is through the internationalization of business faculty and a rise in the enrollment of international students – thus bringing the global village into the classroom. According to Arpan and Kwok (2001), 92% of responding institutions reported a significant increase during the 1990s in the number of business faculty who have lived or traveled overseas. These faculty can now bring their own experiences into the classroom to enrich the curriculum. Similarly, in recent years the number of international students enrolled in business programs has risen. A.A.C.S.B. International reports that over 30% of students in full-time M.B.A. programs in the U.S.A. are neither U.S. citizens nor permanent residents (A.A.C.S.B., 2002)[3]. Thus, students from emerging markets such as China, India, Brazil, or South Africa working in study groups alongside U.S. students expose their U.S. counterparts to some of the realities of doing business in other cultures. The value of such classroom interactions is that they are relatively inexpensive to the institution, but their outcomes are arbitrary and not easily measured. Furthermore, the outcomes depend on students' willingness to learn from such interactions;

unless reflective observation, abstract conceptualization, and active experimentation are encouraged and rewarded by the instructor, students are apt to overlook the benefits of bringing the global village into the classroom. This can be overcome by structuring the in-class experience through the use of a simulation or some other form of experiential exercise, although there are few, if any, such exercises that focus specifically on emerging markets. As mentioned above, *Bafá-Bafá* is an exercise that works well in international business classes: it is relatively inexpensive, easy to operate with a minimum of two administrators, is suitable for undergraduate and graduate courses, and lends itself readily to the E.L.C. model. Alternatively, some instructors are now taking advantage of communications technology to forge links with schools in emerging markets so that students can work cooperatively online on business projects (e.g., Ajami and Arledge, 2003). This type of experience is very promising but, once again, students stand to lose the experiential benefits of this type of cooperation unless the instructor is prepared to structure and reward the experience.

Study Tour

Study tours are the most common form of overseas travel in business schools. Currie and Matulich (2003) found that 41% of M.B.A. programs surveyed in North America have a travel component, but their findings echoed those of Arpan and Kwok (2001) in that foreign travel is required by relatively few business schools -- only 6% of the institutions surveyed. Noting the cost incurred in time and money, Currie and Matulich comment:

> Requiring an international trip is a degree of globalization that many schools are not able to attain, particularly if globalization is not a key strategic initiative of the institution. (Currie and Matulich, 2003, 6)

A criticism of short trips is that they do not give students a realistic picture of what it is like to do business in emerging markets, since they are ferried from the airport in air-conditioned buses and cocooned in deluxe, western-style hotels. In addition, the experiences provided often lack a clear business focus and cannot easily be differentiated from the experiences of a tourist. Even on company visits, students can take a passive role and do not have to interact meaningfully with their hosts. Professor Bob Green of the University of Texas refers to such trips as "…'bubble classes', where you sit in a bus and watch [the country] go by." (Mangan, 1997, A14). Indeed, the gap between the "bubble" and reality is even greater in emerging markets than it is in economically developed nations[4]. At a cost of over $2,000 for a seven day trip, plus tuition if it is taken for academic credit, it is a relatively expensive way to gain a modest amount of international competence. Indeed, the degree of experiential learning achieved can vary significantly, depending on the amount of structure imposed on the trip by the accompanying professor. Recall Dewey's directive that it is "the teacher's responsibility to structure and organize students' experiences" (Dewey, 1938); the study tour experience can be more tightly structured by making it an integral part of a semester-long course rather than by offering it as a stand-alone activity.

Integrated Study Tour

Several business schools now include a study tour as part of a required or elective course, making it an integral part of the course. For example, in the Rollins College M.B.A., *Emerging Markets Initiative* is a semester-long three credit elective course in which students spend one week in the middle of the semester at the Czech Management Center on the outskirts of Prague. Prior to departure, students have background readings on issues in emerging markets, do research, and make presentations on the companies that they will visit in the Czech Republic, and develop a topic for a research paper [*abstract conceptualization*]. At the Czech Management Center, they attend tailor-made lectures presented by local faculty [*abstract conceptualization*] and, through question/answer and class discussion, explore hypotheses and concepts that they have developed about the business environment in the Czech Republic [*active experimentation*]. Daily company visits and interaction with locals in stores, restaurants, and public transportation provide the *concrete experience*. In a recent visit to Škoda Autos, now wholly owned by Volkswagen of Germany, M.B.A. students were sufficiently well informed to pepper senior management with questions about Škoda's cannibalization of the sales of its parent's higher-end models and Volkswagen's reactions to the export success of its Czech subsidiary, filling in the gaps in the students' secondary research and providing not only data for their research papers but also input for a lively discussion on the bus back to the hotel [*reflective observation*]. In a single visit, then, students traversed the entire experiential learning cycle.

Despite the clear advantages of an integrated study tour over the previous forms of foreign experience already discussed, it does have its drawbacks. Time must be allocated during the semester for overseas travel without disrupting students' other classes; unlike a study tour, it cannot easily be fitted in at a 'convenient' time in the academic calendar since the trip is an integral part of the course. (At Rollins College, all M.B.A. classes cease for one week in the middle of the fall and spring semesters, which permits overseas travel.) In addition, the additional cost of travel and local arrangements is out of the reach of many students.

Global Practicum/Project

A global practicum or project is an opportunity for students to work in small teams to apply business concepts and skills to a real-time problem facing a company in an emerging market ("the sponsor") while gaining valuable international experience. The practicum can be organized in a number of ways, but typically it lasts for up to a semester, with time set aside for overseas travel. At the start of the semester, the student group confirms with the sponsor – which could be located in North America or overseas – and the supervising instructor (1) the scope of the project and (2) the final deliverable, which is usually in the form of a written report and/or an oral presentation. Examples of recent global practica are presented in Appendix 1. (See also Alon and Ballard, 2003) for a detailed description of a global practicum.)

Students work on the project during the first half of the semester, gathering secondary data on the country environment, the company and its industry, and on the specific problem facing the company. Before traveling overseas, the group must determine what additional information is required and how to obtain it, and establish clear objectives for the overseas trip. Depending on the nature of the project, the student team might have to identify which countries to visit and in what sequence. If necessary, students will identify and make contact with individuals in the target country or countries and schedule interviews in advance. These contacts could be mid- to senior level managers, entrepreneurs, senior government officials, or heads of trade organizations. Where the sponsor is located overseas, the team will present an interim oral report before returning home to complete the project and to compile the final report before the end of the semester. Each student's final grade is determined by the supervising instructor based on several criteria: (1) the final deliverable as prepared by the student team and presented to the sponsor; (2) the sponsor's feedback on the team's interaction and performance; and (3) peer evaluations of each team member's performance and contribution. Although the program is guided by a supervising instructor, each student's experience is largely self-determined, and the value that each student takes away is in direct proportion to the effort that is made.

The primary advantages for the participating students include (1) enhancing cross-cultural communication skills; (2) developing first-hand experience of the challenges of working in an emerging market; (3) applying business skills to a real-time problem; and (4) cultivating effectiveness as a team member working on an international project. This last point bears emphasizing since the global project is unlike any other activity in which M.B.A. students participate. As Alon and Ballard (2003) indicate, the students are with one another all day, every day, for a week or more. They have to plan their activities together -- where to stay, when and where to eat, how to travel – typically in a cultural, linguistic, economic and geographic environment that is unfamiliar to them. All this can impose a level of stress and discomfort which students must learn to manage in order to achieve a satisfactory outcome for the project. Thus, the E.L.C. model applies to the global project in much the same way as it does to the integrated study-tour, as a continuous learning experience. Furthermore, because of the time requirement – seven to ten days – a global practicum is accessible to part-time as well as full-time students.

The disadvantages of the global practicum are similar to those of the integrated study tour in terms of the resources required. However, in many cases the costs can be minimized by asking the sponsor to help with travel costs or by leveraging cooperative relationships with other institutions; for example, students studying at a local business school have hosted Rollins College M.B.A. students doing practica in Croatia. Another disadvantage is that it takes time to make the initial contact with sponsor companies and to screen projects to ensure that they are appropriate to M.B.A.-level students and that they can be completed in a single semester. Here, the school's alumni network and its contacts with partner institutions can be very beneficial. Finally, global practica are not suitable for undergraduate business students unless a rigorous selection process is in place – after all, the reputation of the school is at stake. Overall, the feedback from students, sponsors, and supervising faculty has been overwhelmingly positive, and many Rollins graduates rate the global project as the best learning experience in the M.B.A. program.

Foreign Language Training

One of the most effective ways to develop cross-cultural communication skills is through the study of foreign languages, yet only 33% of bachelor programs in business and 15% of masters programs require students to take a foreign language course (Arpan and Kwok, 2001); indeed, some school administrators still assume that the emergence of English as the language of business precludes the need for foreign language training by native speakers of English (Mangan, 1997). Foreign language training is ideally suited to the E.L.C. model since language-learning is an inherently experiential activity; furthermore, when combined with a period of residence overseas, it provides excellent training in cross-cultural competence.

However, language training is heavily resource-intensive, and this is especially true of languages in emerging markets which, with the exception of Spanish in Latin America, tend to be less commonly taught in North American schools and colleges. To illustrate this, the Center for International Business Education and Research (C.I.B.E.R.) at Michigan State University has ranked the overall market potential of 24 emerging markets, and the top-ranking markets are Hong Kong, Singapore, South Korea, Israel, and China (Global Edge, 2002). Spanish-speaking Chile and Mexico rank 9th and 11th, respectively. Asian and Semitic languages are rarely taught in North American schools, and when they are, the learning cycle is much longer than for Romance or Germanic languages. Consequently, most business schools prefer to invest their precious resources in more easily accessible languages or in other activities more closely related to the core business functions. A further limitation of language training is that, unless it is accompanied by a business-related activity such as an internship or foreign practicum, it isolates students from the realities of the business world, allowing them no opportunity to practice their business-related knowledge and skills in the foreign environment.

Exchange Program

During the 1990s, business schools around the world expanded their international partnerships to offer more overseas travel and study opportunities to their faculty and students (Mangan, 1997). For example, the Graziado School of Business and Management at Pepperdine University now has 20 international partner institutions, eight of which are in emerging markets in Latin America and Asia; also, Boston University's International M.B.A. includes three months study at Dong Hua University in Shanghai. At first sight, it might appear that such foreign exchange programs offer excellent opportunities for experiential learning. This is true as far as learning to cope with the foreign environment is concerned, but exchange programs suffer from the same limitations as unstructured study abroad programs. There is ample opportunity for students to adopt a passive role, so that an exchange program in China, say, may be little more than *studying* business in an exotic location rather than *experiencing* what it is like to do business in China. In most cases, too, the language of instruction is English, thus giving exchange students little incentive to learn the local language. However, if the exchange is accompanied by a hands-on project or internship, the probability of effective experiential learning is vastly increased. Language barriers can be overcome by teaming U.S. students with local students for specific projects.

Internship

Many scholars have touted the benefit of internships in education (e.g., Spinks and Wells, 1994; Toncar and Cudmore, 2000), though there has been some question about whether they merit academic credit, especially short-term internships lasting several weeks (Ciofalo, 1989). Yet few would question the effectiveness of an overseas internship in developing a student's global competence since it places the student in a real business environment for, typically, six weeks to six months. The E.L.C. operates continuously on a daily basis as students adapt to the local environment and to local business practices. But setting up internships – especially in more remote locations – can be a major drain on the resources of business schools (Arpan, 1995). Also, overseas internships are often unpaid, which can place a financial strain on students. Nevertheless, most students view it as one of the most beneficial aspects of their business training. Internships offer similar advantages to short-term global practica: (1) enhancing local language and cross-cultural communication skills; (2) developing first-hand experience of the challenges of working in an emerging market; and (3) applying business skills to everyday business situations. However, since students are overseas for a longer period, the potential for learning is far greater; offset against this is the fact that internships are not a practical option for part-time students who can take only a short leave of absence from their regular place of employment.

Table 15.1: The Foreign Experience and the E.L.C.

	Activity	**Length**	**Location**	**Applicability to Experiential Learning Model**
1.	In-Class Experience	Any	Home	Limited
2.	Study Tour	1-3 weeks	Overseas	Limited
3.	Integrated Study Tour	1 semester/ 1-2 weeks	Home/ Overseas	Yes
4.	Global Practicum/Project	1 semester/ 1 week	Home/ Overseas	Yes
5.	Foreign Language Training	1-3 semesters	Home/Overseas	Yes
6.	Exchange Program	1-2 semesters	Overseas	Limited
7.	Internship	1-12 months	Overseas	Yes

To summarize, all seven types of foreign experience offer some benefits to business students studying emerging markets, but not all are compatible with the E.L.C. In some cases, the potential for experiential learning is limited unless the experience is carefully structured by the instructor or augmented with additional activities – such as a project or internship – that gives students some *practical* experience of doing business in an emerging market, rather than just reading about it. Table 15.1

summarizes the characteristics of each of the seven modes of foreign experience and their applicability to the experiential learning model (E.L.C.).

CONCLUSION

Just as earning a business degree does not guarantee career success, which depends on performance rather than knowledge, so a brief visit to an emerging market or interaction at home with people from that location does not guarantee that students will acquire the skills that are needed to operate effectively in what is a very different business environment. North American business schools have advanced in internationalizing their programs over the past decade, but we need now to move beyond the levels of global awareness and understanding and provide students with the opportunities to develop global competence in a realistic business setting. As can be seen in Table 15.1, in-class experiences and overseas study tours provide limited experiences for learning about the challenges of doing business in an emerging market. To be sure, they are better than nothing, but they cushion students from much of the foreign environment. This is an especially salient point in emerging markets since there is a much greater gap between the sanitized, western environment that students experience on the typical study-tour in Shanghai, Sao Paulo, or Jakarta and the reality of living and working in the local environment. Similarly, exchange programs that do not include some practical business experience might be viewed as little more than classrooms in exotic locations, offering a limited potential for experiential learning. Overseas internships, in contrast, are highly commendable, but realistically, most students can spend neither the time nor the money to take advantage of this learning opportunity.

Integrated study tours and global practica appear to offer a compromise between minimizing the cost of overseas training and providing both full-time and part-time students with a realistic learning experience. In emerging markets in particular, the cost of local arrangements (hotel, meals, transportation, etc.) is often relatively modest. In addition, the small size of the student group allows students to make their own flight arrangements, seeking the best deals that they can find on the Internet. Where possible, the costs of a practicum are minimized further by asking the sponsor to cover some of the out-of-pocket expenses or by arranging local accommodations through partner institutions. In return for both the integrated study tour and the global practicum, students receive maximum exposure to the foreign environment in a short period of time and are consigned to multiple reiterations of the E.L.C. as they hone their cross-cultural communication skills and apply business concepts, knowledge, and skills to a real situation. As stated earlier, learning by doing is more urgent in the context of China, Brazil, or Indonesia, for example, because students are less familiar with the social, political, and economic context in which business operates. Therefore, social, political, and economic context in which business operates. Therefore, the gap between their assumptions of how business *should* be conducted and how it *is* conducted is much greater than in stable, western markets. In bridging the gap between theory and practice, textbook and reality, experiential learning in emerging markets provides real added value to our students and helps them develop interdisciplinary competence.

However, recruiting faculty interest in supervising these projects can be a major challenge. Where there is a shortage of support staff, faculty might be easily dissuaded from taking on the responsibility for arranging the logistics of overseas trips, but this obstacle may be overcome by having students make their own travel and accommodation arrangements, within parameters provided by the faculty supervisor. In addition, faculty supervisors require adequate compensation, which in itself could be an issue for administrators who fail to appreciate the value of students' first-hand experiences in emerging markets. Therefore, the introduction of these types of experience requires either a strong institutional commitment, a priori, to globalizing the business curriculum, or a willingness on the part of faculty to take on the initial work of setting up integrated study tours and practica to assess student demand. At Rollins College, we have found that when students return from their visits to emerging markets, their experiences stimulate interest and excitement among their peers, creating an internal demand for future courses.

In sum, the opportunities are there to introduce substantive changes in the business curriculum in order to give students meaningful, first-hand learning experiences in emerging markets. It is up to us as business faculty and administrators to seize these opportunities.

NOTES

[1] China/Taiwan, India, South Korea, Indonesia, Mexico, Brazil, Argentina, South Africa, Poland, and Turkey.

[2] It should be noted, however, that Kolb's model is just one of many E.L.C. models: Juch (1987) has identified seventeen experiential learning cycles.

[3] However, since September 2001, more stringent visa requirements have reduced the number of foreign students entering the U.S.A.

[4] I am grateful to an anonymous reviewer for pointing this out.

APPENDIX 1

Rollins College M.B.A.: Global Practica 2003

A. City of Rio Preto, Brazil

Sponsoring Organization:	City of Rio Preto
Contact Executive:	Joaquim Correa-Lima
Location:	Rio Preto, Brazil
Areas of Concentration:	Management, Project Planning, Marketing, Information Technology
Supervising Instructor:	Professor Michael Cipollaro
Financial Assistance:	The Spa Resort will provide room, board, and land transportation for the student team.

Background: Rio Preto is a city of 360,000 people located about 500 km north of Sao Paolo and 850 km southeast of Brasilia. Tourism has never been a priority of the city, and consequently little information is available and almost no effort is made to attract leisure visitors. The city is known for its medical schools and strong medical services. The city government has decided that it must make some significant efforts to attract visitors and would like some assistance in the planning aspects of this task.

Project: The city has to be told what it must do to develop a meaningful tourist industry in and around Rio Preto. The approach to this goal must be defined – the "how to" must be identified – and then information must be gathered that represents the input into any marketing effort. A model should be developed based on what comparable cities have done elsewhere to successfully attract tourists, and the city should be asked to "fill in the spaces" with regard to tourist attractions in the area. A website will be an integral part of the communications plan which also needs to be addressed.

Team: Five students who can devote four to five hours per week for the term plus the project week are needed to complete this project.

B. Shanghai Garment Association

Sponsoring Organization:	Shanghai University of Science and Technology
Location:	Shanghai, People's Republic of China
Areas of Activity:	Int'l. Business, Management, Marketing
Supervising Instructor:	Professor Ilan Alon

Financial Assistance: The Association will pay for student lodging costs in Shanghai.

Background: The Shanghai Garment Trade Association is one of the leading trade organizations in China. It represents not only garment manufacturers and exporters in Greater Shanghai, but also in the developing areas along the Yangtze River. Shanghai, of course, is the primary business province and economic engine of China, and is responsible for more than 50% of all port activity in the country.

The Project: The Association wishes to have a student team research and analyze the garment industry on a global basis. Based upon the findings and the opportunities identified for Chinese garment manufacturers and exporters, students will prepare a series of recommendations on improvements that should be made by the Association's members in terms of their management and marketing systems. In addition, students will have the opportunity to work with Chinese students, to participate in the cultural life of the city, and to provide their host with some observations on business life in America and business school education.

Team: Five to six students will be expected to devote four to six hours per week for the term, plus the project week. A written paper will be submitted to the Association upon completion.

REFERENCES

A.A.C.S.B. International. (2002).U. S.A. M.B.A. enrollment by citizenship, Fall 2001. Retrieved April 24, 2003, from http://www.aacsb.edu/publications/enewsline/archive_data/mbaenroll2001.jpg.

Ajami, R. and Arledge, L. (2003). Forging international linkages: connecting students in an online global classroom. Presented at the ACT6 - Sixth Creative Teaching Conference, Lucerne, Switzerland.

Alon, I., & Ballard, N. (2003). International business education: learning by doing. In Biberman, J., & Alkhafaji, A. (Eds.), *Business Research Yearbook: Global Business Perspectives, Vol. X,* pp. 242-246.

Arpan, J.S. (1995). Personal communication from the Chair of the International Business department, Darla Moore School of Business, University of South Carolina.

------, Folks, W.R. & Kwok, C.Y. (1993). *International Business Education in the 1990s: A Global Survey.* University of South Carolina: A.I.B./A.A.C.S.B.

------, J.S. & Kwok, C.Y. (2001). *Internationalizing the Business School: Global Survey of Institutions of Higher Learning in the Year 2000.* University of South Carolina: A.I.B. Foundation.

Ciofalo, A. (1989). Legitimacy of internships for academic credit remains controversial. *Journalism Educator,* 43 (4), 25-31.

Currie, D. & Matulich, S. (2003). Foreign travel in North American M.B.A. programs. Working Paper, Crummer Graduate School of Business, Rollins College, FL.

Dewey, J. (1938/1997). *Experience and Education.* New York: Simon & Schuster.

Garten, J. E. (1997). *The Big Ten Emerging Markets and How They Will Change Our Lives.* New York: Basic Books.

Global Edge (2002). Emerging Markets Indicators for 2002. Retrieved April 20, 2003, from http://globaledge.msu.edu/ibrd/marketpot.asp.

Joplin, L. (1981). On defining experiential education. *Journal of Experiential Education*, 4(1), 17-20.

Juch, A. (1983). *Personal development: Theory and practice in management training*. Shell International, Wiley.

Kolb, D. A. (1984). *Experiential Learning: Experience as the Source of Learning and Development*. New Jersey: Prentice Hall.

Mangan, Katherine S. (1997) Business schools promote international focus, but critics see more hype than substance. *The Chronicle of Higher Education*, September 12, pp. A14-A15

Manuel, T.A., Shooshtari, N.H., Fleming, M.J. & Wallwork, S.S. (2001). Internationalization of the business curriculum at U.S. colleges and universities. *Journal of Teaching in International Business*, 12, 43-70.

Pepperdine University (2003). Graziado School information and facts: global partnerships. Retrieved April 21, 2003, from http://bschool.pepperdine.edu/facts/globalpartners.html.

Priest, S., & Gass, M. (1997). *Effective Leadership in Adventure Programming*. Champaign, IL: Human Kinetics

Spinks, N., & Wells, B. (1994). Student internships: viewpoints from A.A.C.S.B. schools. *Delta Pi Epsilon Journal*, 36 (2), 81-95.

Toncar, M.F., & Cudmore, B.V. (2000). The overseas internship experience. *Journal of Marketing Education*, 22 (1), 54-63.

Chapter 16
The Use of Global Work-Directed Teams in Promoting International Competence: The Case of Croatia

David M. Currie
Crummer Graduate School, Rollins College

Denisa Krbec
University of Rijeka

Serge Matulich
Crummer Graduate School, Rollins College

INTRODUCTION

Effective education for international business involves three levels: awareness, understanding and competence. The most basic level, awareness, is the most easily achieved, usually by infusion of international elements into academic disciplines. More advanced levels – understanding and competence – are more difficult to achieve because they require some degree of exposure to other cultures and institutions. It has been a challenge for U.S.-based business schools to provide understanding and competence in global education because of the time and expense of taking students outside the U.S.

One method of promoting understanding and competence has been the use of a work-directed team project in a foreign country, in which a team of students act as consultants for a business. For many years academic institutions have used team-oriented domestic work projects as a vehicle for allowing students to implement business principles learned in the classroom. Recently, some universities have begun to offer projects abroad so that students are exposed to another country's business principles, culture, and institutions.

A project abroad has been shown to be an effective method of education as part of active learning. In active learning, the emphasis shifts from teaching to learning as students develop skills in critical thinking, teamwork, problem solving, and communication. In an international setting, active learning adds the dimension of learning about international business. Students learn to adapt to a different culture, work ethic, and behavior.

This paper describes a collaborative effort between a U.S.-based graduate school of business and a Croatia-based economics school to provide students from both universities with an opportunity to conduct a real-world project. The collaboration is modeled after the practicum used in medical schools – an opportunity to practice skills learned in the classroom by applying them to living situations. In the first section we discuss the need for travel abroad as a method for promoting understanding and competence in international business education. Next, we discuss the use of work-directed teams in providing an opportunity for students to apply principles learned in the classroom to an actual business situation and introduce the concept of a business practicum. In the subsequent section we extend the business practicum model into an international setting by describing the collaboration between universities in the U.S. and Croatia. Finally, we provide some lessons learned through the collaboration and evaluate the success of the practicum according to the four stakeholders – students, faculty, the universities, and the government of Croatia.

DEVELOPING GLOBAL COMPETENCE

The goal of international education is to develop executives prepared to make decisions in a world that is no longer limited by borders and nationalities. International education can be thought of as a spectrum of three concepts: awareness, understanding, and competence (Kedia and Cornwell, 1994). As the curriculum moves from awareness to competence, the level of knowledge and ability to function internationally increase, but so do the amount of resources required to provide that knowledge and ability. Global competence is the most advanced level of international mindset, but it requires students to work in a different country so that when they graduate they have a more advanced knowledge of culture, institutions, and business practices. According to Kedia and Cornwell, global awareness can be attained through domestic study and exposure to international students in a domestic setting. Global understanding can be enhanced when students travel abroad for language or study-abroad programs, but to achieve competence, a student must actually work in another country.

When students have awareness, they know that decisions they make as managers have an impact internationally (Kedia and Harveston, 1998). Students with understanding are able to act upon their knowledge of the differences between cultures. When students develop competence, they can work in an international setting, including use of the language.

Nash describes roles that students, faculty, and universities ought to play in globalizing the curriculum (1997). One of his suggestions for promoting international understanding is for universities to offer travel abroad in the form of one- or two-week trips. In a well-publicized indictment of such study trips, Mangan says that the typical two-week trip has marginal educational benefit and amounts to little more than glorified sight seeing (1997). Muuka, Harrison, and Hassan counter by arguing that lectures, on-site industry visits, and cultural excursions "serve many useful educational purposes" (1999, 241). Furthermore, even short visits help students understand the "intricacies of international business through exposure to foreign cultures and business practices" (Muuka, Harrison, and Hassan, 1999, 241). Two-week study abroad trips expose students to many of the basic principles of international business highlighted by Aggarwal: exchange rates; restrictions on cross-border flows of people and merchandise; and the legal, cultural, political, and economic differences resulting from operating in two or more environments (1989). We contend that short trips can be coupled with consulting projects to provide students with sufficient international exposure to move from awareness to understanding.

Kwok, Arpan, and Folks say that curriculum internationalization is a key component of business school internationalization (1993). Curriculum internationalization can be achieved by adding international dimensions to existing courses; by offering an introductory international business course; by offering specialized international courses in disciplines; and by incorporating non-business courses such as history, language, and geography. They say that the most effective way to deepen students' understanding of international business is to offer out-of-country experiences. These can be exchange programs, in which students attend a partner university in another country, or internships, in which students work abroad. Kwok, Arpan, and Folks' survey revealed that although 33% of the universities in their sample offered foreign internships, only 2% of undergraduate and 3% of master's level students took advantage of them. Although the researchers do not offer an explanation for these low levels of participation, we think they may be due to the cost of internships to both the university and the student. It appears that a more cost-effective method must be found to give the benefits of an out-of-country experience to a greater percentage of students.

Another direction for achieving internationalization is through study-abroad programs (S.A.P.), in which students live in another country for a period of time. In discussing the implementation of S.A.P.s, Henthorne, Miller and Hudson point out that students benefit from extensive exposure to a different culture, its history, and its institutions (2001). Douglas and Jones-Rikkers examine the effect of S.A.P.s on students' global perspectives (2001). Not surprisingly, they discover that students participating in S.A.P.s develop greater world-mindedness compared to students without international experience. We point out that world-mindedness is part of global awareness, which is not the same as global competence. Moreover, we believe that because S.A.P.s do not involve work, students do not experience the business culture and decision-making processes of another country, so S.A.P.s are not as valuable as international work experience.

An international skill set requires cultural sensitivity, leadership, and the ability to manage communication and innovation (Kedia, Harveston, and Bhagat, 2001). Clearly, these advanced managerial skills cannot be attained in the absence of work experience in another country. Kedia, Harveston, and Bhagat say that overseas trips and S.A.P.s can help develop global understanding. An unfortunate fact pointed out in the Kwok, Arpan, and Folks' research, however, is that S.A.P.s do not achieve a high level of student participation.

In summary, developing competence in international education requires contact with people in a working environment outside one's native country. It would be best if students were able to work for several months in another country, but this may not be feasible or possible. In the absence of work experience or an opportunity to study abroad for an extended period, a study trip of shorter duration may be an alternative because students still are exposed to aspects of international business beyond what they can experience domestically.

WORK DIRECTED TEAMS

Work-directed team projects, in which students work on a project proposed by a sponsoring company, have been used as a means of imparting international principles for more than two decades. Such projects have had a variety of names in the literature, such as client-sponsored projects (Frear and Metcalf, 1988), commissioned projects (Shi and Siu, 2001), and practica (Kedia and Harveston, 1998). As early as 1980, Richardson and Raveed describe the use of client-sponsored research projects in the form of 'live cases' as a means of allowing students to work on new product introductions for actual companies. Frear and Metcalf expand the concept by incorporating international aspects into research projects in order to help students "acquire an understanding of another country's cultural, political, and economic environments" (1988, 23). Unfortunately, the international project was done in a domestic classroom so that students did not benefit from direct exposure to another country's culture, political, or economic environments. The projects enhanced the students' international awareness but not necessarily their understanding or competence.

Kedia and Harveston propose that business schools become more like medical schools by integrating teaching, research, and practice (1998). They argue that team projects provide a vehicle for applying international business principles, much like a medical practicum, while enabling students to learn and develop skills in international business. Furthermore, work-directed teams are student-centered rather than faculty-centered in that they focus on student learning rather than faculty imparting knowledge. Students encounter problems that tend to be more interdisciplinary, falling outside the boundaries of traditional academic departments. Work projects also focus on application rather than theory, forcing students to apply what they have learned in the classroom. Kedia and Harveston support the contention that overseas trips help students achieve international understanding. The most advanced level of international education, global competence, can be achieved when students are able to live and work in another culture. We point out that work projects abroad enable students to work and live briefly in another country, and so may be a way to move toward competence.

In an article about short overseas programs, Sarathy describes an exchange program between Northeastern University in the U.S. and Ecole Superieur de Commerce, Reims, France (1990). The major team feature of the collaboration is that students work in multi-cultural teams to insure that students are exposed to work habits from other countries. However, students work on a term paper and presentations rather than on a business problem, so they do not benefit from learning how to apply theoretical principles to business situations. Sarathy says that a more advanced step is to organize overseas business internships that would give students the experience of working in a foreign environment. We contend that a business practicum helps realize this goal, albeit for a shorter period of time than an internship.

Saben reviews work-directed projects in a marketing class at Duquesne University in the U.S. (2000). Because the project is oriented toward an actual business problem and a business executive leads students through the process, students gain insight into the application of business principles as well as an awareness of global business. Unfortunately, the course is taught domestically so students do not necessarily develop understanding or competence.

Shi and Siu discuss commissioned business projects in Hong Kong as part of the action learning approach (2001). The advantages of these projects are that students gain practical knowledge, a deeper understanding of business skills, and an increased ability to integrate knowledge from diverse sources. Shi and Siu argue that these projects ought to be an integral part of the curriculum because they allow students to apply what they are learning. We argue that by extending commissioned projects to the international arena, there is the advantage of providing students with work experience or exposure to students and executives from another country.

Action learning means involving students directly in the learning process and causing them to reflect on what they are learning. It includes interactive learning, cooperative learning, case-based learning, problem-based learning, and other pedagogical techniques that encourage students to analyze and think critically, solve problems, communicate, synthesize, and integrate knowledge from various disciplines. Faculty members often act as consultants; they use these active learning techniques to accommodate students' diverse talents and ways of thinking (Kolb, 1984).

We conclude that work-directed teams represent a viable method for imparting skills that students cannot effectively practice in class, so they move beyond accumulation of knowledge. The work effort focuses on application of business principles rather than development of theory. The projects frequently require an interdisciplinary approach, forcing students to think and act outside the bounds of narrow disciplinary constraints. When the work-directed team is global, the skills include communication, management, and coordination across cultures. As we show in the next section, collaborations with students from foreign universities can enhance the learning experience.

GLOBAL BUSINESS PRACTICUM

Since 1991, the graduate school of business at Rollins College in the U.S. has offered a course called Global Business Practicum. Teams of M.B.A. students travel abroad to work on a business problem proposed by a sponsoring company and with the coordination (but not the direction) of a faculty member. Some of these practica have been in developing countries in Europe, Africa, and Latin America. Students receive academic credit for the course, and the sponsoring organization receives a written and oral final report addressing the problem presented in the agreement.

Students have consulted with many different entities, including banks, manufacturing companies, governments, private schools, professional practices, tourist organizations, and hospitals. Projects have included preparation of feasibility studies, financial analyses, marketing plans, business plans, seminars, and social programs. The primary benefit from the student's point of view is the opportunity to apply principles learned in the classroom to a live business problem. They become consultants. Students also benefit from interaction with foreign managers and executives and the exposure to a foreign culture, and they quickly become aware of the difficulty American business executives encounter when working in a country whose language, culture, and business practices they do not understand.

Since the academic year 1999/2000, the Faculty of Economics and Tourism (F.E.T.) in Pula, Croatia has actively participated in a global practicum in which students from F.E.T. collaborate with students from the graduate school of business of Rollins College. The practicum is titled "Collaborative Student and Faculty Experiential Exchange" and was initially supported in part by a grant from the Fulbright Foundation. More than 30 F.E.T. and 25 Rollins students and faculty have participated in the program during the three years it has been in effect. A common characteristic of Pula and Winter Park is tourism. Pula is a tourist resort on the Adriatic Sea; Winter Park is adjacent to Orlando, one of the world's major tourist attractions and the site of numerous theme parks. Students usually work on projects relating to tourism. The program consists of two parts: 1) Rollins College students enroll in the Global Business Practicum course and travel to Pula accompanied by a professor to work with Croatian students on a project for a Croatian client, and 2) students and faculty from F.E.T. travel to Winter Park to study and observe tourism.

For the Collaborative Student and Faculty Experiential Exchange, the host university houses the visiting students with local families. In Croatia, the host usually is the family of the Croatian student working on the project. Living with a host family adds a personal dimension to the experience of living in another country, keeps students out of hotels, and immerses them in the family lives of their teammates. American students develop an understanding of life in Croatia, of the differences between generations raised under communism or under capitalism, and of the language difficulties in a foreign country. (Fortunately, most young Croatians speak English as a second or third language; not many U.S. students speak Croatian.) Students and faculty from F.E.T. in turn live with host families in the U.S. when they visit Winter Park. Living with a host family not only enhances the educational mission, it also leads to close friendships between guests and hosts.

The Global Business Practicum offers numerous desirable features that meet several of the goals described in the previous section:

- Because it is a consulting project, the practicum is learning-centered, forcing students to use many of the skills of action learning such as critical thinking, communication, problem solving, and synthesis.
- Because the consulting project cuts across disciplinary lines, students must utilize interdisciplinary problem-solving skills.
- Because it involves work, the practicum goes beyond a two-week tour of a country with company visits as the focus.
- Because students work outside of the United States, they are exposed to business practices and decision processes of another country.
- Because the out-of-country time is two weeks, the practicum is more cost-effective than an internship, while achieving many of the same objectives.
- The practicum has the unanticipated result of furthering a goal of the government of Croatia to modernize the system of higher education.

EDUCATIONAL REFORM IN CROATIA

Although there are many forces working to reform education in Croatia, there is no doubt that the Collaborative Student and Faculty Experiential Exchange has made a significant contribution toward the goal of reform. As in other Eastern European countries, centralized control, pedantic pedagogy, absence of autonomy, and lack of funding have typified Croatia's higher education system. A common characteristic of higher education in planned economies was that the system was geared toward producing a predetermined number of graduates with training specified by the government (Woodard, 2002). Because government ministries were (and continue to be) the main source of financing for higher education, centralized control permeated the system. Individual universities were left with little autonomy and little authority to make decisions independent of the ministry. This bred a culture lacking innovation and unwilling to take risks (Ledic, Rafajac and Kovac, 1999).

The classroom environment continued the tradition of centralized control. Most classes were directive rather than participative. Professors lectured and students listened passively when they attended at all. The emphasis was on memorization rather than on developing skills in critical thinking, independence of thought, and ability to deal with differing points of view (Bollag, 1996).

Tuition is rarely charged for university education in Croatia, leaving the ministry as the sole source of financing. Because higher education has not been spared from the lack of financial resources facing Eastern European countries, this has led to buildings needing repair, lack of modern equipment and libraries, and low salaries (Bollag, 1999).

The Ministry of Science, Education, and Technology in Croatia has recognized many of these deficiencies and has initiated efforts to reform higher education such as encouraging alternative pedagogical approaches, disseminating the use of technology, and empowering local universities to be creative within the general educational policy of the government (Krbec, 2001). The Ministry funds a significant portion of the cost for students and faculty from F.E.T. when they travel to the United States. The Ministry also has encouraged F.E.T. to develop a master's program in business, which is leading to a more innovative curriculum, modernization of teaching styles and more widespread use of technology.

EVALUATION OF THE COLLABORATION

The collaboration between Rollins College and the Faculty of Economics and Tourism can be evaluated according to four criteria for the four constituencies involved in the collaboration (Table 16.1). The criteria are fulfillment of the educational mission, globalization, usability, and cost. The educational missions of the two universities and the government of Croatia drive the decisions made about programs and curriculum. Two of the strategies of both universities are to internationalize the curriculum and to enhance the global reputations of the universities. Usability is important because the collaboration is beneficial when it leads to results that can be used by students, faculty, and administrators at the universities and the government. Finally, the collaboration must be cost-effective if it is to be viable in the long run and overcome some of the problems associated with international internships. A model that is cost-effective, useful, and furthers the institutional mission can be applied at other universities.

The constituents are students, faculty, the educational institutions, and the government of Croatia. Each of these constituencies has a different view of the outcome and their evaluations may be different from one another. We evaluated the program through several means, including course evaluation forms for students, discussions with administrators and faculty, and feedback from representatives of the government.

The fundamental criterion is how well the program fulfills the educational mission of that constituent. At the student level, the mission is to allow the student to develop skills in critical thinking, to think across disciplinary and national boundaries, and to apply principles learned in the classroom. The educational mission for faculty is to broaden the classroom environment beyond lecturing, to enhance teaching skills, and to learn to teach in English. The university's educational mission is to broaden and modernize its curriculum, to develop a degree of autonomy as allowed by the ministry, and to build a quality graduate program by attracting foreign and domestic students. The government through the Ministry of Science is modernizing the higher education system in Croatia in an effort to improve the quality of education.

Globalization is important enough to be considered as a separate criterion even though it is part of the educational mission, because understanding and competence are higher levels of international education. Students and faculty need to gain exposure to other cultures as part of developing global competency. F.E.T. wants to become a graduate school capable of attracting students from outside Croatia, but to do so it must expand its curriculum and encourage alternative pedagogy. The government wants to prepare Croatia to compete globally, but to do so it needs to develop a cadre of managers trained in modern management.

One measure of the collaboration's success is whether each of the parties uses what it learns. Students develop a skill set they did not have before, which will enable them to become better managers. Faculty learn new pedagogy that they can use in the classroom. F.E.T. can use the collaboration as a recruiting tool in attracting students and faculty. The collaboration benefits the local economy if the results of the projects are implemented by the tourism industry. The government benefits from a paradigm that can be replicated at other universities.

Cost is an important consideration because the goal is to develop a program that can be generalized throughout the curriculum. If the program provides educational benefits that justify its costs, it may be possible to require such experience of all students. The major cost component is travel, including airline flights to the other country and transportation within the country. In-country transportation is especially costly in the U.S., which does not have the urban concentration typical of European cities. U.S. students participating in the global business practicum are charged the total cost of the trip. Because income levels in Croatia are much lower than those in the U.S., it is difficult to charge each Croatian student the total cost of a visit to the United States. Some of the cost is financed from in-kind contributions and a grant from the Ministry of Science and was initially underwritten by the grant from the Fulbright Foundation.

EXAMPLES OF ISSUES RAISED BY THE COLLABORATION

The global business practicum at Rollins and the collaboration between Rollins and F.E.T. provide numerous illustrations of what can be learned about international business by students participating in work-directed projects. The learning experience is particularly enlightening for U.S. students visiting an Eastern European country emerging from a planned economic system. Sending U.S. students to developing countries is highly beneficial to students and can be valuable to the sponsoring organizations. The collaboration also provides insight into the problems facing the Ministry of Science in Croatia as it attempts to modernize the system of higher education.

The Crummer Graduate School of Business at Rollins College offered the first Global Business Practicum in 1991 with a project at Euro Disney in Paris. Beginning in 1992, faculty and M.B.A. students from Rollins College conducted the first of what would become annual global business practica in Eastern Europe by visiting Bulgaria. In 1999, the focus of the practica shifted to Croatia, leading to the collaboration with the Faculty of Economics and Tourism. Visiting both Bulgaria and Croatia provides an opportunity to compare formerly centrally planned countries and to contrast them with the capitalist system. Moreover, visiting a country over a period of years affords an opportunity to witness economic development as it occurs. In the following sections, we provide anecdotes about our experiences with the global business practicum in both countries.

Economic systems

During the Soviet era of central planning, Bulgarian companies were accustomed to setting prices at 20 percent above production cost. After the collapse of the Soviet system, many of these companies lost their captive customers and sales declined. With declining production and high fixed costs, their product cost per unit went up, so in keeping with custom, they raised prices to maintain the 20 percent margin. The student consultants had to teach management that raising prices reduced demand, so to attract customers the firm should cut costs and lower its prices.

In Bulgaria, the manager of a bank plagued by bad debts explained that the defaults were due to the bank's clients selling products to foreign customers on open account. When the bank's clients could not collect the accounts, they had to default on loans to the bank. When students asked why the companies and bank did not use letters of credit, the bank's executives informed them that they did not know what a letter of credit was.

In the case of a Bulgarian manufacturer with four product divisions, our student consultants asked if the company sent representatives to potential customers as part of their marketing program. The president of the company responded that such direct solicitations would not be appropriate: "If they want our products they come to us. It is inappropriate to ask someone to buy our products." The consultants had a hard time explaining that providing potential customers with information about the company's products was a valuable business practice that benefited both the company and the potential customer.

In contrast to the experiences in Bulgaria, students going to Croatia encountered an economy that had a high degree of small-scale free enterprise even during the communist period. In Croatia, students learned about the constraints facing business executives when the state tries to control all aspects of business through laws, regulations, and unimaginable bureaucratic obstacles. Whereas a corporation can be formed in the United States in a week or two, six to nine months is a normal period in Croatia. Simply getting a document notarized can be a burden and is expensive.

In attempting to import a gift of computers for a Croatian university, it was impossible to get a certificate for duty-free import because no Croatian government official could find a law permitting issuance of the certificate. After many delays, the American Embassy in Zagreb located an agreement between the U.S. and Croatia requiring such gifts to be free of duty. When a student showed the agreement to the customs office, the certificate was issued. It was a lesson in the obstacles put in the way of progress by centralized bureaucracies.

Table 16.1: Criteria for Evaluating Rollins / FET Collaboration.

	Student	Faculty	University	Government
Educational Mission	1. Learn to think critically. 2. Gain international competence. 3. Apply business principles. 4. Generalize across disciplinary boundaries.	1. Improve the learning environment in the school and classroom. 2. Develop skills in teaching. 3. Conduct class in English.	1. Modernize curriculum. 2. Develop autonomy. 3. Attract quality students. 4. Build graduate program. 5. Help ensure a quality program.	1. Modernize Croatia's system of higher education. 2. Improve quality of education. 3. Encourage diversity of pedagogy. 4. Disseminate technological innovation. 5. Decentralize authority.
Globalization	1. Gain cross-cultural exposure. 2. Broaden personal outlook. 3. Understand another culture, people, history, religion, language.	1. Gain cross-cultural exposure. 2. Deepen understanding of theory and practice of business. 3. Understand another economic system. 4. Practice or learn a foreign language. 5. Understand another culture, people, history, religion.	1. Develop global reputation. 2. Expand scope of curriculum. 3. Attract foreign students.	1. Prepare the nation for global competition. 2. Develop cadre of proficient manager.
Usability	1. Develop usable skill set. 2. Improve understanding of other cultures. 3. Improve communication skills. 4. Integrate material from variety of courses.	1. Expand pedagogy skill set. 2. Expand global skill set. 3. Expand relations with business community.	1. Recruiting tool. 2. Produce better graduates. 3. Attract and retain qualified faculty.	1. Develop better-educated citizenry. 2. Improve business climate. 3. Develop curriculum that can be replicated elsewhere. 4. Promote the country's culture and attractions. 5. Develop tourism industry.
Cost	Investment in foreign travel yields once-in-lifetime experience.	1. Unique opportunity. 2. Requires effort and preparation.	1. High value means of achieving educational mission. 2. Improve relations with business community. 3. Opportunity for outside funding.	1. Investment improves managers' global skills. 2. Costs shared by partner university. 3. Significant in-kind support. 4. Economic value to the country.

Educational systems

Croatian law requires students to have oral examinations at the end of the year, and this is the sole means of evaluating student performance. Examinations or other methods of student assessment can be given during the term, but they cannot be included as part of the student's grade for the course. Therefore, many students do not attend classes during the term, but focus their preparation for the examination at the end of the year. Faculty members spend an inordinate amount of time on this task because each student must be examined individually. Moreover, students can repeat the examination three times, and many take the first examination without much preparation, just to experience what it is like, knowing that they can return again and again.

Allowing other means of assessment of student performance requires a change in the law on the part of the government. Such a change will encourage faculty to experiment with periodic examinations, class discussions, written and oral presentations, and team projects as methods of evaluating students. Students will benefit as the educational experience moves from merely accumulating knowledge toward higher forms of learning, such as application and analysis of what they learn.

When the Croatians visit Rollins College, one of the requirements is for the students and faculty to attend classes to observe how they are conducted in the U.S. After the first such experience, F.E.T.'s dean commented, "we'll have to change some of our teaching approaches." Another group visited an accounting class in which the professor involves students in considerable discussion. Later the group attended an economics course in which students were making presentations. The Croatian students, who are well trained in economics, but rarely speak in class, participated actively in the presentations by asking questions of the presenting team. The professor in charge of the visiting group observed the increased learning that took place with student participation, and by the next year had incorporated some of the techniques in her class.

Use of Technology

Traditionally, education in Croatia has consisted of professors lecturing to a class of students taking notes. The class might or might not require students to have a textbook to study. Cases, class discussions, study groups, and interaction during class are largely nonexistent. When a faculty member from Rollins College visited F.E.T. in 1999, F.E.T. faculty and students were able to observe the professor accompanying his lectures with a portable projector and laptop computer showing Power Point slides for the class. The class was surprised when the professor asked individual students to respond to a question he posed, then encouraged others to join in the discussion. By the following year, a classroom at F.E.T. had been equipped with a computer and ceiling-mounted projector, and students were able to access at least one professor's Power Point presentations on the Internet.

Development of a Graduate Program

In 2002, the Croatian Ministry of Science allowed F.E.T. to design a curriculum for an M.B.A. program. The benefit to Croatia will be to develop managers with modern, sophisticated skills. Improved teaching and learning practices are clearly central to the achievement of any reform activity. Faculty must learn to lead discussions rather than lecture and have their ideas questioned and challenged without taking offense. If an international student body is desired, classes must be conducted in English, but many of the existing faculty may not be capable of doing so in a credible manner without additional training. The requirement for individual oral examination might have to be changed.

The curriculum must be expanded and modernized. The curriculum ought to train students in critical thinking skills, teamwork, oral and written communication, as well as applying business principles. F.E.T. professors visiting Rollins College have seen the high level of interaction between the business school and the business community, and they realize that such a relationship ought to be cultivated in Pula. The Croatian business community is not accustomed to having a close relationship to academia, nor to providing financial support such as scholarships, internships, and awards for students or professors.

CONCLUSION

Work-directed projects such as the global business practicum promote understanding and competence, the higher levels of education in international business. In working on a project, students go beyond simply reading and discussing international business; they experience it. They learn skills that take them across disciplines and national boundaries.

Collaborating on a practicum with students from a foreign university is a way to enhance the lessons of international business. Now students learn about different work habits, customs, and attitudes that prevail in the foreign environment and how these differences affect business decisions. The collaboration between Rollins and the Faculty of Economics and Tourism has contributed toward global competence in the students and faculty from both schools.

Such collaboration provides an opportunity for a university to encourage educational innovation and global competence. Both participants –

Rollins and F.E.T. – have included in their missions a desire to implement global training into the curriculum. Both universities also encourage broader, innovative pedagogy and want to foster a learning-centered approach to education. The global business practicum helps accomplish those goals.

REFERENCES

Aggarwal, R. (1989), "Strategies for internationalizing the business school: educating for the global economy." *Journal of Marketing Education*, 10, 59-64.

Bollag, B. (1996), "Reform efforts appear stalled at colleges in Eastern Europe." *The Chronicle of Higher Education*, 43, 8, A59.

Bollag, B. (1999), "Reforms in higher education disappoint Eastern Europeans." *The Chronicle of Higher Education*, 46, 15, A55-A56.

Douglas, C. & C.G. Jones-Rikkers (2001), "Study-abroad programs and American student worldmindedness: an empirical analysis." *Journal of Teaching in International Business*, 13, 55-66.

Frear, C.R. & L.E. Metcalf (1988), "International project workshops: merging education with enterprise," *Journal of Marketing Education*, 9, 21-28.

Henthorne, T.L., M.M. Miller & T.W. Hudson (2001), "Building and positioning successful study-abroad programs: a 'hands'-on' approach." *Journal of Teaching in International Business*, 12, 49-62.

Kedia, B.L. & T.B. Cornwell (1994), "Mission based strategies for internationalizing U.S. business schools." *Journal of Teaching in International Business*, 5, 11-29.

Kedia, B.L. & P.D. Harveston (1998), "Transformation of M.B.A. programs: meeting the challenge of international competition." *Journal of World Business*, 33, 203-217.

Kedia, B.L., P.D. Harveston & R.S. Bhagat (2001), "Orienting curricula and teaching to produce international managers for global competition." *Journal of Teaching in International Business*, 13, 1-22.

Kolb, D.A. (1984), *Experiential Learning*, Englewood Cliffs, NJ: Prentice Hall Publishing.

Krbec, D. (2001), "The reform's framework for incorporating 'collaborative learning' activities." Harriger, Alka (ed.) *Challenges to Informing Clients: A Transdisciplinary Approach*, Santa Rosa: Informing Science Institute, p. 330-336.

Kwok, C.C.Y., J. Arpan & W.R. Folks, Jr. (1994), "A global survey of international business education in the 1990s." *Journal of International Business Studies*, 25,605-623.

Ledic, J., B. Rafajac and V. Kovac (1999), "Assessing the quality of university teaching in Croatia." *Journal of Teaching in Higher Education*, 4, 2, 213-234.

Mangan, K.S.(1997), "Business schools promote international focus, but critics see more hype than substance." *The Chronicle of Higher Education*, 44, A14-A15.

Muuka, G.N., D.E. Harrison & S.Y. Hassan (1999), "International business in American M.B.A. programs: can we silence the critics?" *Journal of Education for Business*, 74, 237-242.

Nash, B.A. (1997), "Internationalizing the business school – responding to the customer's needs." *Journal of Teaching in International Business*, 9, 73-85.

Saben, K.A. (2000), "An experiential teaching strategy geared to preparing students for a global economy." *The Journal of the Association of Marketing Educators*, 3, 164-172.

Sarathy, R. (1990), "Internationalizing M.B.A. education: the role of short overseas programs." *Journal of Teaching in International Business*, 1, 101-118.

Shi, Y. & W. Siu (2001), "Commissioned projects in business education: the case of Hong Kong." *Journal of Teaching in International Business*, 12, 1-20.

Woodard, C. (2002), "Once-communist counties make way for the liberal arts." *The Chronicle of Higher Education*, 48, 33, A45.

Chapter 17
Entrepreneurship Education in Argentina: The Case of the San Andres University

Sergio Postigo
Universidad de San Andrés

María Fernanda Tamborini
Universidad de San Andrés

INTRODUCTION

There is a growing consensus that in a knowledge and information society, education is one of the key factors in explaining the emergence of new business (Kantis, Postigo, et. al., 2002). These new ventures have positive effects in economic development, employment generation, and economic dynamism. In relation to this, the growing interest in the relationship between entrepreneurship education, their businesses, and potential of success, show the growing importance of graduates and undergraduates as a 'source of potential entrepreneurs,' especially in terms of encouraging the emergence of new knowledge and technology-based businesses (Veciana, 2002).

During the last few years, several countries have developed and implemented different programs and initiatives oriented toward developing the potential that exists in universities and research institutions for creating these types of businesses.[1] Likewise, numerous universities have grasped the significance of this phenomenon and have included in their undergraduate and postgraduate programs content and initiatives designed to promote a cultural change in their students to value entrepreneurship as a personal and professional development alternative and to encourage closer relations with productive sectors (Postigo and Tamborini, 2002; Kantis, Postigo, et. al., 2002).

Various authors have pointed out an extraordinary increase in the number and importance of entrepreneurship programs, especially in American and European universities, during the last 25 years, as well as the emergence of research centers in those areas.[2] This phenomenon responded to both individual motivation as well as the increasing demand for these types of courses and was implemented through governments, universities, chambers of commerce, and social actors.

In the case of Latin America, it seems to be that the educational system has not contributed to developing the entrepreneurial spirit, and therefore, it is difficult to find universities that teach entrepreneurship. The academic programs of most universities tends to teach students to be "employees" and rarely focuses in developing skills and competencies that enable them to startup a new business (Ussman y Postigo, 2000). Argentina is not an exception. A recent study points out that Argentine society does not promote nor value an entrepreneurial career (Kantis, Angelelli, y Gatto, 2000). The educational system does not generate skills nor competencies for entrepreneurs.

However in the last few years this trend has started to change, and several universities in the region have firm commitments to develop entrepreneurial capabilities (Varela, 1997; Braidot, 2001; Postigo y Tamborini, 2002; Schiersmann, et. al., 2002). In these countries, the role of new business created by university graduates is especially crucial given that the industry structure is composed of firms in traditional sectors and characterized by a relatively low technological content, failing to play an important role as "incubators" of new dynamic entrepreneurs (Kantis, Postigo, et. al.; 2002).

In this context, Argentina appears as a country with a high potential to develop entrepreneurs through university studies, considering the growth of registered students in universities during the last two decades.[3] The percentage of students over the total population that are between 18 and 24 years old increased from 18.2% in 1985 to 21.8% ten years later, and it was estimated that in 2002 the percentage of students would increase to 27.7%, almost ten points above the regional average.[4] (Kantis, Postigo, et. al., 2002).

Given the recognized importance of education in the promotion of the entrepreneurial spirit in business creation, this paper explores the evolution of entrepreneurship education in Argentina and presents the case of a pioneer teaching experience.

LITERATURE REVIEW

The relationship between education and entrepreneurship has been studied in the international literature from different points of view (Robinson and Sexton, 1994; Delmar and Davidsson, 2000; Lüthje and Franke, 2002, among others). A review of the literature allows us to distinguish at least four lines of research. The first refers to the impact that university education has over the economy (Clark, et. al., 1984; Price and Monroe, 1993; Upton, et. al., 1995; Charney and Libecap, 2000; etc). The second focuses on the analysis of instruments and pedagogic methodologies used in teaching entrepreneurship (Sexton and Upton-Upton, 1987; Plaschka and Welsch, 1990; Solomon, et. al., 1994; Laukannen, 2000; etc). A third line compiles research related to state-of-the-art of entrepreneurial education (Vesper and McMullan, 1988; Block and Stumpf, 1992; Kolvereid and Moen, 1997; Gorman, et. al. 1997; Vesper and Gartner, 1997; McIntyre and Roche, 1999; Solomon, et. al., 2002; etc). Finally, the fourth line of research includes reports about practical experiences at different educational levels and countries (McMullan, et. al., 1985; Robinson and Hayes, 1991; Fleming, 1996; Williams and Turnbull, 1997; Levie, 1999; Obrecht, 1999; Louksm, et. al., 2000; Mason, 2000; Levie, et. al. 2001; Lüthje and Franke, 2002; among others).

Despite the great development of entrepreneurship education around the world, in the specific case of Latin America and Argentina there are very few studies about this topic.[5] Therefore, it is important to advance our understanding of this phenomenon at the local level and analyze the existing evidence that justifies the inclusion of entrepreneurship at the university level. According to Klandt, entrepreneurial capabilities are not inborn but can be learned, and therefore he assumes that they may be enhanced or developed by a guided learning process (1993). But what are the implicit objectives pursued by entrepreneurship education? Several authors, such as Korurilsky (1995), Varela (1997) and Veciana (1998), among others, present the following: a) legitimize entrepreneurship and develop an entrepreneurial culture with the purpose of fostering economic growth through the creation of new businesses and employment, b) change the attitude towards the entrepreneurial function, the entrepreneur, and the image of entrepreneurs among students, c) access to the "job creation" option, d) stimulate entrepreneurial capabilities, producing in the medium and long range a new generation of entrepreneurs better trained and informed about when, how, where, with whom, and what is required to start a new firm, e) to prepare students for a dynamic labor market, f) contribute to the development of intrapreneurs, and finally, g) produce knowledge through research.

Taking these objectives into consideration, entrepreneurship education can be divided, according to Laukkannen (2000), into two large areas: education "about" entrepreneurship and education "for" entrepreneurship. The first adopts a more neutral vision and approaches the topic as a social phenomenon. Specifically, it develops, builds, and studies theories about entrepreneurs, the entrepreneurial process, business creation, small and medium firms, and their contribution to the economic development of countries. It is oriented toward undergraduate, masters, and Ph.D. students as well as policy-makers and researchers interested in the area of entrepreneurship.

On the other hand, education "for" entrepreneurship refers to what has to be done to start-up a venture and implies the personal involvement of the student. It also focuses in potential entrepreneurs, nascent and active. These are all those individuals interested in developing abilities and acquiring the necessary knowledge and tools for starting up a business outside as well as within firms. Mason (2000) explains that with this perspective, what is basically looked for is development of key abilities and necessary attributes to facilitate the emergence of a new business.

The fundamental difference between the education "about" and "for" entrepreneurship is that the former builds and transfers theoretical knowledge and the latter's objective is learning and developing competencies, abilities, attitudes, and values. By focusing on different objectives, the teaching methods used usually differ, and as it can be seen in the following table, education "for" entrepreneurship generally uses tools for active learning, based on problem solving and real life experiences.

Table 17.1: Teaching Methods

TEACHING METHODS	"FOR"	"ABOUT"
Listening to lectures	x	x
Student entrepreneurial club	x	
Preparing paper/thesis		x
Written case studies	x	x
Research		x
Special guest speakers	x	x
Role games	x	
Reading books	x	x
Working with entrepreneurs	x	
Writing business plan	x	
Providing consulting services by students	x	
Computer simulations	x	
Watching videos of entrepreneurs	x	
Company visits	x	x
Practical work	x	

Source: Own adaptation from Klandt (1993)

Lafuente and Salas, provide empirical evidence showing that individuals with high levels of education tend to be involved in firms with high survival ratios, especially when technological knowledge is required (1989). They point out that education is an essential asset for those firms, in which can be found a positive relationship between the educational level of the founder and the firms' performance.

From a more global perspective, Kourilsky states that the economic growth of countries will hinge on the ability to create new jobs through entrepreneurship, and he notes that successful entrepreneurship, in turn, would require well-trained aspiring entrepreneurs willing to take the helm of venture creation (1995). Effective initiatives in entrepreneurship education will be increasingly critical for expanding the flow of potential leaders from the systems. According to Laukkanen, the introduction of entrepreneurial education at an undergraduate level can be understood as the strategic response of universities and business schools in a more demanding environment as well as the ongoing evolution of societies that allow for entrepreneurial capabilities and action (2000).

Veciana[6] affirms that education will be a necessary condition, although not sufficient, for business creation and that formal education contributes to the success of new ventures (2002). In relationship with such affirmation, he explains that while the failure rates of new enterprises created by people with low level of education is almost 80 %, in samples that include only university graduates, this number is well below 20%. He also points out that there is an imminent need for venture creation programs as independent fields of study in the same way as finance, management, or accounting programs.

In a study conducted by Varela regarding entrepreneurship education in Latin America, he notes that there are various factors that explain the underdevelopment of the region, among which are a culture that does not promote the entrepreneurial spirit. He also emphasizes the need for significant changes in the educational system with an objective that focuses on changing the culture and its values to stimulate the entrepreneurial spirit. Recently, a study published by Kantis, Ishida, and Komori referenced the role that the educational system should perform as a way to promote the entrepreneurial spirit and the creation of new businesses. Among their findings was the certainty that the educational system in Latin America does not foster vocation and business competencies among their students. It also emphasizes that, given the critical age to create a firm is situated between the age of 25 and 35, universities and other educational institutions should not only be responsible for motivating students, but also for promoting the development of the necessary competencies for starting up a business. In summary, the study reveals that currently in Latin America vocation and business competencies are acquired in the first place with work experience and that the educational system plays a limited role, generally facilitating technical knowledge, but not providing the wider set of capabilities, competencies, and attitudes necessary to being an entrepreneur.

Lastly, an important aspect to emphasize are the differences that exist between education with entrepreneurial orientation versus traditional education[7]. The entrepreneurial approach has the following characteristics:

- focuses on the processes,
- the professor acts as facilitator,
- orientation toward knowing how and knowing who,
- emphasis on the practical relevance of the theory,
- professional training,

- decision making,
- personal action and commitment oriented,
- focuses on pragmatic competencies,
- values real life experiences in the business world, and
- accepts relative situations.

On the other hand, the traditional approach has these characteristics:

- focuses on the contents,
- the professor is the expert,
- orientation toward knowing what,
- emphasis on theoretical concepts,
- generic and humanistic education,
- functional specialization,
- analytical orientation, and
- academic objectives of fairness.

Finally, there is specific evidence relating to the relevance of including centers and courses of entrepreneurship in the university education. In Argentina, the phenomenon is incipient and constitutes a great challenge for the educational system and for those universities committed to the changes and demands of the environment.

METHODOLOGY

The information was obtained through in-depth interviews with key informants (program directors, researchers, and professors). To obtain information about the Karel Steuer Chair in Entrepreneurship, a structured and auto-administered survey was given to 35% of the student population of the university during the second semester of 2002 and the first semester of 2003. The variables included in the survey were: a) demographic characteristics, b) entrepreneurial attitude and motivation, c) perceptions about the process of business creation and entrepreneurs, and d) perceptions of environmental influences.

ENTREPRENEURSHIP EDUCATION IN ARGENTINA

In the last few years, a progressive emergence of courses, programs, and laboratories for the development of business capabilities and other activities oriented toward entrepreneurship in the universities of Argentina has been observed. This phenomenon was happening in both public and private universities. It basically consisted of an increase in academic supply and a change in the traditional concept of the role of the university.

There is a recent study (Postigo and Tamborini, 2003) that analyzes the evolution of entrepreneurship education in Argentina. The results of this research indicate that up until the mid-90s, there were no initiatives focused on the development of entrepreneurial capabilities in the country. Only after 1996 did 4% of the total number of universities in Argentina have programs in the area of entrepreneurship. Nevertheless, at the beginning of 2003, that percentage increased to almost 30%. This increase reflects an important change in the trends of the university system and an increasing interest on behalf of the academic community in the phenomenon of business creation. It is interesting to emphasize that this change, in contrast with what happened in other countries such as Canada and England, was not promoted by government policies, but a response by individual initiatives inside educational institutions as an answer to the demands of the environment (i.e.: high unemployment rates, global trends towards the promotion of policies for business creation, etc.).

Taking into consideration only those universities that introduced courses, seminars, or entrepreneurship programs, the results indicate a concentration of programs at the undergraduate level (80%) and a low concentration at the graduate level (23%). Almost 75% of the courses offered at the undergraduate level are taught in the last years of attendance and are oriented mainly toward the elaboration of a business plan. There are very few cases of programs with compulsory courses in entrepreneurship during the first years of a university education or integral programs that include courses every year. Regarding business plan competitions, approximately 35% of the universities organize them. In regards to geographical distribution, a clear concentration can be observed. The results show that 85% of these initiatives are situated in Capital Federal and the province of Buenos Aires, where almost one third of the total population of the country lives[8].

The principal suppliers of entrepreneurship courses are the universities with orientation in business and economy, followed by some universities of engineering[9]. The average number of students per course is 35 at the undergraduate level and 25 at the graduate level. In relationship to the teaching methods used, a clear tendency to write business plans and analyze cases was observed. This shows a clear bias towards the design of programs focused on education "for" entrepreneurship. Like in other countries, a relevant role is given to entrepreneurs, which is fundamental to transferring the experience of creating a business to a classroom. A significantly low percentage of universities pursued research in the area of entrepreneurship, and approximately 95% of the interviewees and other people that work in each center or program are committed only to teaching.

In conclusion, although there are clear indications of increasing development of entrepreneurship in the university environment, obstacles to its evolution continue to exist. Among the most important:

- the lack of an educational policy oriented toward promoting entrepreneurship,
- strong restrictions from the formal educational system to implement changes in academic programs, and
- lack of support and institutional commitment by universities. In every case, interviewees advocated the acceptance of students to entrepreneurship courses more strongly than the authorities of the university to which they belonged.

Finally, other important barriers are lack of resources and specialized professors in the area.

Despite the barriers mentioned above, the research identifies a set of factors that favor the development of entrepreneurship education in Argentina. Among the most important factors we found:

- incipient but permanent research production,
- the strong cooperation of related institutions, and
- c) the increasing interest of university students and the public in general about the topic of business creation.

Finally, although this research shows the advancement and development potential of entrepreneurship education in this country, it raises the need for confronting issues such as academic legitimacy and insufficient financing for the development of programs and professor training.

THE CASE OF THE KAREL STEUER CHAIR IN ENTREPRENEURSHIP

In this section we will present the experience of the Karel Steuer Chair in Entrepreneurship (K.S.C.), which is the first nominated Chair in Argentina. In the year 2000, the project was consolidated definitively under the sponsorship of a local entrepreneur. Its beginning goes back to 1996, the year in which courses, seminars, and activities related to entrepreneurship began. Since its origin, the main objective has been to promote the entrepreneurial spirit and potential in young university students and the community in general.

A distinctive aspect of this Chair is that it has developed an integral program in entrepreneurship which crosses all academic curricula of all orientations offered by the university. The program is composed of a compulsory course during the first year, special seminars, and elective courses. This is a big difference from other programs developed in Argentina, where isolated courses can be taken only by students in their last year and are limited to certain careers, especially those orientated toward business or engineering.

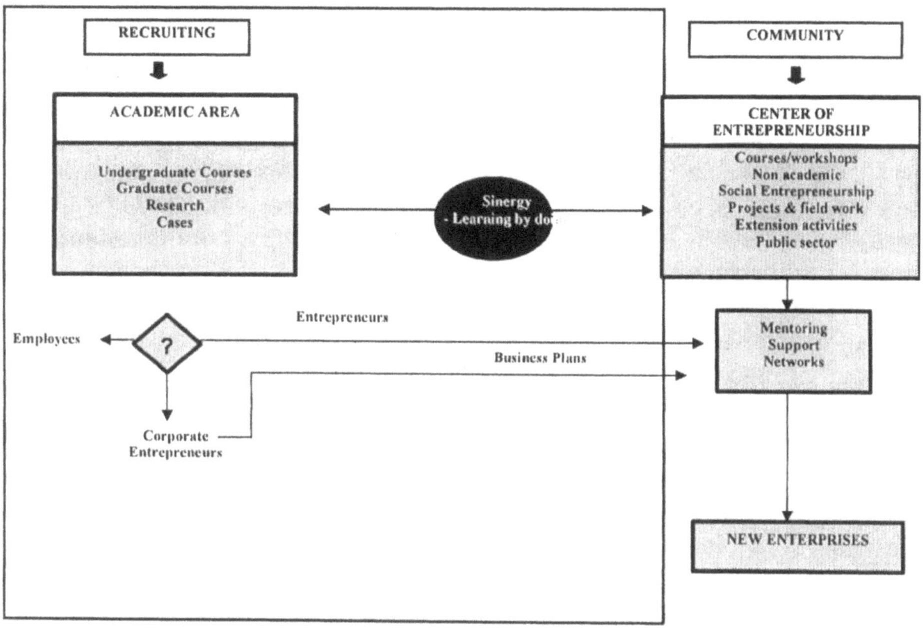

Figure 17.1: The Model.

The K.S.C. offers two types of activities divided into two principal areas. The first corresponds to the academic, and it is strictly related to the activities oriented toward university students. This consists of a) an entrepreneurship program, b) a research program, and c) a unit dedicated to the development of local case studies. The second is the Center of Entrepreneurship that develops and fosters all the links and interactions with the community in general.

The Entrepreneurship Program

With the exception of the compulsory modules in the course *Introduction to Business Administration*[10] required of all students, the remaining courses and seminars are electives; therefore there are no captive students, and activity depends on student interest. During the first course, professors teach theory and basic concepts, and students can choose to develop an entrepreneurial activity. It is in this course that students make their first contact with entrepreneurship topics and the world of entrepreneurs. The main objective is to develop their attitudes, values, and motivations.

The *Social Entrepreneurship Seminar*[11] teaches a set of tools used to create new social ventures and promote in students the concept of social responsibility while developing practice projects for not-for-profit organizations. In addition, the *Creativity and Innovation Seminar*[12] teaches techniques and skills related to opportunity identification, problem solving, and creativity. The course *Entrepreneurial Finance*[13] analyzes tools for project evaluation, financing sources, and negotiation with potential investors. The course titled *Business Creation*[14] is an elective and concentrates on the development of a business plan that is presented to a group of investors at the end of the semester[15]. Lastly, the course *Growth Strategies*[16] analyzes the main challenge faced by every entrepreneur: growth. The students analyze alternative strategies and receive advice from a group of entrepreneurs with extensive experience in business.

Throughout the academic program, topics such as attitude and motivation are thoroughly considered with the opportunity to later develop technical knowledge and specific skills. The teaching methods used during the first year attempt to foster an understanding of business creation at the beginning of a student's university career so that afterwards, students motivated to learn more will choose entrepreneurial elective courses and seminars, resulting in a mechanism of auto-selection. In other courses, instructors seek out students with the desire and potential to be entrepreneurs and actively mentor and coach them. This program is based on a pedagogical model that was developed to satisfy the objective of fostering the entrepreneurial spirit and potential among students while providing all the necessary tools needed to start their own businesses.

The K.S.C. has developed a biannual research program that is fundamentally centered around research fields involving corporate entrepreneurs, entrepreneurship and education, entrepreneurship in emergent economies, small and medium size firms, finance for entrepreneurs, and social entrepreneurs.

Local Cases Development Unit

The objective of this unit is to develop case studies of local entrepreneurs to be used in undergraduate courses and seminars and in graduate courses. During the writing process, the entrepreneur actively participates not only in writing the case with professors and students, but also in presenting it in the course. This task builds a tighter connection between students and entrepreneurs, creating positive role models and exchange experiences.

The Center of Entrepreneurship

The second part of the K.S.C. model is where the entire interaction between the academic world, the entrepreneurial world, and the community takes place. The Center of Entrepreneurship offers a series of conferences referred to as "Entrepreneurship Conferences"[17] which conduct a set of 12 meetings distributed throughout the academic year and developed to target the community. They present topics regarding entrepreneurs and business creation, the objective being to generate a forum for discussion of the problems that entrepreneurs face and to foster the entrepreneurial spirit in society as a whole. It is interesting to point out that these conferences attract approximately 2,000 people each year.

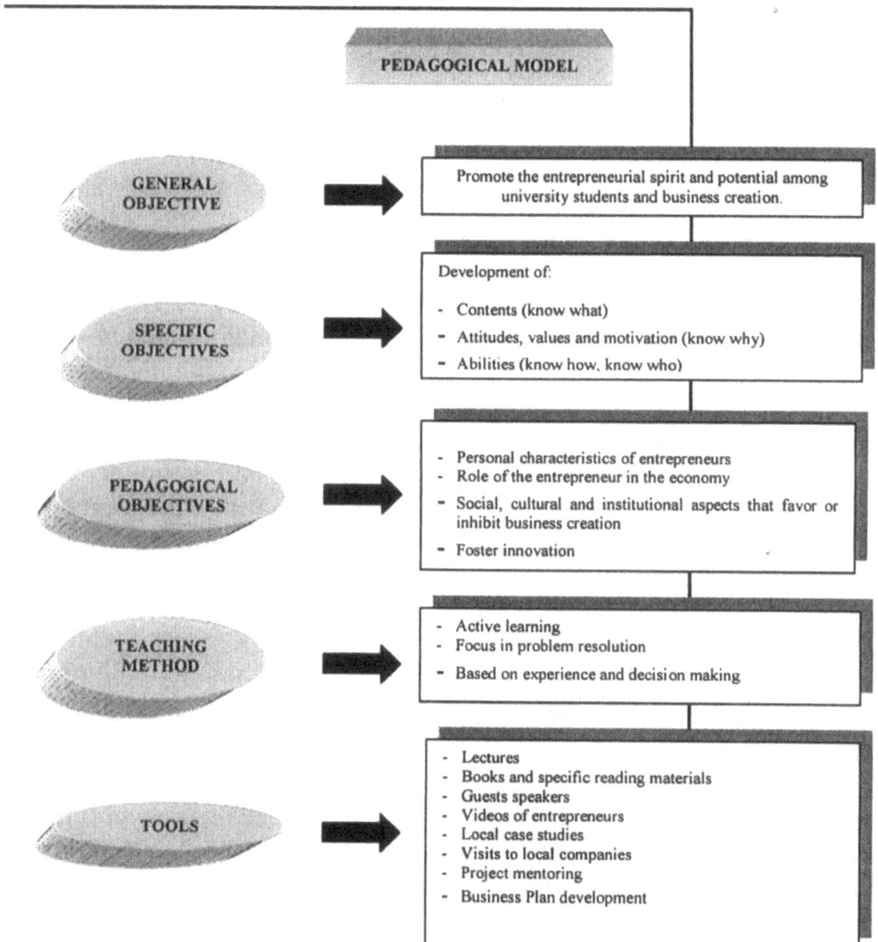

Figure 17.2: Research Programs.

The Center also organizes another activity known as "Entrepreneur's Day,"[18] a day-long gathering of a number of important entrepreneurs of different origins and from different industries who relate to students their "life experiences" in order to stimulate interest in entrepreneurial activities.

Two other programs complete the academic supply to the non-university community. The first is the "About Business Creation" seminar taught in other provinces of the country. The second is "Pioneros," a program targeting young students between 16 and 18 years old that want to develop the necessary skills to start a business. Finally, there are a number of open seminars relating to entrepreneurship organized with other universities and specializing in topics of entrepreneurship, courses for the non-professional, special conferences, programs for corporate entrepreneurs, and a short seminar dedicated to providing strategic support to "start-ups."

Results

Student profiles

Almost 90% of the students that take the courses and seminars in entrepreneurship are between 20 and 25 years old, are mostly male (60%), and are from the business administration orientation (85%). The motivating factor for taking these courses or seminars is based on their interest in starting a new business or social project of their own. They also mentioned that these courses and seminars allow them a better opportunities when job hunting. Lastly, they mentioned their reasons for interest in entrepreneurship. The influence of family role models was very important to this group, the results indicating that 35 % of fathers and 15% of mothers were entrepreneurs, while 70% indicated that some other family member was an entrepreneur.

Impact Over Students

To analyze the impact of the K.S.C. on university students, responses from two groups were considered. The first group was composed of students with an entrepreneurial orientation (S.E.O.) that took at least one course or seminar in addition to the compulsory course. The second group was composed of students with no entrepreneurial orientation (S.N.E.O.) that only took the compulsory course and decided not to take any electives in entrepreneurship.

Related to the entrepreneurial attitude and their perception of this phenomenon, 97% of the S.E.O. considered creating their own business while only 60 % of the S.N.E.O. were willing to do so. When asked about the degree of difficulty in creating a business, the results indicate that 58% of the S.E.O. and 25% of the S.N.E.O. perceived it as easy. This difference could be reflective of the importance of contact with entrepreneurs and their practical experience in developing a business plan in perceiving a lower opportunity cost associated with entrepreneurial activities.

When asked about future career paths, significant differences appeared. Almost 50% of the students that took entrepreneurship courses said they would like to create their own business when they finished their degree, and 78% planned to do so after working a few years. The fact that students, in general, prefer to create a business after obtaining working experience could be related to the deficiencies of traditional formal education in providing practical knowledge and abilities.

The image that students have regarding the entrepreneur changes according to the knowledge they have about entrepreneurship. The S.E.O. perceived entrepreneurs as individuals that contribute to economic growth, create jobs, and are innovative and dynamic. The S.N.E.O. group saw them as persons that possess organization capabilities and financial and management skills.

With regard to motivation, the S.E.O. group agreed that the possibility of implementing their own ideas, unemployment, and achieving economic independence urged them toward entrepreneurship. They said the principal factors inhibiting business creation are insufficient financing sources, legal barriers, bureaucracy, and risk aversion. On the other hand, having ideas, identifying opportunities, entrepreneurial spirit, and education positively affect the emergence of new businesses according to the S.E.O. group.

In terms of self-evaluation of their personal attributes (self-assurance, creativity, perseverance, capacity to assume risks, among others), the results were positive. Most of the S.E.O. group (87%) claimed that the entrepreneurship program increase their knowledge of business creation and improved their technical abilities to start new businesses.

CONCLUSION

In countries such as Argentina, fostering an entrepreneurial culture at the educational level could have, in the long term, a positive impact on improving the image that society has about entrepreneurs, the diffusion of role models, and teaching the necessary tools to create knowledge-based businesses. Altogether, these positives will decrease the perceived opportunity cost of being an entrepreneur.

Although there is no agreement on what is the best alternative to training entrepreneurs, reports show that specific experiences improve existing programs. There are very few programs in the region defined in an integral manner, and where they do exist, they overlook the attitude and early motivation of students so important to the model presented in this paper.

Finally, the introduction of entrepreneurship courses in Argentinean universities should be fostered by governmental education policies that will extend the supply and impact on students and society in general. In this way, issues such as academic legitimacy, financing of initiatives, and specialist training could be resolved.

NOTES

[1] Some examples of this action are implemented in different regions of Germany in the Program E.X.I.S.T., those developed in Scotland as part of the Business Birth Rate Strategy, or in Ireland around the Enterprise 2010 Strategy (Kantis, Postigo, et. al., 2002).
[2] In a study about nine countries, Vesper y Gartner (1997) showed that the number of universities with courses in entrepreneurship grew from 16 in 1970 to 400 in 1995.
[3] According to official statistics, the number of students in the superior level of every 10.000 inhabitants grew from 149 in 1980 to 4,788 in 2000, a 221% increase (Marquina y Straw, 2002).
[4] According to the U.N.E.S.C.O. Statistical Yearbook for 1999, the regional average for Latin America and the Caribbean was at 19.4%.
[5] For example, the studies of Varela (1997), Braidot, (2001), Postigo y Tamborini (2002, 2003), and Shiersmann, et. al. (2002).
[6] In Kantis, H., Ishida, M., and Komori, M. (2002). Empresarialidad en economías emergentes: Creación y desarrollo de nuevas empresas en América Latina y el Este de Asia. Banco Interamericano de Desarrollo.
[7] Own adaptation of Laukkanen (2000) and D.U.B.S. (1992).
[8] Nevertheless, in many cities of other provinces of the country, there are important efforts being made in this matter (for example, in Jujuy, Tucumán, Rosario, and Mar del Plata).
[9] There are isolated cases in universities of architecture, veterinary medicine, and biotechnology.
[10] During the first academic year.
[11] During the second academic year.
[12] During the second academic year.
[13] During the third academic year.
[14] During the fourth academic year.
[15] This is the most demanding course of all the courses offered by the university.
[16] During the fourth academic year.
[17] www.ciclok.com.ar.
[18]www.diae.com.ar.

REFERENCES

Block, Z. & Stumpf, S. (1992). "Entrepreneurship education research: experience and challenge." In D. L. Sexton and J. Kasarda, (Eds.). *The state of the art of entrepreneurship*, Boston, MA: PWS-Kent Publishing.

Braidot, N. (2001). "Educación para la Empresarialidad en el contexto universitario Argentino: ¿Opción o Necesidad?" Universidad Argentina de la Empresa (mimeograph).

Clark, B., Davis, C. and Hornish, V. (1984). "Do courses in entrepreneurship aid in new venture creation?" *Journal of Small Business Management*, 22(2): 26-31.

Charney, A. and Libecap, G. (2000). "Impact of entrepreneurship education." Insigths: A Kauffman Research Series. Kauffman Center for Entrepreneurship Leadership.

Delmar, F. and Davidsson, P. (2000). "Where do they come from? Prevalence and characteristics of nascent entrepreneurs." *Entrepreneurship and Regional Development*, 12(1):1-23.

D.U.B.S. (1992). "An evolutionary study of enterprise education in the North of England. Durham University Business School." Durham University Business School, Durham City, UK.

Fleming, P. (1996). "Entrepreneurship education in Ireland: a longitudinal study." *Academy of Entrepreneurship Journal*, European Edition, 2(1).

Gorman, G. Hanlon, D. & King, W. (1997). "Some research perspectives on entrepreneurship education, enterprise education, and education for small business management: a ten year literature review." *International Small Business*, April/June.

Klandt, H (1993). "Methods of teaching: what is useful for entrepreneurship education?" Conference Internationalizing Entrepreneurship Education and Training (IntEnt 1993). Viena, Austria.

Kantis, H. Angelelli, P., & Gatto, F. (2000). "Nuevos emprendimientos y emprendedores en Argentina: ¿De qué depende su creación y supervivencia?" 5th Reunión Anual Red PyME Mercosur, Córdoba, Argentina.

En Kantis, H., Ishida, M., & Komori, M. (2002). Empresarialidad en economías emergentes: Creación y desarrollo de nuevas empresas en América Latina y el Este de Asia. Banco Interamericano de Desarrollo.

Kantis, H.; Postigo, S.; Federico, J., & Tamborini, M. F. (2002). "The emergence of university graduates entrepreneurs: what makes the difference?" Empirical evidences from a research in Argentina." RENT XVI Conference, Barcelona, Spain.

Kolvereid, L. & Moen, O. 1997. Entrepreneurship among business graduates: does a major in entrepreneurship make a difference? *Journal of European Industrial Training*, 21(4-5): 154-157.

Korurilsky; M. L. (1995). "Entrepreneurship education: opportunity in search of curriculum." Business Education Forum.

Lafuente, A. & Salas, V. (1989). "Types of entrepreneurs and firms: the case of new Spanish firms." *Strategic Management Journal*, 10: 17-30.

Laukannen, M (2000). "Exploring alternative approaches in high-level entrepreneurship education: creating micro mechanisms for endogenous regional growth." *Journal of Entrepreneurship and Regional Development*; 12.

Levie, J. (1999). "Entrepreneurship education in higher education in England." *London Business School.*

Levie, J., Brown, W., & Steele, L. (2001). "How entrepreneurial are Strathclyde Alumni?" International Entrepreneurship: Reasearching New Frontiers Conference, Strathclyde University.

Louksm K., Menzies, T., & Gasse, Y. (2000). "The evolution of Canadian University entrepreneurship education curriculum over two decades." Conference Internationalizing Entrepreneurship Education and Training (IntEnt 2000), Tampere, Finland.

Lüthje, C. & Franke, N. (2002). "Fostering entrepreneurship through university education and training: lessons form Massachusetts Institute of Technology." 2nd Annual Conference of the European Academy of Management, Sweden.

Marquina, M. & Straw, C. (2002); "Datos básicos sobre la Educación Superior. Aportes para discursos, debates y propuestas." Area de Articulación de la Educación Superior, Secretaría de Políticas Universitarias, Ministerio de Educación, Ciencia y Tecnología.

Mason, C. (2000). "Teaching entrepreneurship to undergraduate: lessons from leading centers of entrepreneurship education." University of Southampton. Department of Geography.

McIntyre, J. & Roche, M. (1999). "University education for entrepreneurs in the United States: a critical and retrospective analysis of trends in the 1999s." Georgia Institute of Technology. Atlanta, USA.

McMullan, W. & Long, W. A. and Wilson, A. (1985). M.B.A. concentration on entrepreneurship. *Journal of Small Business and Entrepreneurship*, 3(1): 18-22.

Obrecht, J. (1999). "Entrepreneurship education and training in France: a new challenge to the universities." University Robert Schuman. Strasbourg, France.

Plaschka, G. R. & Welsch, H. P. (1990). "Emerging structures in entrepreneurship education: curricula designs and strategies." *Entrepreneurship Theory and Practice*, 14(3): 55-71.

Postigo, S. & Tamborini, M. F. 2002. "Entrepreneurship education in Argentina: the case of San Andrés University." Internationalizing Entrepreneurship Education and Training Conference, (IntEnt02), Malaysia.

Postigo, S. & Tamborini, M. F. (2003). "University entrepreneurship education in Argentina: a decade of analysis." International Council for Small Business, Belfast, Northern Ireland, June, 2003.

Price, C. & Monroe, S. (1993). "Educational training for woman and minority entrepreneurs positively impacts venture growth and economics development." Frontiers of Entrepreneurship Research, Babson College.

Robinson, P. & Hayes, M. (1991). "Entrepreneurship education in American's major universities." *Entrepreneurship Theory and Practice*, 15 (3).

Robinson, P. & Sexton, E. (1994). "The effect of education and experience self-employment success." *Journal of Business Venturing*, 9 (2): 141-157.

Sexton, D.L. & Upton-Upton, N. (1987). "Evaluation of innovative approach to teaching entrepreneurship." *Journal of Small Business Management*, 25(1): 35-43.

Shiersmann, S., Graña F., & Liseras, N. (2002). "Vocación emprendedora en Alumnos universitarios: el caso de la facultad de Ciencias económicas de la UNMDP y FASTA." 7° Reunión Anual de la Red PyMEs Mercosur, Rafaela, Santa Fe, Argentina, 2002.

Solomon, G. T.; Weaver, K., M., & Fernald, L. W., Jr. (1994) "Pedagogical methods of teaching entrepreneurship: an historical perspective." *Gaming and Simulation*, 25 (3).

Solomon, G., Duffy, S., & Tarabishy, A. (2002). "The state of entrepreneurship education in the United States: a nationwide survey and analysis." *International Journal of Entrepreneurship Education*, 1 (1).

Upton, N., Sexton, D., & Moore, C. (1995). "Have we made a difference? An examination of career activity of entrepreneurship majors since 1981." Entrepreneurship Research Conference 1995, Babson College, USA.

Ussman, A. & Postigo, S. (2000). "O Papel da Universidade no Fomento da Funçao Empresarial." Anais Universitarios. Ciencias Sociais e Humanas. *1990-2000 Yearbook Special Issue*.

Varela, R. 1997. "Entrepreneurial education in Latin America. Center for Entrepreneurship Development." Cali, Colombia: ICESI

U.N.E.S.C.O. (1999) *Statistical Yearbook*. U.N.E.S.C.O., October.

Veciana, J. M. (1998). "Entrepreneurship education at the university level: a challenge and a response." Paper presented at the Rencontres de St. Gall.

Veciana, J. M. (2002). "Comments on the results of a comparative study on entrepreneurship between East Asia and Latin America.", in Kantis, H. Ishida, M & Komori, M. 2002. Entrepreneurship in emerging economies: The Creation and Development of New Firms in Latin America and East Asia. Inter-American Development Bank, Department of Sustainable Development, Micro, Small and Medium Business Division.

Vesper, K. & McMullan, W. (1988). "Entrepreneurship: today courses, tomorrow degrees?" *Entrepreneurship Theory and Practice*, 13 (1).

Vesper, K. & Gartner, W. (1997). "Measuring progress in entrepreneurship education." *Journal of Business Venturing*, 12(5): 403-421.

Williams, S. & Turnbull, A. (1997). "First moves into entrepreneurship teaching in Scottish universities: a consortium approach." The Robert Gordon University.

III. Strategic International Educational Alliances

Chapter 18

India and Business Education: A Model For Curricular Cooperation in Response to New Opportunities

Earl H. Potter, III
Southern Oregon University

Badie N. Farah
Eastern Michigan University

INTRODUCTION

While collaboration between American and Indian business educators dates to the 1950's, the rapid changes of the last decade have transformed the context in which this collaboration is taking place. Not the least of these changes is the increasing strength of business ties between India and the United States (e.g., *New York Times*, June 20, 2003). While these ties are certainly due, in part, to the changing political relationship between the two countries, the increases may have as much to do with the relationships that have resulted from the fact that large numbers of Indians have been educated in the United States (*Chronicle of Higher Education*, 2002). Many have returned to India to lead businesses, but many have also remained in the United States where a goodly number have started business of their own. This situation offers Indian and American business schools a rich set of opportunities and responsibilities. These opportunities come at a time when there are strong calls for change in management education in India and American business educators are looking to internationalize their vision.

In April 2003, the Association to Advance Collegiate Schools of Business – A.A.C.S.B. International -- approved new accreditation standards that resulted from A.A.C.S.B.'s commitment to broaden its membership to include business schools outside of the United States. The new standards both recognize the differences among business programs throughout the world and acknowledge the common commitments that they share. Furthermore, the standards require member schools to demonstrate that they prepare their graduates for the global marketplace.

In demonstrating their effectiveness, business schools must engage their stakeholders in order to understand the requirements of those who will employ their graduates. For the world-class institutions that first entered partnership with Indian universities, this requirement leads to a broad assessment of the global economy. For institutions with more regional missions, this requirement leads to a focus on the peculiar needs of the region from which the institution draws its students. The strategic concerns that drive these institutions to international partnerships will differ from those that shape the objectives of research universities that draw their students from a national marketplace. With respect to globalization, there will be major themes that are common to all business programs, but the character of an institution's approach to internationalization will differ from its peers as its mission and regional economy differs from those of its peers.

In January 2000, the Ministry of Human Resource Development of the Government of India appointed an 18-member commission to develop a Policy/Perspective on Management Education. Five sub-committees of the commission conducted four research studies as well as a benchmarking study in order to assess the current state of management education in India. In commenting on the outcomes of the report, Dayal noted that the All India Council for Technical Education (A.I.C.T.E.), which is responsible for promoting, developing, and supervising technical education, including business education, had been unable to create adequate machinery for: (1) the development and training of faculty to teach courses with applied bias, (2) monitoring quality standards, (3) development of research to make or adapt educational courses relevant for India, (4) encouraging or commissioning development of teaching material on the scale needed, or (5) create an approach that balanced quality control with flexibility (2002). Dayal argues that there are three important changes that must be made for management education to meet the needs of employers in India: (1) application orientation in courses to link practice with theory, (2) testing theories and practices in terms of their relevance to the Indian social, psychological, and cultural milieu, and (3) continuing interaction with work organizations to undertake assignments to better understand and develop meaning/application of classroom teaching (2002).

THE FOUNDATIONS OF PARTNERSHIP

Like many American universities, Eastern Michigan University has signed many international agreements. While some of these have produced tangible benefits to the partner universities and their students, others have produced little practical value for either partner. Osmania University in Hyderabad has had the same experience. Both institutions were determined to approach new partnerships with a comprehensive plan for implementation that avoided the pitfalls of earlier sub-optimal arrangements. Both recognized that international partnerships are difficult to sustain, and both learned that successful partnerships must be founded on the legitimate self-interests of the partners. The Osmania/Eastern Michigan partnership meets this requirement.

Eastern Michigan University (E.M.U.) is a comprehensive, metropolitan university located 40 miles outside of Detroit in Southeastern Michigan. E.M.U.'s College of Business is accredited by A.A.C.S.B. International and enrolls about 3,500 students in undergraduate and graduate programs. Osmania University (O.U.) is a large institution by U.S. standards. It is located in Hyderabad, the capital of the State of Andhra Pradesh and the home of a growing number of high tech companies and institutions. The main campus has an enrollment of 100,000 students. In addition, the university serves as an umbrella to a number of other universities and colleges. In that role, Osmania is responsible for staffing, curriculum approval, and development for all of these affiliate institutions. The total number of students enrolled under the Osmania umbrella, including the main campus, is 300,000 students. Osmania University is a public institution, which provides education and room and board for a nominal fee in comparison to U.S. institutions. Its business management program ranked 37th in the *Outlook* survey of 2001 and was given a grade of B+ (just below the top 25) by *Business India* in 2001.

Osmania and Eastern Michigan University have much in common: (1) both serve students who are drawn primarily from a local region, (2) both are public institutions with a mission that includes preparing graduates for employment in businesses within the region, and (3) neither institution is well-funded in comparison with the leaders in business education, but (4) both must find ways to foster faculty development in international business and increase student exposure to the global economy. Each institution also has different needs that the other can address effectively. Osmania must address the issues identified in the Ministry of Human Resource Development Report on Management Education in India. Eastern Michigan University is committed to the integration of theory and practice in its teaching and has deep experience in designing academic programs in partnership with industry. The majority of E.M.U.'s domestic students are the first in their families to attend college; few have traveled outside the United States at all, let alone to the developing world. Osmania offers the prospect of a stable partnership in which faculty members from both institutions develop relationships over time. Each partner is working with the other to design programs that are tailored to the needs of students that they have taken the time to get to know. Nevertheless, these common traits and complementary interests would not be enough to sustain a long-term partnership if it were not for the economic ties between the regions that each institution serves.

The ties between Southeastern Michigan and Andhra Pradesh are strong. Southeastern Michigan is home to one of the largest Non-Resident

Indian (N.R.I.) populations in the United States. More Indians enroll at Eastern Michigan University than do so from any other nation outside of the United States. E.M.U.'s alums include senior executives at some of India's most prominent companies (e.g., Satyam, India's fourth largest software company) and N.R.I. entrepreneurs who have started businesses in the United States (e.g., Ramsoft). The "Big Three" U.S. automobile manufacturers that, despite diversification, still dominate the economy in the Detroit area have increasing ties to India (*New York Times*, June 20, 2003). It would appear that E.M.U.'s graduates need to understand the implications of these ties in their careers, and there is a large cadre of E.M.U.–N.R.I. alumni and business leaders in the region who believe that this is true.

THE PATH TO PARTNERSHIP

In January 2000, an E.M.U. alumnus led a delegation from the State of Michigan on a visit to the State of Andhra Pradesh. The delegation included politicians, business leaders, and educators. E.M.U.'s Vice-President for Enrollment Management was among the members of the delegation. Initial discussions in Hyderabad led to the return visit of Osmania's Vice Chancellor to Eastern Michigan University in the following summer. For E.M.U.'s part, the initial interest in partnership was driven by the need to increase international student enrollment. Osmania Vice Chancellor D.C. Reddy, for his part, knew that his business school needed the resources of a U.S. partner to address the challenges in the Ministry of Human Resource Development report. The partnership took root because faculty members in both business schools recognized the complementary needs and capacities of the other. Still, the partnership never would have begun were it not for the interest and leadership expressed by Southeastern Michigan's N.R.I. community in broadening the ties with the state that was the birth-home for many of them.

In the winter of 2001, the Dean of the College of Business at Eastern Michigan University and the Vice Chancellor of Osmania University signed a Memoranda of Understanding (M.O.U.) defining cooperation between the two institutions. This M.O.U. called for faculty exchanges, joint programs of studies, curricular development, and student exchanges across both campuses. E.M.U. has many such agreements in place, but this agreement is set apart from others by the speed at which concrete actions followed the signing of the agreement. The first cohort of students entered a joint program in Computer Information Systems nine months after the agreement was signed. The primary reasons for this speed were the strategic imperatives facing both partners. However, the underlying driving force was the call for business schools to learn to operate "at the speed of business" in meeting the needs of business.

Starting in the winter of 2001, visits to Osmania by E.M.U. faculty and administrators created, and continue to create, a fertile atmosphere for cooperation to further the development of this partnership. While E.M.U. faculty members who were born in India made the initial contacts, subsequent visits began to include non-Indian members of the faculty. This development kept the program from being seen as a special interest of only the N.R.I. community. It has been true that the inclusion of non-Indian faculty members has complicated the process of seeking understanding. On the other hand, the cultural and political diversity of India can be somewhat of a mystery to Americans who sometimes assume a false homogeneity among Indian immigrants to the United States. Diversity among the participants in the partnership actually simplified some of the more challenging aspects of the relationships among Indian members of E.M.U.'s own faculty.

THE JOINT DEGREE PROGRAM

The partnership is now entering its third year. A web site (www.cob.emich.edu) at the College of Business provides a variety of information, including academic program specifics, admission information, visa and housing information for Osmania students, and links to detailed and general information about each institution. Frequent news articles in internal outlets, as well as in the regional and national press, build the program's identity. Despite the impact of the events of November 11, 2001, changes in college leadership commitment to the program remains strong. In fact, the events of 9/11 that resulted in the approval of fewer applications from Indian students for study in the United States have increased support for the partnership, the cornerstone of which is still the first joint degree offering -- the Master of Commerce/Master of Science in Information Systems.

PROGRAM STRUCTURE AND CONTENT

In shaping a joint program, Osmania and E.M.U. have been attentive to Dyal's observation that theories and practices taken from the United States must be adapted for use in India (2002). While this may be true, it is also true that joint U.S./Indian business partnerships are creating a common culture for doing business in both nations. It is in this culture that E.M.U.'s and Osmania's graduates will work. The best evidence for this position is the structure of the advisory committee to E.M.U.'s Computer Information Systems (C.I.S.) Department. The committee has included N.R.I. entrepreneurs who do business in Hyderabad as well as Michigan, the Manager of Satyam's U.S. office in Michigan, and Anglo-American entrepreneurs whose companies outsource business operations to Indian companies in Andhra Pradesh.

In shaping this program, both partners have also been mindful of the rapidly changing environment for business education in India. Osmania's programs are approved by the University Grants Commission (U.G.C.) and subject to oversight by the A.I.C.T.E. Eastern Michigan University is accredited by the Higher Learning Commission of the North Central Association of Schools and Colleges, and its business school is accredited by A.A.C.S.B. The A.A.C.S.B.'s standards are changing; the N.C.A. is moving towards a continuous improvement model for re-accreditation, and the A.I.C.T.E. is strengthening its oversight of international partnerships with Indian institutions. All of these interests must be taken into account as plans are made and implemented, and it is not uncommon for the rules to change in the midst of planning.

The MCom/I.S. program structure and course content is based on the content and structure of the M.S.I.S. (Masters of Science in Information Systems) at E.M.U. The model that is in use in the United States is very different from the typical approach to information systems education for business in India. In India it has been the practice to separate I.T. management and business management. Often these two fields are housed in entirely different institutions. The Osmania MCom/I.S. program has been perceived as both unusual and potentially valuable to business (Rajagopalan, 2003). The degree is strongly practical and, in accordance with the advice of the C.I.S. Advisory Board, integrates business strategy and I.T. management skills. It might seem that such a radical shift in approach flies in the face of Dyal's caution (2002). However, the design also follows his advice to make sure that business has a strong voice in shaping new programs.

Osmania and Eastern Michigan Universities chose an approach to a joint program that kept the offerings of both institutions intact, thus requiring minimal approvals for new programs. The program design was driven by E.M.U.'s existing program, which had been developed with the advice of its business advisors. Classroom experience was to be based on the American model of a strongly interactive and applied focus. Students who participated in the program would begin the program at Osmania and have the choice of completing the program in Hyderabad or the United States. As the post-9/11 world unfolded, this feature of the design has proven to be essential. While the U.S. Embassy in India reports that visa approval rates remained near 75% for the last two years, only 33% of students admitted to E.M.U. from Osmania in 2002 received visas. The design of the program allowed them to complete a degree that was substantially the same at O.U.

E.M.U.'s M.S.I.S. program requires the completion of 32 semester hours of study. Twelve of these hours are business foundation courses that can be waived by students who have an undergraduate business degree. The structure and course contents of Osmania's MCom/I.S. program mirror those that E.M.U.'s M.S.I.S. students are expected to complete. The courses taken during the first semester are the business foundation courses: Finance, Accounting, Management, and Operation Management. The courses taken during the remaining three semesters are the core courses of the program: Data Communications, Systems Analysis and Design, Database Management, Project management, Programming, Information Systems Projects, Web Based programming, and E-business. The courses have different titles at the two institutions; however, the contents are comparable.

Whenever the M.S.I.S. program is changed in terms of structure and/or course content, these changes are communicated to Osmania so they can change their program at the earliest opportunity. This relationship addresses one of the chief concerns voiced in the Ministry of Human Resource Development Report on Management Education -- the concern that Indian institutions did not have the resources to keep their programs current. Because of the tight coupling between these two programs, it is essential that the coordinators of the program on both sides of the globe keep in constant communication and that visits take place at least once a year. This allows for constructive discussion, explanation of program changes, and coming to consensus on issues related to the program. In addition, the visits allow the E.M.U. faculty to observe the available infrastructure (computers and communications facilities) for the MCom/I.S.

The M.S.I.S. program at E.M.U. is structured around applying computer information systems to solving business problems. This program prepares its graduates to assume jobs in systems analysis, design, systems implementation, database analysis and administration, data communications, and management of information systems and technology. Osmania's objective for the MCom/I.S. is to prepare students to become systems analysts and produce future managers of I.T. who can handle the challenges of global business (Rajagopalan, 2003). The applied nature of the M.S.I.S.--MCom/I.S. program addresses the charge of the Indian Government to design programs that emphasize project work that involves implementing solutions to real-life business problems (Dayal, 2002; Rajagopalan, 2003).

Scheduling

An Osmania student enrolled in this program completes the first two semesters at Osmania. If he/she elects to join the M.S.I.S. program at E.M.U., the business foundation courses, as well as the Database Management and Programming and Data Structures courses, are waived for the student. The student completes the rest of the required courses for the M.S.I.S. degree at E.M.U. and earns an M.S.I.S. degree from E.M.U. Such a student must have completed a four year undergraduate education. For students with three year undergraduate educations, a bridge program is necessary to bring their status up to E.M.U. requirements. The bridge program requires that students complete 12 credit hours, and may be taken at Osmania or E.M.U.; both undergraduate and graduate courses may be used to satisfy this requirement.

Students who elect to stay at Osmania complete their third and fourth semesters and gain an MCom/I.S. degree from Osmania. In addition, E.M.U.'s College of Business issues certificates to each graduate indicating that the program that they completed at Osmania is equivalent to the M.S.I.S. program at E.M.U.

Admissions

In the first year of the program, 3,000 students indicated an interest in applying for the 40 available positions. Admission to the program occurs in two stages. Students are first admitted to Osmania, then students who want to attend E.M.U. must satisfy E.M.U. admissions criteria as well. All students must have 16 years of education in order to be admitted to the program. Admission to the program at Osmania is based on an entrance test designed by the Osmania faculty and endorsed by E.M.U. Only students with a bachelor's degree in commerce and with a first division standing are allowed to take this entrance test. Students who want to go on to E.M.U. must take the Graduate Management Admissions Test (G.M.A.T.) and the Test of English as a Foreign Language (T.O.E.F.L.). The minima for entrance are a G.M.A.T. of 475 and T.O.E.F.L. of 550.

Scholarships

The Osmania partnership has a high value to E.M.U.; thus, the University has been willing to commit resources to support Osmania students who wish to come to Eastern Michigan University. E.M.U. allocated ten in-state tuition "scholarships" for Osmania students. The selection of scholarship recipients is based upon a set of criteria that was developed by Osmania and E.M.U. that include the following.

Objective Criteria

The objective criteria are based on student's G.M.A.T. and T.O.F.E.L. scores and G.P.A. (B.S. Commerce and M.Com/I.S. first semester marks). These scores are used to rank the students in terms of their eligibility to receive one of the ten scholarships. Subjective criteria are used to break these ties.

Subjective Criteria

The subjective criteria include classroom involvement, communication skills, leadership skills, and initiative. Students are expected to supply recommendation letters from the faculty and administrators to include in their application for scholarship.

The evaluations are finalized after consultation between Osmania and E.M.U. program managers, and the E.M.U. College of Business has the final decision as to who receives a scholarship.

Career Advising

Eastern Michigan University's College of Business holds a career fair each fall that is part recruiting and part educational event. In the morning, faculty and business representatives conduct educational seminars that explore career opportunities in a changing economy. In the afternoon, recruiters meet with potential employees. Osmania, on the other hand, has had no history of bringing students and potential employers together. The partnership has changed this. Contacts with industry are expanding as the new degree model attracts attention. For the first time, Osmania has produced a brochure that presents each of its graduates to perspective employers. In March 2003, Osmania organized an interactive session between the MCom/I.S. students and the heads of prominent companies and organizations that followed the E.M.U. career day model. The E.M.U. team that participated in these activities witnessed first hand the importance of this program to Indian business and organizations.

Academic Program Results

Fifteen of the 40 students enrolled in the first program cohort applied to join the program at E.M.U. in Fall 2002 in order to complete their M.S.I.S. degree. However, due to post 9/11 restrictions in the granting of visas, only five students arrived at the E.M.U. campus in time for classes. The five students who joined the M.S.I.S. program in the Fall semester of 2002 proved to be successful students at E.M.U. All completed their first two semesters of coursework with B+ or better grades. Each Osmania student also obtained employment on campus in positions ranging from hourly work for dining services to Graduate Assistant positions in C.I.S. Although these students could have completed their program of study by taking courses in the Spring semester, all opted to take training in special software packages to enhance their chances in gaining employment. They will be back in the classroom in the Fall semester of 2003 to complete their final semester.

The post 9/11 environment for study in the United States has been discouraging to many Osmania students. This has been especially so because the "success factors" have been hard for them to understand. In order to better advise Osmania students, the Dean of the College of Business met with consular officers in Chennai (the Office of the U.S. Consul that handles visa applications for Andhra Pradesh) in March 2003. At this writing, student visas are being approved, but it remains unclear how many will be approved for the semester that will start in Fall 2003. Nevertheless, more students are planning on joining the program this coming Fall. In addition, students have shown interest in other programs such as the Master's programs in business administration, accounting, and human resources management. E.M.U. and Osmania are now working on establishing equivalencies in these areas.

FACULTY EXCHANGE

Faculty exchanges are essential to the partnership. There are many reasons that this is so, including the need to:

- establish rapport and exchange of ideas between the faculty of O.U. and E.M.U.,
- understand teaching methodologies followed by the faculties,
- provide faculty from one institution the opportunity to teach at the other,
- share research experience and areas of research,
- participate in seminars, panels, and other research dissemination formats, and
- establish possible uniform standards of teaching.

These reasons are essential for the C.O.B. globalization of its programs, as well as for Osmania's objectives in developing its programs in management education (Dayal, 2002).

Thusfar, faculty members from E.M.U. have participated in a seminar offered by the Department of Commerce at Osmania. In addition, some faculty members have lectured to students at Osmania as well as participated in dialogues with industry leaders in Hyderabad and surrounding communities. The E.M.U. faculty members who have participated specialize in strategic management, strategic marketing, and information systems. While the partnership was initiated by E.M.U. faculty members of Indian origin, the shift to leadership by non-Indian faculty has been essential. The inclusion of non-Indian faculty members has been seen as a sign of "true commitment" on the part of E.M.U. In addition, E.M.U. brings a degree of diversity to the partnership that has had a positive impact on the relationship. The participation of a female faculty member was greeted with great enthusiasm from everyone, especially the large number of female students.

The faculty exchange includes identifying certain areas of mutual interest where intensive short-term courses could be undertaken. The details of faculty exchanges relating to time, availability, compensation, lodging, transportation, and meals were negotiated between E.M.U. and Osmania. People from E.M.U. visited the guesthouses at Osmania that will be used to house faculty from E.M.U. for the purpose of faculty exchange. In addition, convenient time slots for faculty exchange for both Osmania and E.M.U. have been identified. The criteria in this case were to minimize disturbing the normal faculty schedule at their home institution. The faculty exchange includes provision of free accommodation in the university guesthouse, food, and local transportation on reciprocal basis.

CHALLENGES

The opportunities and impacts that have emerged as the partnership has developed were not all expected. Efforts could be made to offer training programs for the professionals in the industry. Such programs could support the airfare and honoraria paid to visiting faculty. However, these efforts might also detract from the primary focus on meeting the needs of E.M.U. and Osmania students seeking degrees. In this regard, E.M.U.'s engagement has had a significant impact on how seriously Osmania students are taking the MCom/I.S. program compared to attitudes prior to the O.U./E.M.U. partnership. In addition, the two-day seminar in which E.M.U. participated significantly raised the profile of the Department of Commerce within the University, the city of Hyderabad, and India's professional education community. The importance of these "second order" effects were not considered when E.M.U. began the partnership, but they have become a significant influence in establishing an enduring foundation for the partnership.

In fact, one of the main challenges we have faced is keeping opportunities in perspective. Some opportunities that have emerged do offer the possibility of enhancing the partnership. Others might be characterized as serving legitimate but private agendas that would add less value to the partnership. For example, E.M.U./O.U. faculty members are in discussions regarding the presentation of a business case competition that would possibly be timed with the celebration of the anniversary of the O.U./E.M.U. partnership. This activity would directly benefit the students we intend to serve while also raising the profile of the partnership. On the other hand, proposals to offer contract training to local companies would raise the profile of the partnership but have only a very limited impact on the students for whom the partnership was created.

CONCLUSION

Eastern Michigan University's strategic plan includes a commitment to globalization and a commitment to serve Southeastern Michigan. For the College of Business, these two objectives are complementary. Business in Michigan is international. To serve the region, the College of Business must have strong international programs, and those programs must first relate to the regions of the world where Michigan does business. Among these regions is India. Southeastern Michigan has one of the largest non-resident Indian populations in North American, and business ties between Michigan and India are very strong. Thus, a university partnership that links a public Michigan university to a public Indian university with a similar mission has strong support from the business community.

Such partnerships work best when there is mutual benefit. For E.M.U., the benefits include faculty development, program development, and opportunities for students to experience business as it happens between the U.S. and a developing economy. For Osmania University, the advantages include the acceleration of program development and opportunities for its students to experience U.S.-style education in India.

The key to the success of this partnership has been the recognition by both partners that this relationship is a strategic enterprise that can have far-reaching implications for our students, our institutions, the businesses that we serve, and our communities, if not our nations. The strategic factors that shape the nature of partnerships will differ for other universities in other regions. The importance of building partnerships that take into account the strategic conditions that surround each university is the same for all who would create a successful partnership.

REFERENCES

Celestino, M. L. (1999). Graduate education programs with international vision: how graduate business schools are transcending borders. *World Trade*, *12*, 86-91.

Dayal, I. (2002). Developing management education in India. *Journal of Management Research*, *2*, 98-113.

Harrison, D. M. (2000). The changing face of business education: challenges for tomorrow. *Review of Business*, *21*, 43-46.

Fugate, D. L. & Jefferson, R. W. (2000). Preparing for globalization: do we need structural change for our academic programs? *Journal of Education for Business*, *76*, 160-166.

India's best B-schools. (2001, November 12-25). *Business India*.

India's top business schools. (2001, September 10). *The Weekly Newsmagazine Outlook*.

Rai, S. (2003, June 20). Carmakers around the world are turning to India for parts. *The New York Times*, W1.

Rajagopalan, A. (2003, March 3). Perfect combination: Osmania University, Hyderabad has chalked out a new course, which helps students to more profitably combine commerce with IT skills. *The Times of India*.

Wheeler, D. L. (2002, November 18). As foreign enrollments grow, India becomes the largest exporter of students to the U.S. *The Chronicle of Higher Education*.

Chapter 19
Business Education in Russia: A Siberian Perspective

G. Scott Erickson
Ithaca College

Richard Insinga
SUNY College at Oneonta

Vladimir Kureshov
Siberian State Aerospace University

INTRODUCTION: INTERNATIONALIZING THE BUSINESS CURRICULUM

Internationalization of the business curriculum has been recognized as an important goal for a number of years. The American Assembly of Collegiate Schools of Business (A.A.C.S.B.) has stressed the importance of international content in the curriculum since the 1970s and recently reinforced its commitment in its name change to A.A.C.S.B. — The International Association for Management Education (Fugate and Jefferson, 2001). In spite of this recognition by the highest accrediting agency in the discipline and support for internationalization from scholarship (Fleming, Shooshtari, and Wallwork, 1993; Efendioglu, 1989), progress toward that goal has not always been speedy (White and Griffin, 1998; Kwok and Arpan, 1994; Arpan, Folks, and Kwok, 1993). Indeed, business schools continue to supply an inadequate number of qualified international managers (Webb, Mayer, Pioche, and Allen, 1999). Data suggest that small schools may have particular issues with respect to internationalization (Shetty and Rudell, 2002).

So interest remains in improving the international content of business curricula, both to increase the diversity perspectives of students and to acquaint them with the many additional complications of conducting business abroad. A number of pedagogical techniques have been used to try to better work international issues into courses of study. The most basic solution, of course, is simply to require international courses both inside and outside the business school. More sophisticated approaches include adding international experience to the mix, either directly (U.S. students studying abroad, faculty exchanges bringing foreign faculty to the U.S.,) or indirectly (foreign students in the classroom, U.S. faculty going abroad and bringing back their experiences). Other techniques exist, but virtually all have pluses and minuses. No single technique is adequate for fully internationalizing a business program (Shetty and Rudell, 2002; Fugate and Jefferson, 2001; Praetzel, 1999).

This paper reports on S.U.N.Y. College at Oneonta, a small teaching institution, and its experience with internationalizing its business curriculum through a unique program with the Higher Business School of the Siberian Aerospace University in Krasnoyarsk, Russia. The program combines several facets of internationalization, including student and faculty exchanges in both directions and links with the local business communities. Although issues exist (especially with attracting U.S. students to go to Siberia), the agreement has grown over the years, achieving a certain degree of success.

RUSSIA

Business education in Russia and involving Russia poses some interesting challenges. Any two countries, of course, are going to have differences in terms of the economy, culture, politics, and other such variables. And differences in the objectives and methods of business programs will reflect these differences. The United States and Russia have different situations, with the former possessing a stable, structured economy and the latter a "rapidly changing economy in a rapidly changing society" (Duke and Vitorova, 1998). These differences are also reflected in the educational systems. Compared to the U.S.'s 12-year program with four years of college often following, the Russian system is a ten year model, with a two year specialty degree or five year university Diplome coming after.

A few studies have been conducted on differences in businesspeople and business education in these two nations, but not many. Hazeltine and Rezvanian studied "world-mindedness" of U.S. and Russian students, concluding that no significant difference existed (1998). As a result, openness to trade and other international business transactions should be fairly similar. Various authors have attempted to fit Russian culture into Hofstede's framework (1980), concluding that people are relatively collective (Holt, Ralston, and Terpstra, 1994), accepting of power distance (Bollinger, 1994), and high in uncertainty avoidance (Berliner, 1988).

Sidorov, Alexeyeva, and Shklyarik reviewed the ethical environment in Russia, arguing that the opening of the country in the 1990's created conditions in which business people are seen as highly moral, socially useful agents of change leading the country closer to the Western technologies and products that fascinate a good portion of the population (2000). Further, these authors noted that the future of business ethics in Russia may not be so positive because of the "extremely strange organizations" in place that have vague duties and authority. Sometimes governmental, sometimes private, sometimes allied to a business leader, sometimes allied to a governmental figure, the uncertainty created by such structures is not conducive to developing ethical norms. Business education itself, however, may be able to play an important role in establishing structures and norms within the Russian economy (Kainova, 2001).

Entrepreneurialism in Russia has also been studied (Hisrich and Grachev, 1995), a particularly important topic given the explosion of small business operations in the country (McCarthy, Puffer, and Shekshnia, 1993). Anyone who has visited the country recently knows that this trend has continued, even strengthened, over the past decade. Stewart, Carland, and Carland, for example, collected data from 560 business owners (430 in the U.S., principally from the southeast, 130 in Russia, principally from Irkutsk) (2003). Although some demographic information is of interest (more female participation in the Russian sample), the most fascinating result was that Russian entrepreneurs were more risk aggressive. The study's authors suggest this may come from the more uncertain climate (economic and political) in Russia as well as from the lack of an entrepreneurial heritage and educational programs.

So to our purposes, what this background provides is some guidance as to what the situation is for business education in Russia. A strong interest in international matters, particularly in western technology and business methods, exists. Rapid change is occurring in the economic, social, and political environments. Structures that would normally help police a capitalist economy are still in flux, so ethics and business practices could be molded in positive or negative directions. And entrepreneurialism is being enthusiastically pursued, though again without a strong tradition, educational training, or settled legal structures. Into this environment came the agreement between the New York and Siberian schools.

HIGHER BUSINESS SCHOOL

The Higher Business School of the Siberian State Aerospace University is located in Krasnoyarsk, Russia. Krasnoyarsk, home to around a million Russians, is several thousand kilometers east of Moscow, and 600-700 kilometers north of the Mongolian border. During the Soviet years, it was a closed city where a good amount of the U.S.S.R.'s aerospace research and design, as well as other defense work, was conducted. Heavy industry, based on the Siberian region's abundant natural resources, is a prominent part of the current economy. The city is split by the Yenesei River, a wide, deep, and navigable waterway that flows north all the way to the Arctic Ocean. The city and region possess great potential though it is tempered by the ongoing Russian economic difficulties (double-digit unemployment rates), geographic distance from other major market centers, and lack of experience with a capitalist economic structure.

The Higher Business School (H.B.S.) was organized in 1991, extending the existing economics program at the Siberian Aerospace University (S.A.U., previously, the Siberian Aerospace Academy, S.A.A.). The H.B.S. was recently renamed the Faculty of International Business. The S.A.U. has 400 faculty and 7000 students (4500 full-time), pursuing both undergraduate and graduate degrees. Courses are taught in Russian and English. The H.B.S. is currently pursuing accreditation from the European Council for Business Education and has a long-term goal to be the first school in Russia to achieve A.A.C.S.B. accreditation.

S.U.N.Y. College at Oneonta is part of the State University of New York system, a residential four-year college in the central part of the state, roughly equidistant from Albany, Syracuse, and Binghamton. The college enrolls about 5,000 students, almost all undergraduates. The Economics and Business major is one of the largest on campus.

The partnership between the H.B.S. and S.U.N.Y.-Oneonta started in 1994, with Richard Insinga's visit to Krasnoyarsk and meeting with Vladimir Kureshov. The trip was sponsored by the U.S.I.A. through the National Forum Foundation's American Volunteers for International Development Program. Later funding has come through the Eurasia Foundation Progressively more advanced cooperation agreements flowed from this initial meeing until an Exchange Agreement was signed in 1997 by the S.U.N.Y. Oneonta President, Alan Donovan, the S.A.A. Rector, Gennady Belyakov, and Linda Scatton, Assistant Provost for S.U.N.Y.'s Central Administration. An Articulation Agreement was made in 1998 for a B.A. degree in Business Economics, with later agreements also established in the Food Service and Restaurant Administration and Merchandising degree program and the Fashion Merchandising degree program.

Although originally just an activity meant to provide some expert advice to a small business institution in a developing economy, the program now looks to benefit both schools by better internationalizing their curricula. More and more options are available for the Russian students in terms of a U.S.-based degree completion program, they have an opportunity to take courses in Russia from U.S. faculty (providing a different perspective on course material as well as immersion instruction in English), and their own Russian faculty return from teaching in the U.S. with their horizons broadened. U.S. students benefit from Russian faculty in the classroom and the new perspectives brought by the U.S. faculty who have taught in Russia. The U.S. students also have the opportunity to study in Russia, though few have taken advantage to date.

So the current structure of the program allows for faculty exchanges in both directions. Russian faculty typically come to Oneonta for a semester at a time and teach one or two courses. U.S. faculty typically spend six weeks over the course of the summer (though occasionally a full semester), teaching one or two courses in Krasnoyarsk. All instruction is in English. Students also travel in both directions, though the Russia to the U.S. aspect is much more popular. The agreement allows H.B.S. students to complete a S.U.N.Y. degree by taking designated courses with U.S. faculty in Krasnoyarsk and then spending their last year (at minimum) on site in Oneonta. The first five Russian students received their degrees in Oneonta in May 2002. U.S. students are invited to travel to Krasnoyarsk during the summer (with the visiting U.S. professors), taking a course or two. To date, only a handful have availed themselves of the opportunity. The U.S. professors have also taken a hand in reaching out to the Russian business community, including a new U.S. venture by Kovcheg, a concrete architectural products firm, with assistance from the S.A.B.I.T. program of the U.S. Department of Commerce.

One interesting and instructive facet of the relationship is that it has endured while a separate program withered on the vine. In 1994, Iowa State University was brought into the mix to help provide science, engineering, and agricultural program cooperation. But after an initial flurry of activity, that connection effectively disappeared. Three potential reasons are apparent and instructive.

Initially, the S.U.N.Y.-Oneonta program was driven by faculty and had active participation by faculty members from the beginning. The I.S.U. program was a top-down structure that never fully obtained faculty buy-in. Secondly, the I.S.U. program tried to create a high-level, broad-based relationship from the start. The S.U.N.Y.-Oneonta approach was much slower, in smaller steps, but seems to have established a stronger and more lasting foundation for cooperation. Finally, the S.U.N.Y.-Oneonta and H.B.S. project managers were both personally dedicated to the project and quickly developed a close personal friendship. The project manager from I.S.U. had numerous international relationships and responsibilities, failing to give priority to the Krasnoyarsk work or to developing personal relationships.

CURRICULUM

The curriculum at the H.B.S. is a pretty standard business curriculum, though the economics emphasis (12 credits) found at both the H.B.S. and S.U.N.Y.-Oneonta is a major and unique component. The summer program offered by U.S. faculty varies according to the qualifications and preferences of the instructors, but is taught in English and fits into the curricular structure of both institutions. For Russian students looking to study in Oneonta, these courses are important gateways that serve to evaluate both academic potential and English language skills. Even for H.B.S. students not seeking to study in the U.S., the courses provide an opportunity to practice English comprehension and listen to "American" English.

In general, the English skills of the Russian students are very good, though widely varied. For the majority, the reading and oral comprehension skills are excellent. Writing skills are adequate (the point is usually clear though "a", "the" and other such words foreign to the Russian language are difficult for the students). The students are also somewhat shy about expressing themselves verbally, though their abilities are better than they believe they are. One interesting aspect of the English language training is that it is not only provided by non-native English speakers (the Russian faculty) but that the instructors generally receive their training in an English English tradition — not a true difficulty but a circumstance that can make the accents and usages a more interesting proposition.

The business background of students is also of interest. As noted earlier, Russia's conversion to capitalism is a gradual process. Krasnoyarsk's history as a closed city meant that its exposure to the west occurred later in the game than many other Russian cities of its size, and it is still relatively isolated, being five hours by plane from Moscow, Beijing, and Seoul. That being said, supermarket shelves are now full of branded products, bars and restaurants are present in growing numbers, and outdoor cafes (often supplied with plastic furnishings by beer and soda providers) are sprouting up all over the place. Local television includes M.T.V. Asia and substantial advertising for a wide variety of branded goods by firms such as Nestle and Samsung. The World Cup 2002 soccer matches were overflowing with beer commercials. So while the typical practical examples employed in U.S. classes might not be familiar, close-to-home applications are readily available.

In this paper, we'll focus on one instructor's experience with a specific course, a marketing elective and semi-capstone course (representing the high point of an emphasis in marketing, the major retains a generic business administration designation). Students needed only to have completed a Fundamentals of Marketing course though other marketing coursework certainly helps with the course. The class is structured around marketing strategy, teaching the students the tools of a high-level S.W.O.T. Analysis and resulting marketing mix decisions while providing numerous case examples on which to hone their analytical skills.

INSTRUCTIONAL RESOURCES

The H.B.S. is an interesting mix of up-to-date, state-of-the-art capabilities and barebones facilities. Standard blackboards with wet cloths for erasers are juxtaposed with decent computer technology and, of course, access to the Internet. While the library of the S.A.U. contains 253,000 volumes, the western business holdings (including teaching resources such as video) are limited.

What the Internet link provides, however, is an opportunity to "jump" a technological generation, skipping some of the standard features of western classrooms and moving right to the full potential of the web. Rather than bothering to install video players and overhead projectors, the Russians would probably be better off continuing on their current path and moving directly to newer technologies. Further, given that books, journals, and newspapers can be also be accessed over the web, and that audio and video are available for streaming via the web or C.D./D.V.D., the technology makes some of the other potential physical facilities improvements irrelevant. The existing computer lab also makes possible the use of some other contemporary teaching tools, such as a marketing-based computer simulation. The Russian students seemed to have fine computer skills, executing both Internet assignments and the simulation with virtually no instructor guidance (at least as far as computer issues were concerned). The H.B.S. is also able to provide skilled technicians full time in the computer lab, enabling immediate and effective problem solving.

THE APPROACH

The course was adapted somewhat from the S.U.N.Y. version, conforming to the strengths and weaknesses of the facility and the students. The text was a standard marketing strategy/analysis techniques volume from Rao and Steckel, often challenging for U.S. undergraduates given the quantitative approach but well within the abilities of the Russian students. Other course materials included the marketing simulation PharmaSim from Interpretive Software, Inc. PharmaSim is a brand management simulation requiring students to make the full range of increasingly complex marketing decisions based on environmental circumstances. The software and manuals were shipped directly to Krasnoyarsk for the purposes of the course. Finally, cases were drawn from the online archives of *Inc* magazine, specifically from a regular feature "Anatomy of a Startup."

Grading was allocated to two short-answer essay exams (ten questions designed to be answered in four or five sentences), team-based written simulation reports, and individual case analyses, requiring both a written paper and oral presentation. The variety of written and oral assignments allowed ample opportunities to deliver the course material while pushing the Russian students to develop confidence in their English skills.

The simulation provided some very interesting results. The small class was divided into three teams of three students each. They were responsible for team reports on the ten periods contained within the simulation as they managed the marketing mix for an over-the-counter cold remedy. The periods grew increasingly complicated in terms of decisions, and the simulation provides substantial financial feedback throughout the exercise. I've always liked the simulation because it rewards good decision making while punishing some of the typical but less appropriate choices (such as dropping the price on a premium branded product). Less glitzy but more effective choices, such as maintaining a sizable sales force relative to the competition's, are usually the best decisions and are rewarded. Obviously, this type of exercise allows for some team-building work as well.

The Russian students performed at a far higher level in terms of financial results than I have ever seen on the simulation. Part of this was because there was a ringer — a Russian student who had taken the course before that was repeating it in order to increase his grade. But even with one run-through on the simulation, an undergraduate picks up only so much understanding. The impressive part of the performance was the students' work ethic (a couple of hours spent in the computer lab, minimum, before each update was due) and the teamwork. Invariably, the U.S. version of the course, admittedly with a class not so self-selected in terms of achievers, yields a certain amount of deadweight on the teams. The problem is handled through team evaluations of one another. But in Krasnoyarsk, the teamwork was clearly outstanding and was apparent not just within the H.B.S. teams but across the teams. U.S. students tend to treat the assignment as a competition, but the Russian teams helped one another. The Russian students were both comfortable and accomplished at working in teams. This caused issues in another way when the time came for exams, but nothing that couldn't be handled.

The cases also proved to be very effective for this academic environment. The *Inc* backfiles are available for free online, allowing all the students to have easy access to them without worrying about library holdings or availability. The "Anatomy of a Startup" series tended to focus on entrepreneurial initiatives, explaining the business and the environmental conditions under which each was started. Further, for a long time during the Anatomy series, the pieces included additional comments from outside observers, including competitors, venture capitalists or other sources of money, customers, and other interested parties.

These cases are useful in the U.S. curriculum because entrepreneurism is often not covered in any meaningful fashion, particularly in the typical capstone course. So it provides students with some exposure to small business startups and how strategy relates to them. Further, a number of the firms featured in the articles have some history by the time the students study them, so they can actually research what has become of them since their inception (CDNow, Blue Mountain Arts, garden.com, Excelsior-Henderson, Oregon Chai, etc.). At the same time, the firms are not so familiar that students walk in with any knowledge or preconceived notions concerning the companies (or in this case, any problems with not possessing expected prior knowledge of well-known firms). So they are useful and enlightening in their usual domestic application.

In Krasnoyarsk, their usefulness was even further enhanced. As noted in the literature review, entrepreneurial studies are of interest and important to Russians. They have a saying that Americans are entrepreneurs by choice, Russians are entrepreneurs by necessity. Although the Krasnoyarsk area has a number of businesses of some size (aluminum, utilities, mining, timber), most are left over from the Soviet era and still questionable as to their long-term dynamism and growth potential in a fully free market. The real action in the local economy seems to be coming from small ventures, whether retail/service or high technology. So the interest in and applicability of small business cases was considerable. In addition, all students were starting from scratch with each case, so a lack of knowledge of the usually well-known western firms found in strategy cases was a nonfactor.

The Russians were very good in their analysis of the cases. They were provided a template (macroenvironment, microenvironment, mix decision) but had to adapt it to the individual case. They intuitively understood many of the important issues surrounding a startup and recognized why the issues (e.g. market size, competition, government help or hindrance) were important. And I believe they had a lot more interest in these types of cases than they would have for another case concerning a multibillion dollar corporation.

CONCLUSIONS

The S.U.N.Y.-Oneonta/H.B.S. partnership benefits both partners. In internationalizing both curricula, the program employs a number of methods, not relying on any single technique. To date, the most effective pieces have been the presence of Russian faculty and students and their perspectives in the U.S. classrooms, the presence of U.S. faculty in the Russian classrooms, and the international experiences brought back by all the parties to their own home classrooms. The program makes a case for small institutions cooperating with one another. As noted in the discussion, because the two programs were the top international priority for each other, because the project leaders had significant and frequent interaction (becoming friends), and because the ambitions of the partnership started small, the experience has been a pleasant one for all involved.

In terms of Russia itself, the curiosity, world-mindedness, and interest in the west noted in the literature have all been confirmed by this experience. The Russian students are very eager to experience and learn about western business techniques. These will be valuable as the economic and political structures mature and as the rules of the game become clearer. Some issues with ethics are apparent in the Russian classroom, but the motivations are actually admirable. The students work well in teams in everything they do, and it is natural to them to provide assistance for grading opportunities, even those intended to be individual efforts.

A focus on entrepreneurialism and outreach will be important for the future of the activities in Russia. Even without clear rules for operating, small businesses are popping up and thriving throughout the city. Help for the business owners and for those looking to future startups will be one of the most valuable contributions that the H.B.S. and, by extension, S.U.N.Y.-Oneonta can make to the community.

REFERENCES

Arpan, J.S., Folks, W.R., & Kwok, C.C.Y. (1993), *International Business Education in the 1990s: A global survey.* Columbia, SC: CIBER, University of South Carolina.

Berliner, J. (1988), *Soviet industry from Stalin to Gorbachev: Essays on Management and Innovation.* Ithaca, NY: Cornell University Press.

Bollinger, D. (1994), "The four cornerstones and three pillars in the 'house of Russia' management system, *Journal of Management Development*, 13:2, 49-54/

Duke, C.R. & Victorova, I. (1998), "Exploring joint programs across disciplines and between countries," *Journal of Education for Business*, 74:2 (Nov/Dec), 99-102

Efendioglu, A.M. (1989), "The problems and opportunities in developing international business programs," *Journal of Teaching in International Business*, 1:2, 27-36.

Fleming, M.J., Shooshtari, N.H., & Wallwork, S.S. (1993), "Internationalizing the business curriculum: A survey of collegiate business schools," *Journal of Teaching in International Business*, 4:2, 77-99.

Fugate, D.L. & Jefferson, R.W. (2001), "Preparing for globalization—do we need structural change for our academic programs," *Journal of Education for Business*, 76:3 (January), 160-166.

Hazeltine, J.E. & Rezvanian, R. (1998), "World-mindedness among American and Russian business students: a comparison," *Journal of Education for Business*, 73:6 (July/August), 344-361.

Hisrich, R.D. & Grachev, M.V. (1995), "The Russian entrepreneur: characteristics and prescriptions for success," *Journal of Managerial Psychology*, 10:2, 3-10.

Hofsted, G. (1980), *Culture's Consequences: International Differences in Work-Related Values*. Newbury Park, CA: Sage.

Holt, D.H., Ralston, D.A., & Terpstra, R.H. (1994), "Constraints on capitalism in Russia: The managerial psyche, social infrastructure, and ideology," *California Management Review*, 36:3, 124-141.

Kainova, E. (2001), "Business education," *Russian Education and Society*, 43:7 (July), 42-50.

Kwok, C.C.Y. & Arpan, J.S. (1994), "A comparison of international business education at U.S. and European business schools in the 1990s," *Management International Review*, 34:4, 357-379.

Praetzel, G.D. (1999), "Pedagogical recommendations for internationalizing the undergraduate business curriculum," *International Advances in Economic Research*, 5:1, 137-142.

Shetty, A. & Rudell, F. (2002), "Internationalizing the business program—a perspective of a small school," *Journal for Education in Business*, 78:2 (Nov/Dec), 103-110.

Sidorov, A., Alexeyeva, I., & Shklyarik, E. (2000), "The ethical environment of Russian business," *Business Ethics Quarterly*, 10:4 (October), 911-924.

Stewart, Jr., W.H., Carland, J.C., & Carland J.W. (2003), "Entrepreneurial dispositions and goal orientations: A comparative exploration of United States and Russian entrepreneurs," *Journal of Small Business Management*, 41:1 (January), 27-46.

Webb, M.S., Mayer, K.R., Pioche, V., & Allen, L.C. (1999), "Internationalization of American business education," *Management International Review*, 39:4, 379-397.

White, D.S. & Griffith, D.A. (1998), "Graduate international business in the United States: Comparisons and suggestions," *Journal of Education for Business*, 74, 103-115.

Chapter 20
National Economics University and Boise State University: International Cooperation in Vietnam

N.K.Napier
Boise State University

N.T.T. Mai
National Economics University

INTRODUCTION

The National Economics University (N.E.U.) in Hanoi, Vietnam, and Boise State University in Boise, Idaho (U.S.A.), have been partners since 1994 when Boise State University was invited to offer it's a.A.C.S.B. accredited M.B.A. program in Vietnam. The project was to develop university teachers able to train Vietnam's future managers who would lead the country into a market oriented economy (Napier, Vu, Ngo, Nguyen, and Vu, 1997). The relationship included joint teaching and research, training, and cooperation in creating and building the N.E.U. Business School.

The present paper's three sections examine the history of the National Economics University-Boise State University relationship, the processes of joint project management, ways the universities built a cooperative relationship -- through exchanges and internships -- joint teaching and research, training programs offered in the U.S. and Vietnam, university and college administrative support and advice, and professional staff mentoring and support. The paper closes with comments on "Lessons Learned" from organizational and individual perspectives.

VIETNAM'S RECENT HISTORY

Prior to the relationship, Vietnam had begun to move toward a market oriented economy with the introduction of *doi moi,* or market renovation, in 1986. Prior to and just after this change, Vietnam had traded with and depended heavily upon the former Soviet Union and Eastern Europe for raw materials and goods, as well as job and educational opportunities. When the former Soviet Union fell in 1989, the exchange of goods, materials, and people dwindled, forcing Vietnam to learn to conduct business elsewhere in the world. Vietnam progressed slowly toward a market-oriented economy until the early 1990s when government and communist party officials began to realize the need for educational reform to prepare managers for a global economy (Van Kopp, 1992).

The N.E.U. created a Centre for Management Training in 1990 to provide training for managers of state owned firms in areas of business, accounting, finance, and marketing. Subsequently, the government of Vietnam designated the N.E.U. to begin developing managers trained in modern management and business approaches through a $2 million project funded by the Swedish International Development Cooperation Agency (Sida). The objective was to train thirty lecturers to an international standard, capable of developing their own M.B.A. program for Vietnamese managers. The degree granting institution was a Canadian university, in part because the U.S. embargo prohibited American universities from operating in Vietnam.

HISTORY OF THE RELATIONSHIP

In fall 1993, an opportunistic introduction between the onsite project co-ordinator and a Boise State University professor led to a 12 week train-the-trainer workshop for the Vietnamese lecturers focusing on adult learning, training program design, presentation, and evaluation. Two of the four professors who ran the workshop, from Boise State University, got along well with the project co-ordinator, and offered to help if they could after the workshop.

When the relationship between the project contractor (Hong Kong University) and the degree granting institution faltered, the project coordinator and manager approached Boise State University in July 1994 about taking over the M.B.A. granting responsibilities. By mid-August, the deal was done: Boise State University's M.B.A. degree would be offered at the N.E.U. in Vietnam.

Boise State's quick reaction time is one reason the Boise State University-N.E.U. relationship worked well. Boise State's willingness to take risks that are likely to pay off (Glassman, Neupert, Moore, Rossy, Napier, Harvey, and Jones, forthcoming) and Idaho's small size, making it relatively easy to reach influential players, worked in its favor. Within two weeks of the offer, the Dean of the College of Business and Economics (C.O.B.E.) and the university Provost contacted key players in Idaho (i.e., about 30 key business leaders, the U.S. Senators and representatives, the governor and key officials, the State Board of Education members, and representatives of the M.I.A. and P.O.W. groups) to gauge reactions to the university taking on such a project; the positive reaction led administrators to accept the offer.

During 1994-95, nine C.O.B.E. faculty members taught in Vietnam; five N.E.U. senior administrators visited Boise, met with the governor, the Chamber of Commerce, the Department of Commerce and Boise State administrators and staff. During summer 1995, twenty-six Vietnamese M.B.A. participants spent six weeks in Boise, taking a class and serving in month-long internships at firms such as Boise Cascade, Hewlett-Packard, Ore-Ida Foods, the Y.M.C.A. and others, as well as in several university departments (e.g., Human Resource Management, Executive Development, Physical plant and facilities).

Following a successful first phase, Sida continued the project, ultimately funding two more phases for a total of $7.0 million. Boise State was asked to continue as the M.B.A. deliverer and principal contractor for the final phase of the project.

The relationship strengthened during two more M.B.A. cohorts, bringing the total to 84 graduates by 1999. When Swedish funding ended in 2000, the U.S.A.I.D. stepped in to fund $1.5 million in building capacity and sustainability within the N.E.U. Business School and university.

Over the project's nine years, Boise State sent four professors to teach for at least one semester in Hanoi; nearly twenty others taught in shorter courses, either in Hanoi or in Boise (30% of the College's professors) benefiting Boise State by giving professors an opportunity to learn about another country and culture. Over the years, the cooperation comprised many other activities that strengthened the relationship:

- Placing N.E.U. faculty members in internships in Australia, New Zealand, the United Kingdom, Thailand, the Philippines, and the United States as visiting lecturers and researchers, participated in administrative positions, and conducted specific projects for companies.
- Supporting several faculty members in doctoral studies in Vietnam, the U.K., Australia, Singapore, and the U.S.
- Facilitating visits by internationally known scholars to N.E.U.
- Financing seven research projects between faculty members at N.E.U., and universities in the U.S., the Philippines, and Thailand.
- Creating and publishing a collection of teaching cases and notes for M.B.A. programs in Vietnam and North America.
- Supporting a distance learning masters of research program, delivered by the Graduate School of Management at Macquarie University, Sydney Australia.
- Supporting the design and development of other academic programs at N.E.U. (e.g., Vietnamese language M.B.A., English language M.B.A., two foreign programs – the Henley M.B.A. and Swinburne Masters in International Accountancy) -- and numerous executive education programs.

Interestingly, while not an intent, the project nevertheless helped each organization develop competencies among faculty and administrators (Silins, 2001), including abilities to communicate in a variety of ways, use technology, solve problems, work in teams, and develop cultural understanding. For example, while the Vietnamese are group-oriented, collective people, they rarely work in teams as North Americans think of teams (i.e., a group of people who may not know one another well who work toward a common defined objective). Thus it was critical for both groups to realize that the term "team" had different meanings and expectations so they could learn to work together. (Vu and Napier, 2000).

THE DESIGN AND IMPLEMENTATION OF BOISE STATE UNIVERSITY MBA IN VIETNAM PROGRAM: CORNERSTONE OF COOPERATION

Boise State University delivered its Vietnam M.B.A. three times, graduating 84 participants by 1999. Four issues emerged in the design and implementation of the M.B.A.: (1) program structure and implementation; (2) emergence of problems/solutions; (3) critical success factors; and (4) advantages each university gained.

Program structure and implementation

The Vietnam M.B.A. program structure and implementation comprised four dimensions, discussed briefly: (1) students; (2) teachers and teaching method; (3) program schedule and format; and (4) program management.

Students

The primary audience for the Vietnam M.B.A. was lecturers at the National Economics University. In all cohorts, however, four to seven outside managers also joined, as did lecturers from other Vietnamese universities. The mix was about 50-50% men - women, given the Swedish sponsor's commitment to furthering gender equality. Most of the first group had Russian as their "second language," a few spoke German, Czech, or Romanian, and some had a little English. They all completed a six month intensive English course before beginning the M.B.A. By 1997, the third cohort's English competency was dramatically higher. The first cohort tended to be older, averaging about 30-35; the second group was slightly younger

(27-30 years), and the last cohort was quite young, with an average age of about 26.

Finally, general sophistication and exposure to "the West" differed greatly over the five years of the program. The first group had met few Americans before 1994. Their foreign professors had been Australians, Scots, Canadians, and New Zealanders, and most had never traveled outside of Vietnam, or only to Eastern Europe and Russia. The third group had several members (typically the managers) who had traveled in Asia, America, and Europe. Thus, in four years, the nature and make up of M.B.A. participants changed remarkably.

Teachers and Teaching Method

Initially, foreign professors did all of the teaching (1993-1995), and because this was a "train-the-trainer" M.B.A. program, methodology was part of what the participants learned. In 1994, even "technology" such as an overhead projector was new for N.E.U. participants. Some visiting professors used lectures, but many used interactive, discussion, and case oriented approaches. This was surprising and difficult for some participants initially; they were used to "talk and chalk" teaching (and learning) and were bewildered by classes with little "structure." In fact, one participant admitted he used the "ABC method to teach:" A for advertising, B for brand, C for customer, and so on so students (and the teacher) could follow the lecture.

With the second cohort, the foreign visiting professor led the class, and the Vietnamese (now an M.B.A. graduate) lecturer acted as "tutor," in the British style, sitting in the back of the room and answering student questions later in tutorial groups. Next, the foreign visiting professor and Vietnamese lecturer worked as co-teachers, requiring a significant shift in the relationship (Napier, Ngo, Nguyen, Nguyen, and Vu, 2002). At first, students rebelled, refusing to adjust to a "team teaching format." Yet, given the program's goal of training teachers, it continued. By the time the third cohort began, team teaching was generally accepted, both by teachers and students.

Program Scheduling

The Vietnam M.B.A. experimented with many approaches to scheduling, supported by administration on both sides. The formats ranged from five and six week modules (two classes at a time), to 15 week semesters, to two week intensive courses (all day, one course). Finally, the third cohort spent a full semester in Boise and had another schedule format. They completed ten weeks of course work that was divided into two parts: they were in classes the first five weeks then completed a four-week full time internship with local organizations before completing their last five weeks of course work. Each format had advantages and disadvantages; the important point was that students, teachers, and administration in Boise and in Hanoi supported the variety. That each side was willing to cooperate with experimenting further strengthened the trust and the relationship.

Program Management

Finally, the M.B.A. program management shifted over time from being run by a Boise State University manager (who visited Hanoi regularly, but was not based there full time), to a jointly run program (when the Boise State professor was full time in Hanoi), to being managed mostly by an N.E.U. professor with input where needed from the Boise State person. This process of shifting responsibility allowed for management training and built more trust between parties.

Key Problems and Solutions that Emerged During the Program

Like all development projects, problems arose as Boise State University and N.E.U. cooperated on programs within the project. Three difficult problems emerged as the N.E.U. faculty members became more involved in teaching.

English Language Skills of N.E.U. Lecturers

Although the first group of participants learned English before starting the M.B.A. program, they lacked confidence when teaching in English. This was especially sensitive when the second and third cohorts had stronger English skills than their N.E.U. teachers. The N.E.U. lecturers and their foreign counterparts found several solutions, however. The N.E.U. instructors worked closely with visiting professor counterparts in class preparation, grading, and evaluation, writing and reading student assignments and leading classes in English to gain discipline-related vocabulary and knowledge to boost their confidence.

Limited Business/Organizational Experience of N.E.U. Lecturers

A second challenge for the N.E.U. teachers was their relatively limited business experience (especially since "business" in Vietnam had meant state owned enterprises – S.O.E.s). Most had begun teaching right after graduation from the N.E.U. A few held part-time jobs with S.O.E.s. Only the "outside managers" who participated in the M.B.A. had worked for private or foreign firms.

Again, the solution was multifaceted. First, each N.E.U. instructor experienced an internship (three to five months) abroad in the U.K., Australia, or North America. Many went to universities where they taught, worked on training programs, or conducted research with counterparts. They felt their experiences subsequently supported better teaching (e.g., Sandgren, Ellig, Hovde, Krejci, and Rice, 1999).

Others worked in business firms, such as Boise Cascade. All had done research projects in Hanoi for foreign firms (e.g., Electrolux, A.B.B., K.P.M.G., British Petroleum, Citibank, American Express) and Vietnamese organizations (e.g., Vietnam Airlines, Ministry of Forestry). These experiences gave the instructors insight into other organizations' operations, improved their English, and built a set of networks for future contacts. Finally, N.E.U. faculty members conducted training courses for foreign and Vietnamese organizations and worked on research and consulting projects with such firms.

Cross-Cultural Team Teaching

Team teaching is daunting under the best of circumstances (Fukami, Clouse, Howard, McGowan, Mullins, Silver, Sorensen, Watkins, and Wittmer, 1996) and more so when partners differ on countries, cultures, languages, and methods. The N.E.U. – Boise State teachers developed team approaches teaching in the second and third M.B.A. cohorts. While many of the bi-cultural teams succeeded quite well, others experienced frustration and (near) failure.

Problems ranged from different teaching methods (e.g., lecturing versus discussion) to cultural misunderstandings (e.g., level of casualness with students) to different work styles (e.g., preparing way ahead of time versus at the last minute). The solutions, again, developed over much time and effort, ranged from systematic meetings of team members to meetings of the entire group of teachers, but solutions mostly developed from building trust, adjusting on both sides, and recognizing the impact of actions on the class setting and students (Napier, et. al., 2002).

Critical Factors that Helped the Vietnam M.B.A. Program Succeed

This section discusses three factors contributed to the success of the program and relationship between universities. First, the continuity of program managers (from Boise State University and from the N.E.U.) helped speed learning curves on both sides. The chance for things to go wrong demanded constant vigilance; meeting university and college accreditation guidelines, insuring professional delivery of courses, monitoring student progress to meet regulations and expectations, and even organizing the G.M.A.T. and T.O.E.F.L. exams long distance caused headaches.

Even though much did go wrong, the project managers had an attitude of "making it work," which carried the program through many mistakes. The managers used fax, email, phone, couriers, and visits to keep things working, and most importantly, to maintain the personal relationships that supported the organizational relationship.

Second, the internal staff support from Boise State University -- the"behind the scenes" players – made the project a success. When the project opportunity first emerged, the Provost gathered staff support units (e.g., public relations, registrar, graduate school, admissions, visa processing, continuing education, housing, health care) to ask if they were able and willing to support the program. This was a major commitment because in Phase I of the program, there was no "indirect cost" support. From the start, staff support was consistently positive -- staff members did whatever it took to make the program succeed.

Finally, community support in Boise and Hanoi was a major factor in helping this program and relationship to thrive. The Swedish and U.S. ambassadors came to the N.E.U. to "send off" students to study in the U.S.; the media in Vietnam, the region, and in the U.S. (e.g., *Vietnam News,* National Public Radio's Marketplace, *Wall Street Journal,* C.N.N. Radio, *The New York Times*) profiled the project and the M.B.A. program. Finally, organizational sponsors in Boise and Hanoi repeatedly welcomed the Vietnamese for internships and research projects.

Advantages Each University Gained from the M.B.A. Program Experience

The initial M.B.A. project, and subsequent creation of a business school, gave the Vietnamese faculty members and university the confidence and ability to start the country's first M.B.A. programs; the N.E.U. initiated its Vietnamese language M.B.A. in 1996 and its English language M.B.A. in 2002, patterned after Boise State's accredited program. The methodology and skills that N.E.U. lecturers now use developed from their experiences team teaching with Boise State and other foreigner instructors.

The Business School has offered other graduate programs in conjunction with foreign universities (e.g., the Henley M.B.A. program, U.K. and an international accountancy degree through Swinburne University, Australia). Furthermore, N.E.U. professors have developed case studies, delivered training programs, conducted research, presented conference papers, and published several research and practitioner articles jointly, ranging from comparative research on entrepreneurship, to bi-cultural team teaching, to transition economy management.

Boise State University has also gained enormous experience – both in terms of faculty teaching, research, and administrative experience. A mid-sized state university, Boise State has gained the knowledge and skills to manage large-scale educational projects far away from Boise, which benefit students, the university, the city, and state.

COOPERATION IN CREATING THE N.E.U. BUSINESS SCHOOL

The cooperation extended beyond the M.B.A. program to include creation of the business school in Hanoi – building skills and mindsets for research, academic and executive education programs, administrative practices and policies, capacity in management, and faculty and staff. In the final phase, the N.E.U. Business School also developed a sustainability plan to identify areas of greatest need and impact for the future.

While the relationship between the universities began and grew largely because of the generous Swedish and U.S. funding that supported the creation of a business school at the National Economics University, the funding has now stopped. This section of the paper discusses three key outcomes of the cooperation and the challenges of maintaining a relationship and cooperation "when the money runs out."

Results of Cooperation

One important goal was to extend N.E.U.'s relationships with universities beyond Boise State; the N.E.U. now has links with numerous institutions (e.g., Durham University (U.K.), Seattle University, Utah State University, University of Nancy (France), Indiana University, Bemidji State University, Macquarie University (Australia), Washington State University). These relationships support the N.E.U. Business School through development of clients and programs and co-participation in executive education programs, joint research projects, and university and business school level administrative support. A brief discussion of each follows with emphasis on how the N.E.U. can continue to build relationships and cooperation, even without significant donor support.

Executive Education and Training

Since 1995, the N.E.U. Business School has developed an extensive array of management education and training programs for state and private/foreign customers -- programs critical to the business school's long term sustainability. The training programs have benefited from cooperation with visiting foreign faculty members in several ways, but most notably when foreign faculty have transferred modern training methods to N.E.U. trainers (e.g., team teaching and training, student centered learning, understanding and pursuing more effective marketing approaches).

Research

Research practices in Vietnam do not typically follow international approaches. In Vietnam, senior university administrators usually choose a topic and assign (often up to ten) faculty members to a project. Younger faculty members do the work (which uses secondary data, if that) and senior faculty members' names appear on the finished product. The notion of faculty members choosing their own topics, submitting proposals to a review board, conducting primary data collection and empirical analysis, and then submitting the results to a journal or conference with blind review, is unheard of. Simply reaching the point where N.E.U. Business School faculty members and administrators understood, accepted, and then supported such approaches took years of discussion.

Yet, ultimately, the project was able to help instill a research mindset within the N.E.U. Business School. Nearly all of twenty-seven N.E.U. Business School faculty members have conducted joint research projects. Over half have done research with Boise State faculty members; many have also worked with the more than 40 visiting faculty members who visited N.E.U. over the years. About 50% have presented one or more papers abroad; two thirds have published in academic or practitioner journals outside of Vietnam, in journals such as *The Journal of Management Inquiry, Human Resource Management Review, Organisation*, and *the Journal of International Business Studies*. All faculty members and some manager M.B.A. graduates have published in Vietnamese academic or practitioner journals, and many have written textbooks in Vietnamese for the N.E.U. M.B.A. program.

Boise State faculty members have been able to extend their existing research to Vietnam and beyond or have begun new streams of research (e.g., on entrepreneurs in developing countries). In addition, several jointly written cases have been written. An unanticipated but necessary outcome as well was the shift to a partner/colleague status between researchers (Canto and Hannah,

2001), rather than a mentor-student relationship, which had been typical until the last two years.

Faculty Internships

Another outcome has been N.E.U. faculty internships in Boise and elsewhere. N.E.U. faculty members have worked in Scotland, Thailand, the Philippines, Australia, New Zealand, and the U.S., and they have completed teaching and research internships at Washington State University, the University of Oregon, Utah State University, Weber State University, Oklahoma University, Mahidol University, the Asian Institute of Management, Indiana University, Bemidji State University, and Boise State University. Finally, several have worked in corporations that specifically sought the knowledge of Southeast Asia as they wanted to find new raw material sources or markets for products.

Administrative Support.

Through the project, Boise State supported the N.E.U. university and business school administration through study tours and visits, workshops, and informal "training" that the Provost and other vice presidents (e.g., finance, student services, institutional advancement) have offered. In addition, Boise State provided information about executive education, grants and contracts, auxiliary services, and community boards.

Finally, Boise State has supported the professional/technical side of the N.E.U. Business School, in the area of technology and library science, through joint efforts with information and library experts from Boise State.

FUTURE CHALLENGES FOR THE N.E.U.-BOISE STATE RELATIONSHIP

The strong cooperation between the two universities started from, and has depended very much upon, external funding, which ended in December 2002. Nevertheless, the relationship can thrive in at least three ways, if both parties work toward it. A fundamental shift in the relationship and cooperation is occurring, however. The focus is more at the individual faculty or program level: faculty teams conducting research or programs (e.g., executive education or English language graduate programs) provide the reason for continued cooperation rather than administrator incentives.

Specifically, faculty members within the universities have continued joint research or started new projects. Also, program directors have explored executive certificate programs or other training programs, doing market research for Vietnamese industries and/or U.S. firms or trade associations or conducting study tours for student or executive groups. Finally, foreign faculty members have worked in Hanoi on Fulbright Fellowships, sabbaticals, or on executive education or academic programs, and we expect this to continue – again on an individual level.

LESSONS LEARNED

Although this paper focuses on the cooperation between the two universities, the relationship cannot be divorced from the project which fostered and nurtured it. Working and living together for so long left plenty of lessons.

This section discusses two levels of "learning" that occurred (Table 20.1) -- individual versus organizational – and lessons from project management as well as from the universities' relationship.

Table 20.1: Lessons Learned from the Sida M.B.A. Project.

	M.B.A. Project	N.E.U.-Boise State University Relationships
Organizational Level	How to pursue and manage a large aid project; role of the consultant. How to interact with many stakeholder institutions (e.g., funder, ministries, consultants, each university). How to develop and manage executive education, consulting and research programs. How to manage a business school.	Thinking of each other as partners and "clients." Developing and running academic programs. Importance of inside support. The need for internal "champions."
Individual Level	Ability to "take more control" and "give more control" in work (and personal) settings. Networking internationally.	Teaching and training cross-culturally. Team teaching.

Lessons from the Capacity Building and M.B.A. Project – Organizational Level

Before 1994, Boise State University had never been involved with, let alone managed, a large development aid project. For its part, the N.E.U. had been involved in donor projects but none this large or complex. Over nine years, project managers and administrators (i.e., Director and Dean, Rectors and Provost, support staff in Hanoi and Boise) learned to manage the process by identifying key issues and how to solve them. The process was experimental and iterative, but by the third and fourth phases of the project, fewer problems arose, and those that did were relatively easy to reconcile.

Furthermore, each organization learned how to deal with its internal and external constituencies. For instance, Boise State University's senior administrators dealt with the university and business school accrediting agencies, the State Board of Education, key business and government supports. Likewise, the N.E.U. dealt with Ministries for approvals of academic programs, the official creation of the business school, and formal links with other universities. Also, the university administrators in Hanoi had to deal with rivalries and jealousy of other faculties within the university that did not receive financial and other support that the N.E.U. Business School did.

Lessons from the Capacity Building and M.B.A. Project – Individual Level

The complexity, frustrations, exhilaration, and differences in work and life styles among people within and outside Vietnam generated many learning opportunities for individuals. For example, several N.E.U. faculty members and administrators commented that working with foreign colleagues allowed them to gain confidence in managing their personal and work lives and situations. One faculty member learned to "take more control" over events that occurred in her life. Earlier, she would have given up and "cried because I could do nothing;" but by watching the visitors, she learned to consider expectations rather than "letting things just happen."

By the same token, some "Type A" Americans learned to accept certain events, influences, or limitations without exploding. Rather than expecting to achieve 20 things in a day, they learned to be realistic and achieve just two or three, given problems with fax machines breaking, computers dying, power outages, construction projects in offices, and people not appearing for meetings.

Finally, individuals in both organizations learned about the limitations and cultural challenges of working together. While Boise State University faculty and administrators have long used email, the Internet and even fax machines were new for the National Economics University. Learning how to communicate with others without seeing them (Barrett, 2002), as well as how to build and sustain relationships (for research, teaching, etc.) with strangers was a new skill for the Vietnamese. Further, many people from both universities had never worked abroad, and certainly few had been in the other's country. Through the project, faculty members from both universities came to know each other as well as colleagues from Australia, Europe, Hong Kong, and North America.

Lessons from the N.E.U.-Boise State University relationship – Organizational Level

The N.E.U.'s basic needs were to reform subject curricula to move toward a market economy orientation and to gain knowledge of teaching and learning methodologies. Training N.E.U. lecturers in Boise State University's M.B.A. program was only one way to achieve the above objectives. The cooperation between universities allowed them to identify and carry out more ways to "train" faculty members, especially when each organization thought of the other as a "client." Boise State sought to match student interests with company internships (in Boise); the N.E.U. tried to provide opportunities for Boise State students and faculty members through internships and teaching opportunities.

Also, in working out academic requirements (from the Boise State perspective) and meeting goals of graduating as many Vietnamese students as possible, both sides had to be flexible. Boise State allowed two students from the second cohort a "second chance" after they improved their English skills so they could participate in the third cohort. Despite a desire to want to find a way to keep two students who plagiarized, N.E.U. accepted Boise State's final decision to expel them. Thus, each university learned to try and understand the others' needs and goals and adjust to them.

As mentioned earlier, the need for support inside the universities was critical for both. Such support, especially from within Boise State University, was tremendous. Groups ranging from the admissions office, graduate school, international office, continuing education, housing, meal service, physical education, health center, M.B.A. program office, registrar, and public relations pitched in to support the program. Problems arose in almost every area, yet the people in them repeatedly and generously helped solve them. The program would not have succeeded otherwise.

Within the N.E.U., although the project directly involved the N.E.U. Business School, the project's success required favorable conditions and support from the N.E.U. Board of Rectors and cooperation from the related functional departments (e.g., those where the faculty members had previously taught). At times, conflicts emerged, but ultimately the rector board supported the project's overall direction.

Finally, a lesson for both organizations was the importance of having (or not) an internal champion for the program. For the M.B.A. program, it was the co-authors of this paper. They had taught together, managed the program and its research projects together, and each had support of managers within their universities to make the program a success. As the project progressed, champions emerged for specific program areas (e.g., the English language M.B.A., executive development, and research).

Lessons from the N.E.U.-Boise State University relationship – Individual Level

The N.E.U. faculty members reported that learning about new teaching technologies (other than "chalk and talk") was most useful for them. In the process, they experienced a transformation common in professional teacher development described by Fwu and Wang (2001). The N.E.U. faculty members learned how to use case studies, student projects, discussion and participation, alternative approaches to student papers, exercises, and simulations. The Boise State faculty members, in turn, learned about ways to design and deliver training to non-U.S. audiences and to understand the challenge of working in countries where English may not be the primary language.

Related to this, both sides learned – sometimes painfully – about the challenges of bi-cultural team teaching. Learning to create a balanced and more equal relationship was challenging for Vietnamese and Americans faculty alike. The American faculty members had to learn to "give away" some in-class control and treat Vietnamese counterparts as equal partners. Vietnamese faculty, likewise, had to learn to take initiative and move into a partnership role, which meant they had to lead the class at times, instead of their more traditional approach of following the lead of foreign counterparts.

CONCLUSION

As people on both sides of the ocean admit, the relationship between the two universities has been frustrating and fulfilling, quirky, and perhaps unusual. Still, the benefits of building such relationships and cooperation, regardless of how or how in depth, have rewards that go far beyond a research paper or training program. The friendships, the learning, and the broader views and perspectives have affected people within and far outside the universities.

REFERENCES

Barrett, S. (2002). Overcoming transactional distance as a barrier to effective communication over the internet. *International Education Journal*, 3 (4), 34-42.

Canto, I. & Hannah, J. (2001). A partnership of equals? academic collaboration between the United Kingdom and Brazil. *Journal of Studies in International Education*, 5 (1), 26-41.

Fukami, C.V., Clouse, M.L., Howard, C.T., McGowan, R.P., Mullins, J.W., Silver, W.S., Sorensen, J.E., Watkins, T.L., & Wittmer, D.P. (1996). The road less traveled: the joys and sorrows of team teaching. *Journal of Management Education*, 20 (4), 409-410.

Glassman, A., Neupert, K., Moore, R., Rossy, G., Napier, N., Harvey, M. & Jones, D. (forthcoming). Academic entrepreneurship: views on balancing the Acropolis and the Agora. In *Journal of Management Inquiry*.

Fwu, B. & Wang, H. (2001). Jade's transformation: a case study of teacher professional development in Taiwan. *International Education Journal*, 2 (5), 16-26.

Napier, N.K., Ngo, M.H., Nguyen, M.T.T., Nguyen, T.V., & Vu, T.V. (2002). Bi-cultural team teaching: experiences from an emerging business school. *Journal of Management Education*, 26 (4), 429-448.

Napier, N.K., Vu, D.A., Ngo, T.M.H., Nguyen, V.T. & Vu, V.T. (1997). Reflections on building a business school in Vietnam: falling into an opportunity for "making a difference." *Journal of Management Inquiry*, 6 (4), 340-354.

Sandgren, D., Ellig, N., Hovde, P., Krejci, M., & Rice, M., (1999). How international experience affects teaching: understanding the impact of faculty study abroad. *Journal of Studies in International Education*, 3, 33-56.

Silins, H. (2001). Action learning: a strategy for change. *International Education Journal*, 2 (2), 79-95.

Von Kopp, B. (1992). The Eastern Europe revolution and education in Czechoslovakia. *Comparative Education Review*, 36 (1), 101 - 113.

Vu, T. V. & Napier, N.K. (2000). Paradoxes in Vietnam and the United States: lessons earned: part II. *Human Resource Planning Journal*, 23, (2), 9-10.

Chapter 21
An Emerging Market Player in International Business Education: The Case of Wits Business School

Saul Klein
University of Victoria

Mike Ward
University of Witwatersrand

INTRODUCTION

Economic transition and transformation have been important features of emerging markets over the past decade. In some instances, such as in Central Europe and China, the transition has been from centrally-planned economies to market-based ones, and the key challenges have been to develop managerial skills in market-based economies and post-privatization contexts (see, for example, Spillan and Ziemnowicz, 2001). In others, such as in South America and South Africa, the transition has been more from self-sufficiency and autarky to global integration (see, for example, Klein, 1998). While the different transitions present different, although somewhat overlapping, challenges for management education in affected countries, more attention has been paid to the former type of transition than to the latter. This paper is an attempt to change the balance and put the spotlight on a generally neglected region of the world.

South Africa represents an example of a country that went through a rapid transition from self-sufficiency to globalization. What makes this situation particularly interesting is that economic liberalization was accompanied by political liberalization and pressures to transform the economic and institutional base of the country to make it more demographically representative. It is in this context that the role of a South African business school is analyzed below. We begin with a brief perspective on the nature of South Africa's transition and identify the management development challenges that arose. We then examine the case of South

Africa's leading business school and consider how it responded to these challenges. While the business school has achieved success on many of its objectives, the transition process entails a number of obstacles, both internal and external, that make adaptive change difficult.

TRANSITION AND RE-ENTRY INTO THE WORLD ECONOMY

Until 1994, South Africa was regarded as a pariah state in the global system. Revulsion with the Apartheid policy led to externally imposed global isolation and trade sanctions. The South African economy, in turn, became driven by the necessity for self-sufficiency. Government ownership of what was ostensibly a market-economy was extremely high, and state-owned enterprises were used as a means to protect a White electorate. Economic efficiency was seen as secondary to political stability, and domestic competitiveness was weak.

The year 1994 marked a significant change in South Africa. Following decades of minority-rule and political oppression, the first democratically elected government in the country's history was chosen The new government, under Nelson Mandela, came to power with a mandate for, and great expectations of, major political and economic transformation. Redistribution of income was recognized both as a political imperative and as an economic necessity if the country was to prosper. It quickly became apparent that redistribution required economic growth, and a growth strategy for the country was put in place. Labeled G.E.A.R. (Growth, Employment and Redistribution), the policy was based on trade liberalization, macroeconomic reform, and budgetary conservatism (Department of Finance, 1996). Revised antitrust policy followed in 1998 (South Africa, 1998a). The role of competition in general, and the private sector in particular, in generating economic growth was apparent in the thinking that sought to attract foreign investment and generate exports. This thinking is consistent with the principles outlined as part of the Golden Straightjacket that emerging markets face (Friedman, 2000).

The end of global isolation revealed an urgent need for international management skills. A generation of managers had developed in a largely autarkic environment, with little understanding of and experience with demanding global customers and aggressive foreign competitors. Business had developed practices that served it well in a closed economy, but was largely unprepared for the vigorous nature of international competition. Risks were regarded as experiences to be avoided rather than managed, and cozy, cartel-like arrangements were common domestically. International rankings of global competitiveness, as a consequence, placed South Africa at the bottom of the tables (I.M.D., 2000). While world export volumes boomed in the mid-1990's, South Africa actually lost market share in world markets following her reintegration into the world economy (U.N.C.T.A.D., 2003).

Compounding the skills problem were two other factors: a brain-drain out of the country and political pressure for affirmative action. The early 1990's witnessed a strong exodus of skilled people from South Africa while inbound migration was almost exclusively unskilled. Migration thus exacerbated the shortage of international business skills (Wocke and Klein, 2002). With a political mandate for change, the new government also quickly turned to a transformation agenda that included restructuring the predominately White public sector to become more racially representative and urging the private sector to take similar steps. Legislation followed requiring business to commit to economic empowerment of historically disadvantaged groups (South Africa, 1998b). Unfortunately, the previously economically excluded were also disadvantaged by an appalling education system. Unlike in Central Europe, where math and science skills were developed in the pre-transition education systems, the South African system of Bantu education (for Black children) led to students being ranked last in international comparisons (T.I.M.S.S., 1999).

In short, the 1990s heralded sweeping changes, including affirmative action imperatives, a resulting shortage of Black managers, and the desire of White managers for additional qualifications.

MANAGEMENT EDUCATION IN SOUTH AFRICA

Prior to 1994, seven universities in South Africa offered M.B.A. degrees. By the end of the decade the number of options increased to over 50 with more local institutions entering the market as well as the entry of foreign business schools, some in partnership with local institutions. The increase in the number of suppliers was both a response to and the cause of increased demand for management education. Foreign schools in particular sought to differentiate themselves on the basis of their international origins. Local institutions generally recognized the imperative to develop international management skills.

Relative to their counterparts in developed countries, the established local business schools tended to operate on a broad scope, and their range of activities and programs was very wide, covering the full spectrum from entry-level managers up to senior levels. Internally, they were all relatively small; few (if any) had more than 20 full-time faculty members, the majority of whom lacked Ph.D.s, and they were largely reliant on state funding. Shorter management development programs were essential in order to cope with the financial pressures of falling state subsidies. This resulted in high emphasis being placed on teaching as opposed to research activities.

By the late 1990's rankings of M.B.A. programs began to appear in the business press (see Table 21.1), and the leading institutions began to compete more on the basis of their brands than on generic programs. At the top of the rankings, one business school appears to have carved out a leading position. We turn now to the Wits Business School and examine its changing role.

Table 21.1: Ranked M.B.A. Programs in South Africa (by Financial Mail, August 2002)

1.	Wits Business School
2.	University of Cape Town
3.	Unisa
4.	University of Stellenbosch
5.	Gordon Institute of Business Science
6.	University of Pretoria
7.	University of Natal
8.	GIMT – Henley
9.	Rand Afrikaans University
10.	Potchefstroom Business School
11.	University of Durban Westville
12.	De Montford
13.	Damelin (Oxford Brookes)
14.	Business School of the Netherlands
15.	Bond University
16.	MANCOSA
17.	Heriott Watt
18.	Natal Technikon (University of Wales)
19.	University of the Free State
20.	Technikon SA
21.	Hull University
22.	University of Southern Queensland
23.	Milpark Business School (Thames Valley University

WITS BUSINESS SCHOOL: PAST DEVELOPMENTS

Formally the Graduate School of Business Administration at the University of the Witwatersrand, Johannesburg, Wits Business School (hereafter W.B.S.) was established under the guidance of faculty from Harvard and Stanford Business Schools. W.B.S. began offering executive programs in 1968, followed in 1970 by M.B.A. degrees. By the end of the millennium, W.B.S. enrolled three M.B.A. classes of approximately 60 students each per year along with some 120 postgraduate diploma students, 40 students in a Masters of Management Program, 450 participants in a variety of certificate programs, and saw some 750 participants in its management development courses pass through its doors each year. The load was covered by only 22 full time faculty members and a number of part-time lecturers.

W.B.S. is an example of an emerging market institution that has succeeded in the new South African context. This success, as reflected in rankings of business schools, has developed based on a strong commitment to internationalization. The challenges that it faces going forward, however, are also a direct reflection of its emerging market position and the external forces operating upon it.

Beginning in the mid-1990's with a reconceptualization of its role in the new South Africa, W.B.S. took a number of steps to internationalize its offerings. It did so based on a recognition of the clear need to remain locally relevant and attempted to avoid direct duplication of programs and processes developed in leading business schools in North America and Europe, the risks of which are recognized elsewhere (e.g., Mathews, Rivera, and Pineda, 2001). A concern with global competitiveness characterized its educational efforts as well as its own position. For South African business, it was important to understand export markets and global competitors (*cf.* Kedia, Harveston, and Bhagat, 2001). For the business school, it was important to compete with the best in the world and build a global brand. In doing so, however, pressures from the local environment loomed large. It was felt that it would be difficult if not impossible to obtain recognition through A.A.C.S.B. accreditation, due to the limited number of terminally qualified faculty, and that other approaches would have to be taken.

Faculty

One of the challenges facing an emerging market business school is a shortage of qualified faculty. This problem is particularly acute in South Africa due to the brain drain from the country and extreme salary differentials between state-funded universities and the private sector. Paradoxically, as its graduates were in greater demand, their salaries rose, and the ability of W.B.S. to retain and attract new faculty from its increased pool of graduates diminished.

The academic isolation which characterized the 1980s resulted in a small, insular faculty, many of whom had little international experience of any sort. Academia was not an attractive career option, particularly at the University of the Witwatersrand, which had become a symbol of student unrest and opposition to Apartheid.

One consequence of this situation was a shortage of Ph.D.s. Unlike U.S. and European counterparts, a Ph.D. was never seen as mandatory for faculty in South African business schools. This was partly a consequence of the shortage of faculty and heavy workloads, but also a philosophy that management experience was more critical in an emerging market than academic credentials. Although W.B.S. did embark on a Ph.D. program in the mid 1980s aimed at developing business school faculty, this was of limited success. Efforts to make this a national initiative also failed.

To break the funding dilemma, and to attract foreign educators to help internationalize its programs, W.B.S. was able to procure limited funding for named Chairs and visiting appointments. This proved to be a useful, albeit unsustainable, way to bring in expertise.

W.B.S. has also been able to maintain good relationships with former faculty members who moved out of the country and has established a regular core of visitors from this group. Reliance on this emigrant population brings benefits in that they understand both the local environment and the global context from their own experiences.

Students

As is true elsewhere, a self-fulfilling cycle has developed at W.B.S. High rankings generate greater student interest, allowing the institution to be more selective, leading to better graduates who in turn help sustain high rankings. As part of its applied orientation, W.B.S. generally requires more work experience (typically in excess of four years) for its M.B.A. candidates than do its local competitors. It is felt that students with experience are better able to relate to and apply the lessons learned in the classroom and that their own experiences add an important layer to the overall educational experience. This is reinforced through a cohort model and extensive use of group projects where students are assigned syndicates at the beginning of the program; syndicate composition is constant for all core courses.

Curriculum

As part of a restructuring of the M.B.A. program in 1997, W.B.S. introduced a new core course in International Business. This course was to play a central role in developing the skills of M.B.A. students in areas relating to global competitiveness. Particular emphasis was placed on understanding the role of an emerging market player in the global economy, and recognizing that market selection requires the transferal of competencies. The result was that a focus was placed on other emerging markets in general. The characteristics of such markets, for example, misguided regulations, inefficient judicial systems and information problems (*cf.* Khanna and Palepu, 1997), were ones with which local managers had developed skills in coping. These were also considered the most appropriate markets for South African business to enter, based on an identification of early successes and a consideration of the transfer of local competencies. Not only did other emerging markets represent attractive market opportunities, but they also represented South Africa's major competitors for attracting foreign investment.

The transferal of competencies was partly based on a recognition that emerging markets reward generalist managers as opposed to specialists who are better able to exploit positions in developed markets.

At the same time, South African businesses were attempting to enter foreign markets. This created a new pool of experiences from which lessons could be learnt, about both successes and failures. Executives from these businesses were brought into the classrooms to discuss their strategies and performance, and these were also developed into case studies.

International Study Tours

W.B.S. realized that to play a significant role in the internationalization of South African management, direct experience with foreign countries was essential. This was true both for faculty development and for student education. The first step was to take faculty on study tours to gain a better understanding of foreign markets, first into India, China, and South-East Asia, then into Europe and the U.S.A. and, finally, into South America. Based on these experiences, the study tours were rolled out to M.B.A. students in the mid-1990's, initially on a voluntary basis and then as a degree requirement. While study tours have become increasingly common in M.B.A. programs worldwide, they are rarely mandatory, even in developed countries. Currie and Matulich, for example, found that while 41% of North American M.B.A. programs had an international travel component, only 6% of programs required students to participate (2003).

The model that developed for M.B.A. study tours was based on taking roughly 20 students with two faculty members on two-week intensive visits. The typical visit involves three cities, chosen to reflect different business contexts, and entails a variety of briefings from business, government, and academic experts. In a typical year, study trips are offered to China and Vietnam; Singapore, Malaysia and Thailand; Brazil, Argentina, and Chile; Hungary, Poland, and the Czech Republic; and the U.S.A. A primary focus is placed on understanding other emerging markets, as a reflection of South Africa's competitive and market opportunity set.

Case Development

The twin challenge of remaining locally relevant while becoming globally competitive posed unique challenges for W.B.S. with regard to teaching materials. While international materials were valid for many purposes, they were incomplete in terms of picking up local challenges. Modeling itself on Harvard Business School in this regard, W.B.S. set up a case center to develop and disseminate high quality teaching materials. This was a significant expense for the business school, and one that could not be justified based on sales of materials to other institution in South Africa. It was felt, however, that locally developed cases were essential for effective teaching. Particular emphasis was placed on what was termed "Laboratory South Africa," used to characterize the particular aspects of an emerging economy undergoing rapid transformation. Typical examples of case studies developed included the globalization of a chicken take-away franchise, the demutualization and L.S.E. listing of the largest insurer, and expansion into Eastern Europe and China by S.A. Breweries. The range of cases developed (see Table 21.2), for example those dealing with H.I.V.-A.I.D.S., reflects the uniqueness of the issues being considered. To provide a market-based benchmark for the quality of its cases, W.B.S. arranged for their cases to be distributed through the European Case Clearing House.

Executive Education

Arising out of a critical need to develop its own revenue base and a commitment to remain relevant for the local business community, W.B.S. developed a full suite of executive programs (see Table 21.3). What is remarkable about this list is how many offerings exist, coming out of a small business school, and the range of topics and levels covered. Internationalization also played a part in these efforts, and the study tour model was extended to the school's senior Executive Development Program. Special focus courses, such as Doing Business in Asia, were also developed. The strength of W.B.S. in executive education was recognized by the *Financial Times* in May 2003, when the school was ranked for the first time among the leading business schools in the world. It is noteworthy that only four business schools of the 45 ranked come from emerging markets.

One key initiative was the development of a new senior level executive program (S.E.P.) targeting both public and private sector managers. Developed with and run in combination with Harvard Business School, the S.E.P. created a new venue for developing an understanding of global competitiveness. It also brought in some of the leading educators in the field and allowed W.B.S. to benchmark itself against one of the strongest players in the world.

It may be an important characteristic of emerging markets that public and private sector managers have to work together in order to generate economic growth. Typically, however, different institutions have evolved to cater to the

Table 21.2: W.B.S. Cases (as of 2003).

•	ABSA Free Internet Access – Changing the Face of ISP
•	Amanz'abantu: Water for the People
•	AngloGold vs. Newmont: The Bidding War for Normandy
•	Black Like Me (A-D)
•	Dimension Data: Globalising at Warp Speed
•	Engen and Petronas: Strengthening the Relationship?
•	ERP at IST (A-C)
•	GTKF
•	Hansa Pilsener: From Niche to Mainstream Brand
•	A Human Response to HIV/Aids
•	HIV/Aids in South Africa: What Is an Adequate Response?
•	Identifying Best Practice – Metropolitan and HIV/Aids
•	In Line with the Business – A Human Resources Model for Nedcor Bank
•	Knowledge Management – Designing a Strategy for BSW
•	kulula.com: Now Anyone Can Fly
•	Lechabile: IT as a People Business
•	Management Consulting and SAB: At What Price, Advice?
•	Massmart: Growing the Growth Engine
•	Mozambique and the HIPC Initiative: The Politics of Debt
•	Nando's International: Taking Chicken to the World
•	Nedcor Incentive Scheme
•	Old Mutual: Demutualisation and Listing
•	Office of the Banking Adjudicator: Walking the Tightrope
•	Plates (A) Barry Berman: Assessing the Opportunity
•	RMB
•	Rob Angel: Leading Engen to Empowerment (A)
•	Sasol/AECI: The Right Chemistry for a Merger?
•	South African Breweries: Achieving Growth in the Global Beer Market
•	Strategising to Keep Otis SA at the Top
•	Stride Pharmaceuticals: Employment Equity for Corporate Performance
•	War on HIV/Aids

different sectors. Traditionally, schools of public-sector administration in emerging markets have focused primarily on policy and often provided too little in the way of management skills and understanding of global competitiveness, while business schools have underplayed the role of government policy. The S.E.P. is a unique solution in such environments in terms of developing cross-sectoral content and providing a forum for positive interaction between senior public and private sector executives.

International Partnerships

Another initiative to develop international business understanding was the development of a strong student exchange program. Through membership in

Table 21.3: W.B.S. Management Development Course Offerings (2003)

Senior Management:

- Executive Development Programme
- Senior Executive Programme

General Management:

- Corporate Governance
- Information and Knowledge Management
- Issues in Leadership
- Managing and Measuring Organisational Culture
- Managing a Turnaround
- Managing Corporate Communications
- Strategic Alliances and Partnering

Certificate Programmes:

- Certificate Programme in Business Project Management
- Certificate Programme in E-Management
- Certificate Programme in Finance and Accounting
- Certificate Programme in Industrial Relations
- Certificate Programme in Management Advancement
- Certificate Programme in Marketing Management
- Certificate Programme in Principles of Business and Management
- Certificate Programme in Small Business Management

Finance:

- Finance for Non-Financial Managers
- Integrating Strategy, Budgeting, and Reporting
- International Investments
- Managing a Turnaround
- Strategic Finance

Marketing:

- Principles of Marketing Management
- Product Strategy and Brand Management
- Sales Management
- Strategic Marketing Management
- Strategic Retail Marketing

Human Resources:

- Achieving Outstanding Performance
- Effective Labour Relations and Labour Laws
- Executive Coaching

Other Topics:

- Aligning Operations Strategy
- Aligning Strategy Programme
- Call Center Management
- Internal Corporate Venturing
- IT Leaderships
- Negotiation Dynamics Programme
- New Venture Creation
- Project Management
- Strategic Transformation in a Competitive Environment
- Supply Chain Management

Management Development Unit:

- Certificate Programme in Management Development (In-Company)
- Customised Skills Programme
- Effective Interpersonal Skills
- Self Management for Managers

All courses are run either in-company or at the Wits Business School.

the Program in International Management (P.I.M.) consortium of leading business schools, W.B.S. provides opportunities for its students to study abroad, and in doing so has raised its own profile. By the end of the 1990's, W.B.S. was sending about 1/3 of its full-time M.B.A. students on foreign exchange each year and receiving a similar number in Johannesburg.

The partnership with Harvard in the S.E.P. was an important development in its own right. This partnership provided a vehicle for local faculty to participate in Harvard's case teaching colloquia and learn from and teach with peers ranked at the top of their fields. It also contributed to further brand-building of W.B.S. in South Africa.

Regionalization

By the end of the 1990's, W.B.S.'s model appeared to be working well in its local market; local rankings placed the business school at the top of their lists, and it was approached by institutions in other countries in the region to enter their markets. Executive education programs were drawing increasing numbers of participants, and M.B.A. applications were at an all-time high. Partly out of a recognition that a better understanding of the African context was crucial for its own success, W.B.S. subsequently began offering a number of academic and executive programs in Mauritius and a number of management development programs in Kenya. These developments introduced the challenges of operating in partnership with other institutions and coordinating scarce faculty time in distant locations.

WITS BUSINESS SCHOOL: FUTURE CHALLENGES

By its very nature, operating in an emerging market involves rapid change and enormous pressures. Sustaining a strong position means overcoming a number of challenges that are inherent in such environments. We turn now to look at how those challenges manifest themselves at W.B.S. and what constraints the school faces as it goes forward. The two primary areas of concern are faculty recruitment and institutional structures.

Faculty Recruitment and Retention

Faculty recruitment and retention remains the major problem for W.B.S. As a public institution, the entire University to which W.B.S. is affiliated is under significant pressure to match national demographic profiles for both students and faculty. Black faculty members (particularly South Africans) are virtually unobtainable, given the existing skills shortage and burgeoning opportunities in the private sector. Furthermore, it is difficult to attract faculty from first world countries, in part because of the high risk of living in South Africa and the weak currency. W.B.S. is forced to increasingly rely on three sources: visiting faculty, part-time faculty, and experienced senior business executives taking early retirement (who are predominately White).

Salary differentials between academics and private sector managers are a significant issue in South Africa where skill shortages have driven up managerial salaries to international levels, while university salaries remain highly constrained. In 2000, a full professor at Wits University, at the top of the salary range, earned a complete package of less than US$36,000, including all benefits. Such faculty were being offered two to three times this amount by international competitors, but, to counteract this pressure, a maximum supplementation of 25% could be offered by W.B.S. Entering students, let alone graduates, regularly earn significantly more than their teachers.

W.B.S. has reverted to a Workload Model (W.L.M.) and allows faculty to supplement income by taking on additional consulting work to alleviate the financial pressures on faculty members, but this has serious consequences on research productivity, which remains low. While a typical teaching load on academic programs could involve the equivalent of four to five semester-long courses per year, the true teaching burden is much higher. The workload model does not include work on the school's many executive and other non-degree programs based on the fact that such work accrues extra compensation. Similarly, while the University has rules limiting private work, W.B.S. has tried hard to accommodate and encourage such activities.

W.B.S. continues to seek externally funded chairs, but is vulnerable to donor fatigue, and the business sector is under increasing pressure to make reparations for Apartheid. The ravages of Bantu education were most acute at the primary and secondary education levels, and W.B.S. competes for donor funds with a wide array of other institutions whose needs are often more pressing than is typically the case in more developed environments.

Competitive Environment

The spate of M.B.A. offerings mentioned earlier prompted the Minister of Education to require registration of private education providers and introduce an accreditation process in 2001. The Council for Higher Education's Quality Committee targeted the M.B.A. as their first program, requiring the re-accreditation of all providers (South Africa, 2003). Using E.Q.U.I.S., A.M.B.A., A.A.C.S.B., and F.I.B.A.A. as guidelines, a comprehensive re-accreditation process is currently underway. An immediate consequence was the voluntary withdrawal of several M.B.A. offerings, bringing the competitive set down from 57 to 24 programs. The accreditation criteria include benchmarks relating to faculty qualifications, experience, and publications, and they are likely to re-motivate Ph.D. initiatives.

The accreditation process, however, may also be a double-edged sword. Pressures exist for transferability of credits and multiple academic entry and exit points. These would allow students to switch freely between different institutions and provide recognition for partial completion of studies. The setting of minimum standards could also serve to dilute brand identity and reduce management education to a lowest common denominator by reinforcing the notion of generic degrees.

Institutional Structures

In the late 1990's, the Department of Education sought to tackle the proliferation of tertiary public and private sector providers. In particular, many of the Historically Disadvantaged Universities (H.D.U.'s) and Technikons (Technical Colleges) were merged with their stronger counterparts and rationalized. The University of the Witwatersrand emerged largely unscathed from this rationalization exercise, but faced its own extreme budgetary pressure and also embarked upon an internal re-structuring program. Ten faculties were reduced to five, and more than 100 departments were collapsed into 33 schools. The impact of this on W.B.S. was dramatic.

When it was established in 1968, W.B.S. was set up as a single school in its own facility on a separate campus. This proved a wise move, providing high-level access into university structures, but focus, autonomy and flexibility in operations. The university's 2000 restructuring process resulted in W.B.S. becoming one of five schools in the largest faculty, encompassing Commerce, Law, and Management. The consequence of this has been longer lines of control, a matrix structure, significantly less focus, and reduced autonomy. This represents a significant challenge for the future and a potential loss of W.B.S.'s distinctive competencies.

Rapidly changing career choices in the late 1990's amongst undergraduate students resulted in severe imbalances in staff/student ratios at the university. For example, government heavy-handedness in relation to conditions of employment for teachers made such careers less attractive and resulted in a sudden dearth of students in the Faculty of Humanities, the primary training ground for future teachers. The university's reluctance to face the problem, re-size schools, and close academic posts exacerbated an already imbalanced funding model.

In 2003, W.B.S. finds itself contributing more than 50% of funds generated from its academic programs to other schools whilst facing an increasing deficit on its M.B.A. Paradoxically, W.B.S.'s success in generating its own funds has resulted in it receiving a smaller slice of the university's budget. While the need to remain locally relevant and globally competitive is continuing to increase, the school is forced to operate with fewer resources than its international competitors are able to harness. With academic programs running at a deficit and executive courses generating income, subsidizing faculty compensation, and creating strong brand awareness through aggressive marketing, it is difficult to argue a case for growing the M.B.A. program. The M.B.A., typically the flagship of any business school, stands in danger of being neglected. The school's efforts to change the university's funding model to one based on attributable income have been largely unsuccessful.

Equity

Pressures for affirmative action, created by new legislation such as the Employment Equity Act (South Africa, 1998b) and, more recently, the Mining Charter (South Africa, 2002), have created both an opportunity and threat for W.B.S. Business increasingly requires competent managers from "designated groups" (women, Blacks and Asians). Regrettably, and particularly in the case of Blacks, many potential managers have inadequate educational backgrounds for postgraduate education. W.B.S.'s response in offering intermediate certificated programs, which are in great demand, does not always satisfy aspirations. W.B.S.'s entry requirement for M.B.A. students, in terms of work experience, creates a risk that other M.B.A. programs will draw off students early in their career paths, making these students unavailable to W.B.S. later.

The new legislation has resulted in a shortage of qualified faculty and made it difficult for W.B.S. to meet its own Equity targets. As the market settles these problems are likely to be slowly resolved.

CONCLUSIONS

There are several lessons that may be learned from the W.B.S. experience that may be transferable to other emerging market business schools. These relate to the requirements to build a successful position in a turbulent and fast-changing environment, as well as to the inevitable challenges and contradictions inherent in operating in an emerging market.

Success requirements are very clear. They relate to responding to external change and adapting rather than adopting foreign models. The forces of globalization are acting on all emerging markets, and the necessity to develop globally competent managers is acute. The same is true for education providers, and the importance of globally recognized benchmarks is increasing. The W.B.S. experience demonstrates how this challenge may be met through curriculum changes, international study tours, faculty globalization and international student exchange. Emerging markets, however, are different from developed ones in terms of the management challenges faced and the management competencies required. To address these, an emerging market business school must develop its own teaching materials and ensure that local relevance is maintained. A broad range of programs must be offered and a wide variety of local issues addressed.

The W.B.S. experience also highlights the need for creative solutions to faculty constraints and the dangers of losing institutional independence. Funding will continue to be a pressing concern for emerging market business schools, and state funds cannot be relied upon. The imperative is to develop self-generating income. Doing so through the ambit of executive education programs also provides a market test of whether or not the institution is delivering value. In an environment of scarce resources, however, where universities are chronically under-funded, there is a risk that the business school will be seen as a cash cow and used to subsidize other academic departments. Doing so is likely to lead to the demise of the school, and the overwhelming challenge is to carve out sufficient financial and operating autonomy.

Overall, the challenges are more internal than external. An emerging market business school may be successful through adapting appropriately and responding well to its external market. The internal challenges of organizational structure and decision-making within publicly-funded universities are the ones that can make or break the effort.

REFERENCES

Currie, D. & Matulich, S. (2003). Foreign travel in North American M.B.A. programs. Working Paper, Crummer Graduate School of Business, Rollins College, FL.

I.M.D. (2000). *World Competitiveness Yearbook,* Lausanne, Switzerland.

Department of Finance (1996). *Growth Employment and Redistribution: A Macroeconomic Strategy.* Pretoria, South Africa.

Friedman, T.L. (2000). *The Lexus and the Olive Tree: Understanding Globalization.* Anchor Books.

Kedia, B.L., Harveston, P.D., & Bhagat, R.S. (2001). Orienting curricula and teaching to produce international managers for global competition. *Journal of Teaching in International Business, 13*(1).

Khanna, T. & Palepu, K.G. (1997, July). Why focused strategies may be wrong for emerging markets. *Harvard Business Review.*

Klein, S. (1998, September/October). Competition policy and global competitiveness. *Thunderbird International Business Review.*

Mathews, V.E., Rivera, J.B., & Pineda, R.C. (2001). Management education abroad: adaptation versus a cookie-cutter approach. *Journal of Teaching in International Business, 12*(4).

South Africa (1998a). *The Competition Act, No. 8,* Cape Town: Parliament.

South Africa (1998b). *The Employment Equity Act, No. 55,* Cape Town: Parliament.

South Africa (2002). *Broad-Based Socio-Economic Empowerment Charter for the South African Mining Industry.* Pretoria.

South Africa (2003). *Council on Higher Education Higher Education Quality Committee, MBA Accreditation Manual.* Pretoria.

Spillan, J.E. & Ziemnowicz, C. (2001). Developing new managers after privatization: the case of MBA education in Poland. *Journal of Teaching in International Business, 12*(2).

T.I.M.S.S. (1999). *Mathematics and Science in the Eighth Grade: Findings from the Third International Mathematics and Science Study*, URL: http://nces.ed.gov/pubs2000/2000014.pdf.

U.N.C.T.A.D. (2003). *Handbook of Statistics On-line*, URL: http://www.unctad.org/Templates/Page.asp?intItemID=1890&lang=1.

Wocke, A. & Klein, S. (2002, November). South Africa's skills migration policy. *Development Southern Africa.*

Chapter 22

Final Reflections: The Business Education-Economic Development Nexus in Emerging Economies

John R. McIntyre
DuPree College of Management, Georgia Institute of Technology

Ilan Alon
Crummer Graduate School of Business, Rollins College

INTRODUCTION

The role of higher education in emerging market economies raises complex issues at the macroeconomic and educational policy levels. Without a doubt, the connection between economic growth and professional education and training, as understood in more recent years by the World Economic Forum, the World Bank, and a variety of multilateral development banks and institutions, is a complex one. The 1999 World Bank development report underlined the truism that "poor countries -- and poor people -- are different from rich ones not only because they have less capital but because they have less knowledge" (1999, 1). Knowledge creation is emphasized as a cornerstone in economic and social development.

The Asian Tigers, and particularly Taiwan, Singapore, Hong Kong, and South Korea, invested early and heavily in higher education, and this choice has generally been considered one of the essential ingredients for their economic achievements. The training of a well-prepared, globally savvy, ethically aware and adaptive cohort of managers, executives, and entrepreneurs in emerging market economies poses unique institutional, programmatic, and curricular challenges. Many of the chapters in our book point to exactly this issue and provide guidelines for educators and policymakers to follow.

The relative absence of research literature on the link between higher business education and the emerging market economy paradigm is ample evidence of the complexity of the matter at hand (McMullen, et al, 2000). This is further underlined by the growing importance of emerging markets and their rising G.D.P. (gross domestic product) rates when compared to the growth rates of the Triad-based economies (North America, Western Europe, and Japan). This paucity of literature may be indicative of the tendency for emerging economies to train their top management talents in Triad-based educational institutions until recently.

While this book has not sought to dwell at length on what qualifies a national economy for emerging market status, there exists a continuum between advanced post-industrial countries and underdeveloped economies that is generally acknowledged and authoritatively documented in the annual World Bank's *World Development Report* as well as an agenda with a set of "recipes" to bridge the gap and a broad consensus on what are the most desirable international development goals (World Bank, 2001, 5). Such reports can sometimes underplay the criticality of professional education at the post-high school level and, more particularly, in the business and managerial fields. Our edited volume does not seek to make a contribution to development economics by addressing the essential pathways to economic growth in the early twenty first century using higher education as a singular strategy. We have rather made a contribution in illuminating the conditions that surround business education in selected emerging markets and in bringing together research previously dispersed in multiple academic channels. The gains in knowledge in emerging markets pertaining to business (generally defined) are remarkable, and an initial inventory of these achievements bodes well. These markets are quickly catching up with the state of knowledge in the same disciplines across the developed world.

Emerging market economies usually have a significant level of industrial and economic output and a budding service sector tied to the emergence of a middle class endowed with growing G.D.P. per capita as well as rapidly improving and interconnected technical, legal, educational, public health, and financial infrastructures. Yet emerging economies cannot be simply defined by the size of their economy, as might be the case for China, Brazil, or the larger economies. The Economist Intelligence Unit, for example, includes countries like Chile, Peru, Egypt, Israel, South Africa, Turkey, and the Czech Republic as well as Russia, China, and Indonesia among emerging markets (*The Economist*, 2004, 98). Emerging economies are also typically positioned globally in a catch-up mode to increase societal wealth, economic maturity, and level of integration in the global economy in labor, commerce, capital, and technology flow terms.

Moreover, a further distinguishing hallmark is the force of the transformational processes such economies have undergone in recent years, alongside the well-known dynamic processes of globalization of flows of innovation, production, and distribution in the emergence of homogenized world cultural models. While no consensual definition can be obtained, it can be said that they are economies characterized by large markets, a rising middle class with increasing purchasing power, with rapidly improving infrastructures designed for hyper growth, and, in many cases, increasingly open polities or in the midst of profound political changes. The educational environments in most emerging markets have also changed rapidly, supporting the economic, social, and political changes described above.

The sustainability of economic growth and the requisite diversification of innovation and production patterns depends, in significant ways, on the availability of a sufficiently elastic domestic pool of trained managers and the ready availability of training and educational programs and institutional systems. These factors are closely allied to educational policy responsiveness to the rapid rates of growth transforming emerging markets and to the heightened interdependence with international markets. Business education builds labor's skills and abilities to innovate, compete in global markets, and enable the resulting dynamic growth, not unlike the stages of development process convincingly addressed by Water W. Rostow in the 1960s.

The clear challenge for such societies is to establish and maintain excellence in their professional educational systems which can reconcile the needed local differentiation, cognizant of the specific features of an emerging economy with its unique set of national characteristics, with world-class standards of management, production, innovation, and distribution. The trap to be avoided is the establishment of a variable geometry of business norms, operational ethical principles, and management training pathways: one for the supply chain of customers and partners in the local emerging economy and another for the external and global clients, suppliers, and partners. This was underlined by Dr. Abraham George, President of the George Foundation and Chairman of eMedexOnline L.L.C., one of the November 6-7, 2003 Georgia Tech Research Conference on Business Education in Emerging Economies' keynote speakers.

The further challenge for these societies is to gradually become autonomous in the selection, training, and retention of a world-class, appropriately skilled workforce in the domestic economy, and to produce gainful placement within its own national economic perimeters of domestic managerial talent.

Upward social mobility is an essential feature of the emerging economy paradigm. Securing the essential skills for advancement in a growing and emerging market economy implies not only the inculcation of risk-taking and entrepreneurial values and mindsets but also work habits consonant with those of peers in leading economies. Much remains to be done to secure such attitudinal changes which extol the virtues of competition, quality, openness, responsibility, and risk taking through improvement in the quality and openness of educational systems, the foundation stone of societal and economic change (Lapper and Dyer, 1998, 7-10). The present book highlights the many advances which emerging markets are attempting to make in their educational systems. Most of the changes highlighted, however, pertain to the upwardly mobile, professionally trained, elite group in these emerging markets.

Relatedly, emerging market economies confront a crisis of priorities: how to reduce illiteracy and simultaneously offer advanced managerial, technical training while stoking the furnaces of techno-innovation. This bifurcation of priorities is not necessarily contradictory but requires simultaneous action. In other words, mass education and higher education are interrelated. However, falling behind in the latter will insure loss of needed foreign investment with infusion of capital and technology, further deepening the gulf between the "haves" and "have nots" among competing emerging countries and within the country's own population.

Educational resources are scarce, and perhaps more so in emerging market economies, but the educational opportunities should not be as the new generations seek to achieve higher standards of living, longevity, and attainment. The professional educational challenges of emerging market societies is also that of Western triadic societies as surplus trained labor tends to find external outlets through labor migration if domestic ones are unavailable. That is, countries that focus their resources on the upwardly mobile populations will tend to experience brain drain as opportunities for gainful employment are not available for the educated cadre that result.

Stability, openness, and skilled technical and managerial pools of talent in an emerging market economy are uncontested factors of attraction for foreign direct investment when allied to market opportunities. Country political risk and country attractiveness rankings, as evidenced in the I.M.D.'s and World Economic Forum's annual rankings, as well as country opportunity analytical frameworks all point in this same direction. The work of Michael Porter on the forging of world-class technology and industrial clusters further underlines the essential link between professional education, innovation, external investment, and economic development. Attracting foreign direct investment cannot be taken for granted by growing emerging market countries in competition with each other and requires a readiness to receive the incoming investment on the best of terms and based on global best practices.

The example of the software industry in India throughout the 1990's is instructive. The infusion of software foreign direct investment there required a prior and substantial investment in higher engineering and management education, which is still ongoing, as well as a supporting high tech infrastructure. Similarly, for an emerging market economy to fully benefit from the outsourcing trend of the early twenty first century -- much maligned in certain advanced industrial countries' quarters -- requires a trained workforce willing and able to work to the standards of global industry in design and services.

The success equation is often touted in the simplistic terms of higher education and advanced skills leading causally to targeted foreign investment, which results in higher paying jobs with a multiplier effect, accompanied by technology transfer and diffusion and leap-frogging intermediary stages of economic development. This further underlines that emerging countries, once considered underdeveloped, from necessity derive their competitive and comparative advantages in the modern global economy not so much from natural resources, a large home market, or low wages, but increasingly from offering owners of the factors of production the higher level benefits of a well-educated workforce. The work of Meyer in this regard must be recalled: foreign investment, in and of itself, is not a sufficient cause for economic development unless it is accompanied by an educated workforce able to absorb and diffuse the technology vectored by foreign investment.

Multinationals are usually in the forefront in the recruitment of locally trained managers as home nationals increasingly demands. The 50,000 multinational corporations are an important source of employment growth for the emerging market economies, and these same companies prescribe educational and training standards in business education, encouraging the development of home-grown educational facilities responsive to their specific requirements and standards. The globalization shock dealt emerging market economy systems often engenders a backlash against homogenization of consumption, production, and cultural modes. The development of homegrown business educational systems is a further guarantor or safety valve in the balancing of national or particularistic cultures and global systems, minimizing such backlashes whose rippling effects are deleterious to multinational operations.

Many authors have raised questions about the sustainability of the first wave globalization impacting largely the Triad economies and characterized by deregulation, decentralization, privatization, and the generalization of cyberspace (Samli, 2004). What is often described as the second wave of globalization is the advent of emerging markets, dealing with their "forgotten majority," market potential, and production capacity. This second wave of globalization will challenge the business educational systems of the Triad, focused as they are on Western norms and contents. It will also and concomitantly present new opportunities for developing uniquely tailored business educational systems within the emerging economies as they are carried forward on this second wave of globalization. Clearly, as Japanese management experts are fond of terming it, <u>*nemawashi*</u> (preparing the ground) will be essential to insure that this second wave of globalization does not fizzle and that multinational actors do not retreat to the safety and familiarity of advanced industrialized triad-based economies.

The impact of globalization is most felt in information communications technology, which has revolutionized business and has had a profound impact on the process of business education itself. Almost everyone in emerging economies has been exposed to or heard of the asynchronous tools of on-line tutoring vial e-mail as well as self-taught interactive CD-Rom -based sources and synchronous on-line live courses via the Internet and satellite links. Many assume that it is a foregone conclusion that such information technologies may, in fact, not be appropriate for emerging market economies. It must, however, be noted that China in 2002 had sixty seven state universities in over thirty one provinces offering accredited three-year on-line courses to over 800,000 students.

One of the keynote speakers, Mr. Axel Leblois, President of World Times, Inc., and former CEO of ExecuTrain as well as Bull H.N. Information Systems, and co-founder of the Wireless Internet Institute, noted at the November 6-7, 2003 Georgia Tech Research Conference on Business Education and Emerging Economies, organized by the editors of this volume, that spending on the sole academic segment of e-learning in China may be growing at the rate of 74% per year, reaching $876 million in 2005. He willingly predicted that the best contents, processes, and academic tools will be made available through technology and the Internet in assisting emerging economies to begin closing the academic resource gap that has built over the course of the past century. He further envisions a revolutionizing of business education, as happened in I.T. training, in the emerging economies. While these predictions are debatable, it is certain that the magnitude of the emerging economies' professional educational challenges will require innovation on a grand scale.

This anthology has sought to address emerging market economies' business education strategies, collaborative models, and content choices through a select but broad-spectrum sample of the most representative of such economies: China, Brazil, Ukraine, Israel, Croatia, Argentina, India, Russia, Vietnam, South Africa, and occasionally referencing and using others as exemplars, such as Indonesia, Latin American Spanish-speaking countries (including the case of Mexico), the Middle East, and North Africa's Maghreb.

The emphasis has clearly been on the "how to," the curricular dimensions, the content aspects of business and management education. It endeavors to point the way towards reforms, reviewing the role of executive education as a supplement to embedded business education systems, addressing the nature of business pedagogy (experiential, virtual, case-oriented) in changing contexts, considering the role of government as a provider of higher education and leveraging private and public sector initiatives to foster innovative cooperative educational ventures. It is cognizant of the exigencies of the moment and the need to generate longer term and more permanent solutions for emerging market countries' business education requirements.

The debate as to the means, the best practices, the appropriate pedagogical approaches and curricular contents, and the modeling on Western-based business frameworks cannot be considered apart from the ends and longer term purposes of professional education and its energizing momentum in generating the sources of well-being on which growth, stability, and international peace come to rest.

Dr. Jeffrey Garten, former U.S. Undersecretary of Commerce, has waxed eloquently on the centrality of emerging market economies in the process of continued globalization and the diffusion of its economic benefits (1997). Making tangible progress towards bridging the existing economic gaps between Triad-based economies and the emerging economies of the world may, in fact, be the key to world peace and stability (McIntyre, 2004). These emerging markets and societies can only be ignored at our common peril. Business education is one of the keys to reducing and eventually bridging the gaps, guaranteeing that the economic benefits of the liberal model of globalization are generalized while emerging countries remain true to their national identities and sense of history.

REFERENCES

Garten, Jeffrey. (1997). *The Big Ten: The Big Emerging Markets and How They Will Change Our Lives*, New York: Basic Books.

I.M.D. (2003). *World Competitiveness Yearbook 2003.* Lausanne, Switzerland.

Lapper, R. & Dyer, G. (1998). Brazil. *Financial Times*. 7-10.

McIntyre, J. R., & Travis, E. F.(2004). A framework for understanding the impact of terrorism on international trade and investment. In G. Suder (Ed.), *Terrorism and the International Business Environment: The Security-Business Nexus*. London: Edward Elgar Publishing.

McMullen, M. S, Mauch, J. E., & Donnorummo, B. (2000). *The Emerging Markets and Higher Education: Development and Sustainability*. New York: Routledge Falmer.

Meyer, K. (1998). *Direct Foreign Investment in Economies in Transition*. Chelthenham, UK: Edward Elgar.

Porter, M. E. (1999). Microeconomic competitiveness: findings from the 1999 executive survey. *The Global Competitiveness Report 1999*. Geneva, Switzerland: World Economic Forum.

-- & Bond, G.C. (1999). Innovative capacity and prosperity: the next competitiveness challenge. *The Global Competitiveness Report 1999*. Geneva, Switzerland: World Economic Forum.

Rostow, W. W. (1960). *The Stages of Economic Growth: A Non-Communist Manifesto*. Cambridge, U.K.: Cambridge University Press.

Samli, A. C. (2004). *Entering and Succeeding in Emerging Countries: Marketing to the Forgotten Majorit.*, Mason, Ohio: Thompson-South-Western.

World Bank. (1999). *World Development Report 1998/99: Knowledge for Development*. New York: Oxford University Press.

World Bank. (2001). *World Development Report 2000/2001, Attacking Poverty*. New York: Oxford University Press.

INDEX

FSC
www.fsc.org
MIX
Papier | Fördert
gute Waldnutzung
FSC® C083411

Kolibri 360 GmbH
Ferdinand-Jühlke-Straße 7
99095 Erfurt, Deutschland
produktsicherheit@kolibri360.de